Mildred P. Kindy

Music and Maestros

THE STORY OF THE MINNEAPOLIS SYMPHONY ORCHESTRA

The Story of the

MINNEAPOLIS SYMPHONY

ORCHESTRA

THE MINNEAPOLIS SYMPHONY ORCHESTRA IN 1952

AWARDED A UNIVERSITY OF MINNESOTA FELLOWSHIP IN REGIONAL WRITING

UNIVERSITY OF MINNESOTA PRESS, MINNEAPOLIS

MUSIC AND

MAESTROS

BY JOHN K. SHERMAN

London · Geoffrey Cumberlege · Oxford University Press

Acknowledgments

THE making of this book has been as much a search as a writing assignment, and the search in great measure has involved a rifling of many memories, whose owners have willingly turned over the contents thereof. Without the generous help of the more than eighty persons I have talked to or corresponded with during the past five years, this history would have lacked much of its factual content and its store of incident.

Most bountiful and reliable repository of knowledge about the Minneapolis Symphony has been Carlo Fischer, who more than any other today merits the title of "Mister Orchestra" in the Twin Cities. Mr. Fischer played with the Symphony at its first concert in 1903 and has been a musician, manager, writer, and statistician for the organization for most of the years since. His long experience and willing spirit have made him more than merely an aid in gathering the facts; he has been virtually a collaborator, and ever on call.

Other veterans of the orchestra, including Karl Scheurer, Herman Boessenroth, Al Rudd, William Muelbe, and Henry J. Williams, have supplied much valuable information. Of particular importance have been the recollections of the orchestra's early years passed on to me by William MacPhail, Sr., Eva Blanchard (who worked in the Symphony office in the first decade), Hamlin Hunt, Stanley R. Avery, and the late Richard Czerwonky, who led me to one of my most exciting "finds" — an unpublished autobiographical sketch by Wendell Heighton, orchestra manager in the second decade.

Mrs. Elbert L. Carpenter has been most gracious and helpful in furnishing data on Mr. Carpenter's youthful years and his work with the orchestra, and other members of the Carpenter family have been equally cooperative.

Among the Symphony board members who have told me much of interest and value are John Pillsbury, Sumner T. McKnight, Carl W. Jones, and C. O. Kalman, the latter supplying "eyewitness" documentation on St. Paul's musical life and its early relationships with the orchestra. Past and present orchestra managers, Mrs. Carlyle Scott and Arthur J. Gaines, have filled in much office and backstage history, as has Frank A. R. Mayer, publicity director. Donald Ferguson, program annotator, and Samuel C. Gale, son of Harlow Gale, have furnished me with important data.

I am also indebted to the three Minneapolis conductors I have known for their kind help on biographical questions and for their exposition, during the course of many conversations, of their interpretive ideas. For the Verbrugghen chapter I had recourse especially to the good memory of Jenny Cullen and the gracious and painstaking aid of Madame Henri Verbrugghen.

Research into the Minneapolis Symphony's "pre-history" had firm support and rich sources in Louise Chapman's detailed chronicle of Minneapolis music in the nineteenth century. I bow in gratitude also to Eloise Shryock, Byron Morgan, and Karl Heckrich, to Eleanora Eckstrom and Anna C. Harmsen, daughters of Ludwig Harmsen, and to Frank J. and Eugene Danz, sons of Frank Danz, Jr. Ferdinand P. Schultz's thesis on "Music in the Pioneer Days in the Twin Cities Area" contains authoritative material I have freely purloined. Willoughby Babcock at the Minnesota Historical Society and Gladys Wilson of the Min-

Acknowledgments

neapolis Public Library never once turned down a request for hard-to-find information.

I have drawn liberally on the writings and memories of past and present critics, including those of Frances Boardman and Grace Davies. The reader will note that I have made the critics and their opinions an integral part of the Symphony story. This has put me to the necessity of quoting the earlier Sherman instead of relying on the later Sherman's fading and sometimes nonexistent memory of specific concerts — a seemingly vain maneuver for which I hereby make apology.

Finally my gratitude, a large share of it, goes to the University of Minnesota's Committee on Regional Writing, which provided the original idea and a financial incentive for the book, and to the staff of the University of Minnesota Press for their ministrations on the manuscript. To all the other many friends and helpers whom space forbids listing, I express most sincere thanks.

JOHN K. SHERMAN

Minneapolis
August 15, 1952

Table of Contents

ix

Music and Maestros

☆ Antal Dorati

Illustrations

Music and Maestros

The Oberhoffer orchestra on the Auditorium's stage

Under Oberhoffer: Cornelius Van Vliet, Bruno Labate, and Karl Scheurer

Other members of the Oberhoffer ensemble: William MacPhail, Otto Gebhart, Herman Boessenroth, John Hartl, William Thieck, and Albert Koehler

The "golden era of touring": Richard Czerwonky, E. J. "Bill" Erck, and Wendell Heighton

Rise of the "critical gentry": Caryl Storrs, Harlow Gale, Victor Nilsson, and James Davies

Guest soloists: Ignace Paderewski, Jascha Heifetz, and Albert Spalding

Other "star performers": Marcella Sembrich, Fannie Bloomfield-Zeisler, and Olive Fremstad

Guest conductors during 1922–23: Walter Damrosch, Bruno Walter, and Ossip Gabrilówitsch

between pages 214 and 215

Henri Verbrugghen

Mainstays of the Verbrugghen ensemble: Richard Lindenhahn, Henry C. Woempner, and Georges Grisez

High competence in the strings: Engelbert Roentgen, Jenny Cullen, and Paul Lemay

Mrs. Carlyle Scott and Arthur Gaines

Northrop Auditorium on the campus of the University of Minnesota

Eugene Ormandy

Ormandy as conductor

Sumner T. McKnight, E. L. Carpenter, and John S. Pillsbury

Illustrations

Music and Maestros

THE STORY OF THE MINNEAPOLIS SYMPHONY ORCHESTRA

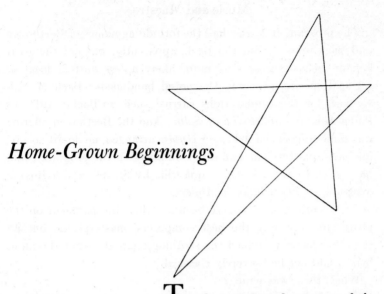

Home-Grown Beginnings

THE first promenade concert of the Minneapolis Musical Society was a fiasco, and no one knew exactly why. The cause of failure was hard to explain, for strawberries and ice cream had been served. Nothing in the annals of Minneapolis from earliest times had indicated that its residents disdained strawberries and ice cream, or failed to show the most zealous civic spirit when those delicacies adorned worthy public undertakings.

Yet on Wednesday evening, June 19, 1872, only a few hardy souls climbed the two flights of creaking stairs of the Pence Opera House for the debut of the eighteen-piece orchestra that unknowingly was the first significant forerunner of the Minneapolis Symphony Orchestra.

What kept the town's concertgoers at home? Were they frightened by the prospectus of the society, announcing that musical standards would be high and that only "masterpieces of the best composers" would be produced? Certainly, by reading farther, they would have been reassured by the promise that "the concert will not be severely classical." But again, their suspicions may have been ruffled by a prim qualifying phrase: "Yet the merely sensational will be shunned."

3

Music and Maestros

The program, it is true, had the forbidding names of Beethoven and Bach upon it. But the Bach, apparently, was not the great Johann Sebastian; he was more likely a less austere local or regional species, probably the noted bandmaster Bach of Milwaukee, for the compositions carried such un-Bachly titles as *Polka Mazurka* and *Polka de Salon.* And the Beethoven offering was something called *A Vesper Hymn,* arranged, no doubt noisily, for brass quartet. The two other numbers on the program could have scared away no one: a quadrille by Strauss and a Rossini overture, to *The Italian in Algiers.*

Such a program may have been a rather slim payment on the pledge to play only the best composers' masterpieces, but on the other hand it fulfilled the soothing guarantee that the numbers would not be "severely classical."

What, then, was wrong?

The admission fee was not exorbitant, only twenty-five cents. And the only competing attraction that night had been the Langrishe Comedy Company's presentation of *Grounds for Divorce* at the new Academy of Music at Washington and Hennepin avenues, followed by Robert Macaire's "Tricks, Changes, Transformations and Comedy Incidents." True, other important attractions of the week may have offered more glamour: the Grand Fabri-Mulders Opera Combination was presenting its typical Verdi mixtures, with costume, and on Thursday the city was to be gripped by the arrival of the Great Eastern Museum, Menagerie, Aviary, and Balloon Show, which featured an elephant named Bismarck and staged a mile-long parade that increased local restaurant business.

But most of this was competition outside the musical field. So the *Minneapolis Tribune,* fervent supporter of commercial and cultural progress in the raucously growing town of twenty thousand, may well have been right in blaming meteorological interference for the failure of the Musical Society's concert. Its post-mortem on the affair said:

"The elements seemed to conspire on Wednesday against the interests of the Minneapolis Musical society. The frequent storms

4

during the day and the threatening aspect of the clouds in the evening affected the public attendance upon their festival quite seriously. The association had provided liberally of strawberries and ice cream, and had prepared a choice program of musical gems for the occasion. . . . Scarcely a corporal's guard was present. The society lost nearly a hundred dollars."

The solicitous *Tribune* concluded its account of the ill-starred opening with the plea that "one hundred prominent citizens of Minneapolis sign a petition requesting the Musical Society to give another concert at their earliest convenience, and thus give them assurance of a crowded house. We see signs of good promise in this home organization and it deserves encouragement now in its early days, not only of the well wishes of the community, but of liberal patronage at its concerts."

This plaintive note of combined urging and optimism was often to be sounded in years to come as Minneapolis' musical organizations came into uncertain being, waxed, and waned. The hundred prominent citizens to whom the *Tribune* appealed apparently did not rise to the occasion or proffer more than their "well wishes," for the Musical Society slowly faded from the scene.

Minneapolis, only two decades advanced from a primitive frontier village of whining sawmills and mud-mired paths for streets, was still feeling its way musically. When the need for music arose, its residents got together and sang, and music, to most of them, meant singing. Orchestral music, in and of itself, was a fragile article during the Grant era, and it is probable that 1872 was not a propitious year in which to unfurl the glories of symphonic literature in Minneapolis. This was the last year of booming prosperity which had begun after the close of the Civil War, for grasshoppers and depression both struck in 1873. While Minneapolis and its older partner across the river, St. Anthony, had been officially "married" and the city had been crowing over its achievements in building and commerce, the status of culture was not yet secure enough to guarantee long life to such genteel dreams as orchestras. The ugly, muscle-flexing little town was

aggressively "on the make," and like most towns that were bene-
ficiaries of the westward tide of settlement, it was predominantly
interested in trade and profit-taking.

But the fact remains that the Minneapolis Musical Society,
short-winded and frail though it was, got itself born and lived
long enough to give three or four concerts in the early seventies.
And a year after its demise, a similar organization, the Orchestral
Union, came into being and gave concerts with decent regularity
for three years.

The town, young and bumptious as it was, knew by this time
that it needed and wanted music, at least as a proper civic adorn-
ment and as social recreation. Its amateur standing as a singing
city was now established; its tradition of professional and semiprofessional music reached back to its beginnings.

The community had sung as it created itself. In the fifties it
imported pianos and melodeons by boat and wagon train to
install them in log cabins and crude frame houses. It plunked
guitars, "that most fashionable of all instruments," according to
George A. Nash, who ran a drugstore. It organized and attended
singing schools, taking indigent music teachers to its bosom and
feeding and bedding them if it didn't pay them. It mingled a
merry note, or a hymn tune, with the staccato of pounding hammers and the high-pitched wail of sawmills. The "divine art" (as
music was called) buoyed up the spirits of the settlers and wove
itself into lives that were fairly devoid of cultural nourishment.

Even in that first decade of Minneapolis' existence (when it
was still a part of the Fort Snelling military reservation on the
west side of the river) there was a modicum of public entertainment that classified as music. Could a symphony orchestra's
genealogy be traced, if tortuously, to B. E. Messer and his production of that pretty fantasy, *Flora's Festival,* on May Day
of 1854 in St. Anthony's Congregational church? Or maybe more
directly to the Quintette Club which appeared four years later?
This short-lived instrumental group harbored the town's two
outstanding teacher-performers, Mr. Messer, who played the
violin, and C. A. Widstrand, a pianist. With three other citizens

who played cello, cornet, and flute, it was the closest approach to an orchestra the pioneer community had heard up to that time.

Messer, a carriage and sign painter by trade, flourished in the small twin cities for about a decade, arriving in 1852 with the usual offer to conduct a singing school and to "teach children without charge." After two years he had brought his group to a sufficient degree of polish to offer *Flora's Festival*. This was a song play concerning the arrival of spring which featured zephyrs, sprites, and fairies in appropriate costumes. The presentation involved considerable effort to mimic the glory of reborn Nature inside the cramped and rough-hewn Congregational church, where flowers and woodsy effects added to the delight of listeners, as it may also have reminded them of chiggers.

The community gave the *Festival* a hearty hand, and the performance proved so popular it was repeated five days later.

When the Hutchinsons, the famous singing family, first visited Minneapolis in 1855, Messer joined them in their first expedition to the site of the town they were to establish, Hutchinson, Minnesota. He took his fiddle along with him, and Hutchinson-to-be was serenaded vocally and instrumentally when the party bivouacked on the western prairie where the town was yet to be born.

Messer returned to the village near St. Anthony Falls and continued his teaching career, taking a prominent part in many musical evenings. In 1858, the year of the Quintette Club's debut, he assumed a conductor's role at the first convention of the Minnesota Musical Association. The Quintette's concert had not been entirely instrumental: Messer laid down his fiddle and sang *Oh! Bury Me Not in the Deep, Deep Sea* and *The Sailor's Daughter*. These poignant lyrics were "rendered," according to the impressionable *Falls Evening News*, "with a fidelity, an eloquence and an unaffected pathos that we have seldom seen surpassed." Two years later Messer departed from the scene, his voice and violin never again heard in Minneapolis.

Widstrand, the town's other leading teacher, was no wanderer. He became a permanent resident and made music both a profession and a paying trade. A music professor from Sweden and a graduate of the University of Uppsala, he opened his class in vocal music in 1854, established the town's first music store, and for seven years was organist for Gethsemane church. His great moment came on a July day in 1856, when he tuned the piano used in a recital by the great Ole Bull and the thirteen-year-old Adelina Patti on their first visit to Minnesota Territory, and forty years later he was still reminiscing of that memorable day:

Ole Bull gave two concerts, one in Edwards hall on the east side, and one on this side of the river in the upper story of Arthur McGhee's grocery store on Second avenue S., then called Helen street, between Washington avenue and Second street. . . . Mr. Bull came over on this side and inspected the very diminutive hall. He discovered what seemed to him a weakness in the floor and insisted that extra timbers be put in so as to make the hall perfectly safe before he consented to play there.

He was very much incensed at what seemed to him to be an extortion when the parties owning the grand piano which had been used in the concert on the east side demanded $50 for taking the piano over to Minneapolis proper. Ole Bull finally succeeded as a makeshift in obtaining the small piano owned by Colonel Stevens. The piano, however, was badly out of tune, and this fact afforded me the pleasure and privilege of tuning it for the great violinist, which it seemed I did to his complete satisfaction, as he gave me a recommendation which I treasure very highly.

In the evening the small hall was packed to its utmost capacity with the elite of the city — we were all elite at that time. A primitive platform had to do service as a stage and a plank was laid from it over to the dressing room, where the concert givers and Miss Patti's father kept themselves when not engaged before the public. When young Patti had to step nearly over the heads of some of the audience and saw the little hall and the packed faces she could not restrain a smile, which was plainly visible and almost audible. She took the audience by storm, however, and there was seemingly no end to the applause and encores.

Then Ole Bull came forward and struck the A on his violin. Mr. Roth struck the A on his piano and off they went. Bull afterwards expressed himself as much pleased with having the piano up to concert pitch, as in the west he had nearly always had to lower his violin to suit the piano. Mr. Bull favored us on this night with his wonderful composition, *Mother's Prayer,* and also, if I remember right, *Visit to the Mountains.* . . . There was no announcement in the papers of the concerts, but both concerts had capacity crowds. . . .

The years into the sixties, through boom and bust, through the war and after, witnessed a steadily growing appetite for music, local and imported. Widstrand kept on teaching, tuning pianos, and selling a line of musical instruments that included not only pianos but melodeons and seraphines. In 1861, music-hungry Germans of the town formed the Harmonia Society. The Congregational church choir, composed of Samuel C. and Harlow A. Gale, brothers, C. M. Cushman, and Joseph Clark, was popular and much in demand for religious and secular occasions. Opera troupes of varying quality descended upon the community with increasing frequency and rapacity. A taste was developed for gaudy-costumed oratorios of Oriental tinge, exemplified by George Root's *Belshazzar's Feast, or the Fall of Babylon,* performed in February 1868 by the Musical Union, a choral group with a small instrumental complement which had sprung into being two years earlier. This had a cast of one hundred assorted Asiatics, and lured numerous sleighloads of music lovers from St. Paul, Faribault, and other towns in the region, and there were long queues at the ticket windows.

Music of all kinds was greatly stimulated by the opening of the Pence Opera House at Hennepin Avenue and Second Street in 1867, when the first and only grand piano in Minneapolis was introduced to a public well aware of the cultural milestone the gleaming Knabe on the platform signified. It was at this opening that concertgoers had their first amazed glimpse of the murals running riot over the opera house's dome and proscenium. These depicted eight cherubim, four angels personifying the seasons, Washington grasping a sword in one hand and the Constitution in the other, Lincoln brandishing a scroll, Andrew Jackson and Andrew Johnson each looking sternly presidential, Shakespeare flanked by two angels posing as Tragedy and Comedy, and over the arch, perched on a shield, an American eagle whose beak held a streamer proclaiming these words: "J. W. Pence, dedicated June 1867."

Progress was progressing so fast in Minneapolis that the Pence Opera House began to seem a little absurd and outmoded by the time Joseph Hodges in 1871 opened his third-floor Academy of Music one block south on Hennepin Avenue. This opening was an event important in the city's orchestral annals because it offered for the first time in local history a symphonic performance: the larghetto and finale from Beethoven's Second symphony, played by the visiting St. Paul Musical Society. The evening was a bit marred by unpleasant weather and a fitful supply of gas illumination. A clue to how the audience reacted to its first experience with Beethoven as a symphonist may be gained from the *Tribune,* which spoke the next day of the society's playing in succession the Beethoven excerpt and the overture to von Suppé's *Banditenstreiche*: "and if we were to select a best piece of the evening it might be the latter of these two. It was one of those overtures that actually rests a somewhat wearied and restless audience."

Reading between the lines, we may surmise that the "Jolly Robbers" overture was a relief after the symphony, that Beethoven lost to von Suppé, and that listeners chafed at music that was not only unfamiliar but serious — as they have ever since.

Music in Minneapolis of the seventies had gained at least nominal prestige with an Academy of Music added to its downtown facilities, even if "Academy" meant only a minute stage with a small seating space attached. The range and diversity of music entertainment meanwhile had expanded. On Sundays there were church quartets and organ playing, on weekdays such things as "parlor" concerts, bell ringers, cornet bands, operatic troupes, and minstrel shows for the lighter touch. In homes, families and neighbors gathered about the piano to sing *Eyes of Black and Eyes of Blue* ("O, eyes of black, you smiled at me . . . O, eyes of blue, how sweet were you!"). In public places, there were the return engagements of Ole Bull, whose increasing age and eccentricity distressed critical listeners, and of the ubiquitous

and popular singing families, including the ever-touring Hutchinsons.

Henri Wieniawski, the French violinist-composer, visited Minneapolis in 1873. In 1875 the Mendelssohn Quintette sang the
bridal chorus from *Lohengrin,* providing a glimpse into "the
music of the future" by that "erratic genius," Wagner. Harlow
Gale, a prominent lawyer and public official, foreshadowed the
"pop" concerts of a later time by instituting in 1877 his dime
concert series in Bridge Square, where listeners strolled about
while listening. In 1878 he found he could not make them pay
even at twenty-five cents admission. Violinists Reményi and
Wilhelmj played in 1879, and the *Pinafore* epidemic was raging
hotly before the decade was out.

Orchestrally the seventies in Minneapolis belonged to two
zealots, two musicians of local repute who possessed the kind of
undismayed hardihood so often found in young communities
where progress is the personal handiwork of strong individuals.
One was Alfred M. Shuey, a grocer by trade and musician by
preference who could play seven instruments with equal facility,
and who was to become one of the city's prominent church organ-
ists. The other was Ludwig Harmsen, German-born musician and
teacher, Minneapolis' first orchestral "maestro" of substantial
standing.

Mr. Harmsen, born in Hamburg and as a boy something of a
trial to his mother by reason of his fanatical habit of practicing
piano ten hours a day, had arrived in Minneapolis in 1868. He
had been a singer as well as a pianist and knew the tenor roles
of twelve operas. But his voice had given way from excessive
use; he had started teaching at sixteen, had crossed the ocean in
1865 to join a brother in Atlanta, and three years later had
struck out from that war-scarred capital for the thriving little
town near St. Anthony Falls. He was then twenty-eight, and an
enterprising and able musician.

He made his pianistic bow in the city at another strawberry
festival, in June of 1868, which was as much a success as the
later one in 1872 was a failure. Managed by the determined

ladies of the Congregational Society, it had charged only ten
cents admission. The gustatory delights of the occasion comprised not only strawberries served in generous dishes with cream
and sugar, or with ice cream (or with both!), but the "best soda
fountain in the state serving all syrups known in the trade."
Those who witnessed Harmsen's debut were a merry throng on
the opera house's parquette floor, plus hundreds in the balcony
seats, and the young Harmsen must have been impressed by a
community spirit which so blithely and generously embraced
music as a part of its social-civic duties.

In any case he decided "this was the place." He became a
permanent resident and resolutely set about acquiring vocal
and piano pupils, becoming the town's first full-time professional
in music.

Harmsen quickly made an impress on Minneapolis' meager
musical life. He was energetic and he was picturesque. Of medium
height, he had an erect bearing that enhanced his stature, and
with long black hair falling Liszt-like on the back of his collar
he was every inch the "professor." He conscientiously dressed
the part. As the years went on, he wore a cape and top hat and
swung a gold-headed cane.

When he took over the conductorship of the Minneapolis Musical Society shortly after its inception, people were impressed
by his authoritative manner on the platform. But not everyone
liked the agitated and wide-sweeping gestures he affected. On
one occasion after he had taken charge of the Musical Society's
successor, the Orchestral Union, an observer from the press, con-
ceding that Harmsen displayed judgment and kept the orchestra
in hand, complained that the symmetry of the performance was
marred by his exaggerated and ludicrous style of waving the
baton, "as if he were pumping the music out."

Conductorial frenzy, even at that early date, pained those
elements of Minnesota's population that preferred a seemly
decorum in public places.

Nevertheless, the concert referred to also pumped out eight
hundred dollars from the public for a charity benefit, which is

evidence that the Orchestral Union was much more a going concern than its predecessor. In 1875 Harmsen was replaced as its conductor for a short time by Emil Weinberg, leading violinist of Bach's Milwaukee orchestra, whose rule was abruptly terminated after a ruction involving receipts. Having weathered this crisis, the Orchestral Union grew until in 1877 it boasted twenty-two instruments in its ensemble and was looking about eagerly for a set of kettledrums. Two years later, however, the orchestra disbanded, largely because its professional members had found enough paying work to make their gratuitous contribution an irking charity.

The Orchestral Union was quite probably the "grandest" home talent orchestra Minneapolis had yet seen and heard. Its ensemble was apportioned to three first and three second violins, two violas, one cello, two basses, one piccolo, one flute, first and second clarinets, three cornets, two French horns, one trombone, and one drum. A program was apt to offer three or four orchestral numbers interspersed with vocal and instrumental solos and choral numbers, and often had a rousing band finale. Typical of an 1877 program was the following:

Overture, "Norma"	Bellini
Orchestra	
Soprano solo, "Wanderer"	Schubert
Mrs. DeWitt (Mrs. A. C.)	
Waltz, "Museum"	Catlin
Bass solo, "The Two Grenadiers"	Schumann
Mr. C. B. Eustis	
———◆———	
Coronation March	Meyerbeer
Piano solo-Fantaisie, "Luciede de Lammermore"	
	Prudent
L. Harmsen	
Soprano solo, "For You"	Willard
Mrs. DeWitt	
Fantaisie — "From the Opera"	
Burt's Band	

Music and Maestros

This program was fulsomely reviewed in the press the next day, the anonymous critic finding that the precision of the players' response to Conductor Harmsen resembled the "faultless unity" of Theodore Thomas' orchestra. This was extreme (if probably prejudiced) praise, for the Thomas orchestra was the Boston Symphony, or Philadelphia Orchestra, of its day, and its name was a byword for orchestral perfection.

Harmsen subsequently shifted from orchestral to choral and organ work, but he always had a large corps of pupils. In later years, in his home on Lake Calhoun Boulevard, he recalled the days when he was the "only teacher here, with pupils in practically every family." He drove a horse and buggy, and in winter a sleigh, in order to serve pupils who were scattered all the way from the east side of the river to Park Avenue and 30th (Lake) Street, which was then in the sparsely settled prairies on the southern purlieus of Minneapolis.

If Harmsen was the dominant batonist of the seventies, Alfred Shuey was the leading musical organizer in the field. Shuey's arrival in Minneapolis in 1866 had preceded Harmsen's by two years, and the grocer-fiddler-cornetist-organist was to outlive the conductor-teacher by fifteen years. He had served in the Civil War, and his military, businesslike bearing was enhanced by a Louis Napoleon goatee and a general air of getting things done briskly and efficiently.

Born in Ontario in 1847, he had studied harmony, counterpoint, and orchestration, as well as violin and cornet, and had come to Minneapolis to make a living at selling food, later entering long service with the Chicago, Milwaukee, and St. Paul Railroad as a ticket agent. His musical training and his energy soon plunged him, willy-nilly, into the town's musical life, and it was largely his organizing influence which in time gave it some semblance of pattern and order. He dreamed up many musical ventures and took part in them in roles ranging from French horn to treasurer in charge of deficits.

The kinetic Shuey had a retentive memory, and in his later years he reminisced of the days when downtown Minneapolis

14

began to dwindle into the outskirts at the site of the present Masonic Temple (Sixth Street and Hennepin Avenue) and when the Bradbury cantata *Queen Esther,* a national favorite at the time, was the chief and recurrent musical sensation of the young community.

It was at a performance of this cantata, conducted by J. B. McGibeny in old Harmonia Hall at Nicollet and Washington avenues, that Shuey made his local bow as a musician. He was first violin at that performance, but he was probably little noticed, for *Queen Esther* was a grand costume piece and attracted as much attention by the garish garb of its fifty singing Jews and Persians who swarmed on the small stage as by its musical appeal or substance. This occasion marked its first local production with an orchestra. Performance of *Queen Esther* assumed unwonted luster in the following winter when its composer, W. B. Bradbury, journeyed to Minneapolis for his health and graciously wrote two compositions for the dedication of Masonic Hall.

Shuey as well as Harmsen must be credited for the creation of the Minneapolis Musical Society, and for keeping the breath of life in it and in the Orchestral Union that followed it. Mobilizing instrumentalists to play together was Shuey's "pet idea." But his interests were varied, and were apt to gallop off in all directions. The streak of fun in him made him a guiding spirit as well as an end man in minstrel shows, and with George B. Eustis he organized a group which was dubbed the "Shueyeustisreevewhitegreenleafplaceiveswhitmoretuckermanmills," an omnibus word, considered humorous at the time, that listed the names of its ten members.

In 1872 Shuey was one of several who played the new organ at St. Mark's Episcopal Church, on Sixth Street between Hennepin and Nicollet avenues, and four years later he became the church's organist, serving in that post for two decades. During that period he found his musical niche as a church musician and an authority on the art and mechanics of the pipe organ.

Crude and small as these instrumental groups of the seventies were by later standards, they were the vanguard then of musical enterprise, the ripe fruit of ambition and progress in a frontier city yearning nostalgically for the wide world's culture and its civilizing influences.

For those who sought elevation and apartness from a rough-and-ready environment, to whom music was a badge of hard-won refinement, concerts by these groups also furnished a kind of bulwark against the unsavory and illiterate portions of the population. In that time, as later, music had its snob appeal. Of the programs given in the early seventies by the St. Paul Musical Society, an orchestral group of high prestige, it was written that support of them was "a sort of crucial measure of social position. . . . Not to be an attendant upon one of these entertainments is to argue oneself outside the pale of 'society'." And it was duly noted on one occasion that "the audience was large and brilliant beyond precedent, embracing the best representatives of all reputable classes of our population."

The Harmsen-Shuey collaboration, which dissolved as suddenly as it came into being, had done much of the spadework that smoothed the way for later musical combinations. Chief of these, dominant through the eighties and nineties, was a father-and-son enterprise that ultimately produced a leader who taught Minneapolis to listen to orchestral music and to like it. That leader was Frank Danz, Jr., the son of the team.

The father, christened Franz but known as Frank as was his son, had come to Fort Snelling in 1877 to lead the Twentieth Regiment Band there. He hailed from Darmstadt, Germany, for many years had been musical director at Manhattan College in New York City, and had married a sister of George Seibert, a St. Paul bandmaster and manager who in years to come was to give many annual series of orchestral concerts in the Minnesota capital.

It was Seibert who devised the plan of organizing the Great Western Band of Minneapolis, which would correspond in general character and usefulness with his own Great Western Band

and Orchestra in St. Paul. The elder Danz, who played the viola and the E flat cornet, was to be its leader.

The first concert of this hopeful organization, garbed in new uniforms, took place May 12, 1880, in the Academy of Music. There had been much fanfare and promotion. The program was garnished with choruses and vocal and instrumental solos. But the instrumental complement on this first night was pathetically small, even with a drum major and two "tubers" included. Nine musicians made up the total, but the Great Westerners of St. Paul added their forces to the Minneapolis contingent and in the *French Comedy* overture of Kelar Bela produced an effect which was described by the loyal *Minneapolis Tribune* as "seldom equalled." Mr. Seibert conducted the combination, and applause was so flatteringly fervent and prolonged that he unleashed a frolicsome encore, the *Tick-Tack Polka* of Johann Strauss. The evening, altogether, was tolerably successful.

The Great Western label did not last long, for before year's end the new organization was known as Prof. Danz's orchestra. It was engaged to play December 6 at the Germania Society's formal opening of the new Turner Hall on Washington and Fifth avenues North. Then and there the Danz name and dynasty were established.

The German Turners and their families assembled en masse on that cold night and admired the spacious auditorium, the handsome drop curtain painted by a Mr. Clausen, and the gas fixtures cleverly designed to resemble ancient brass and wax tapers. The program had the added inducements of singing from the Harmonia Society and its offshoot, the Männerchor Frohsinn, and the Apollo Quartet. Not the least of the evening's attractions were the exercises on the parallel bars by the gymnastics class and some deft twirling of Indian clubs by Prof. Charles Lampe.

In March of the following year, after the senior Danz had played several Sunday concerts in Turner Hall, came the first of a series of alarms which periodically in years to come warned of possible disbandment of the Danz forces or their removal from the city. Danz had been invited by St. Paul citizens to lead an orchestra in that city, and the immediate threat was his leave-taking from Minneapolis, where the box-office returns had been slim.

Efforts were whipped up, principally among members of the German societies, to retain him in Minneapolis, and the solution was the standard one, a benefit concert — in this instance, two of them.

The benefit or testimonial concert had become a familiar institution. It was the conventional but somewhat desperate remedy for depleted finances and yawning and dwindling audiences. On March 22 Turner Hall was moderately well filled to bring some three hundred dollars into the coffers of the Danz organization, and on May 4 the Academy of Music was the scene of a demonstration so enthusiastic and on such a scale as to settle, for the time being at least, the question of the Danz orchestra remaining a Minneapolis institution.

By this time, too, another long-standing custom at Danz programs had been implanted: the interlude by string quartet or orchestra, often the *pièce de résistance* of the concert. The quartet at the Academy testimonial concert was composed of Fred Will, who was to serve many years as concertmaster under both the Danzes, a Mr. Gangelhoff as second violinist, Danz himself as violist, and Clarence Strachauer as cellist.

Slowly the Danz orchestra and the Danz concerts developed a reputation. During the cold months the Sunday concerts at Turner Hall continued, and in the summer of 1882 a brief series of open-air concerts was started at Bridge Square, where patrons drove up with their teams and passers-by lingered to listen to Strauss waltzes, marches, mazurkas, and galops.

The strongest impetus to the cause of orchestral music in the early eighties came as a direct result of parental persuasion within the Danz family, aided by a bit of intramural bribery. It had been the senior Danz's fervent wish over many years to lure his violinist son away from his post as concertmaster for Theodore Thomas and back into the family fold. The father had long been thwarted in that desire by the close attachment between the famous conductor and his star pupil and protégé, and by the obvious advantages enjoyed by a rising young violinist who divided his time between the New York Philharmonic and the Thomas organization, where his rank was high and his position secure.

The bribe was a Stradivarius violin. This was a rare and mellow-toned instrument valued at twenty thousand dollars. It made an irresistible, a clinching, argument. Frank, Jr., capitulated to the fond father and the present that, to a serious violinist, is the gift of gifts. After the close of the 1882–83 season the junior Danz was no longer listed as first violinist with the Thomas orchestra. He had made his decision: the Twin Cities would be his home and workshop henceforth. The first record of the move appeared in the *Minneapolis Tribune* October 7, 1883, when it reported that Mr. Danz's orchestra "has been latterly greatly strengthened by the accession of his son."

A little more than five months later, on March 24, 1884, the younger Danz made his formal debut at the new Grand Opera House (on Sixth Street) as violin soloist with his father's forces. He played the Vieuxtemps *Violin Fantasy* at a complimentary benefit concert tendered the Danz orchestra by its co-laborers of the Philharmonic Chorus, one of the city's leading choral groups. Danz shared the honors of the evening with the first woman pianist of her day, Teresa Carreño, who was making her debut in Minneapolis.

Indicative of the role he was thereafter to play in the town's musical life, Frank Danz, Jr., was presented by the Philharmonic director, David Blakely, with a gold-mounted baton at the conclusion of his solo. His father received a gold-headed cane; his conducting days were over.

So the younger Danz, thirty-two years old at the time, stepped into his father's shoes, while the father, quite content with the turn of events, played viola for a time under his son.

Taking over the sixteen-piece orchestra, the new conductor immediately set about improving it and its repertoire and expanding its service. In addition to its formal concert schedules, he made it available in varying sizes and instrumental combinations for all occasions where music was seemly or necessary. He became, in time, a kind of orchestral jobber managing several units.

Businessmen's banquets were gaily serenaded by Danz's men. The military band contingent oompahed for parades. As time went on, no cotillion or hop, no university ball, acquired its cachet of smartness without the Danz orchestra purveying music from behind the palms. It was a reliable adjunct on countless operatic and choral programs.

As a conductor, Danz, Jr., was not the kind who riveted visual attention by threshing of arms and tossing of a thick head of hair. Facing his orchestra, he had somewhat the phlegmatic authority and weighty stance of Theodore Thomas, his teacher and mentor. His conducting gestures were held close to his chest in quick hand and forearm movements, his tempos beat out in old-style German strictness.

He was a "solid citizen," a family man, indulged in no expletives or profanity, and tended to business. He was respected and admired as a man of his word. He went through the world with a certain sense of the formalities required: a man of courtesy who donned his coat when ladies approached at rehearsals. If his orchestra fumbled during a concert he never turned a hair, and most of the audience never knew it. The offending musicians, however, would probably hear of it afterward. But he was not known to be a severe taskmaster with his men; he was soft-spoken, affable in a quiet way, reserved.

Danz was not an interpretative genius, but it was more important at the time that he was a kind of musical Job, harboring a fixed idea immune alike to assault and neglect. He gave the community, whether it wanted it or not — and there were times when it didn't seem to want it — its first professional and long-time diet of orchestral concerts. More than any other, he set the pattern of regularity and longevity in concert schedules, developing a communal habit of concertgoing that was later to spell long life and self-perpetuation for the Minneapolis Symphony Orchestra.

A stout, moon-faced man with a down-sweeping mustache, Danz was a quiet, industrious, and determined figure rather than a picturesque or sensational one. Brilliance, minus bulldog perseverance, could not have successfully grappled with the city's apathy and nonsupport. He arrived on the scene as a seasoned symphony violinist with a record of ten years' experience in the East. He knew his orchestral repertoire, and he brought to the Twin Cities an experience and technique in that field which were unmatched locally by any of his forerunners or contemporaries.

Through the last two decades of the century, when opera companies and jewel-laden divas and even such formidable rivals as the Thomas and Boston symphonies visited Minneapolis with mounting regularity, the Danz concerts — held every two weeks during the season — played a humble but vital part in developing Minneapolis' own musical identity.

The beginning of young Danz's Minneapolis career was not too promising. In fact his first assignment, the Turner Hall concerts in 1884–85, lost money so lavishly that ominous and well-publicized rumors again spread tidings that the Danz organization would be stolen from an apathetic Minneapolis by an alert and rapacious St. Paul. Civic pride was appealed to and public fear of a sad cultural loss was aroused in order to bolster faltering support. Further benefit concerts were organized, and Danz remained. It is probable that financial stimulants from the fairly prosperous elder Danz often helped override such crises as this one.

The young conductor, beating out time and trying to match expenses with intake, exerted herculean effort to keep his little band intact. But the odds were against him in a small hall on the near north side where the only patrons were the German-Americans of the vicinity and a scattered few from the city at large. In January 1886 a momentous decision was made. It was momentous in that it was life-saving, and life-saving in that a geographical shift brought the orchestra to the town and initiated what were to become, at least at intervals, the palmy days of the Danz organization.

The Turner Hall environment was that of a beer garden — very pleasant for those who liked to sip Pilsener with their music, but a hindrance to program elevation and the support of the well-bred portion of the community, which could not reconcile culture with drinking.

The move was to the new Harmonia Hall, home of the Harmonia Society, oldest choral organization in the city. The hall was a small upstairs auditorium at Second Avenue South and Third Street, and the new quarters had the effect of lifting Danz's music a step up the social scale. At Harmonia Hall no liquors were sold and no smoking was allowed. The change seemed for the best. The *Tribune* reported that the throng attending the first of the series at Harmonia "was an exceedingly orderly and quiet one, and was evidently composed of a class of people who enjoy music for its own worth and do not require the festive lager to assist them in appreciation." And it was recorded that "a number of people prominent in musical circles were noticed in the hall."

Schubert's *Unfinished* symphony was played that day, and the audience numbered only two hundred because of the extreme January cold. On later occasions the hall would hardly hold five times that number of patrons eagerly seeking admission, many of them forced to perch on the gallery rails.

Public prejudice against such worldly phenomena as orchestral music on churchgoing days was widespread in the United States, but particularly strong in a community where Yankee-Puritan influence and cultural interest often went together. So the Danz "Sunday afternoons" at Harmonia were almost invariably and loosely labeled "sacred concerts," regardless of the content of the program and ignoring the fact that frequently nothing of a religious nature could be found on the bill of fare. An effort or two was made to call them "symphonie matinees," but this coinage was dropped, probably because it was too oppressively aesthetic, and certainly secular.

Home-Grown Beginnings

Facing an attentive audience that only sat and listened, that fingered no steins and swallowed no malt, the Danz orchestra soon felt the pressure of a more serious purpose. Two months after the move to Harmonia, it was noted that the group was undertaking and performing "a much more difficult class of music than formerly." Often thereafter the programs contained only one or two sweetmeats by minor composers and more and more of the bigger names. Even in the first downtown season one program offered Beethoven (*Egmont* overture), Saint-Saëns, Schumann, Gounod, Berlioz, Bizet (a *Carmen* medley), and Wagner as represented by excerpts from *Die Meistersinger* —pretty modern for 1886!

This was probably too ambitious. Danz dared not venture too far ahead of his listeners, and he strengthened their trust in him by reverting again and again to their favorites. Against the rusty red background of the small Harmonia stage, he and his thirty-odd musicians would woo audiences with such things as Lumbye's *Visions of a Dream* (with zither obbligato), Labitzky's *Dream on the Alps* (an idyl that ended in an ethereal pianissimo), and Grieg's *Peer Gynt* suite. But they would also venture, at times, into Tschaikowsky and Liszt, and even into such dubious and difficult matter as the prelude and *Liebestod* from Wagner's *Tristan und Isolde,* risking the displeasure of perplexed auditors.

Danz doggedly rode the ups and downs of the public's erratic support. He was a persistent man who took many defeats and swallowed many deficits, and with Germanic calmness he endlessly strove to keep standards at a decent level and receipts at a paying level. It was by no means plain sailing, or a box-office dream.

Truthful James, a sharp-spoken *Tribune* columnist conveniently disguised by a pseudonym, expressed the sentiments of disaffected and unwilling concertgoers when he wrote:

What a glorious thing it would be for the public at large if musicians would be content with playing and singing a class of music that an average audience could understand and appreciate.

23

First Symphony Concert

SECOND SERIES

FRANK DANZ, JR.

Danz' Full Orchestra.

FRANK DANZ, JR., DIRECTOR . . .

. . . GEO. W. TRYON, MANAGER.

Harmonia Hall,

Sunday, February 7th, 1892,

At 3:30 P. M.

For a Danz "Sunday afternoon" at Harmonia Hall

Home-Grown Beginnings

The very great majority of individuals are not educated up to a standard of classical music, and it becomes a bore to them, especially after they have listened to five or six consecutive pieces of this beautiful but incomprehensible music. It is because they persist in doing something that they think will make them appear great, while the audience is not up to the point where they can comprehend the greatness. . . . It is all right for lovers of classical music to entertain each other with that style of music, but it has the same effect on the majority of audiences that a speaker would have addressing an American audience in Arabic.

This protest, a choice example of cultural know-nothingism, must have reflected the unsaid or under-the-breath opinions of many — mostly males who were dragged by their womenfolk to Prof. Danz's elevating afternoons — and was precedent for later complaints against Richard Strauss, Debussy, Stravinsky, Bartók, and their misguided advocates.

Harmonia Hall continued to be home base for Danz, although as time went on he ventured afield to Armory Hall (on Eighth Street between First and Second avenues South) for a series of spring promenade concerts, and in 1888 to the tonier environment of the Grand Opera House. Higher rent at that establishment meant higher ticket prices, which did not please those who had bought the same musical fare at lower rates at Harmonia Hall. Miss Mabel Holden's cornet solo, *Cornet Triumphant*, which featured Danz's first concert at the Grand, was evidently insufficient lure, for the crowd was small.

So the main series of concerts always returned to the lower downtown walk-up hall. There Danz played *Forge in the Forest*, which offered realistic representations of night, daybreak, brook's murmur, and forge's clang; then, possibly made queasy by this and like musical marshmallows, he played the scherzo from the Beethoven Eighth, a first performance, and the Bach *Air for the G String*.

Danz was a conscientious man, and always on call. He composed a *Toboggan March* for the Flour City Toboggan Club. He and his men played at banquets for jobbers and real estate dealers, paunchy men who smoked big black cigars. And violin in hand he stepped forward, after roaring applause at a testimonial concert, to play a solo: a transcription of a Chopin nocturne — this by way of thanks for a floral harp which had been borne to the stage and formally tendered him. "The rich, smooth tone which reverberated through the hall could only come from an instrument in the hands of an ideal artist." So said a nameless, fond critic.

The younger Danz was making his impress on the city, and was building up respect and loyalty, and a tradition. There was some competition from other groups, from the long-established band and orchestra of Wheeler Sidwell, and later from Oscar Ringwald, who conducted with more fire than the imperturbable and sometimes prosy Danz. But no rivals, over the long haul, equaled the class and endurance of the Danz ensemble.

Minneapolis had so far come of age musically by 1890 that Mr. Danz embarked on a daring enterprise: a program devoted wholly to pieces written by Minneapolis composers. There were no geniuses among this group, but it was remarkable that there were enough men in town composing music to supply material for such a program.

The concert led off with a rousing bit of homage in march time, *Salute to Danz*, by J. B. Lampe, which was followed by the overture to *La Fianza* by Willard Patton; two works for string orchestra, E. O. Baldamos' *Valse Lento* and A. M. Shuey's *Après Midi* (which had a far-off chiming effect); two works by Gustavus Johnson, *Reverie* for violin, played by Emil Straka, and *Polonaise*; and two vocal numbers, E. H. Gurney's *Mermen's Song*, sung by A. W. Porter, and Mr. Shuey's *I Know a Maiden*, sung by a male quartet.

This program — the fact that its content had been locally produced, the fact that it was performed at all — bespoke an increasing pride and self-reliance within the music community, a growth of creativity willing to exhibit itself. None of these home-grown works has survived; most of them doubtless were earnest and unoriginal applications of oft-used styles of composition. Nevertheless they were the product of a musical climate that was now salubrious and stimulating, made so by the year-after-year Danz concerts and the influx and activities of many new musicians.

The doughty fiddler-director for seven years had ridden a wave of civic expansion. In a decade's time the population of Minneapolis had more than tripled, from 46,000 to 164,000, and while Danz was involved in what might be called a minor phase of the city's galloping growth, he had started operations at an early stage of that growth and had kept pace with it in his own fashion.

But he could not always hold his advances. The all Minneapolis composers' program he offered in 1890 represented a milestone in musical initiative and public interest from which the following season, 1890–91, retreated most dismally. This was the season that nearly knocked him out. He had expanded his group to fifty members (only ten short of the Theodore Thomas ensemble) and had initiated concerts in alternate weeks at St. Paul's Harris Theater. When the audiences proved slim, he opened a midweek series at the Lyceum Theater on Hennepin Avenue. Then he tried his luck again at the Grand Opera House. He returned to Harmonia Hall. He tried classical music, popular music, music of every school and description. He lowered admission prices. All to no avail. People stubbornly stayed away, and Danz found himself at a loss to explain why last year's enthusiasm had changed to this year's neglect.

Money was lost consistently; the "scare" that the Danz orchestra would finally fold its tents brought only slight swelling of attendance as winter wore into spring. On April 20 came the old remedy, a testimonial concert. The house was tolerably well filled, though not to capacity, and the audience was reasonably enthusiastic.

Danz did not order disbandment. He did not go away. He stayed, and his response to public resistance was an idea that invited, and won, public favor. In May 1891 he started a series of summer concerts at the Lake Harriet pavilion with his uniformed military band, founding what was to be a long tradition and charming custom of hot weather music at that lake, then in an almost rural setting. The streetcar company put on four additional trains to serve the concerts, and ran them every three minutes. Subsequently Danz and his men took their first concertizing tour, playing at Winona and other towns.

And his luck had definitely changed by the time winter again rolled around. The standing-room-only sign was hung out at Harmonia Hall, with standees and latecomers so numerous as to annoy other listeners in the hall. The orchestra's execution was praised: the balance was good, tempos were excellent, and the shadings "exquisite." That hardy perennial, Lumbye's *Visions of a Dream,* was again trotted out, although an accident attended its performance. Mr. Schiefferl's zither, at the moment of its entry, was suddenly disabled by a broken string. "There was only a slight hitch, however, and one of the violins took the zither score and the piece finished in a way that called for an encore," reported the *Tribune.*

An all-Wagner program was offered in February and apparently scored a resounding success. It speaks well for Danz's enterprise that this program came a full year before, not after, the all-Wagner program that Anton Seidl and his Metropolitan Opera orchestra brought to town in 1893.

The Danz concerts continued through the nineties, and by mid-decade Harmonia Hall on Sunday afternoons had become a modest civic institution and a shrine for the faithful. But its appointments were fading and expediency dictated that the Danz orchestra play its final act in another home. It moved its weekly concerts to the new Metropolitan Opera House on First Avenue South in 1897.

These years of the middle and late nineties were the heyday of the Danz organization. It played alternate Sundays at the Lyceum Theater in 1898, and each summer shifted its locale to Lake Harriet. There a smaller group, attired in smart uniforms, serenaded the pleasure seekers who fled for an evening the day's dust and toil and heat.

Viewed from the harassed present day over the gulf of a half-century, those evenings at Harriet with the music floating over the water and sifting through the foliage of elm and oak have an idyllic quality, the pathos of an irrecoverable time. A *Tribune* writer described a Danz evening at the lake:

> The hot sun of the afternoon was tempered by a delightful breeze, and in the evening the air was just cool enough to suggest a light wrap for the ladies. In the evening it seemed as if the whole city had slipped out to Harriet for a gulp of pure air. The great pavilion was crowded by a never ending throng, and a sea of faces confronted the Danz orchestra when the concert began. The shore of the lake was lined for a half mile on either side of the pavilion with countless equipages and pedestrians, and there was plenty of room for all. The bicyclists, judging from the innumerable wheels that were bunched in all sorts of places, had come in a body. The lake was dotted with pleasure boats which presented a pretty spectacle as their white sides flashed in the brilliant electric light. . . .

Outdoor concerts provided ideal summer entertainment, a soothing blend of music and nature, and in his home city (Danz had moved to St. Paul after eight years' residence in Minneapolis) the conductor built up as great a popularity for his series at Como Park as he had at Lake Harriet.

Danz in 1896 initiated a new policy at his concerts, that of replacing vocal soloists with instrumental solos by various members of the orchestra. But continuing in favor were the pieces played by the string orchestra, a regular feature that Danz, a violinist, was as fond of as his listeners seemed to be. In 1898 he played an all-request program. A clue to the popular taste in music at that time may be gained by glancing at the numbers played: Sousa's *Stars and Stripes Forever*; Ole Bull's *Sunday Morning, or the Chalet Girl's Sunday*; Von Blon's *Whispering Flowers,* for strings; Mascagni's *Cavalleria Rusticana,* selections; Liszt's *Hungarian Rhapsody No. 2*; Goldmark's *Rustic Wedding* symphony; Wagner's *Lohengrin,* Introduction to Act III; Von Blon's waltz *My Ideal*; Bizet's *Carmen* suite; and Wagner's *Tannhäuser* overture.

As the new century neared, the Danz orchestra was approaching the end of its life as an ensemble. Its long service in the cause of music in Minneapolis was dramatized on a sentimental occasion on the afternoon of January 2, 1899.

Frank Danz, Sr., aged seventy-one, took up the baton he had not touched for ten years and conducted half a program in the Lyceum Theater. "Probably the hand that guided the forty musicians through the realms of tone did not move as gracefully as in days of yore," said the *Tribune*, "but the precision was there." Here were symbolized a continuity and a tradition that later helped a city symphony orchestra find a solid place on which to stand.

The younger Danz himself was nearing the twilight of his reign, when he was to relinquish conducting honors while furnishing the *sine qua non* — his experience and his men — for the orchestra that would replace and outshine his. He had patiently nourished and strengthened a frail plant — Minneapolis' interest in orchestral music — and could turn over the baton with a good conscience and the sense of a duty performed.

It may be said that along with the faithful and fervent approval which Danz's music drew from its followers there was much lip service, too, much talk that repeated the old saw that Danz had done more for music in Minneapolis than any other musician, and similar true but tired tributes. What did the majority really want, and enjoy most, during the two decades ending in 1900?

For one thing, they enjoyed the visits of Theodore Thomas' orchestra, which gave them heightened and more polished versions of the kind of music the Danzes had taught them to enjoy. Since 1869 Thomas, the country's leading and most persuasive crusader for symphonic music, had taken his orchestra on annual tours, bringing to inland America for the first time the riches of European orchestral literature in progressive-minded programs and commanding interpretations.

This much-traveled organization of fifty-odd musicians made its first venture into the terra incognita of Minnesota in May 1883, and on the twenty-ninth of that month gave the first of three concerts in Minneapolis, playing at the Market Hall on

Home-Grown Beginnings

First Street and Hennepin Avenue and then moving into the Grand Opera House. The opening program, with Julia Rive-King as piano soloist, comprised Beethoven's *Leonore* overture No. 3, two movements from the Schumann Fourth symphony, the Saint-Saëns G minor concerto, the *42nd Psalm* of Mendelssohn with a St. Paul chorus assisting, and Liszt's *Les Préludes* as a dramatic finale.

On the third and last night came the first uncut performance west of the Mississippi of the Beethoven Fifth — a historical occasion to be sure, but no doubt a rather heavy one for a spring night.

Theodore Thomas again came, played, and conquered in the spring of 1885. He was "slightly increased as to avoirdupois and baldness," combined a nonchalant with a businesslike manner, and looked rather bored. In response to applause he nodded curtly to the flower of fashion and refinement arrayed before him in the hall, where all the ladies, it is reported, were dressed formally in white. A pretty vignette of the period is supplied by a newspaper writer: "Many of them wore white bonnets and their attire was in most cases set off by a refreshing bouquet of flowers or a brightly colored fan. They were gracious enough to wear small hats. . . ."

Five years later Minneapolis heard another great orchestra and an internationally noted conductor, the Boston Symphony under Arthur Nikisch. This much-anticipated appearance took place in May 1890 in the echoing Coliseum near the University of Minnesota campus. The concert had only a qualified success. Poor acoustics threw the tone off balance, and the program was deemed trite by many. Liszt's *Les Préludes,* Grieg's *Peer Gynt* suite, the Schumann D minor symphony, and a vocal soloist, Mme. Steinbach-Jahns (who was out of voice), were not sufficient to impress listeners who had expected something more stimulating from Herr Nikisch.

It was a brilliant public event rather than a brilliant program. It caused a traffic jam on the east side, with crowded streetcars and close-packed carriages impeding progress to the Coliseum.

Inside, the newly installed arc lights added to visibility but not to audibility; their hissing competed with pianissimo passages. Conductor Danz was present as an absorbed listener, and after hearing the concert he uttered the conductor's classic complaint: "If we could only have as much rehearsing as these men!"

But Minneapolitans in the eighties and nineties were by no means committed to orchestral fare, which in fact was considered rather intellectual; the popular taste leaned toward opera — grand, yes, but particularly light and comic. This form of entertainment was brought to them by an endless procession of singing troupes: Henry Clay Barnabee's Boston Ideals, later reorganized as the Bostonians; the well-loved Emma Abbott and her companies; the Phillips, Hess, Grau, Mapleson, Carleton, Fay Templeton, Duff, and Calhoun companies; and countless more. Minneapolis music lovers flocked to see and hear Nilsson, Patti, Nordica, Calvé, Eames, Lehmann, Sembrich, Campanini, and the other great chests and throats of the day. (Portly Mme. Nilsson had been an awe-inspiring spectacle in her robe of lemon-colored brocaded satin, her left shoulder bearing decorations from the royal houses of Sweden and Saxe-Coburg. But she was no more gorgeous than Patti, who sang in a costume of heavy shrimp-pink satin garnished with pearls, with long flesh-colored mits encasing her arms.)

Minneapolis audiences welcomed bald, slope-shouldered Reményi and dashing Sarasate with their violins; slouching and unkempt D'Albert and the plump but dainty Teresa Carreño, king and queen of the keyboard; the diminutive and frozen-faced Camilla Urso, violinist; the young Ignace Jan Paderewski; and the boy prodigy Josef Hofmann. They were wild, of course, about band music, especially as played by P. S. Gilmore and later by John Philip Sousa.

And they sang. How they sang! If one wanted to take a hand in making music oneself, and was not content just to sit in a seat and gape, one joined a chorus. Many choruses waxed and waned during the period, but it was especially the Harmonia, the Frohsinn, and the Philharmonic and Apollo clubs in their various incarnations that gave the city's singers opportunity to raise their voices under some sort of discipline.

The fact that for ten years many of the roving opera companies and soloists had a sumptuous setting in which to set off their wares when they came to Minneapolis gave new prestige and a certain cachet to musical entertainment. The Grand Opera House, opened with an elaborate festival in April of 1883, was the finest structure of its kind the city had ever seen. The Grand, as it was familiarly known in the eighties and nineties, was the first ground-floor playhouse in the city's history, with a stage of unheard-of dimensions: forty-four feet wide and sixty-five feet deep. Its décor was both Moorish and lavish. Strangely enough, this handsome house survived hardly more than a decade, in 1895 relinquishing its rank as leading theater to the Metropolitan Opera House on First Avenue South, which had opened the year before as the New People's Theater. By this time the old Academy of Music was ancient history, or at least long extinct; it had succumbed to fire, a spectacular blaze, on Christmas afternoon of 1884.

Minneapolis' booming *fin de siècle* witnessed an avid importation of music, but local production, as we have seen in the outstanding instance of the Danz career, was accelerating too. New and arresting personalities in respectable number appeared on the scene.

Among the most colorful of these was Richard Stempf, jovial and tempestuous director for many years of the Harmonia Society. He was a big German with a booming bass voice, a thick accent, and a dueling scar on his cheek. He writhed and stamped at rehearsals and muttered an agonized "Mein Gott!" when new and raw members sang incorrectly. There was friendly collaboration on many occasions between Stempf's chorus and Danz's orchestra.

One of the more solid figures of the musical community was Hermann Emil Zoch, a rather pedantic and certainly a tireless pianist, who did more for classic piano repertoire than any person before him. Occasionally he played with the Danz orchestra, once performing the Weber *Konzertstück,* and later the Beethoven Fourth concerto, no less. But he was chiefly remarkable, and most awesomely regarded, as a man of limitless memory and endurance who season after season offered recital series devoted to Beethoven, Schumann, Chopin, Liszt, and Brahms. In fourteen years he gave fifty recitals, never once repeating himself, and in 1899 he drew a long breath and started on his second fifty. He reached a score of seventy-three performances before returning to Germany shortly before World War I to live on a government annuity. This war later swept away his insurance earnings, and he worried out his last years in near penury.

Handsome and energetic David Blakely, who for a time had printing and newspaper interests, was active through the eighties and into the nineties as a well-liked choral leader and impresario. The Mendelssohn Club, a small male group he directed, made a plushy debut in 1881, at which time the stage was embellished with rugs, palms, flowers, and a bust of Mendelssohn. Ushers wore full dress and handsome printed programs permitted no advertising. Later Blakely was director of the Philharmonic Club (an early and short-lived chorus), which caused something of a sensation at one of its combination concerts with Gilmore's famous band when the *Anvil Chorus* was pounded on real anvils with real sledge hammers. Blakely eventually became manager for Gilmore, and later for John Philip Sousa.

The brothers Lachmund — Carl V. (pianist, composer, and pupil of Liszt) and Ernest (cellist) — arrived in 1884 and created quite a stir. With their sister, also a musician, they promptly plunged into the musical whirlpool and started concertizing, composing, and teaching. Carl Lachmund achieved astonishing success with children and soon organized a juvenile orchestra that attracted almost as much attention, and probably more curiosity, than many a singer and operetta imported from the East. In 1888 this quaintly monstrous corps of youngsters numbered thirty members, playing everything from xylophones and glockenspiels to harmonicas and jew's-harps. It even boasted a bass viol. This was played by three boys about five or six years old, one of them perched on a high stool to grasp the strings, the other two below pulling the bow back and forth like a two-handled saw.

Hal Woodruff, later a long-time director of the Apollo Club, came in 1886, an organist from Cincinnati, to play at the opening of the Exposition Building, and remained as a church organist and choir director. Gustavus Johnson, pianist, composer, and teacher, was long at the forefront of things musical, and founded a music school bearing his name in 1898. Willard Patton, a singer and composer, made his first bid for fame by conducting a performance of *Trial by Jury* and later took on the Verdi *Requiem*. Popular and active well into the twentieth century, he became most noted for his oratorio *Isaiah* and for a light opera with Cuban setting, *La Fianza*.

Among the violinists must be mentioned Fred Will, the Danz concertmaster, and Emil Straka, soloist for Danz, who had luscious tone and a "Hungarian style." Later, from Chicago, came Heinrich Hoevel, who in 1890 founded the Minneapolis String Quartet (made up of Hoevel, the Lachmunds, and Fritz Schlachter) and remained to become a violin teacher of numerous and notable progeny; and from New York Claude Madden, wayward but brilliant violinist and excellent chamber musician, who conducted the Apollo Club for a short time.

The period also saw the rise of Olive Fremstad, Swedish-born Norwegian mezzo-soprano who was reared in Minneapolis, sang for a time with the Boston Ideals, and by steady and single-minded drive made her way from the Church of the Redeemer quartet to the world's leading opera houses.

During this same decade music schools were sending down roots and increasing their enrollments. The Northwestern Conservatory of Music (becoming the Twin City Conservatory, which was absorbed in 1915 by the MacPhail School of Music) and the Johnson School of Music (followed later by the Minneapolis School of Music and still later the Minneapolis College of Music) were beginning to make the city a place not only to hear but to learn music. The community's foundations for music were becoming more solid.

Music and Maestros

The nineties were particularly notable as a time for births of musical organizations that anchored themselves firmly in the community and lived long and fruitful lives. Their influence on civic musical development plays a crucial part in our story. Two of these groups are alive and thriving in mid-twentieth-century Minneapolis.

One of the two came into being in 1892, when the forty women of the Lorelei Club held an organization meeting, drew up a constitution, and emerged as the Ladies' Thursday Musicale, which later shortened its name to the Thursday Musical. Laura Carroll Dennis, a singer recently returned from study in Europe, was a prime mover in the new organization, which soon grew like the green bay tree, engaging noted artists as soloists and eventually playing hostess to the Chicago orchestra of Theodore Thomas.

The second of the hardy survivors was a reborn Apollo Club, male singing group, which sprang from the remnants of the old Mendelssohn Club in 1895, the creation of W. H. Eichman, General Charles McC. Reeve, and the "singing twins," C. B. and George B. Eustis. Fifty-seven years later it was giving regular concerts to capacity audiences.

But most significant for the future was the start in 1892 of the Filharmonix, an organization which ten years' time and a sequence of events were to make the direct progenitor of the Minneapolis Symphony Orchestra. If the Danz orchestra can be called the mother of the Symphony-to-be, the group of giddy but progressive young men who gave themselves this awful name of the Filharmonix can rightly be called its father.

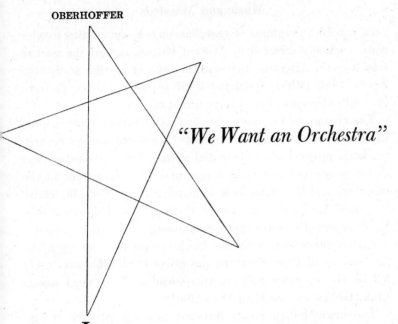

"We Want an Orchestra"

I N THE beginning the membership of the Filharmonix, starting at twenty, was entirely male and amateur, and its purpose was social-musical fun in the homes of its members. In hardly any time at all it spawned the Filharmonix Glee Club, the Filharmonix Mandolin Club, the Filharmonix String Orchestra, a male quartet, and a corps of eager banjo players. Its first two public concerts were invitation affairs and attracted many listeners to a new type of musical variety program. Impressed by their success, the members strengthened their organization, made associate memberships available to those interested, and in a few months' time augmented the string group with reeds and brasses to make a "symphony orchestra," so called, under the direction of B. A. Rose.

This little orchestra, composed mostly of amateurs, performed for four years under Rose's direction and then expired. Changes were afoot, a new orientation was in the wind. From the status of musical playboys who thought that "Filharmonix" was an amusing name, the club, headed by Clarence Strachauer, gradually grew into a solid and serious institution. Its early concerts had been catch-all programs of miscellaneous character. But its glee club, originally directed by Willard Patton, carried the seed of true growth. After the founding in 1895 of a rival group, the Apollo Club (which restricted itself to male voices), Patton's glee club blossomed into a large mixed chorus.

The change to the more dignified name of the Philharmonic Club came in 1897, and the emphasis then shifted almost entirely to choral projects of a substantial nature. The organization was in the process of becoming a new and aggressive force in the city's cultural life. Some talk of merging the two singing clubs, the male Apollo and the mixed Philharmonic, led to nothing. Each, apparently, was eager for dominance.

Patton carried on with the Philharmonic's chorus until the fateful year of 1900, when the possessive eye of the directorate fell on the dynamic and ambitious leader of the rival Apollo Club. His name was Emil Ober-Hoffer.

This tawny-haired young Bavarian had arrived without fanfare in St. Paul in the early nineties as a kind of musical jack-of-all-trades who had been a prodigy violinist in his native Munich and a peripatetic student and teacher of music since. He was born in 1867, the son of Johann Ober Hoffer, musician and composer who had directed opera at Munich and served as court organist in Luxembourg. (The name Ober Hoffer came to be spelled Ober-Hoffer in the nineties and Oberhoffer after the turn of the century.)

Emil had been reared in a musical household, and proved himself an eager listener and learner from the earliest age, with an extreme sensitivity to musical tone. In later years he would tell of the time his father gave a musical soiree at the Ober Hoffer home, when through some lapse of the customary discipline the child Emil was permitted in the music room after his normal bedtime. He had crept unnoticed to a dark corner near the piano-forte, and hid there trembling. He was discovered, later in the evening, clinging to a piano leg in a state of hysteria.

His first venture in conducting, in his early teens, ended disastrously. A traveling Passion Play company informally engaged the young fiddler to conduct a performance, but Emil fled the small hall in fright when the spectacle of the Crucifixion unfolded itself on the stage.

Herr Ober Hoffer gave the boy his first lessons in violin and organ, which were avidly learned, then Emil went on to instruction at the Munich Conservatory, studying under Josef Rheinberger and Cyrill Kistler. It was during these years he learned much of the Catholic service, in which, in later life, he was well versed.

His travels began with his removal from Munich and Luxembourg to Paris, where he studied piano under Isidore Philipp, who was much impressed with his pupil's skill and taste and promise. Meanwhile the Ober Hoffer family had broken up, so young Emil came to America in 1885, becoming musical director at Manhattan College in New York City, playing organ at St. Cecilia's Church there, and serving for a time under Conductor Anton Seidl.

It was one of the many Gilbert and Sullivan troupes then plying the countryside that brought Oberhoffer and his young English wife, a singer, to the Twin Cities for the first time. Legend has it that the company limped into town and halted there because of financial embarrassment. Whatever the cause, the musical couple remained, and for a while their fortunes were at an extremely low ebb.

One night a worried and out-of-funds Oberhoffer called at the Danz home in St. Paul, borrowed ten dollars, and got a job playing viola the next day in Danz's West Hotel orchestra in Minneapolis. Old-timers recollect that the future symphony conductor played in Twin Cities restaurants and saloons during the first impoverished months after his arrival, obtaining these temporary musical jobs from Danz in Minneapolis and Seibert in St. Paul.

Oberhoffer was not long to be cornered in such humble occupations and soon established himself in more dignified and rewarding roles worthy of his talents. He became organist at the Church of St. John the Evangelist in St. Paul and not long afterward he was making himself valuable to that city's leading musical organization, the Schubert Club. He lectured on musical subjects, played in string quartets, gave recitals, and before long had formed a choir and orchestra for the club. Meanwhile he employed his conducting gifts in performances of such fare as *The Mikado* and *The Chimes of Normandy*, the latter bringing him for the first time to general public attention in October 1893.

In 1895 he moved to Minneapolis as organist of the Church of the Immaculate Conception, and now his abilities began to thrust him into prominence. He acquired numerous voice and piano students and was active in programs of the Ladies' Thursday Musicale and its chorus. He assumed the organist's post at the Church of the Redeemer. In late 1896 he was appointed director of the Apollo Club, his first really important post. Here he was able gradually to take on more formidable assignments prompted not so much by others' suggestions as by his own desires and ambitions. By 1900 he was causing much grumbling and head-shaking among the conservatives for his rashness in presenting long oratorios and concertized operas.

These last years of the century were a time of keen competition musically, and there was pulling and hauling in various directions. No love was lost between the rival choruses, but the liveliest and bitterest feud was the personal one between Oberhoffer and a soprano of small build and big ambitions who had arrived, in a state of dynamic ill health, from Europe in 1893. The fourteen-year sojourn of Anna Eugénie Schoen-René in Minneapolis made an eventful interlude in the story of an orchestra's beginnings; though irrelevant in the final stage, it had the great virtue of quickening the formative processes already at work in the community.

Fräulein Anna from the Rhineland and the choral conductor from Bavaria became rivals when events pressed both into positions of authority. Neither had any use for the other, and each was caustic and outspoken in criticizing the other's gifts and personality. At the start it was the energetic and sharp-tongued Schoen-René who took opportunity firmly by the forelock.

"We Want an Orchestra"

Whereas Oberhoffer's ascent was slow and laborious, Schoen-René dramatized her presence in the community without delay, becoming the city's musical gadfly and a self-appointed and zealous promoter of musical culture.

She had come from Koblenz via Paris after preparing herself for an operatic career under the renowned Pauline García-Viardot; she had sung in Beethoven's *Fidelio* and in Mozart opera. Poor health forced her to give up a promising career and she arrived in Minneapolis "a skeleton weighing only 98 pounds." She had come to visit her sister Marie, who was teaching at the University of Minnesota, and to recuperate from what doctors had called a hopeless case of consumption.

In spite of poor health, she paused only three months before presenting herself in public recital. The outcome would have been an outright disaster to any but the invincible Fräulein Anna, for the program was long and taxing and her voice was clouded and roughened by a severe cold. It was an embarrassing evening for those who had come to be impressed and thrilled.

In a year's time the little woman in mannish clothes, driven by a relentless desire to employ her gifts purposefully and to improve the community, had organized the University Choral Union and was directing it in a program, at the People's Theater, that starred the regal Lillian Nordica. This chorus was an amalgamation of student glee clubs she had formed at the University of Minnesota, and represented the first effort to organize music teaching on the campus. In her own words, she "started the university music department" — a statement which mistook the intention for the accomplishment.

The Choral Union's concert demonstrated brilliantly Schoen-René's abilities both as an organizer and as a choral conductor. Her student voices were well blended and rang out true and resonant. It was a pretty tableau when Mme. Nordica was showered with roses and saluted with a rousing "Ski-U-Mah!" by the assembled choristers.

Thereafter the Fräulein, as she was called, expended her boundless energies in many directions, while the bracing Minnesota climate was restoring her health. She staged many festivals, brought many famous singers, violinists, and pianists to the city, and engaged renowned orchestras and opera companies. Usually large audiences attended her attractions, but sometimes they produced small profit. If the advance sale was poor, she signed passes by the bushel and dispersed them far and wide — even to the elevator men in Donaldson's Glass Block. As a buyer of musical talent, she was always a "good loser" when the talent did not sell.

Fräulein Schoen-René had found a mission in Minneapolis. She had arrived in a hinterland community that she regarded as backward musically, and she took it upon herself to correct the situation promptly, raising the city's musical standards by the scruff of the neck, employing all her friendships and connections with the musical world at large to carry out her purpose.

Her aggressiveness and her often autocratic manner frightened many. Some of the town's leading families took her up, but others scampered out of the way when the determined little woman, with a glint in her eye, bore down on them. Her projects were nothing if not ambitious, and sometimes she ran into opposition based, not unreasonably, on Minneapolitans' desire to run their own show. Such was the situation in 1897 when a group of Minneapolis businessmen and musicians had planned a mammoth festival only to find that the redoubtable Fräulein had beaten them to the draw and was planning *hers,* for the same month of May.

A compromise was reached, sparing the city the onerous responsibility of supporting two large-scale musical festivals in one season.

Meanwhile Schoen-René's restless mind was at work on other enterprises. She presented excerpts from operas, founded a dramatic club on the campus, organized a chamber orchestra. In 1898 she was credited with being the first woman orchestral conductor in the country. (She professed not to like conducting. "By my own wish," she later wrote, "I usually contrived to hide myself from the public behind screens of flowers and large palms.") She served as adviser on public school singing. And finally she decided to establish a full-scale, professional symphony orchestra.

In her autobiography, *America's Musical Inheritance,* she relates her unsuccessful efforts to bring such an organization into being. According to her story leading citizens had promised financial backing to the tune of thirty thousand dollars for her Northwestern Symphony Orchestra, which was to serve not only the Twin Cities but a sizable surrounding territory. She proceeded to sign up instrumentalists, engage Walter Rothwell as permanent conductor, and arrange with Walter Damrosch, Emil Paur, and others of equal note to serve as guest conductors. But she went to Europe for her annual vacation, and when she returned she found the bubble had burst. "I was informed a wealthy citizen of Minneapolis had been persuaded to give to that city its own orchestra, and was prepared to guarantee sixty thousand dollars! This, of course, made my backing insignificant, and most of the men I had engaged decided to abandon me for the other."

As this suggests, other events over which Schoen-René had no control were leading to a momentous denouement, and her campaign, for all its worth in stimulating the town's musical pulse and appetite, was fated to run into a dead end.

(After Schoen-René left Minneapolis, her main career as a voice teacher of international reputation began to grow, culminating with her association, in her later years, with the Juilliard Graduate School of Music in New York. Among her students who were to come to prominence were George Meader, Mack Harrell, and Risë Stevens.)

The events which, while realizing Schoen-René's goal for Minneapolis, nullified her personal campaign, may be said to have begun when the Philharmonic Club succeeded in 1900 in luring Oberhoffer away from its competitor, the Apollo Club. Some of the Apollo men were bitter and regarded the maneuver as theft. They felt they had raised their leader from obscurity and by giving him his first important conducting post had earned the right to retain him exclusively. If he had expected to fill both positions, he was disappointed. He resigned the Apollo Club post under fire.

The Philharmonic was now at a high tide of ambition and achievement. Its days of mandolin and banjo twanging and other kinds of musical dabbling were far behind. In December 1900 Oberhoffer conducted his new chorus in a performance of Mendelssohn's *Elijah* which marked "a distinct advance musically for Minneapolis." A published letter to the conductor from W. L. Harris, a Philharmonic Club director, expressed the hope that "Minneapolis will have such facilities in the way of a proper hall and efficient orchestra as to relieve the director of some of his handicaps." Harris' reference to an "efficient orchestra" was the opening gun in a we-want-an-orchestra campaign.

The orchestra for the club was still an improvised, pro tem support for the choral performances. Orchestral musicians were engaged on a haphazard basis: the professionals were paid for piecework; others played for pleasure. The arrangement was neither satisfactory nor businesslike, and it was hardly "efficient." Often as not, musicians who had played at rehearsals were among those missing on nights of performances, lured away by more remunerative assignments. Those who played for the fun of it were hardly more reliable; enjoyment could be a vague and fluctuating compensation.

But Oberhoffer knew how important the orchestral adjunct was to the success of the chorus, and from the time he took over the Philharmonic baton he began to talk, to plead, to persuade. A full-fledged symphony orchestra became his dream and his goal. He visioned the greater possibilities, the wider and more dramatic scope of musical literature, which a symphony orchestra could bring to the people of the city. For the time being, though, he had to make do with what he had.

The Philharmonic's next season, 1901–2, was more than ever ambitious, for it offered two oratorios, *The Messiah* of Handel and *The Creation* of Haydn, and an evening of short cantatas and part songs. At season's close Frederick Fayram, president, announced that the orchestra was to be a regular feature of each of the ensuing season's concerts and that the past season had created a deficit, though not a large one. The fact that business-men supporters of musical ventures were not only facing deficits as a penalty for their cultural enthusiasm, but paying them, was a significant orientation to the problem of financing musical enterprises of civic worth.

The club embarked on its most pretentious effort the following season, and there was portent in the fact that for its performance of *Samson and Delilah* it authorized its conductor to engage needed instrumentalists from the Chicago orchestra of Theodore Thomas. The Saint-Saëns opera was to be given in concert ver-sion, and Oberhoffer spent the summer of 1902 arranging parts so that it could be played with a maximum of forty-five instruments.

The opera was presented November 2 in Swedish Tabernacle. The outcome of Oberhoffer's long labors and the club's expendi-ture of an unprecedented sum of $1600 was impressive not only to the city's concertgoers but to the Philharmonic directors, who now glimpsed what might be done with Oberhoffer's organizing and conducting abilities. The performance clinched the argu-ment, for many, on the need and desirability of a permanent orchestra, and Oberhoffer gained valuable recruits for the cause.

The general response to this *Samson and Delilah* was reflected in the review of Florence Bosard in the *Tribune* the next day: "It is impossible to say what the production of this tremendous work means to Minneapolis. It shows hitherto undreamed of possibilities. It shows that there are the voices, the intelligence, the executive ability, and most necessary of all, the director. The orchestra was splendid . . . [Oberhoffer] directed at once with a subtlety and force . . . magnetic in his influence . . ."

This comment obviously was not routine praise, but arose from excitement and conviction. It was also recognition of the in-creased mastery Oberhoffer had gained over the sometimes reluctant and doughy vocal forces he was trying to shape. At rehearsals he was both a witty wooer and a despotic taskmaster.

He could make sly asides, once alluding to a suave passage from a French composer's work: "Catch a Frenchman writing anything hard." Then, with the suddenness of a thunderclap, he would break out in a blistering tirade against his erring and perspiring singers. A trembling Philharmonic alto one night returned to her home and wrote in her diary: "At rehearsal Mr. Oberhoffer maligned, browbeat, ridiculed and all but bodily attacked the basses and tenors. He got more quiet about 10 o'clock and let us all leave in safety."

The weekly Philharmonic rehearsals were held Mondays in the guild hall of St. Mark's Church on Sixth Street between Hennepin and Nicollet avenues. They were often turbulent sessions, seasoned with sarcastic humor. At one time the tenors were struggling with a Latin phrase. "Where is your Latin?" Oberhoffer cried. "You are singing in Latin, you think?" Then under his breath: "I hear lots of hog Latin around here." He exploded at inattentiveness. Once he rapped a rehearsal to a stop with his baton and furiously snatched his score off the stand, burying his face in it so that only his reddish hair was visible — a ludicrous caricature of a singer with his nose in his music. Then he shouted: "What do you think I am waving this stick for? For exercise? I don't need this exercise. I have an exerciser at home!"

The choristers rallied for new and keener effort after such attacks; they accepted the scathing rebukes as part of their training from a man who intensely wished them to be as good as they could be, and they relished his wit, which was as often playful as destructive. After rehearsals they were wont to crowd around his stand for what further insights and suggestions he might offer. He offered much, and not all of it was technical instruction. His learning and interests leaped musical boundaries; by the time the choristers had mastered *Samson and Delilah,* most of them felt they had taken a course in biblical history.

After its triumph with Saint-Saëns' Bible story in evening clothes, the Philharmonic continued its season with another performance of *The Messiah* Christmas night, of Verdi's *Requiem* February 13, 1903, and of Mendelssohn's *Saint Paul* March 27.

"A pictorial blend of grace and authority"

The Danz men, and Danz himself as concertmaster, had been a vital aid in some of these productions, including the *Samson and Delilah* success, and their functioning under Oberhoffer foreshadowed their role as the heart of the orchestra to come. But the Danz orchestra, as a self-sustaining institution giving its own series of Minneapolis concerts, was being lost in the shuffle in these days of change.

In 1901–2 it had enjoyed a last flicker of glory, but there had been a note of desperation in its promotional appeals. Minneapolis was promised a "new venture," a "mammoth undertaking," a "grand symphony orchestra" which would give eight concerts at the Metropolitan Opera House. Concertgoers were urged to buy season tickets in enough quantity to defray at least a good portion of the expense involved.

The prospectus pledged that some part of a symphony would be given at each and every concert, as well as "overtures of the highest importance." It gave assurance that there was no necessity for music lovers "paying high prices to attend concerts given by visiting organizations, for in Minneapolis was an organization that would give as good as the best." A ceilinged shell was built for the Metropolitan stage and new men appeared in the ensemble. Danz, who had been known, at times, to throw things together in routine fashion, took unusual pains in rehearsal, coaching his reeds and brass sections separately before blending them with the full orchestra.

But the reception at the opening concert was cool, and the faithful scowled and made strained excuses for Minneapolis audiences that by nature were undemonstrative. In early 1902 Danz postponed his sixth concert two weeks to give the concertgoing public a chance to "catch its breath" after a crowded calendar of performances by visiting stars and by bands conducted by Creatore and Innes. The disparaged "visiting organizations" were taking their toll. The postponed concert offered the Mozart *Concertante for Violin and Viola,* a choice that indicates the frequently high caliber of Danz's programming.

But the February 16 concert that followed was more an outright bid for mass support, for it brandished as a lure Signor Liberati, noted cornetist, who promised each lady attending the concert an autographed copy of one of his march compositions arranged for piano, "the same as is sold in music stores."

This was an echo of a provincialism now becoming dated in a city whose musical tastes were growing more sophisticated and whose ambitions were not satisfied by such bait.

Danz himself was about ready to call it quits as a symphonic leader. He was comfortably ensconced as theater orchestra director at the Metropolitan, and the years were teaching him that he loved his violin more than his baton. So the Danz orchestra finally gave up the ghost in the 1902–3 season, and by becoming Oberhoffer's concertmaster for the *Samson and Delilah* performance in late 1902 Danz gravitated to the key position he would hold in his last years.

At the same time the Philharmonic officers saw more clearly the handwriting on the wall. It formed the questions: "Why not a permanent orchestra? Why not an orchestra we can depend upon for both rehearsals and performances?"

Oberhoffer's insistent pleas were being reinforced by developments. As the choral undertakings grew larger and more ambitious, the handicap of the makeshift orchestra became more obvious. The situation finally was no longer tolerable; the time had grown ripe for a bold decision. In the spring of 1903, after the Philharmonic's most successful and brilliant season, the decision was made: An orchestra would be organized for the following fall, and it would be named the Minneapolis Symphony Orchestra.

In arriving at that decision, Philharmonic officers had to reconcile cross-purposes and iron out objections. It was a delicate operation in which the enthusiasm engendered by a big and thrilling idea had to be tempered by diplomacy.

For one thing, the attitude of Frank Danz and his seasoned players could not be ignored. Rumblings had come from the Danz camp, which claimed, with considerable justice, that an old and proven organization deserved civic support rather than one new and untried. When the new one seemed a probability, the Danz men favored their own experienced maestro as its head, reasoning that Danz knew orchestral technique while Oberhoffer had more experience in choral directing. But Danz counseled against any opposition to Oberhoffer, pointing out that the men behind the young conductor were citizens of means whose support meant a surer guarantee of weekly pay. His argument prevailed and there was no further resistance in the Danz ranks.

Nothing in the record, or in the memories of those who knew him, indicates that Danz pined for the exalted position of Minneapolis Symphony leader. The Symphony was Oberhoffer's dream, which became also the Philharmonic's dream and eventual reality. Oberhoffer would have preferred to form his own orchestra and pick his own players, without recourse to Danz and his musicians, but the simple fact was that Danz and his men were needed.

There were misgiving and opposition, too, within the bosom of the Philharmonic Club itself. Among many members there was more than a doubt that Oberhoffer's new project, and his whole-souled zeal for it, boded well for the health and morale of the choral organization.

But objections were overcome and conciliation and persuasion won the day. The club called a meeting of leading citizens and the plan was laid before them, and threshed out. The outcome was a comprehensive blueprint of the orchestral venture, with Oberhoffer engaged for three years as conductor in complete charge of programming and performance.

To take care of the additional responsibilities of the new orchestra, the Philharmonic's board of directors was increased to twenty-five members, and among the new appointees were E. C. Gale, J. S. Porteous, Horace M. Hill, Fred B. Wells, H. J. Burton, Eugene Stevens, R. P. Woodworth, and — portentous addition — a young lumberman who had once dreamed of being an opera singer, Elbert L. Carpenter.

Nine committees were named by President Fayram, and a season of six concerts by the orchestra, plus the regular concerts by the club, was announced. Artists of international reputation were promised. Season ticket prices were established: for the orchestral series $5 and $7.50, for the choral concerts $2.50 and $3.75, for the combined series $6 and $10. And a campaign to raise a guaranty fund of $10,000 a year for three years was successfully consummated.

This was something new to Minneapolis — a new concept and a new procedure. It had its precedents in other American cities which already supported their own symphony orchestras: in Chicago and New York, in Cincinnati and Philadelphia, and in Boston, where Henry L. Higginson in 1881 had first devised the plan which enabled civic orchestras to play music of high standards at reasonable admission prices, without worrying about the wolf at the stage door. Higginson, a music-minded financier, had set up a fund of $1,000,000 for the Boston Symphony in anticipation of yearly deficits of $50,000. Before the end of the century his example of private wealth making good the inevitable financial losses of symphony seasons had been widely followed.

The Minneapolis Symphony would soon find its Higginson, but meanwhile the first fund campaign involved an unprecedented marshaling of civic forces and moneyed men and interests, all in behalf of a cultural enterprise of hoped-for community value. The drive signified a revolutionary shift from individual to group enterprise in support of a musical organization. It instituted, for the first time, committee promotion and control of an orchestral venture in place of one-man management.

The Danz orchestra had been a private venture, striving for profit or at least solvency against fluctuating odds. It had pleaded but never campaigned for support. It had made no attempt to organize a city-wide patronage as insurance against calamity, and it had little power to do so.

The new plan had its roots in the growth of a large and influential organization, and one of the keys to its success lay, quite simply, in numbers. An all-city chorus had sprung up and flourished during the last decade of the Danz regime. The chorus in time needed a permanent orchestra, and through sheer numbers and the prestige and influence of its guiding spirits, it could reach out into the community as no thirty-man orchestra, and as no individual leader, could do on their own initiative.

Minneapolis at last wanted something that no one man or organization could afford. It wanted something that could no more pay for itself or show a profit than could a public library or an art museum. So the device of the guaranty fund, a citizens' subsidy, was adopted, amounting in essence to a self-imposed tax by people who were public-spirited and also wealthy enough to pay the assessment.

All the Philharmonic officers and directors worked on this fund campaign, but Edmund J. Phelps and T. B. Janney were leading spirits in the project, together with Fayram and other club officers such as Charles N. Chadbourn, Fred Smith, and W. L. Harris. Fifty-four guarantors, representing much of Minneapolis industry and wealth, were gathered into the fold that first season.

There was not yet complete realization on all sides that "guaranty fund" spelled "donation," or was anything but a temporary arrangement. A newspaper editorial called on the people of Minneapolis to prove their appreciation of what had been done for them by giving the orchestra a decent support, because "guaranty funds cannot be relied upon indefinitely." The author of that statement proved a poor prophet. Time would teach all contributors that sums contributed against *possible* deficit would eventually become guaranty against *certain* deficit. Minneapolis would maintain its proudest cultural institution through deficit financing, but to the canny it constituted a civic advertisement well worth the cost.

In June Oberhoffer with his wife went to Europe on a special mission, to hear concerts in various music centers, but more important to seek out and sign up needed instrumentalists and to procure scores for the orchestra's scanty library. He returned in September, having engaged two French horns (E. J. "Bill" Erck and Franz Baltrusch), an oboe (Paul Hofman), and a bassoon (Henry Cunnington). He brought with him more than a thousand dollars' worth of music, mostly novelties, including several scores by Richard Strauss which at that time could be obtained only through contact with the master himself. He had heard Fremstad, whom he compared favorably with Nordica, and Schumann-Heink, the "idol of Munich" in 1903. He was bubbling over with ambition and high spirits, and came back to Minneapolis with the conviction that in America "the great music of the future is to be developed."

Twenty-five Twin Cities musicians had already been contracted for, and the conductor promptly went about signing up others to make up a complement of nearly fifty. The orchestra's music library, even with Oberhoffer's purchases, was sadly inadequate, and now in addition to Danz and Danz's men, the Danz music was called upon, and freely handed over. (Some of this music still reposes in the Symphony's library.)

Sectional rehearsals started within a week or two after Oberhoffer's return, and by mid-October the whole orchestra was practicing three times a week in the old Holcomb Dancing Academy on Fourth Street between the *Tribune* and *Journal* buildings. In all there were nine rehearsals for the opening concert.

At the very start the conductor ran head-on into temperament trouble. Friederich von Wittmar, the orchestra's titled bass player, discovered when he arrived for the first rehearsal that his stand was number 2, and he refused outright to play in that subordinate position. It was a crisis that good-natured Ed Schugens solved quickly by relinquishing his status of principal to the baron.

It may have been a distinction to play with the new Minneapolis Symphony, but it was no road to riches. Musicians were paid $1.50 per rehearsal and $6 per concert. As time went on a Symphony musician could make as much as $20 to $25 a week.

In rehearsals, concertmaster Danz proved a great help in the suggestions he gave for phrasing and effects. Often Oberhoffer would hand over the baton to Danz, asking the older man to conduct a passage so that he might hear how it sounded. In those days, of course, there were no symphonic phonograph records and no radio, no way of hearing orchestral sound except from the living body of musicians that produced it.

The conductor, who believed in the concert hall proprieties and wanted no middlewestern gaucheries to mar his opening program, was particularly intent on observing all the niceties, all the punctilio, the occasion required. With that in mind he lectured his men on stage deportment at the final rehearsals. He adjured them not to cross their knees or talk among themselves while on the platform, and gave them explicit instructions on how to file to their seats before the concert started.

The orchestra's debut was set for Thursday night, November 5, 1903.

A soothsayer might have called it a propitious time for a new civic orchestra to introduce itself. The waning year had had its share of momentous events and changes and beginnings. Theodore Roosevelt was president. Before the year's end Wilbur and Orville Wright, near Kitty Hawk, North Carolina, would make their first shaky hen's hop in a mechanical flying machine. The first motion picture with a plot, *The Great Train Robbery,* had been filmed. The Ford Motor Company was founded. Serbia's king and queen and assorted relatives had been efficiently assassinated on the night of June 11, and Panama had shaken off Colombia in a quick revolution.

Fictional best sellers that year were Mrs. Humphry Ward's *Lady Rose's Daughter* and Thomas Nelson Page's *Gordon Keith,* but many were still devouring 1902's most popular books, *The Virginian* by Owen Wister and *Mrs. Wiggs of the Cabbage Patch* by Alice Caldwell Hegan. In the parlor around the piano the new tunes that were sung and strummed were *Sweet Adeline, In the Good Old Summer Time,* and *Under the Bamboo Tree.*

There was a landslide for the Republicans that first week of November, with Mark Hanna's Ohio candidate riding easily into the governorship of that state. But Tammany had won again in New York. The Crow Indians were raiding sheep herds in Wyoming and making life exciting but uncertain for sheepherders.

"We Want an Orchestra"

Enrico Caruso made his debut in *Rigoletto* at the Metropolitan Opera House and critic W. J. Henderson, with the sound of cheers still in his ears, wrote with a steady hand that the new tenor "made a thoroughly favorable impression, and will probably grow into firm favor with the public." Sergei Rachmaninoff had recovered from a paralyzing spell of lethargy, had composed his brilliant Second piano concerto, and was being badgered to play on every public occasion a youthful error, the lushly gloomy Prelude in C sharp minor. Richard Strauss's fecundity of ideas was beginning to show signs of depletion in his *Sinfonia Domestica*. Claude Debussy in France was engaged in composing his orchestral masterpiece, *La Mer*. Dimitri Mitropoulos, a seven-year-old boy in Athens, was playing his scales on the piano and occasionally worrying his watchful mother by wandering off into improvisations of his own.

The style profile for women emphasized two swooping downward curves, fore and aft, but showed no more than an instep at the lower level, and there was a passionate concern with neck decoration and long feather boas, some of which terminated in a series of little fur balls bouncing about not more than a foot above the sidewalk.

Washburn Crosby had not yet hit on "Eventually, Why Not Now?" for its Gold Medal flour but was edging closer to it with "No doubt about it."

In Minneapolis that year were portents of increased acknowledgment of the values of culture. William Mentor Crosse, a New Zealander with lofty ideas of what listeners should be encouraged to hear, had given all-Bach and all-Beethoven piano recitals, and the New England Furniture and Carpet Company had expressed its considered view that "the increase of the demand for Oriental rugs in a community is a sure index of, and coincident with, its growth in artistic inclination."

The pianola and the Victor talking machine ($3 down and $1 a week) were much advertised. Fashionable home interiors were heavily draped, and on Sundays contented householders unfolded their newspapers to read George Ade and Peter Finley Dunne while the children made a grab for Happy Hooligan, Buster Brown, and the Katzenjammer Kids.

The town at large, that opening week of November, was still firmly in the grip of football fever. There had been an epic game October 31 in which Minnesota had achieved a hard-fought tie, 6 to 6, with its old enemy, Michigan, outplaying Fielding Yost's point-a-minute Wolverines and apparently out-bruising and out-slugging them too.

At the Bijou Theater that week were Belasco's *Zaza* and Sudermann's *Magda* with Eugenie Blair, a large woman better equipped to emote as Magda than to sparkle as Zaza. Hall Caine's *The Holy City* (deprecated by the Catholic clergy) played to packed houses at the Metropolitan, the Ferris stock company offered *Colleen Bawn* at the Lyceum, while the Kentucky Belles displayed more than an instep at the wicked Dewey on Washington Avenue. Walter Damrosch and David Bispham, baritone, took the pulpit at the First Baptist Church to explain and sing the themes of Wagner's *Parsifal* and the *Ring*.

It was against this background of events large and small that the newborn Minneapolis Symphony Orchestra and its conductor, Emil Oberhoffer, tremulously faced their first-night audience in a makeshift concert hall.

A huge cluster of chrysanthemums, an exclamatory blob of pink, shared the stage's center with the dark, svelte figure of the conductor on the platform. Above and around the half-hundred seated musicians was festive green that rebuked the November chill outside, with potted palms tracing waxy curves and a festoon of yellow blooms making a blithe border around the stage.

The town had mustered more than a quorum to see and hear its new musical baby, cribbed in the windy expanses of the Exposition Building on the east side. The temperature had dipped to freezing, but raw weather kept only the faintest-hearted away from the exciting première. "Everyone" was there—everyone from society's upper realm, everyone from the circles of the music-wise and the music-mad.

The interior of the big, crude structure, which had resounded to hammering and sawing for many weeks, was only half in readiness for the high and eloquent art of the symphony. Drafts and echoes swept and caromed about the place. At one end of the hall, a billowing canvas curtain blotted out several acres of unneeded space. Skeletal beams and woodwork had been camouflaged with bunting and temporary walls.

Before his first downbeat that Thursday night, Mr. Oberhoffer was still a bit breathless on the platform. He had made a tardy arrival at the Exposition Building, delayed by the press of traffic moving over the bridge toward the hall, and blocked at the hall's entrance by a conscientious but confused doorman until he was identified and permitted to go inside.

He was a portrait of elegance. Oberhoffer never would be one to neglect the proper and picturesque habiliments of his profession. He laid down his gold-headed cane, doffed his topper, whipped off his silk-lined cape, pulled off his white gloves, and then made his entrance to the welcoming hand-spatter of nearly three thousand concertgoers.

Below at his left sat stout, sleepy-eyed, dependable Frank Danz, concertmaster and principal of the eight-man first violin team. Heading the cello section of four players was Carlo Fischer, brilliant young instrumentalist who had just been signed up by the Cincinnati orchestra for three years, but who was playing this first concert before his departure. He was to return to Minneapolis later and take an important role in the orchestra's development.

Among the first violinists were old Fred Will, bearded, aristocratic in bearing, a Danz veteran whose career went back as far as the senior Danz's first concert in 1880; the floridly handsome Claude Madden; and next to Danz in the first stand a skinny stripling, Albert Rudd, who had studied under Danz and taken charge of the Bijou Theater orchestra. In 1934 Rudd was to return to the symphonic fold after a career of many years as the city's best known theater orchestra leader and violinist.

In the second violins was another promising youngster, William S. MacPhail, a Madden pupil and Danz man whose European studies were still ahead of him, and still farther ahead his founding of the music school bearing his name.

The personnel was reasonably professional, considering the times and the limited amount of money available for musicians' salaries. But some of the men were only part-time musicians: Ed Schugens, bass, operated a shop that sold and repaired musical instruments and served as a gathering place for the musical fraternity. Julius Blakkestad, cello, was a salesman in his brother's musical instrument store. P. J. Lawrence, flute, was a lawyer. Cragg Walston, second violin, was in the lumber business with his father. As time went on, the orchestra would number in its ranks a mathematics professor who played bassoon, a paperhanger who played bass, and many another who divided his time with an outside trade or profession.

Some doubling was necessary, and at least five men in the ensemble were versatile enough to be able to shift from strings to wind instruments — from cello to bass clarinet, from string bass to tuba, from string bass to flute — and back again. Danz in the front chair, plus Danz men strategically located in all parts of the ensemble, formed the nucleus of the new organization, without whom Oberhoffer could hardly have mustered a corporal's guard.

The first performance of the new orchestra needed a big and costly name, preferably a singer's name, as an ace-in-the-hole guarantee of its success and as lure for that sizable portion of the populace that might be more name-conscious than symphony-hungry. The orchestra's backers were willing to spend $500 for such a name. Minneapolis' own Olive Fremstad, who in the last three years had become the darling of European operagoers, would have filled all specifications. But she was not available for the opening night and could only be engaged for a later appearance. The choice finally narrowed to the noted Anton van Rooy, Dutch baritone who had sung at Bayreuth, but a week before the concert van Rooy canceled his engagement, pleading that his attendance at Metropolitan Opera rehearsals, held earlier than usual, prevented his coming.

"We Want an Orchestra"

Only two well-known singers were available at that late date: Charlotte Maconda at $175 and Marcella Sembrich at $1800. The latter was fearfully expensive, but after prolonged discussion by the Philharmonic's board and the guarantors' committee, she was engaged, on the theory that the first concert demanded the best guest artist available, regardless of cost.

Sembrich was being trumpeted as the "successor of Adelina Patti" and had become the rival of Lillian Nordica as the prima donna then most in the public eye and ear. The imperious Polish coloratura, who had retained so much of girlish spirit and grace, had appeared a year earlier in Minneapolis, but her program, devoted wholly to song, had withheld from her hearers those highly ornamented arias in which she excelled and for which she was famous. This time, with great acclaim, she sang with the orchestra *Ah! fors e lui* from Verdi's *Traviata* and the Strauss waltz aria *Frühlingsstimmen,* and to Oberhoffer's piano accompaniment three songs by Schumann, Arne, and Richard Strauss.

Without question Sembrich added allure to the orchestra's première, exuding that regal aura that the idols of opera's golden age always carried with them as an almost tangible stage property. One of the chief values of her appearance was the attention it diverted from the obvious flaws of the orchestra's performance.

She had come for rehearsal earlier that week, and because her own scores had not yet arrived, she rehearsed the songs from Oberhoffer's scores and over his shoulder, beating time with a lorgnette sometimes at rhythmic odds with the conductor's stick, hissing in passages played too loud, giving quick nods of approval when the men responded alertly. With generous good will and not a little prescience, she later told inquiring reporters from the press that "the tone quality of the new Minneapolis orchestra is splendid, and in Mr. Oberhoffer you have a leader who is not only a cultured musician but an extraordinary conductor."

On the night of the concert, after the *Unfinished* symphony was performed, Mme. Sembrich was led gallantly from the wings by the maestro himself, the two walking onto the stage with fingertips just touching in a high and elegant handhold.

Music and Maestros

The first-night program was as follows:

1. Prelude to "Die Meistersinger von Nürnberg"......Wagner

2. Symphony in B minor........................Schubert
   a. Allegro Moderato (B minor)
   b. Andante con moto (E major)

3. Aria from "Traviata"...........................Verdi
   "Ah, fors e lui"

   Madam Sembrich

   WITH ORCHESTRAL ACCOMPANIMENT

4. Symphonic poem "Les Préludes"..................Liszt

5. Serenata ....Moszkowski

6. Songs with Pianoforte accompaniment:
   a. Der Nussbaum...........................Schumann
   b. The Lass with the Delicate Air..................Arne
   c. Ständchen ....Richard Strauss

   Madam Sembrich

7. a. Aragonaise from the Ballet Suite in "Le Cid"..Massenet
   b. Overture to "William Tell"....................Rossini

8. Waltz Aria, "Frühlingsstimmen"..........Johann Strauss

   Madam Sembrich

   WITH ORCHESTRAL ACCOMPANIMENT

How did the orchestra sound on that faraway November night of its birth? Thin, presumably. By today's standards it certainly must have sounded thin, with the strings, hardly more than half the personnel, drowned out when the brass blasted. This was pointed out in the critical post-mortems. Apparently Oberhoffer's stratagem of bringing the double-basses forward, close to the first violins, was not enough to make the strings hold their own in the tuttis.

But the violins, at least the firsts, were a sound and seasoned little body of men who could carry on acceptably even in a crisis, and in the Moszkowski morsel for strings they gave testimony of their finesse and coordination. This little serenade, in fact, was the most avidly greeted of the orchestral offerings, and Mr. Oberhoffer, with a raising of eyebrows that plainly said "it can't be helped," was persuaded to play it a second time.

The brass and woodwinds were less secure, their tones sometimes rough and their phrasing hesitant.

It was Oberhoffer who, after Sembrich, reaped the lion's share of the kudos. Henry B. Curry of the *Minneapolis Journal* alluded to the artistic repression and tasteful thoroughness of "the self-possessed conductor," while the orchestra was credited with precision, dynamic variety, and consistency.

The same Mr. Curry (who was soon to forsake music criticism and move to St. Paul to write a drama column for the *Pioneer Press*) had other things to say about the program: "The *Meistersinger* prelude did not 'appeal,' as the pastors put it. Neither did the technical difficulties, the transcendental melancholy, of Liszt's symphonic poem, *Les Préludes*. Yet everyone was charmed with the simple beauties of the Schubert symphony in B minor, thanks somewhat to its familiar harmonies. . . . And the *William Tell* overture, with its masterful 'cello solo by Carlo Fischer, completed a most favorable impression."

The *St. Paul Dispatch* sent a reviewer to cover the opening in Minneapolis, and from this writer's report we get another first-night reaction: "Mr. Oberhoffer is definitely gifted. If he sometimes gives preference to the song element and ignores the note of tragedy, he is only following the bent of a nature to which music spells happiness, and to which the music stands always in a glorified light."

The foregoing was signed M. K. B. for Minna K. Bailey, who covered a wide gamut of subjects for her paper, ranging from gardening to fine art, and who in the late twenties, as critic for the *Kansas City Star,* was to be the prime mover in launching that city's Marion Talley on her short-lived career as a Metropolitan Opera star. Miss Bailey also had complaints about the orchestra's balance and blanketed string tone: "The brasses will be more subdued when they are not so placed as to aim their tones directly toward the center of the house. The violins, which are of fine quality, will have greater power and body of tone when they are placed more compactly."

The *Minneapolis Times* stinted no praise: "What Mr. Oberhoffer has accomplished in so short a time . . . is little short of marvelous. There is a smoothness, a finish and unity of spirit altogether remarkable, and unexpected by even the orchestra's most sanguine supporters, and the tonal balance and quality are fine. Mr. Oberhoffer's work with the orchestra has more than ever convinced his friends that he has all the requirements for a great director."

So ran the morning-after comment. With all the fault-picking, and considering the inescapable hazards of a first try in an improvised auditorium, the orchestra's bow was auspicious. Many of course wondered whether the whole project wasn't another flash in the pan; there had always been a high mortality rate in the city's new musical organizations. First-night dazzle had often been followed, in an alarmingly short period, by last-night fizzle.

But the officers of the Philharmonic Club allowed themselves no dark premonitions, no more than did the man who overnight became a full-fledged symphony conductor. A dream had materialized, a comfortable pot of money had been raised, and a question had been answered: the question of whether a paid and permanent orchestral accomplice of the club could be set up and made to stand on its own feet.

With the tensions and satisfactions of the opening concert behind them, conductor and musicians plunged into preparations for the second concert, to be given December 1, when Harold Bauer, pianist, and Dvořák's symphony *From the New World* (then just ten years old) would be the major attractions.

Oberhoffer had taken on the chore of writing program notes, and his comment on the *New World* betrays his feelings, which were both positive and warm, about certain developments in popular music that had gained wide following: "It is scarcely within the scope of this note to inquire how far Dvořák was right or wrong in his acceptance of Negro tunes as typically American, but in the light of the recent popularity of the 'ragtime' (which is said to be of African origin by those best informed) it would seem that he hearkened aright, only where he,

with the skill of the master, could construct a musical edifice of
lofty dimensions, the same material less skillful builders have
prostituted into a sore affliction to our popular music — the ragtime."

It is interesting to note that Oberhoffer, long before a saccha-
rinity called *Goin' Home* had been made of the symphony's largo,
quoted a writer who had termed that slow movement a "Moonlight Night on the Plantation." One wonders whether he had
heard of the greater geographical shift given it by Anton Seidl,
first conductor to present the symphony, who called the largo
"Desolation of the Prairie in the Far West." Dvořák, needless
to add, was responsible for neither title.

The *New World* was quite unfamiliar and struck some listeners
as a bit revolutionary, or at least undignified. For that matter,
dignity was not served in the program's opener, Elgar's *Pomp
and Circumstance* march, which ran into technical trouble at the
very start. The beat-and-a-half rest at the opening was ignored
by the overeager brass, which came in fortissimo ahead of the
strings and fought with them — a measure apart — all the way
to the change of theme in the trio.

This accident disturbed critical listeners, who were even more
annoyed by the brasses' excessive volume; some called it noise.
Their complaint was often to be reiterated in the future; the
orchestra was long known in some quarters as brass-happy and
obstreperous. But criticism in that first year took odd and
apparently unjustified tangents. What seems now an innocuous
and amiably sentimental work, the *Rustic Wedding* symphony
of Goldmark, was played January 29, 1904, and was termed fantastic, bizarre, and ultramodern by the knowing Caryl B. Storrs
in his first signed review in the *Tribune*. The "tremendous difficulties" (!) of this work, he wrote, were attacked with courage
and evident enjoyment in "an artistic if not perfectly finished
interpretation."

By this time the orchestra was uprooted, a wanderer in search
of a home. The International Auditorium at the Exposition
Building, despite M. W. Savage's efforts to disguise it as a con-

cert hall, had proved its inadequacies. The first three concerts of the season were played there, but then Oberhoffer and his men found another refuge, though one hardly better suited to their purposes: Wesley Methodist Episcopal Church. There the fourth and fifth concerts (January 29 and February 16) were played, with the orchestra personnel, and the audience too, overflowing into the Sunday school rooms and other chambers adjacent to the main auditorium of the church. The arrangement, though unavoidable, was obviously bad, and the musical sound was so churned up and thrown about by the semi-dividing walls that listening was a baffling experience.

It was in Wesley Church that Beethoven's *Pastoral* symphony was given complete for the first time by the orchestra.

The sixth and final concert of that first season, on March 23, 1904, reverted to the International Auditorium. Olive Fremstad, absent from her home city for ten years and now laureled with success, was the soloist, singing *O Don Fatale* from Verdi's *Don Carlos*, four Norwegian folksongs of Grieg, Wagner's *Träume*, and the *Seguidilla* from Bizet's *Carmen*. Frank Danz took a bow for his fine obbligato in Handel's *Largo*, and everything was in the best of order until the program's epic finale.

This finale was the blood-curdling *1812* overture of Tschaikowsky. A special set of chimes had been imported to lend added luster and magnificence to the climax of the work, where the Russian hymn finally quells, in a triumphant din, all opposition from the French *Marseillaise*. The chimes were resplendent in gold leaf and elaborately decorated with sportive cupids, and they were given a position of honor and prominence in front of the orchestra. Joseph Frank, who played viola and ran a music store on Sixth Street, was assigned to play them.

At Frank's very first stroke the head of his hammer flew off and rolled under the chairs of the first violins. It was quite irretrievable, particularly at that cataclysmic moment when the Muscovites had Napoleon on the run. The *1812* rolled on to its jubilant finish, without benefit of chimes. Mr. Frank, feeling and looking foolish, stood it out with a stick in his hand.

"We Want an Orchestra"

The first season was over. It had been gratifyingly successful, and the second season was already in preparation.

The Minneapolis Symphony thus became, in 1903, the eighth major orchestra to be established in the United States (two of them in New York City). This was only three years after the birth of the Philadelphia Orchestra, six years before the San Francisco Symphony was organized, and fifteen years before the Cleveland Orchestra was founded. In four short months the Minneapolis orchestra had established permanency against odds that must have been formidable, considering the fact that a city ranking eighteenth in population was now one of seven in America possessing orchestras of their own.

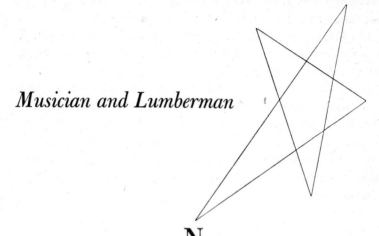

Musician and Lumberman

NEITHER audience nor orchestra could be satisfied for long with the awkward makeshifts that were all the city could offer for use as concert halls. From the time of the orchestra's birth there had been brewing a novel and daring scheme to create a fitting domicile for the new musical organization. W. F. Bechtel, president of the Northwestern National Life Insurance Company, had been approached with a proposal to build a downtown music and assembly hall, and in collaboration with a committee headed by Fred G. Smith had hatched a most unconventional plan for financing the project.

Mr. Bechtel's company offered to erect and maintain on the property it owned at Eleventh Street and Nicollet Avenue a $150,000 structure housing a music hall and company offices, in exchange for $2,000,000 in insurance policies sold by Minneapolitans before April 1, 1904. It was promised that ground would be broken immediately if the quota was reached by that date, with the building scheduled for completion the following November 1, in time for the opening of the orchestra's second season.

All the town's musical organizations entered with zeal upon a city-wide insurance selling campaign, with orchestral musicians and choristers and businessmen not only taking out policies for themselves but soliciting others. The quota was raised and construction was started on a building to be modeled as far as possible on Boston's famed Symphony Hall, but the promise of completion by November 1 turned out to have been too optimistic. It was not until early March 1905 that the new home of the Symphony was ready.

Meanwhile the orchestra was a migratory entertainer. Turning its back on the condemned International Auditorium and the inadequate Wesley Church, it found another temporary diggings at the First Baptist Church, giving the first four concerts of the 1904–5 season there, and skipping over to Swedish Tabernacle for a special performance with the Philharmonic Club of *The Messiah* December 28.

The gala opening of the new Auditorium took the form of a four-day festival, a musical spree which aroused in all participants and spectators a thrilled if fatigued sense of pride — pride that the nuptials of civic spirit and music had, at last, been grandly solemnized.

The orchestra's entry into its new and permanent abode on Eleventh Street was in the nature of a second birth, and entrenched it at a time when continued vagrancy might have spelled dissolution. It now entered with appropriate fanfare and revitalizing acclaim the Doric temple which had been called into existence mainly because the orchestra, to those who believed in it, was too precious a possession to be left adrift and homeless. The Auditorium was almost directly a result of the orchestra's creation, a materialization in masonry of the city's impulse to have and hold its symphonic institution.

Even so, the orchestra and its colleague, the Philharmonic Club, very nearly were jockeyed out of front-and-center position in the opening week's festivities. Old rivalries had been silently at work. Too much had been taken for granted by the Symphony people, and to their consternation they discovered that the Apollo Club had engaged the opening night. Apollo Club members who were friends of the insurance company, it was said, had manipulated the coup.

This could not be. Pressure was brought to bear — and the

Symphony-Philharmonic forces could exert pressure — to correct the lamentable situation by at least including the orchestra and its choral partner on the first-night program. W. L. Harris, leading businessman and Philharmonic bigwig, helped to work out the compromise, and all who were involved eventually saw the wisdom of having the city's three outstanding musical organizations share the stage on the Inauguration Musical Festival's opening night.

When the Auditorium doors were formally opened on that gala Wednesday night, the interior design and décor aroused excited comment. Nothing so spacious or so chastely simple in concert hall design had been seen in Minneapolis. Architects Arthur M. Chamberlain and George E. Bertrand had practiced their craft with a restrained and cultivated hand, offering a commodious interior with a minimum of that ornamentation so dear to the hearts of those reared amid Victorian rococo.

The assembled spectators gazed at the Acropolis pictured on the curtain, noted the discreet tan and cream color scheme of the interior, with the green cushions of the chairs, the red carpeting, and the dark mahogany of the woodwork as tasteful accents. They observed, with a mixture of awe and guarded approval, that "there wasn't a curved line" in the place.

"It seemed impossible there could be so many carriages in the city," wrote a reporter present at the scene. "They drove up with a constant whirr of wheels," and to that sound were added "the calls of drivers, the slamming of doors, the ripple of laughter from the gathering crowd."

Inside, waiting for the Acropolis to rise, was the cream of fashion and wealth on the lower floor and in the boxes, with many unnamed in newspaper accounts swelling the total and confirming hopes that music was for all the people. While most of the ladies' gowns were high-necked there were a number of "beautiful throats" unencumbered by collars, many white shoulders on which gems gleamed. There were fluttering of fans and quivering of aigrettes, and "above all, that indefinite cosmopolitanism of perfume that goes with a stylish audience."

And when the curtain lifted, an impressive array of choristers and orchestra players met the audience' gaze. The stage, which had been hailed as "almost the largest in the country," was seen to hold a multitude of such size that it looked, at first, as if a second audience had assembled to watch the first one. The men, white-bosomed, were massed in the center, with the Apollo Club members standing in front, all with carnations in their lapels. Behind them were the Philharmonic men, and on each side were banked the white-garbed Philharmonic women. Seated in front was the great orchestra, in readiness for the conductor's down-swinging baton.

Soprano Charlotte Maconda had been imported for the first program, and Maud Ulmer Jones, a local favorite, sang with the Apollo Club. The mayor, governor, and other dignitaries and their consorts were ensconced in dignified prominence in improvised boxes occupying spaces later to be filled by the new forty-ton Kimball organ. Dr. Marion D. Shutter, Universalist clergyman, gave the dedicatory address and said that "the difference between provincial and metropolitan is spelled out in these lofty columns and over these ample walls." The corps of fifty ushers had spent the preceding week studying the seating plan and distributed all patrons efficiently and without error. At intermission, trumpets summoned the chattering concertgoers back from the foyer, which had been decorated with bay trees.

It was an evening full of import. On the front page of the *Minneapolis Tribune* was a boxed "Greeting to Music Centers" proclaiming Minneapolis' willingness to "extend the hand of fellowship to all cities where temples rise for the worship and practice of the most social of all the arts."

The Minneapolis Symphony, merely a service unit in this glamorous debut of the Auditorium, came into its own on the second night, when Vladimir de Pachmann, pianist, and Mme. Maconda were soloists with the orchestra. Its program was of festive rather than substantial character, "affording sensuous delight rather than intellectual stimuli." De Pachmann was chided in reviews the next day for mannerisms which in years to come were to grow into outlandish eccentricities. The *Tribune* reported that he "allows his personality to obtrude itself too much into his program, so that one is constantly and abruptly brought back from the idealism suggested by the music with an airy wave of the hand to the orchestra or the audience, or a pause as he raises an arm and beats time to his own music." The orchestra splashed pleasantly in the shallow waters of Goldmark's *Rustic Wedding* symphony and Liszt's *Les Préludes*.

The festival's third night offered a concert version of Verdi's *Aïda* with imported soloists, one of whom was destined to climb to operatic heights as a star, and later as manager, of the Metropolitan Opera Association. His name was Edward Johnson and his role was that of Radames. The Symphony and the Philharmonic chorus were assistants on this occasion.

On the fourth and last night one thousand Minneapolis school children — four hundred massed on the stage and three hundred in each of the balconies — raised their piping voices in song, and with the collaboration of the Philharmonic chorus and the Orpheus Singing Society, produced a fairly ear-shattering evening.

The week had been an exciting and expensive one — it had cost $30,000 — and markedly successful in making music a major issue in town. W. L. Harris, Philharmonic officer, had staged two elaborate banquets during the festival week, feeding and lauding everyone connected with the concerts from Emil Oberhoffer to the office secretaries.

When the furor eventually died down, the orchestra went into rehearsals for its sixth and final concert of the season, which was given March 14 with Johanna Gadski as soloist. Some postseason chores later brought it back to the Auditorium, for the Philharmonic's performance of Rossini's *Stabat Mater* and Haydn's *Creation* in April and for the baptism of the new organ on May 4.

What was the caliber of the music during the Symphony's first two seasons? Could it be said that Oberhoffer made a clean break from the caramel-stuffed programs of pre-Symphony days and drastically uplifted the city's musical tastes? The answer (with which Oberhoffer certainly would have concurred) is that he did not.

What he did accomplish was to negotiate a smooth, slightly graded ascent, rather than a break; he wooed his public while he himself put his conducting feet under him. The two seasons, nevertheless, had respectable landmarks. They had offered three Beethoven symphonies, which included, amazingly enough, not the perennially popular Fifth, but the First, the Sixth, and the Second (the latter, for some reason, minus its first movement!). There were as yet no Brahms or Tschaikowsky symphonies, but Mozart was represented with the E flat and the *Jupiter*. Liszt, Wagner, and Saint-Saëns were liberally drawn upon. Debussy was still caviar, and missing from the menus.

Among the repeated favorites were Dvořák's *New World*, Goldmark's *Rustic Wedding*, and Schubert's *Unfinished* symphonies, Liszt's *Les Préludes*, Wagner's *Meistersinger* prelude, and the overture to Weber's *Oberon*.

Almost all the programs — and this indicated Oberhoffer's theory of gradualism — were generously sweetened with such items as Moszkowski's *Moorish Fantasy* and *Malagueña*, Anton Rubinstein's *Rêve Angelique*, and Bolzoni's *Minuet* for string orchestra. Such winsome pieces, long since buried in the Symphony's library, served to soothe rebellious hearts and keep in line those who asserted that the one thing they liked in music, by George, was a good tune. And there is no evidence that Oberhoffer did not enjoy playing such items. A romanticist, he took no stern stands against melodious sentiment, yet his programming rarely lacked substance and backbone.

In two seasons' time Oberhoffer had worked out a definition, at least a preliminary definition, of what a civic symphony orchestra should be and at the same time his person and personality had grown into a kind of civic symbol of musical culture. He looked like what he was, and wished to be. His ruddy hair made a misty aureole above a broad, high forehead and swept backward in the Paderewski style. Its color was a clue to his temperament and tenacity. He was a dreamer, but an energetic and purposeful dreamer. The touch of red in his mane and mustache was a visible sign of his inner fire; the far-gazing eyes spoke of imagination and vision.

The miracle of Oberhoffer was not so much that he was self-made as that he was both self-made and home-made. He acquired his conducting technique in a city that offered no other training course than that of an orchestra on constant public display. It was self-education under a spotlight, with the neighbors looking on.

That fact had the double effect of putting him on the defensive and of making him a humble and eager votary of the art he was determined to master. More keenly than anyone else was he conscious of the lacks in his background, realizing that his training as batonist had not been the standard, thoroughgoing apprenticeship that the great European conductors had undergone. He knew that what he was to learn must be learned by his own efforts in a musically isolated American community.

This accounted for his zeal, industry, and resolution in teaching himself what no man or school had formally taught him. From visiting artists and conductors he gleaned what he could, and applied it to his own technique.

So he was always a student, and always studying. Behind this ability and desire to absorb was something of far greater value: the artist who could build from the notes in front of him a warm and moving artifice of tone. Always, to Oberhoffer, music was tonal poetry, and he was enough the child of the nineteenth century to bring to music romantic ardor rather than classical austerity. He was a man in whom music and feeling were always closely joined.

While the Minneapolis Symphony Orchestra was his training school, Oberhoffer was no shy student therein, but maintained from the start a proud and conscientious leadership that made his position more than titular. The art of music to him always partook of the elevated and noble, and he reflected that belief in his own rather aloof and aristocratic demeanor. The aloofness indeed may have been partly a shield to protect his feelings of inadequacy on the score of scanty training. But there is no questioning the high seriousness and spirit of consecration with which he took his role. This attitude withdrew him somewhat from the town's social circles and social entertaining.

As time went on and the orchestra he led gained prestige in and out of the Minneapolis region, Oberhoffer grew increasingly conscious of his position as musical leader. He came to visualize community growth in musical culture in terms of outstanding individuals who took the major burdens on their shoulders. He subscribed to the "great man" theory in this field at least.

On tour he would arrive in a city or town and his first question would be: "Who's your man here?" In other words, who was the Emil Oberhoffer of Fresno, California, or Alton, Illinois?

If he was the proud master of the Minneapolis Symphony, he was also its devoted servant, and his sense of responsibility toward it sometimes caused real sacrifices. He was invited once to conduct the St. Louis Symphony in a guest engagement that necessitated a substitute to take charge of the Minneapolis rehearsals for a concert he would conduct after his return. He left for St. Louis, but after brooding long hours on the southbound train, finally got off at a junction point and returned posthaste to Minneapolis. Arriving home in time to take over the rehearsals, he contritely confessed that he had almost deserted his orchestra for a mere fee and bit of prestige in St. Louis, but had speeded back after realizing where his duty lay.

Oberhoffer's conducting, in addition to poetry, had sweep, drama, and an urgent eloquence as he acquired greater control of his craft. It strove to re-create the music's spirit rather than give a precisionist's graph. As one critic said, it "never shirked the impact of a big musical thought." There was no niggling attention to detail as such, and sometimes the detail was blurred in the uprush of tempo and volume, and at such times numerous notes fell by the wayside.

But the broad design, the clear melodic line, the victorious progress to his climaxes, more than balanced such minor losses. Oberhoffer's was the grand conception always, spurred by a vaulting imagination that occasionally asked for more than the orchestra could give.

His tone was often commented upon, often praised for its sweetness and clarity, its "roundness," its virility and power in the fortes. That power was sometimes too much; then there would be objection to his unreined and strident brasses.

On the platform Oberhoffer was a picture of grace and authority pictorially blended. It was said that he practiced conducting before a full-length mirror, but whatever the means, conscious or instinctive, of attaining the visual effect, the figure on the podium presented a most persuasive and ingratiating portrait of a conductor in action.

Oberhoffer in his personal and social contacts was witty and cultivated, charming in manner, a brilliant conversationalist of wide-ranging interests. His humor was keen-edged but usually good-willed, and there was a playful streak in him, a love of mischief and mimicry when surrounded by bosom friends. His sarcasm could take a quick edge when the cooperation of his players faltered, and became a rapier thrust when parrying a snub directed toward the orchestra, which was his child, his whole *raison d'être*.

His musical interests and preferences were broad, discriminating, and wholly unprejudiced. Far from betraying a nationalist bias toward German music and conducting methods, he bent the other way, showing a decided and lifelong liking for the French spirit in thought, in music, in those transparencies and balances in tone and texture wherein the French excel.

This inclination was rooted in the fortunate influences of his youth, which had given a young and susceptible German a Gallic orientation, first in Luxembourg and later in Paris.

So at the head of Minneapolis music was a man of true sophistication in taste, bound to no objective except that of playing good music, and intent on winning friends for it by all the personal, artistic, and technical arts at his disposal. He may have been high-handed in his role of musical arbiter, but he was a diplomat too — a wily diplomat in introducing new works judiciously surrounded by familiar works, and in presenting programs of novelty, contrast, and color.

In program-making Oberhoffer was unquestionably an artful practitioner, a musical chef wise in the ways of flavors and balance and succulent side dishes. He once told the writer: "It is easy enough to pick a Brahms or Tschaikowsky symphony for your program, but what will go with it? That's a more difficult matter. It's like a chicken dinner — you pick the chicken, but often the dessert or entree will make the chicken taste so much the finer."

He understood well the psychological demands of the program, devising his musical evenings as astutely as a composer arranging his symphony movements for individual contrast and overall unity. He could take a soloist and make him or her the diamond in a craftily designed setting. In all this he was an undisputed master.

The main goals were never lost sight of. Before the advent of Oberhoffer, there was only a potential audience in Minneapolis for Beethoven and Brahms, which is to say a nonexistent audience. What the orchestra was to give was outside the experience, and only on the fringe of knowledge, of all but a handful. It was Oberhoffer's dextrous spoon-feeding that built up, in the Twin Cities, sizable audiences for Beethoven and Brahms, and also of course for Tschaikowsky, Dvořák, Franck, and in time Sibelius. Creating and maintaining a symphony orchestra was only half his assignment. He had to create, and rear, that listening body without which the performing body could not live, or be. He accomplished this by keeping a step ahead of the orchestra and two steps ahead of the audience, never admitting how far ahead he was but never failing to keep his lead.

A conscientious conductor could do all this, could build an organism that grew steadily stronger musically, and yet that organism could remain economically a will-o'-the-wisp. If this was to be avoided, the time had come to set up a firmer business base for the orchestra, and give it a more professional management.

The organization was acquiring artistry on the one hand and esteem and support from the public on the other; it was obvious that both acquisitions were investments that needed protection.

So for the third season, 1905–6, a new business manager was hired: R. J. Collins of Chicago. And, more important, a new controlling body was organized: a committee of management headed by Elbert L. Carpenter, a young Minneapolis lumberman. The choice of a chairman could not have been more propitious.

While young Emil Oberhoffer was preparing for a life of music in Munich, young Elbert Lawrence Carpenter was dreaming of a life of music in a small Iowa town. The young Iowan's dream was never to materialize in its original terms, but it was to prove as potent and constructive a musical force as the young Bavarian's scales and exercises.

Elbert Carpenter was the oldest of a family of seven children, the son of a lumberman, Judson E. Carpenter, who had come west from New York State to the river town of Clinton, in eastern Iowa. There the family had a sash and door plant, the Curtis Brothers Lumber Company.

The young Elbert sang a dependable baritone in the church choir, could find his way around the organ keyboards, and learned to play the flute proficiently. In the long Iowa evenings he joined the family and visiting neighbors when they gathered about the Carpenter piano, as they often did, to sing favorite songs.

He had a natural and consuming love for music, even as a boy. He was blessed with a good ear — an asset he was to retain all his life — and he found joy in making music. His private air castle was a career in music. He would be a musician, and he would travel to far places as a musician.

So strong was the impulse that at the age of thirteen, Elbert did in fact become a musician, an authentic, working musician. And he did travel, but not to far places. One day a small orchestra troupe arrived in Clinton, fluteless. When he heard of the opening, Elbert immediately applied for it. He was taken on, and forthwith left town as a full-fledged member of the group.

But in the excitement of obtaining his first paying musical job, he had neglected to get parental permission. His absence from the Carpenter home was quickly and apprehensively noted, and father Judson immediately went into action. He picked up the trail and followed the orchestra to Cedar Falls, its next stop. When Elbert, by this time nervous and homesick, played the flute that night, he looked out into the audience and to his amazement and relief saw his father sitting there.

His father did not indulge in the classic gesture of leading the errant son home by the ear but instead insisted that the youngster play out the remainder of the orchestra's short tour. Thus early in life was impressed on Elbert the sound doctrine that a contract, verbal or otherwise, must be fulfilled.

A few years later Elbert was sent to Lake Forest Academy near Chicago, and there his impressionable mind and quick imagination were fired by a vivid, unforgettable experience. He heard for the first time, and then many times thereafter, the famed Theodore Thomas orchestra. Whenever he could not legally absent himself from school, he took French leave to Chicago and came back on the milk train.

So marked an impression did the Thomas concerts make on Elbert that for many years after he returned to Clinton, he assiduously saved enough money to travel to Chicago regularly to hear Thomas play.

Meanwhile he began to plan more definitely a career as an operatic singer. A voice teacher heard him sing and encouraged him by saying that he had the potentialities of a fine Wagnerian baritone. He took some voice instruction in Chicago, and his thoughts began to turn to Germany and the possibility of doing what all young American musicians did or dreamed of doing if they were serious about their music: go to Europe to study.

But the dreams and ambitions built up over the years were suddenly demolished by the practical demands of the family's business in Clinton. Elbert's father fell ill, and the student was needed back home to lend a hand in the affairs of the lumber firm. This meant not only abandonment of his musical ambitions but an abrupt end of his academic education. Oldest of the children and conscientious in his role as "big brother" of the family, he went home without complaint and went to work at the sash and door factory.

Young Carpenter developed in time into a salesman of unusual drive and ability. He began to travel for the firm, and his trips often took him to Minneapolis. In 1887, at the age of twenty-five, he was sent to Minneapolis to manage a branch of the Clinton firm, and not long afterward Thomas H. Shevlin invited Carpenter to join him in forming the Shevlin-Carpenter Company, thus launching what was to grow into one of the major lumber concerns of the country.

There followed a period in which Carpenter developed his gifts of leadership, his insight into men and affairs, his skills in finance and management, his position as a prominent figure in lumbering circles. It was a period, too, when the demands of business, and the birth and expansion of the thriving new company, pushed the old dream of musical achievement into a far corner of consciousness. It did not die, but it did undergo a change in form.

E. L. Carpenter publicly entered the lists of Minneapolis music supporters in 1903, when his name was aligned with those of twenty-four other substantial citizens comprising the Minneapolis Symphony's first board of directors. But for years before that time he had followed the town's musical activities with keen eye and ear. No longer regarding himself as a musician, present or potential, he had become an experienced and judicious listener, keeping always his amateur standing as a music lover, to whom the tone art was the greatest inspirational value of life.

From the time of their marriage in 1890, he and Mrs. Carpenter (Florence Welles) kept fully abreast of musical events, and it was in the late nineties that they first heard a rising young musician play the organ at the old Church of the Redeemer. (Though a regular churchgoing Presbyterian, Carpenter often crossed denominational lines and visited other churches to sample the music they offered.) The organist was Emil Oberhoffer.

Musician and Lumberman

Thereafter Carpenter often heard Oberhoffer play, and his admiration and respect for the young man's musicianship steadily grew. On an evening in 1902 (probably the night of the *Samson and Delilah* performance in November) the Carpenters went to Swedish Tabernacle to hear the fledgling conductor direct an orchestra and a group of singers, and they returned home with a deepened conviction of Oberhoffer's power and personality as a musical leader.

The following year Carpenter joined the Philharmonic Club board, which had been expanded when the Minneapolis Symphony was created, and subsequently gave more and more of his time to it until, in 1905, the committee of management was established. As chairman of that committee, he was well embarked on his lifelong career as the orchestra's guide and guardian, its rock in time of trouble, its chief advocate and father confessor, its family doctor who administered a financial hypodermic when the patient had sinking spells.

The conjunction of E. L. Carpenter and Emil Oberhoffer in the formative years of the orchestra's life supplied the major motive power in its development and hardihood through lean years to come. It might be said that the present symphony orchestra—like the healthy individual who picked his ancestors wisely—owes its stout constitution and long life to these two "ancestors" and the happy chain of circumstances that brought them together at the right time.

It was, altogether, a dynamic collaboration and partnership. Each complemented the other in temperament and specialized skills, and each harmonized with the other in thinking about long-range purposes and standards. Each, in his way, was a dictator, but both men were doggedly and single-mindedly devoted to the orchestra, its well-being, and its goal of quality and superiority.

Carpenter quickly and conscientiously took the reins after becoming chairman of the management committee. His industry and determination in the affairs of the orchestra, and his knowledge of how to make an orchestra survive, were of a kind never before seen in a city where musical management had always been a matter of part-time attention to a part-time interest.

As the years passed, it was evident that no one on the board was better versed or more keenly interested than Carpenter in the specialized business of operating an orchestra. No one showed more balanced judgment in decisions. Certainly no one, with the possible exception of E. J. Phelps and Charles N. Chadbourn, who worked in close collaboration with Carpenter in the early years, gave more time to the affairs of the orchestra.

Eventually the others began to bank on Carpenter as the man closest to the Symphony and its problems, and his suggestions often enough were ratified with little argument. "Leave it to Bert" was the refrain. It came to be taken for granted that Carpenter was the man who knew most what he was talking about, and what ought or ought not to be done.

It was a case of a man eager and willing to work getting the job. It was a case, too, of a man finding his dearest hobby and playing at it harder than most men work. The Minneapolis Symphony became Carpenter's life. It was his pastime (an expensive one at times), his chief avocation, his in-hours and after-hours obsession.

Yet there was enough balance in his nature, a deep enough sense of civic responsibility, to save the orchestra from developing into what it might have become in the hands of a man with less vision and more vanity — a private plaything, a one-man manipulation. Constantly Carpenter sought to give the orchestra heavier ballast in the community and wider use as a community asset. The orchestra, he felt, should be shared; its support should be shared. With a calm aggressiveness that lacked all conceit he placed himself, for three decades, in the front line of the money raisers — of those with the thankless job of raising guaranty funds and the more thankless one of collecting money for deficits.

And there were deficit years, many of them. Carpenter and his colleagues worked hard at finding the money with which to carry on, and the search sometimes failing, he would take out his checkbook and perform the basic gesture. In the darkest years his attitude at board meetings was unfailingly a stoic optimism. "All we have to do is go out and raise the money" he would say, and he would spur his associates into another joust with resisting contributors.

This optimism, and the absence of bluster and egoism in an enterprise where Carpenter was really running the show, plus the Carpenter prestige in financial and social circles, which made his requests for funds hard to turn down — these were the things that kept the orchestra functioning. These were the things that spelled continuance when all the evidence pointed to the wisdom of disbandment.

In the early years the orchestra had far fewer workers than it has now. It was not an easy thing to "sell." Today sheer length of life of the orchestra is one of the best arguments for its perpetuation, but in the first years the Symphony in the minds of many was a costly experiment, a luxury the town could ill afford.

There was more than a little justification in this complaint. No city the size of Minneapolis was supporting an orchestra of corresponding size and cost. It was turning into a heavy piece of nonprofit property.

Often Carpenter with one or two of his associates would go out into the town and by door-knocking and a bit of desk-pounding would raise most of the necessary funds. Carpenter was wont to leave the details of the fund campaign to the committee, while he loaded himself with fifty or sixty subscription cards for a personal campaign that tackled the biggest donors, and the biggest resisters.

Some of the regular donors of large sums laid down curious conditions before making their contributions. Herschel V. Jones, publisher of the *Minneapolis Journal,* was annually asked to give to the guaranty fund, and annually he extracted a promise that the orchestra play Paderewski's *Minuet* once during the season in return for his check. John Pillsbury, one of the leading spirits of the organization and an industrious fund-raiser, told in later years of the wealthy and aged contributor who requested that solicitation in his case be delayed until January 2 of each year.

If he was alive on January 1, he made his donation on January 2. But after his death the contributions continued, paid out of a charity foundation he had set up during his lifetime.

More than once the orchestra was close to foundering, and in desperation the proposal was sometimes made that the board engage a lower priced conductor, cut down the size of the orchestra, and try to operate it as a paying institution. Carpenter stood adamant against all such suggestions, and the board always came around to his viewpoint that no orchestra at all would be better than lowering its standards.

There were times, decades ahead, when the question before the meeting was the blunt and ugly one which the realities of the situation imposed: Do we carry on, or do we liquidate? The problem could not be solved by simple Pollyanna formulas of faith and hope in the orchestra's destiny, yet invariably it was threshed out to an affirmative finish on not much more than faith and hope — and hard work.

Carpenter's hard work in his first season (1905–6) in charge of the Symphony's back office and finances did not show markedly at once. The four-month series between November and March offered only three programs with the Philharmonic chorus and six orchestral concerts, the latter of uneven merit and rather dim public appeal.

Emil Oberhoffer had spent six weeks in the East before the opening, attending concerts and auditioning musicians, had returned with a new first flutist, Max Guetter, and had bolstered his ensemble in the string and woodwind sections. Christian Erck was cello principal, and Frank Danz was still concertmaster. The orchestra now numbered fifty-eight positions.

Separate rehearsals of the strings, reeds, and brasses were scheduled daily to bring the orchestra to letter-perfection for the opening concert, which was to launch the season with a stiff and really high-minded program: the Beethoven Fifth symphony and the Beethoven violin concerto, cheek by jowl, with Hugo Heermann as the soloist.

Musician and Lumberman

This combination may have proved indigestible to the concert-goers who assembled at the Auditorium November 7; they were distinctly undemonstrative, and their applause was grudging. With four other numbers scheduled, the evening proved altogether too long, and Oberhoffer was criticized for not rising to the climaxes in the symphony. And again the strings were smothered by the brass.

Nor was criticism quieted at the next concert, December 13, when the trombones became unruly and Raff's *Im Walde* symphony seemed to get out of hand technically. The evening was saved, however, by Alfred Reisenauer, German pianist, and by the orchestra's support of him in the Liszt A major concerto.

Reisenauer, a big-chested, round-faced German, appeared to be pleased and rather impressed by the midwestern orchestra's performance in the Liszt. "No rehearsal was necessary," he told the press with a shoulder shrug. "It was simply a case of running through the composition."

The César Franck D minor symphony, since grown to be one of the commonest of concert hall staples, was brand new to Minneapolis on the night of January 23, 1906. "A great modern work," it was called, but again the orchestra and its conductor were politely heckled in the critical post-mortems. Lack of precision and a coarse and overbearing brass were noted, along with a failure to rear a mighty climax when such was called for.

The latter, however, was blamed on the size of the orchestra and its physical inability to cope with sonorities and sustain them. But the faultfinding continued. At a later concert the Liszt Polonaise in E was "indifferently played," and Howard Boardman, critic of the *Journal,* grumbled over the revival of the increasingly popular *New World* symphony, in which, he said, Dvořák had lifted syncopated themes "from the gutter to the housetop." The third movement, particularly, offended the rather proper Mr. Boardman, who referred distastefully to its "bizarre reminiscences of New York Bohemia." He averred that it was this movement which would "most frequently be passed under the ban."

But the season ended with a real pulse-quickener: the Grieg piano concerto played by Raoul Pugno, a stout, picturesque Frenchman with a magisterial beard, a broad brow, and a primly perched pince-nez. The concerto had not been played locally since 1891, and as often happened when a prominent soloist shared the platform, the orchestra and Oberhoffer were stimulated into giving more than their best. After it was over there seemed to be general agreement that the orchestra had made the grade at the finish, that the direction had a surer touch, and that the ensemble was smoother and less marred by individualistic malpractice in the ranks.

The season had also offered several performances of the Philharmonic Club, and interspersed were visits by Emma Eames and her company, Emma Calvé (who failed to sing *Carmen* December 13 because of illness but returned January 3 to make amends), and the New York Symphony under Walter Damrosch. This last, hailed as the "event of the year" for Minneapolis music lovers, was noteworthy for bringing to the city the first performance of the Tschaikowsky Fifth symphony, a subsequent best seller.

Indeed, when the fourth symphony season, 1906–7, was launched in November, the Tschaikowsky Fifth was the opening gun, occupying the central position on the initial program. And this was the first of more than thirty performances of the work in the next four decades.

In spite of some blurring in the last movement, the 1906 reading of the Tschaikowsky opus was evidently a rousing one. But something more than the orchestra's success with that symphony accounted for the tonic atmosphere at the Auditorium on that and later nights.

Audiences began to increase in size and enthusiasm and, while still dominated by fashionable "society," cut a wider swath through all classes of the population, with many students in evidence. The newspapers spilled new adjectives in their critical columns. And a phrase was coined: "the new and greater orchestra." Improvement was noticeable, dramatically noticeable, in the work of Oberhoffer and his men.

After three lame seasons, formative but occasionally fumbling, the orchestra apparently had taken a new lease on life. Greater *esprit de corps* and a readier response to the baton were evident. The string sections had been augmented and showed a new precision of attack. The wind instruments were beautifully blended, and even the naughty brass had been tamed, so that its work "demonstrated strikingly Mr. Oberhoffer's correction of what has always been the weak point in his orchestra."

This new quality in orchestral performance and the new enthusiasm among hearers had a realistic explanation. The guaranty fund had been raised from $10,000 to $25,000 a year, and the campaign to raise that sum had brought in $28,000 without much difficulty. The ante was then upped to $30,000, which was easily reached. The pledges covered three years, thus ensuring the orchestra's operation for that period and allowing Oberhoffer to expand, strengthen, and tighten his ensemble, with more qualified professionals at key points. Doubtless, too, Oberhoffer and Carpenter had put their heads together to bring about a more earnest purpose and a firmer grip on responsibilities.

On December 16, a little more than a month after opening night, the Sunday afternoon popular concerts were inaugurated. The experiment was regarded as risky in some quarters, the contention being that Sunday amusement seekers could not be weaned away from the downtown theaters by orchestral music. After the series started, a different kind of objection came from another quarter. A delegation of church people called on Mr. Carpenter to lodge formal protest against the shocking innovation of Sunday concerts and to express grave concern that such concerts would break down the Sabbath. Carpenter suggested to the petitioners that some Sunday they post themselves at the Auditorium's doors and observe the faces of the people leaving the concert. "You will see uplifted expressions," he said. "You will see that the music has done them not harm but good."

They would also have seen the largest and most enthusiastic crowds that had yet attended Minneapolis Symphony concerts. The popular series met with instantaneous success and acclaim. With tickets priced at twenty-five and fifty cents, the public took to these matinees so rabidly and in such numbers that sold-out houses quickly became the rule.

For the first time in the Symphony's history, people who wanted to hear it play were prevented from doing so because there was no place to seat them. Long queues formed on Eleventh Street and often were dispersed before the anxious waiters reached the lobby. Inside the hall were scores who had never heard a symphony concert before. The orchestra had at last begun to make contact with the man in the street and the lady of the house.

The popular concert series was taken on not with any hope of profit — the bargain-rate admission precluded that — but more from a sound impulse to amplify and build up the symphony audience. The evening programs were still too rarefied and too expensive for the great majority. The Sunday matinees were designed more as a preparatory course for the "higher education" in music the Friday nights offered.

The "pops" started out biweekly, but the reception they received was so eager and clamorous that on February 11 the committee decided to make them weekly. Ten in all were played during the season. These, with the six regular evening concerts and the five joint appearances with the Philharmonic Club, made this November-to-March season the busiest in history. The orchestra, it could rightly be said, was now "in production."

The Sunday menus were motley miscellanies of classical and semiclassical material. Many a toothsome lure of that time has since gone to the warehouse: Bolzoni's *Minuet* for string orchestra, Kretschmar's *Coronation March*, D'Albert's overture to *Der Improvisator*, excerpts from Moszkowski's *Boabdil*, and the sweetly sentimental *Scènes Pittoresques* of Massenet with its tolling of the Angelus.

The popular concerts were Oberhoffer's idea, and he had some firm theories about them. One was that Sunday patrons should not be privileged to buy for fifty cents what the Friday-nighters spent a dollar and a half for. He wished to keep the Sunday and Friday repertoires entirely separate. His intention was to play music "within the understanding and enjoyment of the average person" while keeping the programs "of a high standard and of a dignified character."

Quantity and variety were the guiding principle, and as many as twelve pieces were programmed for a single afternoon. The soloist was usually a singer. The only exceptions were Carlo Fischer, who had just returned from Cincinnati to head the cello section and was twice presented as Sunday soloist, and Hermann Zoch, the city's foremost exponent of classic piano literature. This indefatigable pianist shattered the relaxed and tuneful Sunday tradition by playing the Beethoven *Emperor* concerto in its entirety.

These Sabbath music festivals were hugely enjoyed by those "average persons" the management committee wanted to please, and to educate. But whether the audience took the aforementioned *Emperor* concerto to its collective bosom is a matter of doubt. It was wary of "education," and it was apt to bridle at songs sung in any language but English. When baritone Harry Phillips sang Leporello's aria from Mozart's *Don Giovanni* in what was referred to as "a foreign tongue" (i.e., Italian), it was suggested that such a feat was "proof of thorough preparation, but somewhat irksome to the average audience attending a Sunday afternoon concert."

Oberhoffer also offered one of his own compositions at a popular concert: *Hora Novissima,* a "vocal scene" with orchestra, the poem (sung by Maud Ulmer Jones) telling of the last hours of a dying child at whose side the mother is watching while the bell tolls.

The subscription season, too, had its highlights and landmarks. A curious novelty was Mendelssohn's incidental music for *A Midsummer Night's Dream,* performed in conjunction with the Philharmonic ladies' chorus and a reading of the Shakespeare comedy by George Riddle. The latter assumed all the roles, raising his voice for Titania, lowering it in *buffo* effects for Bottom. This occupied an entire evening.

There was also an all-Wagner program, and there was the first local performance of a work by Brahms, only ten years deceased. This was the *Academic Festival* overture, which apparently enjoyed only a *succès d'estime,* for one critic applied to the performance that damning phrase, "an adequate reading." This adequacy was all the more remarkable, he went on, because it was the orchestra's first attempt with Brahms, "who is anything but obvious."

Fannie Bloomfield-Zeisler, that seemingly frail pianist who crouched and swayed over the keyboard as she played, performed "prodigies of execution," her weaving brown arms and flickering fingers creating pianistic magic in a Moszkowski concerto. Two noted baritones also were among the guest soloists: Emilio de Gogorza and Giuseppe Campanari. And one of the year's ambitious undertakings was *The Beatitudes* by César Franck.

A large wreath of roses, a gift from the orchestra to Oberhoffer, was presented at the final evening concert March 15, signalizing the feeling of friendship the season's success had engendered. And at the final Sunday event, aging Frank Danz played the violin solo in Saint-Saëns' *Danse Macabre* and one thousand people were turned away.

The orchestra had been honed to a keener edge these last five months. Tempos were sometimes temperamental, too dragged or too hurried; there were moments of confusion in complex passages; the brass sometimes fell into old errors of blatancy. But the teamwork was definitely improving, and the bonds between the orchestra and the town had been widened and strengthened.

This firmer attachment of orchestra with public was soon followed by further work on the foundations: an important and lasting change in the character of the orchestra's "holding company." At the beginning of the fifth season, 1907–8, the Orchestral Association of Minneapolis was incorporated under the educational laws of Minnesota, with a membership comprising the one hundred fifty subscribers of the $30,000 guaranty fund. Carpenter became president of the corporation and held the post until his death in January 1945.

The incorporation move had a dark significance for the Philharmonic Club which had fathered the Symphony. It was an outright bid for independence, and it began to confirm the fears expressed by club members four years before that a professional orchestra in their midst would jeopardize their own musical objectives. Time would soon reveal that the Philharmonic, by capturing in 1900 the most promising conductor in sight and making him its own, had unwittingly signed its own death warrant. As the orchestra gained in skill and prestige, the club found itself outshone by a potent rival for the public's affections. It continued to give concerts well into the second decade, but its fate was sealed by the setting up of the Orchestral Association in 1907 and by the final and complete severance of orchestra and club two years later.

Ironically, the Apollo Club, which seven years before had lost Oberhoffer, was destined for long survival. More clannish and firmly committed to its all-male identity and repertoire, the Apollo would build its smaller niche and stay in its shelter in all the coming years.

Meanwhile the Philharmonic's "second fiddle," its instrumental assistant, became first. The child outgrew the parent and finally pushed him off the stage.

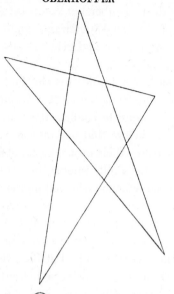

Orchestra-on-Wheels

O NE more important step had been taken in the fourth season. Packing up its fiddles and clarinets, the orchestra for the first time went calling on the neighbors. It visited Moorhead, Grand Forks, and Duluth on its maiden tour in the spring of 1907. The group did not then, or for some time afterward, travel full strength, but was cut down to a skeletonized, easily transported edition of the home ensemble.

This brief junket established a precedent and a part-time way of life for the Minneapolis Symphony, starting it on a 200,000-mile journey that has taken it to every state of the Union but five, to Canada, and to Cuba. Touring gave the orchestra a new mission in life, opened a new source of revenue, and made Minneapolis an exporter of symphonic music to innumerable towns that had never heard it.

It was Oberhoffer who initiated the tours, rushing in where management feared to tread. The Orchestral Association, wary of the risk of increasing the annual deficit, declined to sponsor such speculative ventures; so Oberhoffer with his own money financed the first three tours, in the spring seasons of 1907, 1908, and 1909. After the success of the first one under his personal management, he decided in the winter of 1907–8 to employ Wendell Heighton to arrange the itinerary for the next one. Heighton was a semiprofessional cellist who edited and published the *Western Musical Herald* in Des Moines and had had some experience in artist bookings.

Oberhoffer engaged Heighton on a trial arrangement calling for a salary of forty dollars a week as cellist and expense money on the portions of the tour he arranged, plus a bonus if the tour proved financially successful.

The plan worked out. Heighton earned a bonus of one hundred dollars on a twelve-city tour in 1908, and at the start of the 1908–9 season was called back to handle all tour bookings. The arrangement this time was a better one for Heighton: a profit-sharing plan by which two thirds of the proceeds went to Oberhoffer and one third, plus traveling expenses, to Heighton.

The third tour in 1909 marked an amazing advance in number of bookings and length of route, and it also constituted the true beginnings of the far-flung conquests of the orchestra. A six-week trip extended as far south as Kansas and Missouri and as far east as Galesburg, Illinois. In the short period of three years the Minneapolis Symphony had established its hold on a wide front as a successful and popular musical organization.

Now the Orchestral Association was ready to assume sponsorship of the annual trips, and did so in 1910. At the same time it employed Wendell Heighton to replace R. J. Collins as business manager, with primary responsibility for arranging the tours. For many years thereafter the tour receipts were distributed three ways: to the association, the conductor, and the tour manager. Oberhoffer made much of his income by this arrangement. In 1912 the association, to make a good thing better, instituted an annual midwinter tour to supplement the established spring jaunt.

Although to Heighton goes much of the credit for building up the itineraries and making the 1910–20 period a golden era of touring, it was Oberhoffer who had the good idea at the right time. He and his musical troupers took to the road seemingly at the precise moment when the Midwest discovered it lacked, needed, and wanted the product they purveyed. There was little, if any, competition for the Minneapolis orchestra in the scores of communities it visited. The days of Theodore Thomas' touring were long over; Thomas had died in 1905 after fourteen years as conductor of the Chicago Symphony. School and college orchestras had not yet learned to tackle symphonic music. Radio was yet unborn and the best the phonograph could offer was tinny reproductions of Caruso, Melba, and their contemporaries singing arias against a background of vague and shallow instrumental noises.

So the unaccustomed sound of a symphony orchestra, in itself, was an alluring and even exotic importation for towns whose musical culture was sustained, if at all, by local choruses. These choruses, incidentally, were a large factor in the success of the orchestra in building up its tours, for they were eager to sing with instrumental support and spent many weeks before the orchestra's visit in preparing Mendelssohn's *Elijah,* Handel's *Messiah,* or some other of a wide variety of oratorios, cantatas, and concertized operas.

But with or without choruses, the orchestra served many towns' yearning for an annual music festival in the spring months, and its visit in many cases *was* the festival. Often several days were spent in a single community, with the musical diet varied by recitals given by the vocal and instrumental soloists of the orchestra.

The spring tours, as time went on, became heavy-laden with festivals, music teachers' conventions, college musical fiestas, and matinees for, and by, children. In the late summer of 1911 the orchestra played a two-week festival in Ravinia Park in Evanston, and six years later it became a regular feature of the Chicago North Shore Festival, terminating its spring tours with a week of concerts there for three successive seasons. For these engagements the fifty-four-man touring orchestra was augmented by most of the rest of the personnel, brought down from Minneapolis to make an eighty-man team.

Orchestra-on-Wheels

The spring tours carried the lightest complement of musicians. More men were taken, as a rule, on the midwinter trips. For the four eastern tours during the decade of 1910–20, as well as three to the South and the Pacific Coast, the full orchestra of ninety men was used. A Canadian Pacific tour in the fall of 1920 used about seventy-five.

With the orchestra, for more than a decade, went also the vocal soloists, who customarily were engaged as a unit and sang at most of the concerts. A straight orchestral diet was too severe, as yet, for Des Moines, Deadwood, and Keokuk.

These soloists, representing the four vocal registers — soprano, contralto, tenor, and baritone or bass-baritone — worked in handily for oratorios and cantatas, could toss off the quartet from *Rigoletto,* and were ready to sing a half-hour of encores with piano accompaniment, which often set the seal of rapturous approval on programs otherwise deemed austere.

In addition to the specially engaged singers, section leaders of the orchestra were regularly called upon for solos. Cellists Carlo Fischer, Cornelius Van Vliet, and Hermann Beyer-Hane, harpist Henry J. Williams, violinists Richard Czerwonky, Karl Scheurer, and Guy Woodard frequently assumed these assignments and shared billing with the vocal stars.

Often, too, at the larger centers the orchestra would collaborate with noted musicians in concertos, songs, and arias, such combinations drawing that added complement of listeners who more willingly paid for music when it was associated with famous names in the flesh.

From the beginning the Minneapolis orchestra-on-wheels was prepared to play anywhere and under all conditions, come snow, high water, or railroad wreck. Bad weather, primitive concert hall accommodations, traveling hazards, all made the life of these musical barnstormers an arduous one.

The itineraries led the orchestra from whistle-stops to college towns, state capitals, and the larger centers of business and culture — and back again. Audiences were warm and enthusiastic, cool and perplexed, cold and sophisticated, noisy, courteous, large, small, and sometimes minute.

The means of traveling was soon standardized and given a modicum of comfort. The first tours were taken in railroad coaches, but before long Pullman cars, two of them, became regular equipment for the Symphony "special," with a baggage car ahead to carry the instruments and the trunks containing scores. Pullmans permitted concurrent traveling and sleeping, and the night hops made possible more solid booking.

But in spite of the Pullmans, traveling was often rugged. The tour manager always set up a "tight" schedule which on paper may have left ample time for transit from one engagement to the next but which in practice often came into conflict with acts of God and careless brakemen.

In February 1912 the musicians were stalled in a Wisconsin snowdrift for five hours. In May 1913 they were caught in the Indiana floods and manager Heighton was marooned and separated from his orchestra for two days. On two occasions, in 1909 and in 1916, the orchestra found itself separated from imminent concert hall dates by large bodies of water, in the one case the Missouri River, which lacked a bridge, and in the other Lake Michigan, which also lacked a bridge. The 1909 concert was in Lexington, Missouri, and the personnel and baggage were transported *in toto* by truck and ferry in time to play the concert, while the cars were rerouted by a roundabout rail route via Kansas City. The Lake Michigan crossing in 1916 was also made by ferry, which this time bore the Symphony Pullmans and baggage car across the lake in time to make an Appleton matinee that otherwise would have been missed.

In January 1917 the orchestra started its midwinter tour beset by howling gales and heavy snowfall, with a snowplow clearing the way eastward and two locomotives requisitioned to pull the train through the blizzard.

In 1918 the Minneapolis Symphony train, coasting slowly down a long grade in eastern Nevada, collided with a westbound express before it could reach a siding for a prearranged passing.

Fortunately, the special's engineer sighted the westbound train approaching at some distance and promptly applied the brakes, though he could not stop in time to avoid a collision. Fourteen musicians were injured, including Oberhoffer, who acquired a nasty lump on the forehead. A concert was scheduled that evening at Logan, Utah, and the five-hour delay occasioned by the wreck made it unlikely the date could be filled. But concert managers have an inherent horror of canceled engagements, and the conscientious Heighton kept wiring Logan at intervals that the orchestra would arrive "as soon as possible" and play its program.

"As soon as possible" turned out to be 11 P.M., but the audience was there, and waiting. The intervening time had been passed in community singing and a few speeches, and some of the audience had pieced out the evening by going to a movie. On arrival, Heighton rushed to the hall and told the audience the concert would start as soon as the instruments could be brought to the hall. The concert began at 11:30 and was over a little after 1 A.M.

If traveling was beset with delays and accidents, concert hall conditions often made concert-giving a valiant but absurd exercise in doing the impossible. Visiting many communities that had never heard symphony music and had no proper place to house it, the orchestra took potluck in accepting and making the best of what facilities were available.

It played in gimcrack corn palaces, creaky opera houses, tents, churches, high schools, lodge halls, armories, Shrine temples, cattle barns, gymnasiums, and (in Duluth) a curling club arena. It played in all manner of nondescript structures whose only redeeming virtue was space enough for fifty to ninety musicians at one end and an audience at the other.

As the years passed the orchestra learned that there were few large places claiming four walls and a roof that could not serve as a concert hall. Once it played in a fruit warehouse in Oregon where the platform was built of planks laid on crates and the listeners sat on apple boxes. On the same western tour it performed in style in a state penitentiary for a locked-in audience of convicts.

It played in drafty sheds in village outskirts adjoining cow pastures. It played in firetraps where every member of the orchestra, caution intensified by long touring experience, looked around for the nearest exit before sitting down to play the overture.

The Symphony's concert-in-a-tent took place in 1916 in Edmond, Oklahoma, a small town fourteen miles north of Oklahoma City which had no theater, no auditorium, no church — no building of any kind to house an orchestra. A large circus tent was procured by the town's fathers, and there the orchestra played on a hot May Sunday afternoon.

(Thirty-three years later, in 1949, it played again in a tent, this time at Aspen, Colorado, for the Goethe bicentennial convocation. This tent, designed by Finnish architect Eliel Saarinen, was acoustically perfect in fair weather, but the frequent mountain showers, which struck usually at concert time, set up such a drumming on the canvas that playing a symphony often meant waging a losing fight.)

In 1914 another hot May afternoon in Omaha found the orchestra playing to a half-empty hall. A dust storm blew outside, keeping potential concertgoers at home, and the heat was so oppressive that Oberhoffer was obliged to ply a palm fan, waving it quite as much as he did his baton.

Another nonmusical accessory once used by Oberhoffer on the platform was an umbrella. During a concert in the old Corn Palace in Mitchell, South Dakota, a drenching rainstorm swept the city and the roof of the building began to leak. Oberhoffer was put to the ludicrous necessity of conducting with one hand and holding the umbrella in the other. But a far greater problem on this damp occasion was that of keeping track of the orchestra, whose members were constantly shifting their positions to avoid being rained on. Finally the sections were so thoroughly scrambled that the conductor was cuing the violins for oboe passages.

Concert stages could be hot, they could be dripping, sometimes they were too cold for comfort. Chilled instruments were a frequent wintertime hazard, but an unheated stage was worse. Once, in Canada, portable stoves were installed on the platform so the musicians could keep from freezing as they played. On another frigid occasion no stoves were available and the only solution was to play the concert in hats and overcoats. The audience, exhaling steam, was dressed likewise that night.

Stages were often too small to hold the orchestra and platforms had to be built over the pit. Frequently border lighting systems had to be set up in theaters equipped only with footlights, whose use was banned because of glare that prevented the players from watching the conductor.

It was at Aberdeen, South Dakota, that accidents happened twice in the same place. In May 1910 a local chorus was massed for *Creation* on a terraced platform on the stage, with the orchestra below on the main floor. During the overture the supports of the rear part of the platform buckled and crashed, dumping a number of surprised bassos on the floor below. No one was seriously hurt, and after a pause in which Oberhoffer quickly surveyed the wreckage and saw no corpses, the overture was resumed, the bassos brushed themselves off, and the concert proceeded.

The other accident in Aberdeen, in the spring of 1914, was more amusing than dangerous. The conductor had raised his baton for the quiet opening of the *Tristan und Isolde* prelude when a piercing whistle shattered the calm that had fallen over the hall. One observer later wrote: "At first people mistook the sound for some new and startling Wagnerian effect, but when they had about concluded that either the French horn was having a fit or the bassoon a brainstorm, it dawned upon them that a passing locomotive was responsible for the sound." Here, again, the conductor let his baton drop and waited. The whistle dwindled into the distance, the tittering subsided, and the prelude was resumed as soberly as the situation permitted.

Extraneous noises are a common nuisance in concert halls, and the touring orchestra had its full share of this kind of interference. On its first trip to Chicago in March 1911, a fair-sized audience had assembled in Orchestra Hall to hear the young orchestra from Minnesota. Midway in the program opener, the Beethoven *Leonore* overture No. 3, the building suddenly shook to a prodigious slamming of doors. The audience jerked in its seats and looked about apprehensively. Several women rose to leave the hall. "But the orchestra," wrote composer-critic Eric DeLamarter later, "kept on playing as if Mr. Oberhoffer were using a new edition of the score with hitherto unsuspected dynamic effects." The house quieted down as the conductor calmly carried on. It was later learned that a powder mill in southern Wisconsin had blown up and had broken windows all over Chicago.

Another novel noise of extraneous source punctuated a program at Fort Dodge, Iowa, where the orchestra found itself lodged on the fair grounds. At the first note of the concert a discordant chorus of howls, yelps, and roars broke out next door. A small circus had winter-quartered its wild livestock on the grounds; the animals' vocal protests continued through the program.

Outside noises such as locomotive whistles and explosions and animal cries — and the high-pitched lawn mower in Sioux City that once provided an obbligato for Czerwonky's violin solo — were beyond the control of Oberhoffer and his musicians. They ignored them as best they could and kept on playing with straight faces, just as they learned to keep the music going when the lights went out, as they often did in the early days of touring. (The *Gavotte* from *Mignon* and the *Barcarolle* from *The Tales of Hoffmann* came to be standard blackout repertoire.) The men became quick-witted enough to handle almost any crisis. They could play in the dark, and they could hurdle thirty-two bars as nimbly as a rattled soprano once did when she lost her place in a solo.

But when intruding noises were of audience origin, Oberhoffer was not inclined to be patient. In 1911 at Logansport, Indiana, one of the children in the audience was particularly and annoyingly noisy. The orchestra was playing the Beethoven *Eroica* and at the end of the first movement the conductor lowered his baton and turned around to face the audience.

"Don't misunderstand me in what I am going to say," he began. "I love children, indeed I love them very much. But I cannot see that their talking is necessary during a performance of the *Eroica* symphony. Unless it is stopped we cannot go on. It not only disturbs our work but it interferes with the pleasure of the audience."

The child stopped talking but the noise jinx was not laid. Later in the program a workman calmly tacked a curtain outside a window of the hall while soprano Lucille Tewksbury was engaged in a solo.

Later, at Hibbing, Minnesota, there was more vocal interference, this time from crying babies in arms in various parts of the audience. These, combined with the talking and walking about of several "rowdies" in the hall, caused the conductor to stop the music several times until the noise had subsided.

In Louisville in 1915 Oberhoffer introduced a long pause that was not in the score of the Beethoven Seventh to allow an epidemic of coughing to wear itself out. He was not so patient in Duluth four months later, where, in a belligerent mood, he started the Beethoven Fifth symphony on the dot and made the first three movements of that work a processional for the seating of two thousand tardy patrons in the curling club arena.

How did the men of the orchestra spend their time while traveling? In the small compass of their berths they tried to surround themselves with the comforts of home. Tobacco cans, books, magazines, pictures, and stacks of mail were within easy reaching distance, and there were secret caches of food delicacies tucked in corners. After concerts, with the train under way, poker games would be resumed, and on mornings when there had been no stop for breakfast, the travelers were wont to assemble around thermos bottles for doughnuts and coffee bought the night before.

An innovation in the early touring period was the combination kitchen, beer repository, and dance floor in the rear end of the baggage car. Here the men, usually after a long siege of small-town stops and a prolonged diet of ham and eggs, would gather to cook their own meals. Three kerosene stoves and an assortment of pots and kettles enabled the amateur chefs, including Oberhoffer himself, to fry steaks and chicken and enjoy the luxury of "home cooking."

Although some thirteen nationalities were represented in the orchestra personnel, the musicians were a homogeneous group, being mostly Germanic or German-trained, and there was a camaraderie that made them a close-knit family. More than once a space was cleared in the baggage car and impromptu dances were held with music supplied by oboe, tuba, and bass drum. On these evenings the soprano and contralto members of the entourage were in great demand as waltzing partners.

The 1912 spring tour was noteworthy for producing the *North Pole* symphony, which had its première in the Symphony's baggage car but was never heard elsewhere. Caryl B. Storrs, the *Minneapolis Tribune* critic who frequently accompanied the orchestra on its tours, described this masterwork in fulsome terms: "One of the men's favorite stunts is the performance, in the baggage car when refreshments of a German character are passed around, of the *North Pole* symphony, a mighty orchestral work composed by George Koehler, clarinetist and postmaster, with program notes by 'Bill' Erck, French hornist. . . . A few extracts from the program notes may convey a faint idea of its scope and purpose:

" 'The majestic opening strain, Allegretto Eskimono, of the *North Pole* symphony depicts the hardships and suffering George Koehler endured. For days he has been living upon blubber and gumdrops, hearing no sounds but the wailing of the Eskimo women, which will be noticed in the "leit-motif." . . . The second movement is the longing movement in the minor key, *lamentoso con afraido*. It reminds George of home, and not knowing the date (the calendar being frozen) he imagines it is Christmas. A bowl of steaming soup with red hot wieners surrounded by mountains of sauerkraut, runs through his brains. . . . His third movement, *Presto Home,* a giddy and gay 12/8 movement, heads again to the first and second movements. The entire symphony winds up with two extra measures to show how the expedition breaks up.' "

The following year Mr. Koehler, impressed by the success of his *North Pole* symphony, started working on a companion-piece, the *South Pole* symphony. His work was held up, however, pending the invention of a double-contra-bassoon which was to introduce the theme illustrating the breaking up of an iceberg.

The aforesaid Bill Erck had a vein of prankish humor that found vent in more than the writing of program notes. A professional clown in his youth, Erck was a solemn-faced Hollander with a gift for practical jokes that temporarily demoralized the orchestra without causing permanent damage or ill feeling.

Once at an afternoon concert in St. Cloud the orchestra was playing the Tschaikowsky Fifth and had reached one of its crashing climaxes which normally is followed by a pregnant pause. On this occasion Erck filled the pause by dropping a length of heavy chain.

Erck's tricks became legend. At one of the Minneapolis rehearsals he tied a string to the scroll of one of the basses during intermission, affixing the other end to a large dishpan, which crashed to the floor when the bass player swung his instrument into position. At another rehearsal, this time of Tschaikowsky's noisy *1812* overture, the impish Mr. Erck unpacked a revolver he had brought along and shot blank cartridges during the din of the finale.

Oberhoffer at one period contracted the annoying habit of extending the rehearsal session beyond the prescribed three-hour period ending at 12 o'clock noon. The men were averse to making a formal complaint, and Erck solved the problem with an effective if not-too-subtle maneuver. At precisely noon one day an alarm clock started ringing under Oberhoffer's platform, followed by a half-dozen bells ringing from other clocks secretly installed around the stage. The conductor was startled, then amused, and he took the hint. Rehearsals thereafter ended at 12 o'clock sharp.

One of the tour soloists in the early years was Arthur Middleton, noted bass-baritone, and one of his favorite arias was the *Largo al factotum* from Rossini's *The Barber of Seville*. During the course of this song the barber's name is called several times, "Figaro, Figaro, Figaro," and at one point is followed by a pause. At this point Erck once responded with "yes, dear" in a feminine voice, nearly disrupting proceedings.

The long spring tours could be boring, especially to a couple of spirited girls — Jean Cooper and Leonora Allen — who in 1916 were the contralto and soprano members of the vocal quartet that went along with the orchestra. To relieve the tedium of travel they conceived the playful idea of sprinkling catchew powder in the Pullman quarters of the orchestra men, enrolling the porter in the plot and assigning him the task of distribution. The outcome seemed funny at first but became almost disastrous when the wind players, seized with prolonged fits of sneezing, lost the lip control which enabled them to play their instruments properly. Somehow the perpetrators of the prank were identified, and a cruel revenge was planned. Richard Czerwonky was conducting some of the tour concerts, and the two singers were allowed to overhear his directions to the orchestra one day: "Let's put the contralto up tonight and the soprano down" — in other words, play in too high a key for the low voice and too low a key for the high voice. The girls were paralyzed with fright, and although the orchestra did not carry through its act of retaliation, the threat had its effect and the singers were sufficiently chastened to forswear practical jokes for the rest of the tour.

Symphony musicians' fondness for nocturnal poker caused considerable embarrassment for four of the men one warm night as the Symphony train was leaving Kirksville, Missouri. For comfort's sake, the four had donned their pajamas before adjourning to the baggage car where the poker games were habitually held.

Upon arriving at a junction point early the next morning, the two Pullmans were attached to another train heading for Kansas

City, but the train was a heavy one and the baggage car was left behind to be hooked onto a later train. It did not arrive in the Kansas City yards until noon the next day, at which time four discomfited men, pajama-clad, could be seen scurrying over the tracks in search of their Pullman home and daytime clothes.

In general it may be said that Symphony musicians of those days liked beer. After the concert was played and the time for relaxation came, often it was beer that was uppermost in their minds. There was an elaborate beer party at the Rosebud brewery in Yankton, South Dakota, in the spring of 1910, when violinist Czerwonky celebrated his birthday and invited all his colleagues to partake of brew and sandwiches.

A more memorable evening in connection with beer is still a subject of fond reminiscence by veterans of the orchestra. It happened in Fargo. After the concert the men were exceedingly thirsty, for it was a hot, dry night, and a group of them headed for a saloon. The 11 o'clock closing hour came too soon and caught them, unfortunately, before their thirsts had been slaked. The bartender allowed them to remain on condition they keep quiet, but the men found that rule hard to obey, and after much noise and more admonitions from the barkeep, their libations were interrupted by a portentous knocking on the door, followed by the entry of the local constabulary. Chastened and fearful, the musicians were herded into a closed wagon that had been drawn up to the door, and then were carted away into the night, presumably to the jailhouse.

The miscreants could see nothing at all, but they heard their conveyance rumble across a bridge and enter what seemed to be a large building, whose doors were opened to allow entry of the wagon and closed after it was inside. The lights were turned on, the wagon doors were opened, and the sheepish men filed out — into a large brewery. There the governors of North Dakota and South Dakota greeted them with brimming steins, and there also was Oberhoffer, grinning from ear to ear. The conductor loved a good joke, particularly if washed down with beer.

Such escapades relieved the tedium of traveling, of playing the same compositions day after day, and of long separation from homes and families. They were invariably post-concert diversions, which provided release from the tension and scrupulous sobriety that prevailed before and during programs.

In Deadwood, South Dakota, an elaborate party was given the musicians after a concert played in that uninhibited town. The party did not break up till 4:30 A.M., at which time the musicians started walking back to their home-on-wheels. It was a balmy, moonlit night. En route, one by one the carefree players unleashed their instruments — first a piccolo, then a clarinet, then a trumpet — to form a band and improvise a march. Spying a drowsing horse hitched to a wagon, they detached it and hoisted Oberhoffer onto its back. Then all marched, parade-fashion, in a noisy procession to the railroad yards. Legend has it that when they reached the train, the maestro expressed a wish to ride the horse into his Pullman, but was dissuaded from doing so by the more practical-minded of his men.

Another famous party took place at the Deutscher Verein in Logansport, Indiana, in 1912. A hundred members of the Verein entertained the men, an impromptu vaudeville show was staged, and Oberhoffer assured his hosts he had turned down a remunerative Indianapolis engagement to come to Logansport. "What's money compared to good fellowship?" he asked. A feature of the evening was Czerwonky's playing a violin solo while accompanying himself on the piano, a feat for which he had long been noted.

In its travels the orchestra was constantly a target of hospitality, good will, and refreshments from friendly communities that had come to regard Oberhoffer and his men as their own. In San Antonio, Texas, in 1917 a welcoming party of formidable proportions was on hand when the Symphony special pulled in at 9 o'clock in the morning. Committees from all of San Antonio's musical organizations were present, together with the entire personnel of the San Antonio Symphony and, to cap the climax, the First Minnesota and Second Wisconsin Infantry bands, which serenaded the visitors with *Hail Minnesota*.

The regard for Oberhoffer throughout the region often came

close to idolization. A cab driver in Kirksville, Missouri, a frequent stop of the orchestra, confided to manager Heighton that his expectant wife intended to name her baby Emil. Whether or not the baby turned out to be a girl named Emily, the record doesn't show.

Some of the praise that appeared in the smaller newspapers was rhapsodic to the point of incoherence, as this gem from the *Mason City Globe-Gazette* attests:

Emil Oberhoffer is a man six feet two with a large head full of musical genius, with the face of a scholar and kindly philosopher and with a magic wand that resembles the geography pointer of the public schools of a quarter century ago. . . . His arms are long enough to surround his orchestra of 50 in loving embrace and coax the deliciousness of a Goldmark bridal song, or with the same arms send every instrument scampering in excitement with sob and blare and clarion call and deep diapason in a Wagner overture or a Liszt Rhapsodie. . . . It is useless to attempt to write a critique of the program. It was so superlative in every particular, in action, in spirit, in delicacy of tone, in what a layman calls velvet or fever, when he is thinking of deliciousness and color, in sweeping crescendo and crashing smilax [sic], the whisper of a zephyr and the roar of the tempest with the man on the box lashing the orchestra to fury or lulling the tempest — what's the use of mere words? Let it go at that. . . .

Whereupon the ecstatic critic continued in the same vein for another third of a column.

Salina, Kansas, evinced great admiration in 1917 for the restraint in Oberhoffer's conducting: "His directing attracts attention by its freedom from violent gesticulation and gymnastics. Oberhoffer needs only to lift a finger when other directors are beating the air. He moves his baton across a foot of space when other directors disturb at least a square yard of atmosphere."

This observation agrees with the remark of the *Cleveland Plain Dealer* that Oberhoffer indulged in "no shivers a la Stokowski" and with the shrewd but admiring estimate of the *Louisville Courier-Journal*, which in 1915 spoke of Oberhoffer's sensitive left hand "unfolding tones like a flower, or snipping them off peremptorily," coupled with an "evocative baton calling the trumpets to arms."

This oft-mentioned subtlety and economy in platform style was confirmed by the *Louisville Times*: "He plucks at the air with two fingers and draws out of the atmosphere a thread of sound fragile as spun glass; he seems to snatch fragments of tone from some invisible source and scatter them with his fingers; he points his baton and an accent leaps out like an electric flashlight; he waves a sweeping palm and billows of thunderous tone surge in response."

These rather flowery prose pictures of a poised and assured conductor do not harmonize, however, with references elsewhere to Oberhoffer's "spasmodic mannerisms," his "chalk-talk gestures," and to that "mesmeric gesticulatory exuberance" which (in the opinion of one critic) the orchestra could get along, and play as well, without.

These discrepancies in the reactions to Oberhoffer were caused by the shifting winds of critical opinion, by the disparity between rapturous admiration in the "sticks" and sour fastidiousness in the musical capitals, and also by the fact that Oberhoffer, over the years, changed and mellowed his conducting technique.

In the earlier years of the century the rural areas were too greedy for music, and too unversed in it, to have developed an alert or finicky ear. The reviews from these outposts for a decade constituted a vast wave of ecstatic approbation, with only here and there a sour note. Their praise was as untechnical and slapdash as were their ways of manhandling Oberhoffer's name, which at various times and places came out in print as Max Oberhoffer, Emil Aberhoffer, Emil Obderhoffer, Emil Oberteuffer.

Back in 1910, in Deadwood, South Dakota, the impending visit of the Minneapolis Symphony was hailed as the "biggest event of the kind in the history of the Black Hills as well as the biggest drawing card in the history of Deadwood." And there was a note of gratification in the statement that the orchestra would "bring to Deadwood the better class of ladies and gentlemen from all the towns and villages within a radius of at least 80 miles, all arrayed in their finest, making a scene of rich splendor."

At Devils Lake, North Dakota, in 1913, an unusual tribute came from the audience after the performance of Tschaikowsky's *Pathétique* symphony. There was not a sound in the house after the end of the last, long, hushed note. When Oberhoffer, wondering what was wrong, turned partially around to glance furtively at the audience, he discovered that the entire throng had quietly risen to its feet in what was obviously a spontaneous expression of heartfelt praise for the performance. This silent homage, an observer felt, vividly measured "the extraordinary progress within the memory of men now living of a section overrun by buffalo and the same tribes of Indians found there by Lewis and Clark." Silence after Tschaikowsky was thus interpreted as a gauge of the civilizing influence which had come over North Dakota.

Devils Lake also provided one of the most startling headlines the Minneapolis orchestra was ever granted by a newspaper covering one of its concerts. In sledge-hammer capitals across the top of the front pages was printed:

ONE OF THE GREATEST ORCHESTRAS IN THE UNITED STATES PLAYING IN SMALLEST CITY IT EVER APPEARED IN CERTAINLY HAD THE MOST APPRECIATIVE AUDIENCE IT EVER PLAYED TO

Only in the subhead was there a qualification:

PROGRAM WAS ALMOST TOO HEAVY FOR MAJOR PORTION OF AUDIENCE

That qualifying complaint seemed to stem from contralto Barbara Wait's choice of a song, the *Brindisi* from *Lucrezia Borgia*, which, "while beautifully rendered, was 'clear over the heads' of at least 90 per cent of the audience." Apparently the printed program did not make it clear that a *brindisi* was nothing more esoteric than a drinking song.

Music and Maestros

In the same year the orchestra played in Cedar Rapids, Iowa, and featured on its program the *New World* symphony, which Dvořák had worked on during his sojourn on a relative's farm in northeastern Iowa, near Spillville. Dvořák had been known to many who attended the concert, and relatives of the master occupied seats of honor.

Restricting the orchestra to the rural circuit in mid-America did little to build its national reputation; the Symphony could endlessly pound the Corn Belt trails and never be anything more than a hick orchestra for hicks as far as the East was concerned. Its Chicago concert in 1911 was its first big-city date, but this had no national vibrations.

Only a year after the Orchestral Association assumed responsibility for the tours, a bold adventure was decided upon. The orchestra would step upward and eastward and enter the national scene. "National" meant New York, the center of music-making and music-publishing. Advertising space was bought in the musical magazines, Oberhoffer was pictured on the cover of the *Musical Courier* of March 1912, and the Minneapolis Symphony made its first sortie into Manhattan.

The decision to assault the cultural bastions of the East had been reached in the fall of 1911 after due consideration of the hazards and possible long-time benefits involved. The businessmen of the orchestra's board, led by E. L. Carpenter, acted on the theory that easterners knew Minneapolis made good flour and good lumber, but did not know Minneapolis made music, and it was time they learned.

The financial profit of such an adventure would be nil, but the possibility of gaining for the Minneapolis Symphony a standing among the major orchestras of the country was worth aiming at and working for.

"For 50 years the tide of American music had been flowing from east to west," critic Caryl Storrs pointed out, "and now a serious musical organization from the banks of the distant Mississippi river, where but yesterday the buffalo roamed unmolested and the only music was the song of birds and the pine tree symphony played by the wind, was to start the first wave of the new tide from west to east."

Oberhoffer approached his first conducting appearance in the world's most critical musical arena with a trepidation not un-mixed with fatalism. "Heaven only knows what they will do to us," he said, "but I am willing to learn. We are going to do the best we can — and take what we get." He reminded himself, and others, that the orchestra was only nine years old, having started out as "nearly an amateur organization."

So there were some who knew that the trek to the Atlantic seaboard would probably not be a rose-strewn triumphal march. That a young midwestern orchestra would conquer New York was a secret but slender hope.

New York, the great importer of music, was accustomed to look across the ocean, or to the immediate vicinity of Philadelphia or Boston, for its musical wares — not to "the far west" beyond Chicago. This was long before the day of frequent prestige visits to the metropolis by American orchestras from far afield, and in the East puzzlement was voiced that the Minneapolis ensemble should spend the time and money to go to New York and swell the already overburdened concert schedule there. The venture, to New Yorkers, seemed foolhardy and ill-advised and prompted by vanity if nothing worse.

Any orchestra member or sponsor who had been lulled into complacency by the unstinted praise and glowing adjectives that trailed the ensemble in the hinterland was due for a rude awakening in Manhattan, where the adjectives, some of them, burned instead of glowed.

Oberhoffer's left hand was too obtrusive for the *New York Post*'s taste, although it was granted that he got the results he aimed at, "as Nikisch used to do in Boston, where they criticized his arms, his hands and even his cuffs."

The *Evening Globe* found that Oberhoffer obviously sought dramatic effect and shattered the music's design by so doing. The Brahms First symphony was a rough-and-tumble hurly-burly, the Strauss *Death and Transfiguration* was rude and noisy, and *Eine Kleine Nachtmusik* came out heavy-handed and un-Mozartean.

The *New York Press* conceded that Oberhoffer was one of the most picturesque conductors local concertgoers had seen in years — "slender as Toscanini though considerably taller"—but the orchestral tone lacked sensuous beauty, the violins were harsh and wanted body and fullness. But his left hand, contrary to the *Post*'s view, was free and expressive, used at times as a rhythmical index, with a beat that was strong, sweeping, and sharply incisive.

There seemed to be objection to the orchestra's inability to play pianissimo, and to Oberhoffer's tendency to take the slow passages too slow and the fast ones too fast. The *New York Tribune* took a rather lofty perch in announcing, in effect, that the Minneapolis Symphony played as well as could be expected but that the manner of the conductor was extremely distasteful to "the veteran concertgoers of New York."

But the *New York Sun* seemed to sum up with notable shrewdness and fairness the first-night impression on cultivated ears: "If the tone as a whole is heavy and somewhat rough, if the strings are a little raw and the brass too rude, if the dynamics lack most of all a sonorous and smooth moderato, there are on the other hand a fine vigor in all the playing, a tumultuous forte and a good piano, a bold attack and a general unanimity which command praise. . . . His personal style is certainly overdone, but perhaps his men require this. Much of his conducting is devoted to those physical graphics which old observers cannot help believing do less for the players than for the audience."

When the Minneapolis orchestra paid its second visit to New York in 1913, its coming aroused more than a little petulance. The irritated *Musical Leader* asked: "Why does the orchestra of the Northwest go out of its beaten path to challenge comparison with the Boston Symphony, the Chicago Symphony, the New York Philharmonic and the New York Symphony? It is mistaken ambition and no one is deluded as to the means employed for obtaining audiences." (An obvious reference to the time-honored method of marshaling an audience: distributing free tickets.)

The *New York Times* chimed in with a rather pained and sarcastic refrain: "The Minneapolis Symphony orchestra seems to have a 'wanderlust' or mania for traveling far from home. It has come some 1,200 or 1,400 miles, as it did last year, to give an orchestral concert in New York, which is already fully and more than fully supplied with all the orchestral concerts it needs. This week orchestral concerts are given within the confines of this city by four different orchestras."

The *Sun* declared that "it was difficult to determine what benefit the local public, which is now overburdened with orchestral concerts, can reap from such visits." Returning to the attack, the *Musical Leader* waspishly remarked that "the young Lochinvar-from-the-west argument is all right if his steed is the best, but should he bring only a fresh young untrained colt, then he had better go back to the place whence he came."

The right of the Minneapolis Symphony to play in New York quickly became an issue, and a hot one as musical issues go. The *Musical Observer* sprang to "Lochinvar's" defense and asserted it was exceedingly regrettable that "the New York daily press did not treat the second visit of this excellent organization as fairly as it should have done. The patronizing tone of some of our papers was entirely out of place to say the least. . . . When an admirable organization like this Minneapolis orchestra visits us, when undeniable proof is given of the liberality, enthusiasm and artistic spirit of a comparatively small western community, with no other view than the gaining of a foothold or an appreciative word, our critics reward them with a few remarks that the wood-wind section might have been better, that the brass at times was somewhat noisy, that the strings at times played well or they didn't, and that the conductor, Mr. Oberhoffer, was a man of some talent."

Tolerant, too, if somewhat flippant, was the appraisal of the Pied Piper in *New York Town Topics*: "From out of Minneapolis came that city's symphony orchestra, and under the guidance of Emil Oberhoffer treated us to some XXX best brand readings of orchestral classics. Why outside symphonic bodies love to invade New York and give our local organizations the harmonic ha-ha is not quite clear. . . . Can they possibly have found out the truth, that musically speaking, our metropolis is the most provincial city in the United States? At any rate the Minneapolis men played their Northwest passages extremely well, and Emil, the guide, led them with skill and understanding, even if he lacked the necessary fire to thaw the icicles from Brahms' *C minor* symphony. Many musical jokers who had gone to the Minneapolis orchestra concert to scoff, remained to cough."

This seesaw of eastern opinion — with Philadelphia impressed by the strength of the orchestra as an entity rather than in its separate choirs, and Cleveland remarking acidly that the orchestra "seldom gives anything with striking artistry" — proved fairly baffling to the man most keenly eager to read a clear verdict of success or failure.

"I cannot learn anything from these eastern criticisms," said Oberhoffer in the spring of 1913. "They have said that every section of the orchestra was superb and that every section was rotten; they have called me great, original and poetic and they have called me mediocre, imitative and sordid. I would really like to learn my strong points and my weak points, but I cannot do so from these criticisms."

Oberhoffer was not the first musician to learn that the attempt to add up the unrelated and individual reactions of many observers results in no clear-cut, tangible total.

But there was no indication that the city fathers back in Minneapolis were dissatisfied. In March of 1913 the Orchestral Association took out a $50,000 insurance policy on the life of Emil Oberhoffer, and the eastern trips continued. New York was visited again in 1914 and 1916, and in the latter year the orchestra made its first expedition to Boston.

Sarcasm remained rife in Manhattan. "The Minneapolis orchestra once more enters the domains of the effete east to shed sweetness and light in those places where orchestral music is yet in its infancy" sniffed the *Sun*. But there were fewer reins on the praise, when praise was forthcoming. The *New York Press* could not recall having heard at any of the season's concerts, including those of the Boston orchestra, a string tone "so full, so mellow, so vibrant, so expressive."

The impudent *Town Topics* spoke up again, one of its writers asking, "Why is it that New York has no local orchestra to equal some of our visitors? It does no good to pat ourselves on the back and be satisfied with our own organizations. I assert, with a confidence born of long experience in Europe, that no New York orchestra could repeat the fine performance of the Minneapolis Symphony orchestra in Carnegie Hall last Saturday evening."

A burst of toleration came from the *Evening Post,* whose critic said there was real value in "broadening our view, to show us there are first-class orchestras in other cities than New York and Boston," and there was even an affectionate reference in the *Sun* to the "Big Minnie" band and the fact that it had mellowed perceptibly since its last visit.

From Boston came the authoritative voice of H. T. P. (H. T. Parker) of the *Boston Transcript,* in a studious critique which was neither praise nor blame, but analysis. He spoke of Oberhoffer's "sharp, clear and almost angular beat, never [used] displayfully but always in full mastery of his purpose with the music and in full ability to impose it concentratedly upon his orchestra. Obviously he seeks above all intensity and puissance of voice. . . . [His hand] worked in broad strokes, not in adroit shadings. . . . like Mr. [Max] Fiedler before him, he played more upon the nerves than the other perceptive faculties of his hearers."

The war years found the orchestra quite as active on the road as in peacetime. It played *The Star-Spangled Banner* at the start of every program and *America* at the close. It displayed prominently its service flag of five stars (one of them gold) and it refused to argue the war issues backstage or on the road.

In 1917 the orchestra took its first turn through the Southwest, then on up the California coast, and back through the mountain states, and in 1918 it repeated the itinerary. In September and October 1920, with soprano Florence Macbeth as soloist, it invaded the northwestern United States and the adjoining provinces of Canada for the first time, adding such towns as Saskatoon, Edmonton, Calgary, Vancouver, Seattle, and Walla Walla to its lengthening timetables.

Oberhoffer took substantial programs on the road. Even in the earliest days of touring (1909) his travel repertoire included four symphonies — the Beethoven Fifth, the Tschaikowsky Fifth and *Pathétique,* and the Schubert *Unfinished* — and by 1914 the trunks in the baggage car held the scores of no fewer than fifty-four orchestral compositions, including eight symphonies, twenty-seven pieces for the soloists, and five vocal productions including oratorios, concertized operas, and opera scenes.

The Tschaikowsky *Pathétique* was a tremendous favorite from the start, both at home and afield, and so was the Dvořák *New World.* In 1912 the Brahms First went into the touring repertoire, causing a critic in Springfield to remark that "all the conductors have caught it [the Brahms First] like the measles."

Of Beethoven's symphonies the Fifth was oftenest played, but the *Pastoral* was soon added, and later the Seventh and the *Eroica.* The Sibelius First was occasionally performed, and in 1913 the Franck D minor vied with the Beethoven *Pastoral* in popularity. In 1915 the Rachmaninoff Second entered the lists, and in 1917 the Kalinnikoff First (since interred) started a long run lasting through several succeeding seasons. Mozart's G minor appeared in the 1919 concert menus, representing a significant break from programming almost entirely from the romantic period.

The high incidence of cantatas, oratorios, and concertized operas on the tour programs of this period reflected the end of an era rather than the beginning of one. The war speeded the breakup of many civic singing organizations by removing their young male members. Few small-town and college choruses any longer ambush visiting orchestras for assistance in the performance of such choral works as Coleridge-Taylor's *Hiawatha's Wedding Feast,* Grieg's *Olaf Trygvason,* and Saint-Saëns' *Samson and Delilah.* The taste for them has virtually disappeared.

But many worthy projects in the choral field were successfully undertaken. The Verdi *Manzoni Requiem,* a great and difficult work, was the major attraction at the Denver music festival in 1910, with the Minneapolis Symphony in support. (The approval on that occasion was not unanimous: the *Denver Times* saw no entertainment in a requiem, and remarked that "the people didn't want to be pallbearers of the late Mr. Manzoni," even if the composer of *Trovatore* did write the piece.)

Of major caliber, too, were the oft-repeated *Elijah* and *Saint Paul* of Mendelssohn and Haydn's *Creation.* But the Beethoven Ninth was not attempted, or the Brahms *Requiem,* or anything by Bach.

Although the tour programs were liberally strewn with such encores as *Danny Deever* and *Träumerei* and *From the Land of the Sky-Blue Water,* Oberhoffer made room for these tidbits (as he did for his own orchestration of Dvořák's *Humoresque)* on the theory that they were appetizers to go with a solid musical meal.

He knew what was best for his hearers, even if they did not. "Sometimes people ask us to play waltz tunes by popular composers," he once said. "But it would be like throwing valuable time away. I don't mean that such pieces aren't all right in their place, but we don't pay an orchestra $125,000 a year to play them. It is our aim to raise the cultural and educational standards of music, and we shouldn't lower them by giving the people light, flighty things which they often desire."

Touring was expensive, but while frequently there were small houses and bitter self-accusations on the part of communities where attendance lagged, the end-of-the-season balance sheets usually showed gains, even when prestige visits to New York and long hauls to the Pacific Coast were taken into account. Manager Heighton in 1911 estimated that the orchestra's touring cost $1000 a day and a tour of eleven weeks $75,000. Since then, the figures have mounted to $3500 to $4000 a day, and the increased touring costs have narrowed the margin of profit.

During its first decade of travel, the Minneapolis Symphony Orchestra had impressed itself, its name, its prowess, and its musical message over a large terrain. It had become, in a measure, a national and even international orchestra. It had brought good music to a hundred and seventy communities that had never heard a symphony before. It had become "our orchestra" in scores of towns and cities which welcomed it back every year or two with fond fanfare and a civic glad hand.

The organization which the *Fargo Forum* once called "a kind of brass band adjunct of the Civic and Commerce association" was now termed (by *Metronome* magazine) "one of the three great orchestras of America."

Oberhoffer's reputation during that period not only had extended itself to the geographical limits of the Symphony's "empire" but had gained considerable elevation as well. His gifts were discussed and praised in the same breath with those of noted rivals in his own field. Beside him, said Charles E. Watt, editor of Chicago's *Musical News,* Theodore Thomas seemed "cold and artificial, Walter Damrosch amateurish and ineffectual."

All this had been accomplished while the orchestra and its conductor were solidifying their position as a habit-forming satisfaction of cultural need in the Twin Cities.

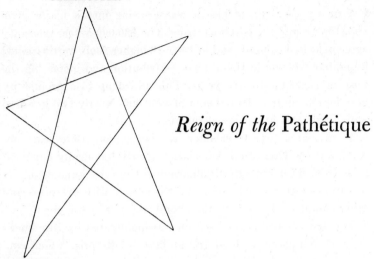

Reign of the Pathétique

THE Minneapolis Symphony's music-on-the-road was a projection and repetition of its music at home, and the concerts on Eleventh Street were taking on a glory of their own. The second decade of the century, as Oberhoffer gained greater control of his instrument and power over it, was a period of rich fruition in orchestral art in the Twin Cities.

The formation of the Orchestral Association in 1907–8 had initiated a season headlined by the idolized Ignace Paderewski in the Beethoven *Emperor* concerto, Teresa Carreño in the Tschaikowsky B flat minor, and Maud Powell, greatest violinist of her sex, in the Bruch G minor. David Bispham had sung *Wotan's Farewell.* The popular series had brought forward violinist William MacPhail in solo position and increased the local fame of Clara Williams, soprano, and Heinrich Hoevel, violinist.

Paderewski returned the next season (1908–9), Lillian Nordica sang Isolde's *Liebestod* for the first time in Minneapolis, and Albert Spalding, America's entry in the violinists' hall of fame, made his midwestern debut on a December Sunday afternoon. The subscription series contained a noteworthy Wagner-Beethoven program, and the season terminated with a sentimental flourish in an "acted" performance of Haydn's *Farewell* symphony.

Music and Maestros

Year by year the orchestra was growing into a major civic investment, and the cost was rising. The $30,000-a-year guaranty agreement had run out, and in 1909–10 higher goals were visioned by adding $20,000 to the annual contribution and increasing the term of guaranty to five years. This added up to a promissory note for the unprecedented sum of $250,000. Nearly two hundred individuals and firms signed that note.

At the same time Oberhoffer was put under a five-year contract and the Orchestral Association gently but firmly cut itself loose from its parent, the Philharmonic Club, by announcing its intention of giving only orchestral concerts, with oratorios and other choral works "left to the choral societies of the city."

The first $50,000-backed season was highlighted by Bruckner's Seventh symphony (a bold and ambitious enterprise which chagrined most of the backers), Ernestine Schumann-Heink's local bow, and Minneapolis' own Fremstad returning to sing Isolde's love lament.

The following season brought greater quantity — thirty concerts in twenty-two weeks — and a quality that could be measured by such progressive ventures as a first performance of Sibelius' First symphony, an all-Schumann centenary concert, and the orchestra's first all-American program. This was the season Oberhoffer conducted the Brahms Fourth symphony without a score, a feat he afterward often repeated in other works. Olga Samaroff, a rising young pianist, was introduced in the Grieg A minor concerto, and Nellie Melba, termed by critic Storrs as still the "most phenomenal vocal machine in the world," sang a poor list of songs poorly, although her famous trill continued to thrill.

The immediate future of the orchestra — its guaranty backing, its audience "draw," its programming policy — had thus far always been the urgent concern. But in 1911–12, the first look was taken at the far future of the orchestra and its support. The children's concerts were started: six programs that illustrated the instruments of the orchestra, the story of the symphony, and narrative music. A new organization was set up, the Young

Ludwig Harmsen,
Minneapolis' first real
orchestral maestro

Two musical zealots of the 1870s

Alfred M. Shuey,
musical organizer
extraordinary

*Early concert
halls in
Minneapolis*

Pence Opera House

Harmonia Hal

Frank Danz, Sr.   Frank Danz, Jr.

The Danzes, father and son,
taught Minneapolis to listen to orchestral music and to like it

The Danz musicians garbed in summer uniforms

Bridge Square, scene of open-air concerts by the Danz orchestra

Anna Schoen-René,
energetic gadfly
and promoter of
musical culture

1897 NORTHWESTERN 1897
May Musical Festival.

A. E. SCHOEN-RENE, Director.

Exposition Building, Minneapolis, May 17 & 18

3=Superb Musical Events=3

Only Appearance in the Northwest
OF
The World's Greatest Cantatrice

Mme. Emma

CALVE

Mme. Lillian Blauvelt
—AND—
SIGNOR G. CAMPANARI

Mrs. Katherine Bloodgood
Miss Jennie Mae Spencer
Miss Rose Stewart
Miss Minnie Little
Mr. Barron Berthald
Mr. Heinrich Meyn
Mr. J. H. McKinley
Mr. Charles Morenhout.

THE BOSTON FESTIVAL ORCHESTRA,
CONSISTING OF FIFTY PERFORMERS, UNDER THE DIRECTION OF MR. EMIL MOLLENHAUER,

CHORUS OF 400 SELECT VOICES

SPECIAL EXCURSION RATES HAVE BEEN ARRANGED BY ALL RAILROADS.

ADVANCE SALE OF
SEASON TICKETS
Dyer's Music Stores, Minneapolis and St. Paul,
April 19 and 26 and May 3.

Parquet $6.00
Private Boxes { Six Persons $36.00
               { Eight Persons $48.00
Dress Circle $3.00, $3.50, $4.50, $5.00
Balcony $3.00, $3.50

Regular Ticket Sale
Commences at Dyer's Music Store,
Minneapolis, May 10.

Monday Evening $1.00, $1.50, $2.00
Tuesday Matinee, All Seats $1.00
Tuesday Evening .. $1.00, $1.50, $2.00, $2.50, $3.00

To insure prompt attention, all mail orders for seats to be reserved, and requests
for copies of our Illustrated Souvenir Program Books (to be issued about April
15th), should be addressed to
HARRY GAY, Business Manager,
Post Office Box 15, Minneapolis, Minn.

Playbill for one of Fräulein Anna's musical festivals

Emil Oberhoffer, "discreet emulsion of sentiment and intellect"

Elbert L. Carpenter, for four decades the orchestra's stanch
patron, guide, and guardian

Oberhoffer on the podium, "a portrait of elegance"

The Auditorium, home of the Symphony from 1905 to 1930

The Oberhoffer orchestra on the Auditorium's stage against the woodsy backdrop that was facetiously called "E. L. Carpenter's pine forest"

Under Oberhoffer the orchestra in its second decade was blessed with exceptional stability and quality of personnel

Cornelius Van Vliet, cello

Bruno Labate, oboe

Karl Scheurer, violin

William MacPhail, violin   Otto Gebhart, trombone

Other members of the Oberhoffer ensemble

The trumpet section: left to right, Herman Boessenroth,
John Hartl, William Thieck, Albert Koehler

Richard Czerwonky, concertmaster, was a frequent
soloist

The practical jokes of E. J. "Bill"
Erck relieved the tensions of
constant traveling

Wendell Heighton, tour manager, built up the itineraries

*The decade from 1910 to 1920 was
the "golden era of touring"
for the orchestra*

Caryl Storrs of the *Tribune*   Harlow Gale of the *Daily News*

*The growth of the Symphony was accompanied by the
rise of the "critical gentry"*

Victor Nilsson of   James Davies of the *Daily*
the *Journal*   *News* and *Tribune*

Many artists of later fame were young when they first appeared as soloists with the Symphony

Ignace Paderewski, "giant of the keyboard"

Jascha Heifetz, a musician of "almost appalling accuracy"

Albert Spalding, "America's entry in the violinists' hall of fame"

Minneapolis heard almost all the "star performers" of the period as guests during Oberhoffer's conductorship

Marcella Sembrich, soloist at the first concert of the Symphony

Fannie Bloomfield-Zeisler, the seemingly frail pianist whose fingers could make magic

Olive Fremstad, home-town soprano who became "the darling of European audiences"

Minneapolis enjoyed a succession of guest conductors during "the interregnum," 1922–23

Walter Damrosch "came for a holiday and enjoyed himself"

Bruno Walter was touched by the warmth of his reception

Ossip Gabrilówitsch offered an easygoing account of the Brahms C minor

Reign of the *Pathétique*

People's Symphony Concert Association, and Mrs. George Chase Christian became its president. Mrs. Christian was to be a loyal, long-time supporter and generous patron of the orchestra.

Unquestionably the most popular symphony in the repertoire of the orchestra in these years, its one indispensable and ever-reliable staple, was Tschaikowsky's *Pathétique,* introduced in 1907 and featured thereafter at least once every season, except one, during Oberhoffer's regime. The general music public loved it and could never have enough of it, but its excessive repetition brought considerable grumbling and protest from the journalistic sidelines.

As early as 1911 a rebellious voice was raised. Stuart Maclean of the *Minneapolis Journal* said of the *Pathétique,* "It is morbid, it is awful, under certain circumstances its effect may well be dangerous."

Harlow Gale in the *Daily News* in 1913 wrote: "The orchestra plays this hectic and lugubrious *Pathétique* remarkably well, and had made it its parade and exhibition piece, at first at home and now on its tours. But is this good reason why we at home should be annually harrowed by its unhealthy paroxysms?"

The *Pathétique* was indeed lugubrious (it still is), and recent inquiries into the life of the woman-shy composer give some justification to Gale's peevish allusion to its unhealthy paroxysms. A provocative problem for the sociologist or psychologist, possibly even for the psychoanalyst, would be that of explaining the grip this neurotic work that expires on a note of forlorn defeat had on the contented pre-World War I community the country over.

It is a question, perhaps a flippant one, what Emil Oberhoffer and the Minneapolis Symphony would have done in their period of greatest growth had there been no Tschaikowsky and no Tschaikowsky symphonies. For while the conductor offered a wide-ranging musical diet and never neglected the solider, older fare, it was Tschaikowsky, and again Tschaikowsky, that brought out the crowd. Not only the *Pathétique* but the two other favorites of Tschaikowsky, the Fourth and Fifth symphonies, were regularly and frequently programmed, with no indication that the concertgoing public tired of them, even if some critics did. For many listeners the intense, dramatized emotionalism of the Russian created a concert hall experience that gave excitement and thrills while still spelling "classical music."

Tschaikowsky seemed to be the great leveler of the natural barrier between symphony music and those afraid or in awe of it. Many a reluctant intruder at the Auditorium on Friday nights and Sunday afternoons overcame his doubts about "highbrow" music when the orchestra unleashed the self-pity, the lovely melody, the spine-tingling climaxes of the ingrown Slav.

In the second decade Tschaikowsky's stock was high, probably at its peak. His music was almost modern then; the "stories" and programs behind his works and his oft-quoted comments on his state of mind while in the throes of composing — "confessional" literature of a kind not often encountered in program notes — gave added if extraneous interest to merely listening to Tschaikowsky. In the public prints reams were written about the chills and fevers of the Tschaikowsky ego as reflected in his music. The fact that no composer hitherto had brought such deeply personal documents to the concert hall, or cast them in more palatable and rousing musical idiom, made his symphonies "must" material for every concert schedule, a trustworthy magnet for audiences.

In the eleven seasons between 1911–12 and 1921–22, the *Pathétique* was played fifteen times in Twin Cities concerts, and its repetitions on the road multiplied that number several times. In the same period the Fourth ran up a score of ten, the Fifth had twelve performances, and other Tschaikowsky works — the *1812* overture, the *Marche Slave,* the violin and the B flat minor piano concertos, and the *Casse-Noisette* suite — were aired at frequent intervals. Many who were young then have never forgotten the goose flesh and spine tingle that Oberhoffer's far from restrained treatment of Tschaikowsky gave them.

Most of the critics complained some of the time about this emphasis on Tschaikowsky; some complained all the time. Caryl

Reign of the *Pathétique*

Storrs of the *Tribune* called the Fourth symphony a wild, weird, and sinister work, "based upon a false premise and struggling vainly to make truth of falsehood." James Davies at the beginning of the 1916–17 season declared (after a performance of the Fourth) that "it was apparent we are in danger of becoming Tschaikowsky-ized this season." But the strongest and most outspoken stand against Tschaikowsky was taken by Harlow Gale, who also was pained by Italian opera. In 1914 he deplored the disappointingly small audience that attended an all-Beethoven program, because, he said, he felt that "some 1,500 souls are missing their musical salvation, and will be condemned to the everlastingly hot and cold torments of Italian opera and Tschaikowsky."

Gale, who wrote for the *Daily News* until 1916, decided finally he could stomach the *Pathétique* no longer and went on strike against it. Whenever the *Pathétique* was programmed, he stayed home. By so doing he achieved the double purpose of sparing himself discomfort and registering public protest in the strongest terms at his command. Absence from the concert hall was the snub direct, the snub dramatized.

Gale was absent but not silent on these occasions. Each time his "review" was written at home on his trusty Blickensderfer No. 5, and each time he congratulated himself, publicly, on the privilege of keeping to his cozy den while the "hectic and dismal *Pathétique*" unfolded itself at the Auditorium. He was particularly incensed when, as often happened, an entire program was given over to music by this "pathological Russian."

Tschaikowsky was rated ridiculously high, he argued. "Isn't it a sacrilegious distortion of all art values to make an all-program triumvirate of Beethoven, Wagner and Tschaikowsky?" he asked. "Is an all-Mendelssohn or Mozart program only good enough for children? Aren't Bach and Brahms as worthy as Tschaikowsky? For one I cannot endure the adulation of this morbid, hectic, dismal composer, in his being played by our orchestra far more, in proportion to his works, than any one of his ten vastly higher forerunners."

So Gale stayed away because he had something much better to do: playing cello with his chamber music colleagues, performing "the lovely, pure and romantic string quartets of Mozart and Schumann. . . ."

Gale, son of that elder Harlow Gale who instituted the "dime concerts" back in the seventies, was typical of a new breed of local music critics who were devoted to the art of music and brought more literary craft and keener discrimination to the subject than their forerunners had done. He was in his fifties at the time, and had taught psychology at the University of Minnesota for ten years. He had gone to Yale as a youth, and later spent four years in Leipzig and Berlin in the early nineties, when the dead Wagner and the still-living Brahms dominated the Continental musical scene. His particular god was Beethoven, but Wagner and Brahms had made a deep impression on him during his maturing years.

Gale wrote mostly as he pleased, and he went farther than his colleagues in refusing to suffer at concerts he did not want to hear. But he resembled them in his large capacity for music and for discussion of music, and with them built a new demi-profession in Minneapolis: that of press critic meeting frequent and regular deadlines.

The influence wielded by this new journalistic gentry was a powerful one in creating and increasing public interest in symphony music. This interest was inevitably a minority one, but it constituted a germinal element in the city's prestige and its pride. The relatively small group that contributed to the guaranty fund and regularly attended concerts created sympathetic ripples far from its little circle, so that all of literate Minneapolis was conscious of its symphony orchestra, realizing dimly or consciously that it was "high class" and lent distinction to the community.

The newspapers and their music writers were cooperative, the former now beginning to allot an untold number of columns to the cause of music, the latter writing as if the space at their dis-

posal were limitless. Gale in the *Daily News* — probably because
the paper was physically smaller — was generally briefer and
more pithy than his confreres.

Caryl B. Storrs of the *Tribune* was probably the most picturesque of the critics, and of them the most active and versatile
proponent of good music during the second decade. For many
years he wrote the analytical notes for the symphony programs.
He accompanied the orchestra on many of its tours and conscientiously sent reports of its victories afield back to the home
paper. (In Logansport, Indiana, he once dutifully assumed the
job of reviewing the Minneapolis Symphony concert for the local
newspaper, when told that no one on its staff was competent to
cover it.)

Storrs was born in Michigan, was trained as a physician, and
started his journalistic career by contributing verse and prose to
a small-town weekly newspaper in his native state. Virtually
abandoning the profession he had earlier elected to follow, he
became a member of the *Tribune*'s staff in 1901. Three years later
he turned to music and drama criticism, and stayed with it till
the day of his suicide in January 1920.

Storrs was a cultivated man, and when he started writing
music reviews in 1904 it was obvious that something new — a certain distinction of style and a penetration and piquancy of judgment — was being injected into the formerly haphazard and prosy
business of concert commentary. His writing sometimes took
rather heady flights, but exuberant prose linked with lofty sentiment was deemed appropriate for music, at least in the environment of newspaper columns filled with factual accounts of the
day's happenings. If today there is less loose rhapsodizing about
such things as the soul in discussing music, it may be because
we are not so sure as we were of the whereabouts of the soul,
or whether indeed we have brought it along to the concert hall.
At any rate, Storrs had a lively facility with words and apparently no subject, for him, better deserved the freest, the most
devout, and the most flourishing use of words than music. His

love affair with the Minneapolis Symphony Orchestra was deep and long-lasting, and yet he preserved jealously his independence as an objective and frequently chiding onlooker.

His integrity as an independent observer was not always understood by those within the orchestra's circle who preferred to regard him as a promoter and press agent, and who interpreted his sometimes caustic critiques as a kind of betrayal. Storrs was not aloof and above-the-battle as a critic, and he therefore came to know the difficult position of working heart and soul for an esteemed civic institution, of being close friend to many of its members and practitioners, yet of playing square with his own conscience and the audience by saying honestly what he thought as often as possible.

William McNally, another newspaperman who later became a critic, novelist, and playwright, was an office colleague and close friend and neighbor of Storrs. He has described the critic as a bluff, witty, and boyish-spirited man, enthusiastic, sensitive, with a great conversational flow and real skill as a raconteur. Storrs was a fervent amateur pianist and would often join McNally in four-handed performances of Beethoven symphonies in the early morning hours before the two left their Hampshire Arms apartments for their jobs at the *Tribune*.

Like Gale, Storrs could be easily irritated by vocal intrusions at symphony concerts, particularly when occasioned by the high-voiced sisterhood. Of Alice Verlet, a Belgian singer who appeared with the orchestra in 1915, he wrote that "a chapter in every treatise on psychology should be devoted to the mysterious relation existing between coloratura sopranos and sartorial conspicuity." Describing her as clad in a gown that clung closer to her figure than ivy to a tower, he said that "the explanation probably is that as compositions for the coloratura voice ignore the art of real music in order to center aural attention upon vocal acrobatics, the possessors of this kind of voice feel justified in centering ocular attention upon their physical charms."

But Storrs did defend, most of the time, conductor Oberhoffer's right to play as much Tschaikowsky as he pleased, taking tacit

issue with Gale on this sore issue. His argument was that repeated playings "enable us to better understand music that is
difficult at first." (It comes as a shock to realize that Tschaikowsky probably *was* difficult to understand at first.) But he did
suffer somewhat from the Tschaikowsky dyspepsia of his brethren, as we have seen, and he declined to approve of that composer's *Manfred*. In it, he wrote, "the artistic control which saves
the *Fifth* and *Sixth* symphonies from shocking bewilderment is,
in a measure, lacking." Storrs saw Tschaikowsky's symphonies
as autumnal, decadent: "The danger of this passionate music
lies in its very glory. . . . Through the autumn of Tschaikowsky
let us never forget the springtime of Mozart or the full summer
of Beethoven."

The blithe but discriminating *Tribune* critic did not capitulate
meekly to many modes of music and compositions which today
we have learned to accept, and even discount, from long familiarity. Of Liadoff's moderately modern *Kikimora* he said that
"it was without form, beginning nowhere, going nowhere and
getting nowhere"; of the Berlioz *Fantastique* he complained that
it was obvious and full of cheap tricks; and Richard Strauss's
hot-blooded *Don Juan* he rather puritanically described as an
"attempt to drag music from heaven to earth and make her perform a sordid and unworthy task."

This puritanism of viewpoint was not exclusively Storrs'; Gale
had ridiculed the effort, in *Don Juan*, to derive inspiration "from
the amorous sports of this frisky adventurer," and Victor Schof-
felmayer, who wrote about music for the *Journal,* went even
further. He declared that "the revolting incidents around which
is woven Lenau's lascivious poem [the literary base of *Don Juan*]
cannot inspire music of true worth."

The writer has a single recollection of Storrs. One morning
the critic was guest speaker at a high school auditorium period,
wearing the pince-nez with broad black ribbon he often affected
for public appearances. Seating himself at the piano on stage, he
set out to demonstrate for the assembled students the difference
between classical and popular music, taking a classical melody,

playing it straight, then "ragging" it. Unfortunately he failed to make his point that the classical theme was good, true, and beautiful and that the ragtime arrangement was a cheap corruption. The young audience howled its approval of the syncopated version.

The other Minneapolis critics who came into prominence during this decade and were destined to become veteran recorders of the musical scene were Victor Nilsson and James Davies.

Nilsson took over the music post for the *Journal* in the midyears of the first decade, after two years with the old *Times,* and he remained there until his death in 1938. Born in Sweden, he was a courtly and courteous personification of culture, a gentle soul who praised more easily than he blamed, who preferred to analyze rather than judge. For a newspaperman his learning was wide and deep in the arts and humanities. He had come to Minneapolis as a youth of nineteen in 1886, and in the nineties had attended the University of Minnesota not long after founding a commercial newspaper, the *Progress,* which later became the *Progress-Register.* He was an ardent and loyal proponent of Scandinavian culture and was twice knighted by King Gustaf of Sweden for introducing and promoting Swedish artists and musical organizations in America.

Nilsson was probably the least belligerent and most scholarly music critic in the city's history, and his appetite for music was literally bottomless. He was catholic in his tastes, accepting and understanding many modern works that nettled and offended his colleagues, although Debussy's *La Mer,* first played in 1921, found him the sole dissenter: "It has not the brine of the sea or the mystery of the depths."

On the whole, and over a period of three decades, the dignified and patient Nilsson took all music to his bosom — and asked for more. Every concert, down to the humblest exhibition of panic-stricken students, found him present (usually with his sister Emma) and sitting it out till the last encore was sounded.

He was a bachelor, reserved and introspective. Tall, rather bleakly handsome, always immaculately dressed (with white pip-

ing along his vest), he would attend concerts with perhaps a
volume of Ibsen's plays in hand, humming quietly to himself in
the intervals between numbers. His reviews were usually long-
winded and sometimes hardly readable, but they always gave
thoughtful and sympathetic consideration to the music and those
who performed it. In later years a throat affliction reduced his
voice to a piping whisper, making him seem more than ever a
withdrawn, quiet oracle.

James Davies succeeded Harlow Gale on the *Daily News* in
1916 and four years later followed Storrs on the *Tribune*. A
stocky, quick-moving man, he was a rare blend of peppery
temper and warmheartedness. He adhered hotly to firm opinions,
wrote at breakneck speed, and was wholly unaffected; he was
much liked for his forthrightness and camaraderie. By temperament he was almost the opposite of Nilsson in his bluff and
hearty approach, his sharp, unqualified judgments. He, too, had
a voracious appetite for music, but showed little patience for
singers who mispronounced the German language (which he
taught), for show-off modernism that flouted, as he thought, the
rules of sense and beauty, for the "melodic nonentities from
Verdi's operas" on symphony programs.

(Almost all the critics waged intermittent war on singers who
interrupted symphonic proceedings with Italian arias and sometimes reduced them to absurdity with fatuous encores in English.
Many prima donnas sang with the orchestra, and Oberhoffer was
bothered by them far less than the critics were. By his own admission, he knew how to handle them. "They are not difficult
to manage," he once said. "To me they are so many pathological
cases, and I deal with them as though I were an alienist. They
are perfectly manageable if you treat them like children and coax
them along, never getting irritated at their moods.")

Davies was born in England of Welsh and Irish ancestry, came
to the United States alone at the age of seventeen, and was
graduated from Boston University in 1900, receiving his master's
degree there five years later. He had a good voice and earned
part of his way singing in church choirs, concerts, and light opera.

Later he attended the University of Leipzig, where he received his doctorate in philosophy and lectured on English literature and where, too, he met and married a violin student, Grace Golden, sister of Verna Golden, who later became Mrs. Carlyle Scott. (Mrs. Grace Davies was to carry on as newspaper critic after his death in 1940.) Davies joined the University of Minnesota faculty in 1909, teaching German there until his retirement in 1938.

H. A. Bellows, who replaced Robert Griggs Gale as music commentator on the old *Bellman* magazine, became the *Daily News* critic when Davies moved over to the *Tribune,* and proved he had a mind of his own. Later Bellows was to take on Storrs' old chore of writing program notes.

The rise of the critics — qualified reviewers who took their mission seriously and wrote with increasing discernment and style — came in natural response to the rise of the orchestra as a plastic and skillful playing unit. The orchestra grew into a great instrument in the mellow mid-years of Oberhoffer's reign, and between 1914 and 1918 reached its first high peak of endeavor when ensemble, repertoire, experience, and technical brilliance all combined to produce exceptional music and programs.

Davies once remarked that Oberhoffer could have done better in developing the Minneapolis Symphony if he had not had to train four orchestras during the years of his conductorship. This reference to shifting personnel is not markedly applicable to the mid-teens orchestra, which achieved considerable stability and waxed strong because of outstanding instrumentalists at key posts.

These made a redoubtable team. Replacing Frank Danz (who spent his last years giving concerts at St. Paul's Como Park and Mozart Hall, and who died in 1911), Richard Czerwonky began a long reign as concertmaster in 1909. This German violinist had been brought from Berlin by Karl Muck for the Boston orchestra; he was a virtuoso performer who functioned equally well as soloist and instrumental leader. Cornelius Van Vliet, arriving in 1912 as cello principal, became one of the orchestra's pillars. Franz Dicks presided over the second violins, and Frank Kuchynka, probably at that time the finest soloist on his instrument in the country, headed the basses. Karl Scheurer, a first-rate violinist from Germany, took charge of the viola section for five years; for almost the whole span of the orchestra's life he has been a knowing and skillful leader in the string sections, in 1951 second violin principal.

In 1914 the orchestra acquired one of the finest woodwind players in its history: Bruno Labate, oboist, who remained until 1920, when he went to the New York Philharmonic as first-chair man. Labate was a round-faced, smiling Italian, so diminutive that one of his colleagues, watching him walk on stage at a rehearsal one morning, remarked that "Bruno would make a fine watch charm." He was so short that his feet barely touched the floor when he sat down. Labate had a large and glowing oboe tone which is still legend among the older concertgoers.

Completing the roster of exceptional musicians who lent luster to the Oberhoffer orchestra were Carl Woempner as first flutist, succeeded by Leonardo de Lorenzo; Henry Cunnington as bassoonist and William Thieck with his silver-toned trumpet; Pierre Perrier, clarinetist with exceptional beauty of sound and phrase; Richard Lindenhahn as number 1 horn with rich timbre and faultless technique; Otto Gebhart, an able Theodore Thomas trombonist who died in 1920; John Sperzel with his deep and mellow-voiced tuba; William Faetkenheuer as that dependable punctuator, the tympanist; and the always popular and much applauded soloist, Henry J. Williams, harpist.

An unobtrusive newcomer joined the Minneapolis Symphony in 1913 in the double role of second violin and fourth trumpet, and ten years later inherited one of the orchestra's most exacting and grueling duties, that of librarian. He was Herman Boessenroth, a versatile man whose talent for detail and whose tasteful skill in orchestration made him one of the few "indispensables" of the organization.

With the orchestra bolstered by first-rate musicians playing first-rate instruments, with problems of financial support only

moderately onerous, the repertoire became increasingly sophisticated and venturesome while keeping its firm foundations in the
classic masters. Despite the free rein given the Tschaikowsky
mania, the great symphonic composers were not overshadowed
by it; they were liberally represented in the orchestra's programs.
No season went by without Beethoven and Brahms symphonies,
which were and are part of the basic repertoire of all self-
respecting orchestras. There was a smattering of Mozart, not so
much Haydn. New works came with reasonable regularity, and
by the end of the decade Oberhoffer was constantly tackling
modern works and peppering his programs with local and often
American premières.

The Minneapolis conductor was growing up. He was acquiring
full mastery, and his musical personality flowered. This "discreet
emulsion of sentiment and intellect," as Percy Hammond once
called him, was developing the power that dramatized the intellect and gave backbone to the sentiment. He finally found his
accomplishments beginning to catch up with his ambitions and
dreams.

His desire to give his best was strongest when confronted with
the things he regarded as best, so that he worked harder and
longer on these than on lesser works. If a Brahms symphony
was the week's major assignment, he would devote most of rehearsal time to it, skimping the rest of the program. At the
concert he would not only play the Brahms magnificently but
pull from his players, by some combination of urgency and mag-
netism, a compelling performance of the other numbers on the
program. Afterward, many a musician would look at the score
he didn't know too well and wonder how he had played the notes.

Oberhoffer was close as a father to his men, and he spanked
them verbally when they played sloppily or lapsed into low
stylistic habits. He was not above coarse allusions when empha-
sizing what he was after. "There are two kinds of music — music
above the navel and music below the navel," he once said at
rehearsal. "How do you want to play it?" He could give a nasty
rebuke to a lazy musician: "Go back to the Dewey!" (a cheap

burlesque house on Washington Avenue). He alluded sarcastically, and pointedly, to slack players as "chair warmers." His sense of platform decorum was particularly outraged by a cellist in the ranks who for a time tried to smoke a cigar while playing at rehearsals.

The Minneapolis orchestra in the fall of 1914 put a new city on its traveling schedule, a city whose patronage was to prove far more important than that of any other community, large or small, distant or near, on the Symphony's circuit. That city was St. Paul. For the first time Oberhoffer and his men began to serve St. Paul regularly and became thereby a true Twin Cities institution.

St. Paul had had its own orchestra for eight seasons, but was never too happy with it, or lucky either. Conducted by Walter Henry Rothwell, a pupil of Gustav Mahler, the St. Paul Symphony had been founded more from motives of rivalry with and emulation of Minneapolis than from an irresistible demand by St. Paul music lovers for an orchestra of their own.

It had been maintained at an expense of $40,000 to $50,000 a year with deficits ranging from $15,000 to $20,000, taken up not too cheerfully by the city's businessmen. The first season had run up a scandalous $50,000 loss and resulted in an appeal for help to C. O. Kalman, a financier who at that time took over its financial guidance and began his long and valuable service to the Twin Cities' musical community.

The orchestra, like its opposite number in Minneapolis, gave local concerts and went on tours, the latter for a time arranged by Charles L. Wagner, who was brought in as manager. (Wagner later went to New York and became a prominent figure in the concert agency world.) At times there was brisk competition between the two ensembles for tour dates, and for a while an "orchestra war" threatened. The St. Paul group made a profitable journey through Canada, but a subsequent tour of the eastern United States proved ill-advised and consumed the profits of the earlier trip.

The old and stupid rivalry between the cities was whipped up by boasting on both sides of the river. On the Minneapolis side the danger of the St. Paul orchestra's moving in on Minneapolis' tour territory was smugly shrugged off as nonexistent. On the other side it was pridefully reported that St. Paul was spending more per capita for music than any other American city — and specifically sixty-two cents as against Minneapolis' thirty-eight cents!

In the fall of 1914, at the start of World War I, the guaranty fund expired and St. Paul businessmen, faced with the necessity of adding $20,000 to the new one, decided they had spent enough. The orchestra's affairs were forthwith liquidated and its debts paid. J. McClure Bellows, music writer of the *Pioneer Press,* lamented that "with orchestras springing up around us in smaller places, such as Minot, our humiliation is complete."

Efforts had earlier been made to consolidate the Minneapolis and St. Paul orchestras, for obviously it was foolish to have two such expensive organizations serving cities whose aggregate population was little more than 500,000. (Curiously enough, Richard Strauss, the noted Austrian composer, once voiced his views on this situation. On one of his two visits to Minneapolis he expounded on the absurdity of Minneapolis and St. Paul both trying to operate symphony orchestras.) No support for the consolidation plan could be developed in the capital city, even with a proposal that two thirds of the cost be borne by Minneapolis and one third by St. Paul.

The truth of the matter seems to be that St. Paul had little enthusiasm for its own orchestra but less for "buying in" on the orchestra of its sister city, even though the latter, by general agreement, was giving better concerts under a more magnetic maestro. A drastic reduction of top season ticket prices from $22 to $12.50 in the 1912–13 season had not served to make the St. Paul orchestra any more popular and only worsened its box-office malady.

It was E. L. Carpenter who in August 1914 suggested that the Minneapolis orchestra duplicate its Friday night performances on Thursday nights in St. Paul. Eight of these Thursday nights were finally agreed upon for the series across the river. Guest artists could be had for both concerts for one fee or a little more, and the orchestra's St. Paul appearance could be construed, by music union regulations, as a rehearsal.

St. Paul at first greeted the fortnightly calls of Oberhoffer's musical squad with mixed emotions. Why, some citizens asked, should we support a Minneapolis institution when we couldn't stand back of our own? Why should St. Paul backers of these concerts put themselves in the position of boosting a Minneapolis product? "Why not get the Association of Commerce," one chauvinist suggested bitterly, "to advocate the removal of our Auditorium to the sister city?"

But these hurt feelings were eventually assuaged, or ignored. The Minneapolis orchestra's concerts had a strong "angel": the St. Paul Institute, many of whose members had been guarantors of the old St. Paul Symphony. Mr. Kalman, former vice-president of the St. Paul Orchestral Association, took over the chairmanship of the Institute's concert committee. In later years George F. Lindsay became one of the orchestra's firmest friends and largest contributors in St. Paul.

Also, nine former musicians of the St. Paul orchestra were immediately taken in by the Minneapolis Symphony, bringing to twenty-one the number of onetime players in the defunct organization who now belonged to the Minneapolis ensemble.

Critic Bellows assured his fellow citizens that "the Minneapolis orchestra comes to us not as an invasion but as a neighborly loan in time of need," and soon the concerts were hailed as signs of an entente cordiale bringing to an end the period of intercity bickering. A new era of good feeling was foreseen, and Harlow Gale made an inspired suggestion. Minneapolis, he said, should be magnanimous enough to change the name of its orchestra to the Minnesota Symphony Orchestra.

Unfortunately his idea was not acted upon. The year the idea was broached would have been the time to make the name change, before the "Minneapolis" trademark had grown as familiar and famous as it later became, and as entrenched as a long-time investment.

St. Paul's annual quota of concerts was soon raised to ten, then to twelve, and finally to sixteen, and before long the city's press — the *Pioneer Press* and the *Daily News* — developed a critics' corps that matched the Minneapolis scribes in acumen and readability. Indeed, in sophistication and literary charm the writers from St. Paul often outshone their colleagues across the river.

One of the St. Paul critics was an unusually gifted author, Charles M. Flandrau, master of delightful and witty prose of a quality not often seen in newspapers. Son of a judge and member of an old and prominent family, Flandrau had written a book, *Viva Mexico!*, which was and still is one of the most sparkling and personal of travel chronicles. With this slim volume and his *Diary of a Freshman* and *Sophomores Abroad*, Flandrau had developed a small but solid literary fame, appreciated by a discerning few. Educated at Harvard, much traveled, this dilettante in comfortable circumstances turned to music reviewing as a kind of diversion, an outlet for occasional writing.

He wrote first for the *Pioneer Press* and later for the *Daily News*, bringing to his reviews the approach of a literary man interested in and stirred by music but not deeply versed in it, or pretending to be. His writing occasionally had a languid and condescending tone, but was graced always with wit and temperament, and reflected the viewpoint of a sensitive, indolent, and cultivated man.

Flandrau's opinion of the much-played *Pathétique*, at variance with the grousing of some of his colleagues, illustrates his independence of mind, his refusal to be badgered into a viewpoint not strictly his own.

"In spite of all the sob-artists of all the silly program notes pertaining to Tschaikowsky's lovely *Sixth* symphony," he wrote, "this work has really never been the welter of unbridled grief that they would have one believe. In proof of which, all that is necessary is a pair of attentive ears and the symphony itself.

What do we find? Four movements, of which part of one (the andante of the first) is pleasantly melancholy, and a whole movement (the fourth) most of which is sad, I grant you, but by no means agonizing unless the conductor deliberately sets out to make it so. All of what is left is positively joyous."

It seems a shame to leave buried in yellowing newspaper files some of the Flandrau mots and mischievous phrases with which his reviews abounded. He spoke once of "the almost appalling accuracy of Jascha Heifetz." The season opened one fall in a refurbished concert hall and he wrote: "The Auditorium's new decorations are going to be prettier than they smell."

Again: "As for the waltz movement [of the *Pathétique*] it suggests absolutely nothing more than a large corps of cuties pirouetting around a stage in white silk tights." And "Goldmark's overture to *Sappho* is a somewhat flashy and empty work that might just as well have been entitled *Julius Caesar, Carrie Chapman Catt* or *Mary Pickford*." And again: "To say that Mr. Oberhoffer takes liberties with him [Beethoven] merely means that the objector has heard some other conductor play Beethoven differently." Of the performance of Boëllmann's *Fantasie Dialogue* for orchestra and organ Flandrau wrote that he hadn't been present at so truly grand a noise "since the last time I heard a battleship saluting a secretary of the navy."

When Flandrau went to the *Daily News* in 1919, Wilbur Webster Judd took over at the *Pioneer Press,* bringing another artful if somewhat windier and less sparkling style to the business of concert appraisal. Judd had his carefully nurtured enthusiasms, a watchful ear, and a curious hobby of birds, domesticated birds, which he kept in many cages in his apartment.

These two rather precious bachelors, Flandrau and Judd, set a tone of fastidious cultivation in critical journalism in St. Paul, but in the same period another reviewer, Frances Boardman, took her first flights in what was to be a much longer, more conscientious, and eventually more astute service to the cause of good music. She made a respected profession of what in the past had qualified as diversion or sideline.

Music and Maestros

In the 1914–15 season Emil Oberhoffer initiated an extra series of all-Beethoven concerts on six weekday afternoons, during which all the nine symphonies and three of the concertos were played. A special Beethoven program book was printed for the series, which was climaxed by a performance, second in the city's history, of the Ninth symphony, with a select corps from the Philharmonic Club singing the choral portions. The series started out weak at the box office, with only half a house out front, but it built up attendance and drew a capacity throng for the choral finale.

The same season saw first performances of such rarities as Berlioz' *Harold in Italy* and Tschaikowsky's *Manfred*, and each season thereafter offered local premières that kept the customers, and the critics, on the *qui vive* and sometimes on the fence. The thirteenth season (1915–16) introduced the Borodin Second symphony, Delius' *Dance Rhapsody*, and Tschaikowsky's *Francesca da Rimini*.

Even more exciting was the year that followed. In the Friday series of twelve concerts were heard Stravinsky's *Fireworks*, Glazounoff's Sixth symphony, the finale of Richard Strauss's *Salome* (with Marcella Kraft in the solo role), Rachmaninoff's *Island of the Dead*, Strauss's *Alpine* symphony, Kalinnikoff's First symphony, the Chausson *Poème* for violin and orchestra (with Thibaud), Grainger's *In a Nutshell* suite, and John Alden Carpenter's *Adventures in a Perambulator*. This high incidence of modern works, many of them major, in a twelve-concert series has rarely been equaled by the orchestra since.

Virtually all the great instrumentalists and singers of the period appeared with the orchestra during the decade. Representatives of opera's "golden age," some whose voices were in decline, were on the list: Hempel, Gadski, Fremstad, Melba, Destinn. Other singers just starting slow or swift ascents were orchestra guests, among them Amelita Galli-Curci, first heard locally in March 1918, and Gladys Swarthout, who was a girl of eighteen with a curl on her forehead when she sang at a Sunday "pop" on December 7, 1919.

Reign of the *Pathétique*

Among the great composers and teacher-composers who appeared in Minneapolis in that era were Ferruccio Busoni, Eugène Ysaye, and Alfredo Casella. The young Kreisler played the Beethoven and Brahms concertos. Elman had been a favorite since he arrived in 1908, "the wonderful Russian boy violinist," a curly-headed prodigy. Rachmaninoff played his C minor concerto in 1919. A memorable evening was one in which Gabrilówitsch and Bauer played a Mozart two-piano concerto. Myra Hess and Guiomar Novaës, who were to become the two outstanding pianists of their sex, made their first bows in this period.

In 1916, the engagement of gifted Jean Vincent Cooper as contralto soloist for the spring tour was to bring to Minneapolis, a few years later, a much admired Symphony soloist and a new member of the Carpenter family. Miss Cooper came from Jackson, Mississippi, had a voice that critic Storrs termed of "pure and golden quality," and became the wife of Lawrence, son of the E. L. Carpenters. Thirty-five years after her first songs with the Minneapolis Symphony, her son Vincent Welles Carpenter was carrying on in his own way the family's musical interest and traditions, as composer-in-residence at St. Paul's Macalester College.

Two curiosities of the decade were Grainger's aforementioned *In a Nutshell* suite, introduced and buried in 1917, and the appearance of Carlo Liten, Belgian tragedian, in a reading of his poems. Grainger was mercilessly ribbed for the strange collection of noisemaking devices he assembled for his suite: steel and wooden marimbaphones, a nabimba, a stand of Swiss bells, a celesta, a glockenspiel, and a xylophone, all clustered about the conductor's dais like a "herd of queer-looking monsters."

The *Tribune* had said of the *Nutshell* suite and its composer, "If you don't care for the shell, go and enjoy the nut." The Minneapolis critics read off the performance rather brusquely, Davies declaring that "one thing is certain, such a composition has no business on a symphony program." Flandrau in St. Paul claimed he was unnerved when a small army of attendants carted on stage a kitchen range, a soda water fountain, twenty-six stovepipes, three dozen brand-new coffee pots, an icebox, and "a small but perfectly appointed operating table." But he found the Grainger suite, despite its odd hardware, a "work of extraordinary interest and fascination."

The lean and ascetic-looking Liten, who seemed to personify the sorrow of overrun Belgium, in December 1918 intoned several patriotic Belgian poems with orchestral accompaniment — a strange union of speaking voice and music. He had been engaged while the war was on, had been forced to cancel his November date, but finally was able to appear a month after the armistice, when the psychological-emotional value of his performance had diminished.

This unavoidable piece of poor timing was only one of the distresses that began to beset the Minneapolis Symphony in 1918–19. The western tour was canceled that season. And as the war overseas rolled into its final phases and thousands of doughboys were dying on the fields of France, anti-German sentiment waxed hot and personal, and the orchestra with its heavy enrollment of German players was, if not suspect, vulnerable to the hatreds and suspicions of the time.

In the inner circles of orchestra management there had been some concern because Oberhoffer, like Karl Muck, was German-born. In 1917 Muck, conductor of the Boston Symphony, had allegedly refused a request to play *The Star-Spangled Banner* at a concert in Providence. (It was later brought out that Muck had never received the invitation to play the anthem, and that he included it in his programs thereafter.) He was arrested in March 1918 and interned as an enemy alien "dangerous to the public peace and the safety of the United States."

The policy as to Oberhoffer was to meet possible public criticism and suspicion head-on, and his unquestioned patriotism (soundly based in a south German's abhorrence of Prussianism) was pointedly referred to in the public prints. He was once a German, it was frequently mentioned, but he had long been an American and was "intensely patriotic," eager to use his orchestra "to promote patriotism at all times." And on tour, manager

Heighton always hastened to add that there "are no slackers in our orchestra — every man is an American citizen and we speak only the English language." Oberhoffer had earlier insisted that no German be spoken by his musicians in public or backstage. So the *Decatur Herald* editorialized: "The leader of one great orchestra has been jailed for sedition, and the Minneapolis Symphony orchestra is recognized as a great patriotic force. What a contrast!"

But there was some nasty publicity about an allegedly disloyal member of the orchestra, charged, rather hysterically, with having pictures of the kaiser, kaiserin, and the Austrian royal family hanging in his home. The suspected musician, after investigation by the Department of Justice, was cleared of the charges, and the damning pictures were found to have been those of Franz Joseph and Empress Elizabeth of Austria, both deceased and therefore to be regarded only retroactively as enemies. The musician bought a couple of Liberty Loan bonds and was reinstated.

During the war period the orchestra played several programs for servicemen, offering what some still recall as fearfully wooden treatments of *Smiles* and *There's a Long, Long Trail*. And at the start of the 1918–19 season, all the orchestra members were required to sign loyalty pledges, which they did to a man. They also bought $20,000 worth of bonds in the fourth Liberty Loan.

All this patriotic breast-beating, plus the long-standing regard the orchestra had earned from its constituency, brought the Teutonic-complexioned Minneapolis Symphony safely through the hectic period when even Beethoven symphonies were frowned on as subversive and possibly treasonable.

A piece of light verse written in this difficult period by Caryl Storrs of the *Tribune* conveys some sense of the temper of the time and place in its mingling of wartime sentiment with friendly affection for the orchestra, whose roll, in part, it calls.

"Oh Say, Can You See?"

When the symphony's done, and the musikers rise
  "The Star Spangled Banner" to play,

Music and Maestros

There's a thrill in the heart and a beat in the pulse
    Of which there is little to say.
Oberhofferan skill with the magic baton
    Does nothing more potent than that;
And it moves every soul in the upstanding throng,
    Save the lady who can't find her hat.

Mr. Faetkenheuer's tympani roll with a will,
    Del Hoskins is there with the drum,
And Rudolf stands ready, with cymbals all poised,
    Awaiting the crashes to come.
The cellists abandon their wondrous technique
    For it's hard to do much on their feet,
But none in the band make more loyal attempts
    Than Carlo, Chris Erck and Van Vliet.

Jimmie Williams sits down, but that doesn't mean
    He is not patriotic, oh, no;
But he can't change the chords on his Wurlitzer harp
    Except with the pedals; and so,
We'll have to excuse him from rising, and feel
    That his motives misjudged will not be;
Just think of the discords that Jimmie would make,
    If unable to alter the key.

The basses stand always, so Baron von Witt
    And Kuchynka are quite at their ease;
But Sperzel, the tuba man, pity deserves,
    For he can't hold his horn on his knees.
The audience sings till it's red in the face,
    And follows as close as may be;
It does pretty well, save when Trumpeter Thieck
    Takes that jump on "the land of the free."

There are those that contend that the national hymn
    Isn't in it with Mozart and Brahms;
Mebbe not, but it gets you, just now, where you live
    And tingles your reddening palms.
Its form may be wrong, and it's darn hard to sing,
    But that part of the show can't be beat
When Emil waves both of his arms in the air,
    And the orchestra springs to its feet!

The exciting news of the armistice brought a halt to symphony
rehearsal on November 11, when the elated Oberhoffer dismissed

the men after summoning them to mount their chairs and play
The Star-Spangled Banner.

Meanwhile the influenza epidemic had resulted in a ban on all
public gatherings, and for six weeks the orchestra existed only
as a rehearsing organization, with no early prospect of an audience, while it awaited the lifting of the health board sentence.
The oft-postponed opening concert took place finally on November 18, with Mischa Elman as soloist.

The next squall to rock the Symphony's barque in this stretch
of bad weather and shoals came in February 1919, when for the
first time since the organization of the orchestra, the conductor
took sick leave, going east for a month for his health. This was
the first visible sign that the strain of being the prisoner as well
as the director of the organization he had built was beginning to
tell on Oberhoffer. An insight into his state of mind at this time
is found in his response to an inquisitive caller in New York:

"I am hungry for music of somebody else's making," he said.
"The planning, the studying, the rehearsing, the meditating on
all the programs I give — the little triumphs of one day followed
by despair the next, when one falls short of the ideal sought —
this constant giving out, without any taking in, brings one sometimes to the brink of musical bankruptcy. I crave to feed on
what I have been doling out."

So Oberhoffer took "the musical cure," as he called it, under
Drs. Damrosch, Stransky, Campanini, Polacco, Monteux, and
others, listening with that attentive but carefree attitude one
may take when observing a familiar task performed by others.
In Minneapolis Adolph Weidig, a Chicago composer-conductor,
and Artur Bodanzky, New York conductor, took over the baton
while Oberhoffer was enjoying his busman's holiday in the East.

The roving maestro returned to Minneapolis in time to hear
Bodanzky conduct the home organization and to call it "the best
orchestra I ever heard." On March 7 he resumed his duties a relaxed man. Perhaps too relaxed. His performance of the Brahms
C minor symphony showed tempo retards in every movement,
with sluggishness of feeling in the first, reported Davies.

141

The ensemble stability of the orchestra's serene and fruitful years had begun to buckle this season, and for a time most of the replacements were short-lived. A severe blow was the simultaneous leave-taking of two popular men, the concertmaster and the principal cellist, who had been with the orchestra so long it was hard to imagine its functioning without them. Czerwonky, who had been engaged to head the violin department in Chicago's Busch Conservatory, was succeeded by Guy Woodard, and Van Vliet was replaced by Hermann Beyer-Hane at the cellists' first desk. The following season Michael Kasanoff came in as new viola head and personnel manager but he died in a year's time. In 1920–21 the shakeup continued to the point of disruption: Franz Dicks, long-time second violin principal, Labate the oboist, Perrier the clarinetist, and trumpeter Thieck, all departed.

It was a time of shift and transition; the magic composite of the years before had been disturbed and in a measure lost; the search was now on for a new and dependable blend of personnel. The trial-and-error method resulted in several mistaken and unsuccessful choices, and also in several valuable acquisitions in new men.

Among the latter were Engelbert Roentgen, who followed Beyer-Hane's short reign as cello principal; Henry Woempner, first-flutist son of Carl, an earlier flutist; and Alexandre Duvoir, an oboist of great distinction. The following year (1921–22) saw the arrival of debonair Paul Lemay as first violist. Lemay was an American of French ancestry who flew British planes in the 1914–18 war and now pursued aviation as a hobby. He was to die on a reconnaissance flight in World War II, after founding and conducting the Duluth Symphony Orchestra.

The disruption of personnel was intensified to a dangerous point by the most critical emergency the orchestra's management had faced up to that time. This was the conflict with the American Federation of Musicians in the spring and summer of 1921.

The unusually short season of 1920–21, brought about by the abandonment of the four-week spring tour because of high railroad rates, had impelled the management to seek other means to give the men their normal guaranteed employment of twenty-six to twenty-eight weeks at home and four weeks on tour. The Minneapolis park board had offered the Orchestral Association $5000 a week for an eight weeks' series of summer concerts at Lake Harriet. To make up the difference between that figure and the amount due the men, a ten-cent admission was to be charged seatholders at these concerts.

But the AFM flatly rejected the plan on grounds that the park board was currently employing a non-AFM or outlaw union group (Barrett's Band) for neighborhood park concerts.

A great hue and cry was raised. This was the first time the increasingly strong AFM had interfered with the plans of the Symphony management on a major issue. The four-month struggle that ensued found the orchestra musicians in the middle, mute but hoping for the best. All of them were loyal union men (members of AFM's local unit, the Minneapolis Musicians Association), and yet there was no doubt that they needed the extra employment the summer series would give.

E. L. Carpenter and the Symphony board took a stand that was both firm and indignant, insisting on the right of the orchestra management to make a contract with the park board. The national union insisted with equal vigor that the Minneapolis parks, being on the "unfair" list, were out of bounds for union musicians.

Wrath and wild rumor accompanied this first sparring match between businessmen in music and musical businessmen. Reports of the orchestra's imminent disbandment were rife, and the newspapers, not notably union-minded at this time, took up the cries of outrage and doom. "Union Rules May Cost Minneapolis Great Orchestra," announced one, and in June the *Tribune* went so far as to headline a news story, "Minneapolis Symphony to Be Abandoned."

This report of the Symphony's death proved to be greatly exaggerated but its future was uncertain and looked black indeed. No contracts had been entered into between the management and the orchestra musicians for the season to come, and none was to be signed until the authority of the Orchestral Association to book its orchestra for engagements in Minneapolis parks or anywhere else was recognized.

The deadlock continued through half the summer. Carpenter talked with Joseph M. Webber, AFM president; calamity seemed around the corner when the fate of the orchestra, as the press reported, was finally "put up to the guarantors"; and the *Daily News* started printing a daily column labeled "Keep Symphony Orchestra Going." This was a catch-all for hundreds of fervent postcard messages sent in by citizens who had been invited to write to the newspaper.

There was a great communal sigh of relief August 7 when Webber relented and announced that he had taken the Minneapolis parks off the "unfair list." But the orchestra, with no contracts signed, was actually nonexistent. It was too late by this time to proceed with the Lake Harriet concerts, and it was almost too late to marshal the personnel with which to open the 1921–22 season. Carlo Fischer, now resident manager, was recalled from a vacation in Canada to put into quick motion plans for the coming year. Fifty musicians were called up for auditions, for there were many gaps in the ranks left by players who had bowed out when the Symphony's foundations began to shake.

Oberhoffer, after months of suspense and dread, was "a new man" upon hearing the news. "The death of the orchestra would have been a crushing blow to me. I am very, very happy," he said, and went on to declare that the men "will now earn steady incomes, without having to go away to earn their summer money." (He was overoptimistic. The earning of summer money thirty years later was still a serious problem for orchestra musicians hired for only a half-year's term.)

With renewed zest Oberhoffer again made the trek to New York to find a concertmaster — Woodard having taken leave after three seasons — and to round up other musicians for his decimated band. The new concertmaster he picked was Vladimir Graffman (who did not last long either), and he engaged no less than six other section leaders in the strings, reeds, and brass. Cellist Roentgen was elevated to a newly created post, that of assistant conductor, and after the first rehearsal Oberhoffer announced that the nineteenth season would open with the "best personnel the orchestra has ever possessed." This time, he said, he had personally tried out and engaged every new man himself, instead of leaving part of the job, as in the past, to agents.

The season that followed was a notable one, truly one of the finest in Symphony annals, full of surprises and not a few landmarks. One might have expected Oberhoffer's energy and enterprise to flag a bit after nineteen years in the same post. They seemed instead to flare up in a final burst of brilliance. He played five of the nine Beethoven symphonies, all the four Brahms ones, also the three Tschaikowsky favorites, the Fourth, Fifth, and Sixth. His first-performance list was distinguished and ambitious, including Atterberg's *Ocean* symphony, the Busoni violin concerto, d'Indy's *Symphony on a French Mountain Air* and *Istar* variations, the Mahler Fourth, two Mozart concertos previously unplayed, and two of the major works of modern times: Debussy's *La Mer* and Stravinsky's *Firebird* suite.

Performance of the latter, particularly the clashing dissonances and pounding rhythms of Katschei's infernal dance, fanned the flames of controversy, with critic Davies in full cry against that "finicky futurist who has wandered so far from rationality in his compositions that he has become the laughing stock of the musical world."

Stravinsky in moderation was not such a terrible person, conceded Davies, but "gusts and eddies of tone mean nothing to the average listener, and when these are produced by the stutterings of cornets, the shrieks of trombones, with string instruments glissandoing frantically from one figure to another, and the reeds gallantly adding their quota to the general cacophony, then we have chaos, musical madness of the most awful kind."

Bellows was more lenient and receptive, finding nothing subversive of musical morals about the *Firebird*. "It uses," he wrote, "occasional chords and combinations of sounds which the conventionally trained ear rejects as unpleasant, but it does this for a definite purpose, and mostly to depict an exceedingly unpleasant person. Now, if art can represent nothing but pleasant things, what are we going to do about Shakespeare and Dante and Michelangelo and Hogarth and Molière? What, for that matter, are we going to do about Wagner, whose horrible cacophonies and utter lack of beauty were the table talk of fifty years ago?"

So raged the argument on the most explosive modern piece Minneapolis had yet heard — an argument repeated with variations by embattled concertgoers in the Auditorium lobby, on the way home, and for days afterward. It was a healthy debate. Oberhoffer soon repeated the *Firebird* at a Sunday concert, and since 1922 the composition has won its way into the standard modern repertoire. Today it sounds almost dulcet to ears habituated to the shrill onslaughts of latter-day jazz.

The season was star-studded as few had been in the past, presenting at its Friday and Sunday programs an unprecedented parade of newcomers among the guest artists, who numbered thirty in all. This was the year Twin Citians first saw and heard Myra Hess and Erika Morini, Hess making her bow at a "pop" and Morini arriving in town heralded as a girl prodigy and an enthusiastic Coué disciple who had found the every-day-in-every-way incantation a morale builder. It was the season that brought two noted composers in performances of their own works: Alfredo Casella and Selim Palmgren. It was the season in which Harrison Wall Johnson, fresh from piano study abroad under Ferruccio Busoni, played the Saint-Saëns F major concerto, and young Donald Ferguson (who was to become the most brilliant musicologist and most inspiring music teacher the University of Minnesota ever nurtured) conducted his own *Symphonic Waltz*. (Years later Ferguson recalled the Sunday he directed that work as the time he was washing his car and entirely forgot the morning rehearsal at the Auditorium.)

Fate was kind in making this 1921–22 season such a brilliantly successful one, for it proved to be Oberhoffer's last with the

Symphony. And the season was a good farewell, well worth re-
membering him by.

There was no hint until March 1922 that the parting of the
ways between Oberhoffer and the orchestra was imminent. On
March 10 it was reported that the conductor had been granted
a year's leave of absence to study and listen to music abroad,
but this announcement gave no warning of the bombshell thrown
by Oberhoffer a week later, when he declared his intention to
sell his home and quit Minneapolis for good. Rumors flew of
friction between him and the board on the issue of the orchestra's
spring tour, which this year had been abandoned. On April 8 his
resignation was summarily announced, its acceptance by the
orchestra board being based on Oberhoffer's "irrevocable" intention to leave.

The break was a bitter one for the music community, and there
is evidence that it was bitter for the two principals involved,
Emil Oberhoffer and E. L. Carpenter. But it was inevitable, and
it arose not from one immediate issue but as a culmination of
many differences that had developed between two leaders whose
bond of mutual interest and purpose had held firm, and warm,
for so long.

Oberhoffer had the irritabilities of a man of temperament, and
the impatience, as he grew older, that made it difficult to repress
them. During his last years as conductor he took exception, more
and more, to Carpenter's influence in policies and decisions he
regarded as within his own domain. In his three last seasons he
"resigned" regularly, or threatened to, and was increasingly
upset by problems involving compensation, improvement of personnel that he wanted and could not get, and control of programming. Carpenter's patience and diplomacy kept the situation
in *status quo* for a long time, but eventually there had to be a
showdown between two men who could no longer come to terms.

The Minneapolis Symphony Orchestra for nearly two decades
had been the child of two fathers — two doting, possessive fathers
who had worked hard and prodigally spent their energies and
resources to bring up the child properly. Unavoidably, there was

147

jostling. This kind of situation, over a long period, had in it the danger of disagreement, collision, and cleavage.

Oberhoffer's struggle to build a fine orchestra and a body of responsive listeners had been for him an engrossing but often disheartening task. Toward the end of his conductorship, when he sank into dark moods, he voiced discouragement and told of trying to "educate the people here to music, but it hasn't done much good."

These were the pessimistic thoughts that a high-strung man fell victim to when the strain and elation of the concert were over, the applause died away, and the victory seemed yet to be won. Oberhoffer had always aimed at a high goal, and he was conscientious enough to feel that either he had not reached it, or by reaching it had not set it high enough.

He had made his great contribution by 1922; his act of orchestral creation and nurture into flowering had been consummated. He had given nineteen years to the Minneapolis Symphony — as long, certainly, as any conductor without unlimited energies should spend with an orchestra without risking a breakdown and a lessening of powers. He had spent his talent and temperament as a spendthrift spends his money; he was nervous and tired, and his health had been in decline. He was fifty-five, he needed a rest, and it may be assumed he wanted a rest. He could afford one, because, being a thrifty German, he had accumulated a comfortable competence. Minneapolis, fond of him, may have wanted more from him, but the demand for more would have been an unnatural and greedy one, regardless of his feelings in the matter.

In the Friday night audience of April 7, 1922, most of the old subscribers and orchestra friends were well aware of the crucial turn of affairs. But on the face of it, this concert was only a farewell to a leader who was soon departing on a year's leave of absence, as reported in the papers.

Oberhoffer had written a farewell message he intended to read to the Friday-nighters, but he was too overwrought to attempt speaking. His feeling for the drama of the occasion impelled him to choose Strauss's *Death and Transfiguration* as a swan song,

148

but the pull of its pathos, as he later admitted, was "too much for me, and fearing I might make a sorry exhibition of myself, I refrained."

His statement, published Saturday along with the announcement of his resignation, alluded to the magnanimous aid of the guarantors, bespoke the gratitude he felt toward his audience, his co-workers, and the officers and directors of the Orchestral Association. And it reminisced of the days a quarter-century before: "When I suggested to the choral society (which eventually gave birth to this orchestra) to offer two oratorios in one season, I struck a snag. 'Such things had been tried before and had always failed' — 'The city was not ready for such heavy music,' were the comments. I received anonymous letters warning me of the danger of such undertakings. And one dark night the president of the society, accompanied by the director of a conservatory, sought me at my home and tried to reason with me, but failing to convince me of the impossibility of the thing, counseled me to leave town before I had disturbed the placid musical serenity of the city too much.

"Ladies and gentlemen, the other evening you sat through a complete Brahms program, and I notice you did not even make for the fire escapes when we played Stravinsky, and I am glad I did not follow the advice of my musical (?) brethren of long ago. . . ."

Green vines wreathed Oberhoffer's podium on the Friday night these words were written but not spoken. Just before intermission a huge basket of roses, a gift from the orchestra men, was taken to him, and at that moment the trumpets sounded a flourish, the other instruments joined in, and the audience rose spontaneously and broke into a roar of applause that lasted ten minutes.

The final Sunday concert on April 9, after news of the resignation and Oberhoffer's "farewell address" had been published, developed into a more emotional demonstration. It was an affecting occasion for all concerned, on both sides of the footlights. The program featured the Tschaikowsky Fourth symphony and was climaxed by Kaun's inspirational *Festival March and Hymn to Liberty.*

Before starting the latter, the conductor mounted his platform, hesitated a moment, and then turned diffidently to the audience. In low tones he said that the composer, ending his piece with *The Star-Spangled Banner,* had suggested that the audience rise at that point and join the orchestra in singing the national anthem. "I pass this suggestion on to you, in the hope you will respond to it. Needless to say, it will make me happy to step down from this platform for the last time carrying the sound of your voices."

Nothing could have moved that tense and devoted audience more than such a request for such a reason, and when the opening measures of the national anthem sounded, everyone rose and Oberhoffer turned about to face his hearers. His pale face was set in stern self-control, and he sang as he conducted. After the last note died down he stood for a moment, looked about him uncertainly, then stepped down and hurried to the wings.

The audience broke into a storm of cheers and clapping, the orchestra unloosed a brassy fanfare with drum roll, and after a minute or two the conductor returned. As the applause went into a wild crescendo, he stood there, bowed, wanly smiled his gratitude, then fled to the wings with a handkerchief to his eyes. This time he did not come back, although the standing audience refused to move and continued its adoring clamor for several minutes.

Emil Oberhoffer never conducted the Minneapolis Symphony again. The break with his orchestra was clean, permanent—and sad. That April afternoon the audience filed slowly out of the Auditorium wiping eyes and blowing noses. The first chapter of the orchestra's history had ended on a note of tears and a deep sense of loss. It was the mood of the last movement of the *Pathétique.*

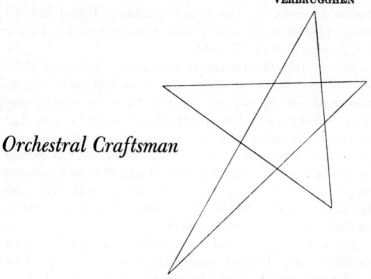

Orchestral Craftsman

OUR next hero is a spry and genial Belgian who "looked like a Frenchman, spoke like an English-man, and acted like an American." Henri Verbrugghen, second conductor of the Minneapolis Symphony Orchestra, was diminu-tive in stature and aquiline of feature. He sported a pair of fiercely waxed mustaches, loved Beethoven, chamber music, and horses, collected old musical instruments, and smoked vile French tobacco in a meerschaum pipe.

The engagement of Verbrugghen in 1922 marked a shift in policy in harmony with the Symphony's hard-won standing in the major league of American orchestras. Oberhoffer had grown up with the community and was a product thereof. He was a prophet in his own country, learning how to be a conductor in the place where he first conducted. But from now on conductors were to be an import commodity, selected from the best the world market offered in this rare species. And the price went up accordingly. The new maestro was engaged for $25,000 per an-num, a considerable advance over Oberhoffer's stipend.

In contrast to Oberhoffer, who never quite shook off the am-biguous role of village genius, Verbrugghen came from afar, trailing an impressive banner of accomplishment behind him. He lodged himself in Minneapolis after an odyssey that had taken him literally around the world.

Born in 1873 in Brussels, he took eagerly and early to his lifelong instrument, the violin, making his first public appearance at the age of nine and four years later becoming Eugène Ysaye's star pupil in the Brussels Conservatoire. A spirited as well as a talented lad, he was once awarded a second prize — instead of a merited first — for the unbecoming antic of dancing on the piano before his performance. Ysaye went to London for his first appearance there in 1888, and he took with him young Henri as a kind of prodigy exhibit, introducing him to concert audiences in England and Scotland.

This first trip to England began to orient the fledgling fiddler to British life and British music-making, so that he became for most of the years of his life a Belgian-Englishman. He crossed the Channel again the fellowing year to give joint recitals with Jean Gerardy, a noted cellist, and then returned to Brussels to graduate with a *premièr prix* from the Conservatoire.

Henri's father was a wealthy Brussels textile manufacturer who had been unable to coax his son into entering the family business. The inclinations and gifts Henri inherited from his mother's musical side of the family were compulsive, and they deflected him not only from textiles but'from a suggested alternative, the medical profession. Family pressure was strong, and it was only through the combined urging of Ysaye and Joseph Wieniawski (brother of violinist Henri) that the parents finally were convinced that their son should prepare for a violin virtuoso's career.

Henri grew up in a fertile period of Franco-Belgian music-making, and the Verbrugghen home was a regular rendezvous for local and visiting artists. One of his proudest boyhood moments came when he was chosen to turn César Franck's pages at the first private reading, by Ysaye and the composer, of what became one of the classics of modern chamber music: the Franck A major sonata. After young Henri left home to start his career as violinist (proudly refusing financial aid from his parents) he played under such noted batons as those of Saint-Saëns and Charles Lamoureux, founder of the Paris concerts bearing his name. But Henri's first firm handhold on an orchestral career was gained at the age of nineteen, when he was engaged by the Scottish orchestra in Glasgow, just founded by August Manns.

This was in 1892, and subsequently through the nineties he played off and on with the Glasgow orchestra, finally joining it in 1900 as assistant concertmaster under Wilhelm Kes. Later, in 1902, he was promoted to concertmaster under Sir Frederick Cowen, whose assistant he became and whose place he frequently filled. (It was accepted tradition for the concertmaster to be also deputy conductor, occupancy of the former position implying the requisite skill for the latter.) In the same year he started a four-season term as concertmaster for Sir Henry Wood's famous summer promenade concerts in London.

Meanwhile, in the years before and after his marriage in 1898, he had convinced himself that conducting was more his métier than virtuoso violin playing and at the same time he developed the skill to support that conviction. The mid-year concert seasons at two seaside towns in North Wales — Llandudno and Colwyn Bay — provided him for nine summers the opportunity to conduct with increasing regularity. After five seasons at Llandudno he shifted to nearby Colwyn Bay, where he conducted through 1903, in charge of an orchestra made up of sixty-five of the best English and Scottish instrumentalists who regularly summered at that resort town.

A period of hardship and penury followed soon after his marriage, a happy event quickly clouded by two misfortunes: illness which denied him a much-needed concert assignment in Helsingfors, and the bankruptcy of his father, who suddenly needed financial succor. For several grim months, the temptation to accept a well-paying job at a London restaurant proved nearly irresistible, for it would have taken the worried couple out of a dreary attic and shortened the periods between meals. But the temptation was valiantly resisted and the bleak winter was somehow ridden through with the help of an indulgent landlady.

Music and Maestros

Verbrugghen's permanent winter post after 1900 (and until 1915) was with the Glasgow orchestra, and his fortunes began to improve as his performing and teaching duties multiplied. His quick rise to concertmaster position was followed, in 1910, by another important step up in his career—succession to Sir Henry Coward as conductor of the Glasgow Choral Union, which represented not a changed position but an added one. The Belgian's star was now in rapid ascent. *Le petit Verbrugghen* of the nineties had become a commanding personage with flaring mustaches and goatee, and a musician greatly in demand. The string quartet to which he attached his name played the length and breadth of the British Isles, and in London he presented a complete cycle of the Beethoven violin sonatas. His guest conducting calls took him to Belgian centers and to Berlin, Munich, Copenhagen, and St. Petersburg.

He transported his Glasgow chorus to a Paris music festival and came back with a *premièr prix*. He led this group in virtually every number of the choral repertoire of that place and time, and he conducted operas at the city's conservatory, called the Glasgow Athenaeum, which drew generous patronage from the lay public.

The climactic stages of his British career were approaching. In 1914 he presented a Beethoven festival in London, whose success was so great that he was back again in 1915 to conduct a Bach-Beethoven-Brahms festival. Then out of a clear sky, when World War I was closing on Britain, came an invitation from New South Wales to undertake the exotic but arduous task of developing musical culture in Australia. He accepted with alacrity.

A labor government had recently been voted in at Sydney, and at its head was Premier William Holman, a man of artistic inclinations who for several years was Verbrugghen's mainstay and chief supporter in government circles. Sydney, that "Paris of the southern hemisphere" with its more than a half-million population, was by no means in a musical backwash, but its musical activities had never been organized or given direction. It had no permanently established symphony orchestra; there was much music teaching, but no conservatory.

Verbrugghen was given virtual carte blanche to found in New South Wales a music school of the highest standards, out of which a symphony orchestra might be born. At his disposal were put the former and now-converted government stables near Government House, a quadrangular structure enclosing a roofed central courtyard that soon became the school's auditorium.

With zeal and high ambition, Verbrugghen straightway set about establishing a music school that would embody his theories on musical education while conforming in general organization with the Conservatoire he had known in Brussels. He visualized the school developing from a nucleus of chamber music study and playing, an activity that would give natural birth to an orchestra, and to this end he asked for, and received, permission to send for his colleagues of the Verbrugghen quartet. The three arrived from Scotland in a few months and forthwith became key members of the staff.

The symphony unit quickly grew out of this situation, and at the start everybody, professors and instrumental students alike, was required to play in it. It mushroomed from forty-five members the first year to ninety-six members in its third year. In the last season of Verbrugghen's tenure in the early twenties, it gave one hundred and eighty concerts in Sydney, Melbourne, Adelaide, and other Australian cities. By this time too it had toured New Zealand, and had run up an astonishing record of thirteen performances in three years of Beethoven's *Missa Solemnis*.

One of Verbrugghen's special triumphs had been a Beethoven cycle in Melbourne, lasting one week, and offering as a grand climax the Mass in the afternoon and the Ninth symphony in the evening! Verbrugghen had almost a gluttonous appetite for these formidable projects and he often made them pay, much to the amazement of the Sydney officials. He came back with a profit of £1000 from that Melbourne Beethoven festival.

In 1922 two circumstances led to the severance of his bond with the conservatory and orchestra he had brought into being and reared. One was a combination of fatigue and disillusionment brought on by long years of hard, unremitting, and largely thankless work — interrupted only by a working trip to America in 1918 to compare conservatory curriculums. (He made his first American appearance on that trip, conducting the Detroit Symphony at the invitation of Ossip Gabrilówitsch.) The other was the increasingly dim view taken of subsidized conservatories and orchestras by a slothful and indifferent bureaucracy.

Verbrugghen was persuaded to take a leave of absence to restore his health and spirits, and he departed for Europe, going eastward by way of New York. It was in that city that he met E. L. Carpenter, who in the crucial spring of 1922 was casting about for a new conductor.

Carpenter had already decided on an "interregnum" for the 1922–23 season in Minneapolis, a transition period when the orchestra, for the first time, would have no permanent conductor but be led instead by a series of guests. Immediately impressed by the Belgian and his record, he at once invited Verbrugghen to begin the parade of visiting notables.

From the viewpoint of the audience, the season under five noted maestros taking their turns on the platform was one of rare interest and varied challenges. Minneapolis had never heard so many conductors in so short a time. For the orchestra, too, it was a time of stimulus, along with the strain of adapting itself to different conducting styles and demands.

The Minneapolis organization has never been conductor-resistant, even when led by less than masterful and knowing men. Unlike the temperamental and testy ensembles of the East — orchestras that reputedly can make or break a conductor — it has consistently been a friendly and malleable ensemble. Whatever private and scurrilous opinions of the man on the box have been expressed by individuals, the group as a whole has been traditionally responsive, working with a will for all and sundry batons.

The five conductors of 1922–23 were Ossip Gabrilówitsch, Walter Damrosch, Albert Coates, Bruno Walter, and Verbrugghen. At first glance it appeared to be an exhibition of candidates for the vacant post. As a matter of fact, only two of the five, Walter and Verbrugghen, had been under serious consideration, and not long after Carpenter met and talked to the peripatetic Belgian, the field narrowed to one man.

The season was only two months old when Henri Verbrugghen was announced as the new permanent conductor, with a three-year contract. But contrary to the belief expressed in some quarters, he had not been signed up before the season started. His attachment to New South Wales had not yet been broken when he opened the Minneapolis Symphony series. The Sydney officials had extended his leave to permit this period of guest conducting, but they had made no further concession. Verbrugghen had asked for financial guaranty or severance of his conservatory from the uncooperative ministry of education, and he cabled for definite assurances that either one or the other action would be taken. The replies were evasive, voicing intentions but no promises.

This wasn't good enough for Verbrugghen. He cabled his regrets at the vague response and his decision to sign the contract in Minneapolis, which he did forthwith. The conservatory he had left behind him soon relapsed into a routine English school, and the orchestra became a mere adjunct thereof. In mournful commentary on the loss of the "great little man" from their midst, the Australian *Musical News* paid tribute to his accomplishing so much "with governments that cared not for art, with politicians to whom music and all connected with it were a nightmare, and with ministers who loved neither Verbrugghen nor his music."

It was considered odd, at least by critic Nilsson, that Verbrugghen for his bow in Minneapolis should have picked the Tschaikowsky *Pathétique* — "not a cheerful work for a gala evening," and too closely associated with Oberhoffer and his recent leave-taking. But there was agreement that the orchestra under Verbrugghen's hands had good balance, clarity of detail, and fine string work, Davies' only qualification being that the contrasts of hope and pessimism in the Tschaikowsky work were not clearly enough drawn. Nilsson called it a dramatic rather than a romantic interpretation.

At a succeeding concert the Minneapolis audience heard Verbrugghen's little souvenir from the antipodes: *Waiata Poi* by Alfred Hill orchestrated by the conductor. This short piece with its final trombone glissando, based on Maori song and ritual as observed by Verbrugghen and Hill in New Zealand, was a bit of jocular shock for the hyperboreans of Minnesota. Critic Bellows thought it an excellent fox trot, but suggested that the trombone phrase was less a shout of enthusiastic ecstasy, as the program note called it, than the sound made by a Maori dancer suddenly hit in the pit of the stomach. The sound effect of reed skirts slapping against dancing girls' thighs was uncannily simulated by the percussionist's shaking a pillowslip filled with peanut shells. Verbrugghen formerly had produced that sound by paper bags filled with dry hops, but dry hops apparently were in short supply in Minneapolis and so the peanut shells were substituted.

"Jazz" had recently entered the American vocabulary, and the slippery trombone exclamation in *Waiata Poi* was quickly but rather loosely identified as jazz: its first intrusion in a local symphony hall. Verbrugghen claimed none of the prejudice against jazz that Oberhoffer had often voiced, and had even admitted it was "beautiful" when well played. It is likely, however, that Verbrugghen had heard only the polished concert jazz exemplified by Paul Whiteman and not the more authentic but then-obscure Dixieland variety.

At his first Sunday afternoon concert the little Belgian introduced his protégée and long-time pupil, Jenny Cullen, concertmistress of the Sydney orchestra, who was returning to Australia via America. And on a later Sunday he rather daringly gave the "pop" audience its first stiff dose of Bach, playing with Miss Cullen the double violin concerto, with Engelbert Roentgen conducting.

In November Verbrugghen stepped down for Mark Twain's son-in-law from Detroit, the high-collared and dignified Ossip

Gabrilówitsch, who offered an easygoing account of the Brahms C minor. Verbrugghen resumed for a four-week stint before the arrival of Damrosch, who was followed by Coates and then Walter. The guest season was pungently summarized by James Davies in correspondence to the *Christian Science Monitor,* and also was the subject of pithy analysis by Judd in the *St. Paul Pioneer Press.*

Damrosch "came here for a holiday," Davies said, "and enjoyed himself thoroughly." In that mood he did not make the orchestra work strenuously and some of his performances were rather loose. Judd termed him an exponent of the "old school of Theodore Thomas." Gabrilówitsch made no marked impression, wrote the Minneapolis critic, playing the Brahms First amiably and "missing its granite-like features with unerring accuracy." Judd thought the Detroiter's execution was "dreamed rather than projected."

Coates gave one of his stock performances, with a good deal of the prima donna in his methods and "too little economy of motion." (Coates had conducted his one concert without score, and Nilsson had noted his extremely energetic beat and the tracing of "strange hieroglyphics" with left-hand fingers in his playing of *Schéhérazade.*)

Bruno Walter, who remained in Minneapolis for three weeks, made the deepest and most favorable impression. Obviously he was the greatest of the season's five conductors, and without doubt the finest conductor Minneapolis Symphony patrons had heard up to that time. Davies scoffed at the theory that the excellence of the performance under Walter was due largely to Verbrugghen's preliminary training.

At any rate, with Walter at the helm the orchestra played with magnificent spirit and beauty, the interpretations were finely tempered, and at Walter's last appearance there was audience enthusiasm of a kind seldom approached in the orchestra's previous history. Concertgoers stood and cheered. The modest Walter was touched by the reception he received (which in truth outdid in warmth his New York welcome), and later he wrote in his autobiography, *Themes and Variations,* that "a particularly enjoyable period of my first stay in America was spent in Minneapolis. . . . So cordial a relation between me and the orchestra and so personal a contact with the audience was established during that time that in that icy part of the United States I was made happy by the surprising, the exciting warmth of the musical atmosphere."

When Minneapolis settled down to Verbrugghen again, it soon learned that he was a meticulous orchestral craftsman. It has been said that the orchestra had never been better technically than it was under his baton, but some thought the schoolmaster had replaced the poet, and that care in crossing t's and dotting i's had taken some of the old spirit and glow out of the orchestra's playing.

There is no record of Verbrugghen's announcing his belief in the theory that if honor and devotion were given to the letter, the spirit would take care of itself, but the concert hall evidence often pointed to such a belief, conscious or not. His exacting preparation of scores for public performance, his tireless attention to detail, and his sometimes fanatical respect for the notes on the page were signs of a scrupulousness that sometimes left no room for the lift of a big idea.

A clue to his methodical approach may be found in a statement he once made about Beethoven, "the most sane and balanced man who ever composed music." In Beethoven, the conductor said, he found "the perfect grammarian, who speaks a language so purely that each tone and inflection has its proper place and value. He feels emotion but with the refined erudition of a mature mind."

Discounting what may have been a reporter's distortion of a remark made in an interview, Verbrugghen's fascination with the grammar, the orderliness, of music perfectly put together is nevertheless evident. One of his aims — no small one — was to project that orderliness, that perfect balance of parts, with a clarity that would win its own argument and be its own reward.

The method had its hazards. As Lawrence Gilman wrote in

1924, Verbrugghen was "a shining example of those excellent conductors who are sometimes held up to us as models because they 'let the music speak for itself.' Sometimes it seemed to us he was a bit too humble in his attitude. After all, music does not speak for itself — it never has and never can. . . . We could not help wondering if Mr. Verbrugghen respected the notes of Mr. Brahms [in his C minor symphony] more than he loved the stirring and beautiful and mysterious spirit that is perpetually struggling into life behind them."

Further confirmation of Verbrugghen's didactic tendencies as interpreter came from the astute Cyril Arthur Player of the *Detroit News,* who in 1925 made a critical survey of middle-western orchestras. He found the Minneapolis Symphony one of the most careful and painstaking orchestras he had ever heard. He felt that Verbrugghen had a special affinity for the classic period: "he has that searching deliberation which, while eschewing the flights of too rash adventure, bestows priestly devotions on the accepted divinities of art."

Player implied that the ensemble was controlled but not inflamed by its leader. "In discipline the orchestra was loyal, but without quite that instantaneous and electrifying positiveness which marks the supreme orchestral organization." It was fairly flexible, but not supple. Its single conspicuous failing, he went on, was a certain paucity of inspiration, "something that has nothing to do with the efficiency of the personnel, the quality of instruments, the correctness of score reading, but which is or should be the benediction of every worthy work."

Nonetheless, Verbrugghen's contributions unquestionably widened the orchestra's scope as well as the city's musical horizons. Having spent seven years building a conservatory with high and severe standards, where students were required to learn and know much more than the special skills they had elected to acquire, Verbrugghen came to Minneapolis in the role of creative educator as well as conductor.

His interest in Bach, well based in his experience, introduced a neglected and important element into the orchestra's repertoire.

Oberhoffer's Bach contributions had been scanty; he had played the *Brandenburg* No. 3 only once, away back in the fifth season, and had thereafter relied mostly on the ethereal *Air for the G String* from the D major suite. But Verbrugghen played more than a score of Bach's works during his nine seasons with the orchestra, and to the Twin Cities at least he made Bach familiar, if not popular, several years before Leopold Stokowski's suave Bach arrangements on phonograph records gained general circulation.

Verbrugghen's passion for chamber music, too, soon made itself felt, when he gathered around him the three who had followed him from Scotland to Australia and then to America: Miss Cullen as second violinist, David Nichols as violist, and James Messeas as cellist. Soon to be added to the town's musical fare were regular concert performances by the Verbrugghen String Quartet.

In addition, he restored life for a time to the dormant choral forces of the community and forged a close connection between the newly organized Minneapolis Choral Society and the Symphony. No conductor who had spent the years Verbrugghen had in Great Britain could be anything but a choral enthusiast and authority. His long experience with choral performances in the British Isles and Australia now had to find vent in the new environment.

For ten years, too, he had been developing and putting into practice new and revolutionary orchestral techniques as applied to the classic repertoire, particularly the symphonies of Beethoven. The modern orchestra and modern concert hall, he claimed, had both become so large as to throw out of balance the figure patterns and interplay of instruments and instrumental choirs as heard in Beethoven's day. The string sections, greatly augmented since the beginning of the nineteenth century, were particular offenders in this disbalance.

Verbrugghen's remedy, in part, was to diminish the sound of the string sections when they merely supported solo episodes in other parts of the orchestra. This he accomplished by allowing only alternate desks of violins to play repeated accompanying figures when the woodwinds, for instance, had important solos. Sometimes the division would be at each desk, inside men playing continuously and the outside men, those nearest the audience, contributing only the accented notes.

The method amounted to a manipulation of the orchestra rather than a tampering with the score, its aim being only to bring out clearly and in proper relationship all the "voices" of a symphony as transmitted by the modern ninety-piece orchestra. In a way it was a means of producing "guaranteed sound" by new distribution (and omission) of instrumental parts rather than by trying to suppress and amplify various parts of an undiminished ensemble.

One of the most vivid word portraits of Henri Verbrugghen in his first years as Minneapolis Symphony conductor comes from Deems Taylor, the critic and composer, who early in 1923 was engaged on an inspection tour of middlewestern orchestras. He saw, heard, and met Verbrugghen in Milwaukee, where the touring Minneapolis organization was giving a concert.

In type and temperament Verbrugghen reminded Taylor of Arturo Toscanini. He was a "personage," a rather spare and small man with dark hair peppered with gray, but with "dark eyes so bright and keen that despite lines about them they convey a sense of inextinguishable youth." He was one of "those short men who produce a tall effect upon the beholder."

Others noted the massive, leonine, yet delicately formed head on the small frame, the quick perceptions and ready conversational flow, the intellectual curiosity that made him impatient of specialized training in music and other fields. He was a stubborn advocate of general knowledge and culture for everyone, including musical performers. "Knowing history, philosophy, and other things helps make a good musician," he once said. "Most performers practice too much and think too little."

Taylor was as taken by Verbrugghen's conducting as by his physical appearance: "Everything he does is the projection of a strongly individual personality." The composer-writer spoke admiringly of the "almost architectural quality" of his readings, the clarity and sharp definition that bespoke clear intellect and a strong will.

The bantamweight maestro was no placid time-beater on the platform. Many observers were impressed by his vigor, flourish, and fury. They called him "that flaming little volcano," the "little Napoleon of conductors," a "small bundle of temperamental energy and forcefulness." He had a wide gamut of gesture, from the slashing swoop of his long baton to the neatest, most delicate motion of his small hands for the fine-tooled passages, where the baton seemingly became a pencil drawing miniature designs.

In the roaring climaxes Verbrugghen's long hair would cascade over his eyes and his coattails would fly. He held the reins tight in these tonal crises and often gave the impression of great power under steady control. Again, his gyrations seemed to have little relationship to the music under his hands. The "perspiration and paroxysm" mentioned by one observer sometimes had no tangible effect on the sound he produced. Pitts Sanborn once listened to Verbrugghen's account of the Brahms C minor symphony and afterward wrote that "never did conductor toss about more wildly, never did band appear to labor harder than in the celebrated finale, and never did that finale sound so small and so tame."

Verbrugghen by his own admission employed his gestures consciously and with calculated effect, not on his audiences but on the men who played under him. He firmly believed that orchestras, even the best of them, would not react effectively to a sluggish leader. So he deliberately used a mimetic art that called for the lowering and elevation of eyebrows, a wide radius of gesticulation, the leaping ability of a mountain goat, facial expressions that ranged from the scowling to the coy. All these, he once said facetiously but with serious intent, were the necessary means of making orchestra players respond.

"The conductor whom you see behaving like a crazy man is not showing off," he said. "He is using every fiber of his physique

FROM THE BIRMINGHAM NEWS

"No placid time-beater"

and his personality to deploy his players like a gigantic musical instrument."

For building pleasant relationships with the musicians and maintaining orchestra morale, Verbrugghen had a simple rule: "Keep your men in good humor." Discipline could be put on a basis of good fellowship. He believed too, as many other orchestra leaders have believed, that a good conductor is like a good actor, able to project himself into the personalities of many other people.

For the fundamental problem that transcends conducting mechanics and the task of "getting along" with your men — the problem of conveying great music greatly — he placed thinking far above practice. It was Thomas B. Sherman, perceptive critic of the *St. Louis Post-Dispatch,* who put Verbrugghen into what he called the "cerebro-dramatic school" of conductors. He observed that Verbrugghen had developed his orchestral forces to an admirable state of responsiveness, but "disdains the use of voluptuous coloring and goes in for firm outlines and strong contrasts." Sherman found the ensemble noticeably lacking in transparency, "that golden glow which proceeds from an orchestra when all its members are virtuosi, when they are all well rehearsed, and when they have been playing together under one man long enough to have become as parts of a single organism."

Before the guest season of 1922–23 passed into history, the orchestra had its first rendezvous with a new invention, a new means of mass communication which already was immobilizing astonished listeners in thousands of American living rooms. Two years after the founding of America's pioneer broadcasting station, KDKA of Pittsburgh, the Minneapolis Symphony played a program into the microphones of WLAG, the "Call of the North" radio station, quartered in the Oak Grove Hotel.

At a cost of $5000, more than two miles of cable were laid between the Oak Grove and the Auditorium, and one hundred dollars in prizes were offered for letters from radio listeners reviewing the program. The concert, sponsored by the L. S.

Donaldson Company, took place March 2, 1923, under the direction of Bruno Walter, and offered a Schumann symphony, some Mozart ballet music, excerpts from Wagner's *Tristan und Isolde,* and Weber's *Euryanthe* overture.

The concert marked not only the orchestra's but Walter's first contact with radio, and the conductor was enthusiastic. "Imagine playing to an audience all across the continent, with thousands listening!" he exclaimed. The broadcast reaped five hundred letters from half the states of the Union and numerous telegrams. And the thing that impressed many listeners was the fact that the applause and cheers for Walter could be heard just as distinctly as the music! Audience sounds, in those days, seemed the acme of realism to the owners of crystal sets.

The orchestra, along with the rest of the country, performers and listeners both, was now entering the era of mechanical and electromagnetic reproduction of music. A little more than a year after its first encounter with Marconi's invention it had its introduction to Edison's (and Berliner's). On its eastern tour in April 1924 it remained in New York City for Easter week to make four phonograph records for the Brunswick-Balke-Collender Company.

Negotiations with Brunswick had been pending for several months. In signing up the Minneapolis organization the firm was taking on its second American symphony orchestra (the first having been the New York Philharmonic under Mengelberg), and it was entering a field of competition dominated by Victor with its Boston and Philadelphia orchestra discs and Columbia with its pressings of European orchestra recordings. The company was therefore cautious. The step was expensive enough and the competition keen enough to make Brunswick officials wary of buying what might prove an unsalable commodity. It had to count on more than home-town sale of Minneapolis recordings.

So the company officials decided that the reception of the Minneapolis Symphony by the New York audience would decide the issue. If the orchestra drew enthusiastic approval at its Manhattan concert, the contract would forthwith be signed. E. L. Carpenter went east to await the outcome.

The concert proved highly successful, at least from the audience standpoint; orchestra and conductor received big ovations. Carpenter signed the contract and the work of recording started immediately.

The sessions extended over three or four days and were tense, lengthy, and difficult. The players were ranged on a steep grandstand to bring them in huddle formation close to the large horn and recording apparatus, and there were many "takes" to ensure a flawless product.

Tonal balance was hard to attain. The double basses did not register and the tuba was substituted. The bass drum made not even the faintest thud. This, of course, was in the days of acoustical recording.

These first records by the Minneapolis Symphony — now collectors' items — were Massenet's *Last Dream of the Virgin,* the *Melodrama* from Guiraud's *Piccolino,* Weber's *Der Freischütz* overture, and Alfred Hill's *Waiata Poi,* the Maori dance overture.

The orchestra made a few more waxings for Brunswick in subsequent years, and some of the sessions in the twenties took place in Chicago in an empty nightclub, near a busy street intersection. At one of these sessions the orchestra repeatedly attempted a Weber overture, and each time it reached a certain dulcet horn passage a policeman's shrill whistle from the outside joined the horns inside. So, though the overture was recorded, it was never issued; the traffic whistle was ruled out as an anachronism in Weber's measures.

After the 1922–23 guest season was over, Verbrugghen spent a recuperative summer in the Canadian Rockies, Mme. Alice Verbrugghen (a singer who specialized in British ballad and folk song) arrived to join her husband, and the orchestra prepared to celebrate its coming of age. It was twenty-one years old.

It reached its majority in the fall of 1923 with an acoustical improvement — a newly constructed stage at the Auditorium, a heptagonal reconstruction of the old "flats" which served as a better sounding board and also gave improved visibility from the house. And Verbrugghen, for his first season as regular conductor, gave full vent to his pedagogical instincts and decided to stage a cycle of Beethoven programs: six consecutive concerts, not as an extra series, as Oberhoffer had done in 1914–15, but as part of the Friday night series.

This ambitious project, involving all the nine symphonies, several of the concertos, and a few songs and arias, proved to be a tactical error. Verbrugghen had underrated the musical experience of an audience that had been taught its Beethoven lessons often and thoroughly by Oberhoffer, and overestimated its capacity to absorb a solid diet of Beethoven for six successive weeks.

Before the cycle was completed in mid-December listeners were showing signs of restiveness and boredom, many feeling they were being patronized. Davies concluded that "we can get too much of a good thing" and suggested that better results would have been obtained had the six Beethoven programs been scattered through the season.

Flandrau in St. Paul insisted that the intensive Beethoven course had not been a mistake, as many had called it, affirmed that the "six orgies were wonderful," but conceded that a Beethoven cycle was the sort of cultural crime one has to commit just once. Later he expressed the hope that "on no single occasion shall we be inundated and overwhelmed by two symphonies. . . . It isn't fair to the listener, to the orchestra, to the conductor, or to Beethoven."

Verbrugghen himself played the violin concerto at the second of the Beethoven concerts, garnering polite approval rather than fervid acclaim. He played it dryly and without flourish, probably suffering the same extreme nervousness that had always beset him when performing a solo. As far back as the nineties, when he decided that the glory of virtuoso playing was not worth the torture that preceded a performance, he had regularly been ill for days before every solo appearance.

The Beethoven series came to a big climax with the Ninth

symphony. A precedent was established when that massive choral-orchestral work was repeated at a "pop" concert on Sunday — another daring but in this case successful maneuver.

Verbrugghen was not thick-skinned, and he was chagrined at the dissatisfaction caused by his Beethoven experiment. He chose to regard it as a concertgoers' revolt against serious classics in general and Beethoven in particular, and he let it be known that the following season would see a marked shift in program policy. If novelty was preferred to classicism, novelty would be the order of the day.

Wild reports that the 1924–25 season would contain nothing but modern symphonies or no symphonies at all disturbed and alarmed Nilsson, who sounded the warning that excommunication of the classics would be a hundred times worse than "too much Beethoven." He pleaded for reconsideration of any rash decisions to play only music of the hour, claiming that "to abandon or even neglect the classical symphony repertoire would be a grievous mistake to make in a metropolitan city like Minneapolis."

Verbrugghen's sense of proportion, or wise counsel, or both, eventually prevailed, and the following season saw no ban on Beethoven. Quite the contrary, in fact. Three Beethoven symphonies, two of his piano concertos, two of his overtures, and several of his shorter pieces were performed, placating Nilsson and others who had taken Verbrugghen's threat seriously. Revived this season, also, was that charming orchestral tableau introduced by Oberhoffer years before: the Haydn *Farewell* symphony done with candles on the stands and the musicians walking off one by one, leaving only the conductor and two violinists on the dimly lit stage at the end.

Concession to "music of the hour," however, brought a surprising number of first performances, eight of them premières of interesting modern works by such composers as Honegger, Bloch, Ravel, Holst, Stravinsky, Respighi, and Richard Strauss.

The Honegger opus, *Pacific 231,* a descriptive piece that paid shrill homage to a heavy locomotive, was the season's chief shocker. It gave Minneapolis its first sampling of the product of the Paris Group of Six, and like that other realistic portrayal of machinery, Mossolov's *Iron Foundry*, it enjoyed a brief moment in the spotlight and then went to the musical graveyard. (It was exhumed once, twenty-six years later.) But its first hearing induced a controversial flurry as well as a peculiar buzzing in concertgoers' ears.

That testy defender of orthodoxy in music, James Davies, was the most furious dissenter to Honegger's screaming steam engine. He insisted that if Verbrugghen had laid his baton down and told his musicians to play at will, using every distortion and key they were capable of, the result would have differed little from what the Swiss-Frenchman had put into his score. "I have heard the elevated railways of Chicago, New York, and Boston sing better music than this," he wrote. "I have lived through the terrors and strain of boiler works, but never, no never, were my nerves rasped to such tatters as when listening to this unhallowed musical slander."

Frances Boardman in St. Paul noticed that several persons left before the piece was performed, probably because they were susceptible to car-sickness. She thought *Pacific 231* overused imitative sounds, aligning itself "with those vaudeville tricks in which a handsaw is made to sound like a ukulele, and a ukulele like something else." And N. B. Abbott in the *Daily News* delivered the opinion that, conservatively speaking, "this number is about 7,000 light years from anything resembling music."

Donald Ferguson, in later comment on *Pacific 231,* told of the rumor that Honegger had been a passenger on the North Coast Limited when it made its famous first run from St. Paul to Seattle, and was inspired by that experience to compose the work. The run was made in 1900, the locomotive was numbered 231, but Honegger was only eight years old and presumably not among those present. "Yet the title of his piece would never have coupled the word *Pacific* with the actual number of that engine," Ferguson said, "had not some striking facts about that notable trip been brought to his mind."

Other premières of that season were more substantial, and some were of compositions almost as provocative but destined to wear better. Modernism was in the saddle as Verbrugghen brandished the "novelties" which were his answer to last year's bored-by-Beethoven faction. It was altogether a constructive and enterprising answer. Ravel's glistening and intricate *Daphnis et Chloé* suite No. 2 bemused the old guard and fascinated the few who liked new and complex sounds. Bloch's passionate *Schelomo* was introduced, and Richard Strauss's *Don Quixote* was performed with Engelbert Roentgen and Paul Lemay in the solo cello and viola roles. There were also Respighi's *Concerto Gregoriano* with Albert Spalding and that magical evocation of carnival atmosphere in the mock-sad story of a puppet, the *Petrouchka* suite of Stravinsky.

Verbrugghen's approach to Stravinsky was more petulant than sympathetic and patient. He admitted that in the *Petrouchka* suite all a conductor could do "is give the opening beat of each measure and leave the rest to the players. That is all that can be done when, with his fatuous ideas of rhythm, Stravinsky changes the time signature with each measure."

The season was stimulating to those who wanted new things. But all was not contentment in the ranks of those who listened. There never was (never will be) unanimity of satisfaction with symphony program content. The rumbling of protest that greeted the Beethoven cycle in 1923 shifted to another sector of the audience in 1924–25, and E. L. Carpenter took it upon himself to demolish a brash proposal that programs be selected by a committee representing the subscribers.

This suggestion had been prompted by an unconventional concert containing a dated and dullish symphony (the Raff *Lenore*), a strange concerto for string quartet and orchestra by Emanuel Moore (featuring the famous Flonzaleys), and the rasping but original modernism of the three dances from de Falla's *Three-Cornered Hat.*

Carpenter painstakingly proved that a committee of laymen could not possibly perform the specialized job of picking programs, and he pointedly asked, "How many people in Minneapolis know anything whatsoever about the new works which have never been played before?" How many, he went on, could read a score well enough to gain the faintest idea of how it would sound when actually played? Carpenter contended that "a committee, no matter how carefully selected, would mean absolute stagnation, for it could do nothing except 'play safe' and recommend the relatively few works with which its members are familiar."

Not a murmur rose thereafter from the proponents of committee programming. Carpenter had squashed an absurd notion. But in taking the trouble to squash it he submitted a programming philosophy and procedure which are still sound, and which showed incidentally how deeply and intimately this businessman was versed in the care and feeding of symphony audiences.

The making of symphony programs involves three things, he said: (1) a judicious use of the relatively few numbers which are both "classics" and genuinely enjoyed; (2) the employment, more sparingly, of numbers less popular than they once were but having inherent musical value; and (3) the addition to the repertoire of new works of real significance.

How keen was his musical judgment can be seen by the examples he cited for each of the three classifications. In the popular classics he included the *New World* and *Pathétique* symphonies and the Grieg piano concerto; in the solid but not-so-popular classics were Franck's *Symphonic Variations* and Bach's *Brandenburg* concertos; in the new and significant works, the *Petrouchka* and *Daphnis et Chloé* suites.

With this support from Carpenter, Verbrugghen achieved a very presentable record of "firsts" during his tenure. Through him and his orchestra the Twin Cities first heard, in addition to the works already mentioned, Richard Strauss's *Ein Heldenleben* and *Also Sprach Zarathustra*, Schönberg's *Verklärte Nacht*, the Bruckner Fourth, the *Pastoral* symphony of Vaughan Williams, and the First symphony of Shostakovitch — who in 1930 spelled his name the Polish way, Szostakowicz. (The

Verklärte Nacht première in St. Paul in 1925 had a rather sanguinary touch. Verbrugghen's swinging hand smashed his watch crystal on the rack and bled freely as the conductor carried on, undeterred, to the finish.)

It was inevitable that the jazz of the twenties would provoke a mildly raucous echo in the concert hall. In its sweep of the country jazz had enlisted advocates who hailed and defended it as a peculiarly American expression, indigenous to our land, the new folk music made in the U.S.A. During the decade there were several timid ventures in presenting jazz in properly dignified (and inflated) symphonic investiture. Stravinsky's *Ragtime* in 1924 was really pre-jazz and hardly counted except as a red flag to critic Davies. Later, DeLamarter's *Symphony after Walt Whitman* revealed noticeable jazz tendencies, but the Belgian Bourguignon's *Jazz Triumphant* was shrugged off as an aimless and alien attempt to make jazzlike sounds by putting saxophones and odd percussion noises in the score.

The main impact of jazz was made by Paul Whiteman's orchestra, which first visited Minneapolis in March 1925. The much-publicized "king of jazz" brought his virtuoso band to the Kenwood armory and played a program climaxed by George Gershwin's *Rhapsody in Blue*. The impression made by the concert, and especially by the *Rhapsody*, was vivid and to many a revelation. Jazz suddenly became respectable and at the same time exciting. But three years elapsed before the Minneapolis Symphony risked its reputation on Gershwin's impudent, good-natured assault on concert hall canon.

Then the result was rather heavy-handed. Verbrugghen had taken it upon himself to deodorize the *Rhapsody* and make it conform to symphonic etiquette. He deleted what he called the "tomfoolery" and "squeaky sounds" and "wah wah business on trumpets and trombones." James Bliss, a Minneapolis pianist and teacher, played the solo role with sincerity and humor but with rather stiffish precision.

The *Minneapolis Star*'s critic called the performance a hybrid that was neither jazz nor valid concert hall material and said the pomposities of symphonic handling "gave it a guilty conscience." And Verbrugghen's elimination of the "wah wahs" brought prompt needling from the alert contingent that wanted its jazz effects unmolested. One anonymous heckler made public complaint that "if 'wah wah' means something to the work — and Gershwin probably had a reason for inserting it — the 'wah wah' should be left in. One could as easily make fun of an Elgar overture for its 'oom-pah-oom-pah' or a Wagner prelude for the 'blah-blooey' of its tubas, and as reasonably ask for their deletion on grounds that these horn sounds, translated into words, sound and look silly, or that on hearing them for the first time, people are inclined to snigger."

Thereafter the *Rhapsody* was shelved for the remainder of Verbrugghen's term. Two seasons later, however — in 1929 — he introduced *An American in Paris,* for which real French taxicab horns had been imported. These rubber bulb sound-makers with their high-pitched bark were lost in transit, but arrived in the nick of time on the morning of the final rehearsal. From such emergencies were newspaper feature stories fashioned and public curiosity piqued.

Verbrugghen's interest in novelty and experiment was spurred more by exploration in the classic field that he knew and loved than by the radicals and the jazz-tainted among the new composers. His fondness for old musical instruments made him an eager collaborator in the performance, in 1923, of a Haydn concerto for a two-manual clavecin played by Lewis Richards. Though the orchestra was reduced to eighteenth-century size, the clavecin's tone barely reached the tenth row and Davies concluded that the collaboration was more suited to chamber music setting.

In 1927 Twin Cities concertgoers heard their first harpsichord in a symphonic environment, tinkling authentically but inaudibly in a Bach concerto. The *Star* irreverently reported that the effect was that of Bach being smothered under a blanket, "uncomfortably reminiscent of moonlight at Waikiki." Davies decided that harpsichord tone had no more force and far less character than an up-to-date mandolin.

Other strange and unfamiliar sounds issued from time to time from the orchestra during Verbrugghen's rule. The saxophone crashed the symphonic ensemble for the first time (except for its use in the infrequent jazz works) in 1926 in Bizet's *L'Arlésienne* suite, whose *minuetto* has a part written in for Adolphe Sax's invention, and it behaved very prettily and modestly. The next week another and later invention was introduced: the so-called sustaining piano devised by John Hays Hammond, Jr. This was a conventional grand piano whose strings were covered by a series of shutters operated by a fourth pedal, a "reflecting modulator" that produced effects of diminished, sustained, or augmented tone as the shutters were opened and closed.

Everybody thought the effect was impressive in the Rachmaninoff C minor concerto, but the sustaining piano never returned to the Minneapolis Symphony platform.

The phonographic nightingale in Respighi's *Pines of Rome* burbled for the first time the following season, reminding the *Star* of "those water whistles used in theater orchestras while playing *Listen to the Mocking Bird*." Probably the loudest assisting noise the orchestra could claim in this period, at the opposite extreme from the whispering of the clavecin, was Michael Jalma's university military band in Tschaikowsky's *1812* overture, which old residents maintain made an even more deafening clamor than Oberhoffer's by no means muted version. The overture's pulse-stirring effect was enhanced by blank cartridges fired from a gun into an off-stage barrel.

In the middle and late twenties, after the shakeups and changes of the transition period, the orchestra developed a core almost as solid as the sound nucleus which made Oberhoffer's group of ten years earlier such a superior organization. For a while there was some restless shifting about in the concertmaster position: Elias Breeskin followed by Gustave Tinlot followed by

Orchestral Craftsman

Pierre Henrotte in one-season spurts, with E. Joseph Shadwick finally holding the post two seasons and then Harold Ayres coming up from the ranks to begin his long tenure. The rest of the strings had leaders of high competence: Paul Lemay, viola, who in 1930 became assistant conductor; Engelbert Roentgen, cellist and part-time conductor who left in 1930 for New York, where he soon played at first stand with the Metropolitan Opera orchestra; and Frank Kuchynka, double-bass principal and occasionally a dexterous soloist on his growling instrument.

A valuable addition to the woodwinds was plump, polished Georges Grisez, who arrived from the Philadelphia Orchestra in 1923 and who became the first clarinetist ever heard as soloist with the Minneapolis Symphony. The rest of the woodwind corps remained constant in personnel and of high quality in musicianship for a considerable period: Alexandre Duvoir, oboist; Henry C. Woempner, flutist; the Cunningtons, Henry and Syd, playing bassoon and contra-bassoon; Roger Gauthier as English horn. Richard Lindenhahn led the French horns for many years; Glenn Cooke (later personnel manager) played tuba; and two veterans remained at their posts: Henry J. Williams, harpist, and William Faetkenheuer, tympanist.

These, with the three members of Verbrugghen's String Quartet, were the mainstays of his orchestra, some having been part of the Oberhoffer combine and some carrying over into the Ormandy administration to come. All were experienced and dependable musicians, whose combination of skills was as important to the orchestra's product as the conductor's leadership.

Orchestra policy during the decade continued to lean hard on the fame and drawing power of guest soloists of high repute, old and established or new and exciting, for whom there was an increasingly brisk competition in the flush spending years of the twenties. The Verbrugghen era saw the Twin Cities' debut of Alexander Brailowsky, José Iturbi, and Vladimir Horowitz among the pianists. (The enterprising Schubert Club in St. Paul had snared Horowitz for its 1927–28 season — two years before the orchestra presented him — and his recital in the old People's

Church was probably the most exciting "one-man show" in that city by any musical artist in the twenties. Those who were present still recall how the floor of the church building shook during his furious crescendos and fortissimos.)

Popular and oft-returning, among the pianists, were Harold Bauer, Myra Hess, and Rudolf Ganz, and of the older giants of the keyboard, there were Moriz Rosenthal, Fannie Bloomfield-Zeisler, and Ignace Jan Paderewski. The return of Mme. Bloomfield-Zeisler in 1925, in her fiftieth anniversary year as a concert pianist, was a dramatic occasion. She was sixty-one years old then, dressed all in black, and some of her former emotional drive was lacking. But her performance in a Chopin concerto was clearheaded and persuasive, and Nilsson, who could unburden without forewarning an oddly picturesque metaphor, hailed her as "the American lioness of the piano, but one with silken paws."

Jascha Heifetz and Joseph Szigeti, of the young and brilliant generation of violinists, created sensations then as now. The debut in 1929 of chubby, towheaded Yehudi Menuhin, twelve-year-old *wunderkind,* roused audience and musicians to raptures. The boy lost his way in the second movement of the Brahms violin concerto, but this lapse endeared rather than shocked, particularly after Verbrugghen turned around to explain that Yehudi was playing the Brahms for the first time in public. A half-hour later the lad in blouse and velvet breeches was sobbing quietly in the corner of the greenroom, deaf to assurances of solicitous elders that he had not committed a heinous crime.

Among the other violinists Zimbalist, Seidel, Thibaud, Elman, and Spalding were frequent visitors, and Carl Flesch made three calls. It was after Flesch's first appearance with the orchestra, in 1925, that Nilsson made a mot, perhaps unconsciously, that has lived long in the recollection of concertgoers of that time.

When Flesch arrived he was temporarily lamed by neuritis in the legs, and was forced to play the Brahms violin concerto installed in a chair. Nilsson wrote of his performance: "In a sitting position Flesch soared to the skies . . ."

Singers' names, of course, crowd the programs of the period. Althouse and Tibbett, Thomas and Jeritza sang in Minneapolis, and Sigrid Onegin in 1924 incited what became a prolonged and rapturous adulation by a large contingent of concert-goers, terminated only in 1937 when her heroic contralto voice suffered a dimming of its old power and eloquence. Helen Traubel, a pretty young girl from St. Louis and a protégée of Rudolf Ganz, made her first appearance in the relatively lowly circumstances of a Sunday "pop" in 1926, just as Gladys Swarthout had done in 1919. In the twenties Traubel was "built like Diana" (according to the *Daily Star*) and all the critics lavishly praised her gifts, Davies commenting on "the feeling of plenty of reserve power" in her singing. His phrase was prophetic. No singer has shown a more abundant reserve power than Traubel in the last quarter-century.

The talents of Twin Cities musicians were liberally drawn upon in those days, more so then than later. Among the pianist stars at the "pops" were William Lindsay, Harrison Wall Johnson, Mr. and Mrs. James Bliss, Gabriel Fenyves, Elsie Wolf, and Mary Louise Bailey-Apfelbeck. Local singers who were frequently heard and warmly greeted were Agnes Rast Snyder, Meta Ashwin Birnbach, Agnes Griswold Teasdale, Berthold Busch, Mabel Pelletier, Inez Chandler Richter, and Annette Yde Lake, whose daughter Harriette was later to reach stardom as Ann Sothern, the film actress.

After the rash of guest conductors in the 1922–23 season, there was little interference from imported maestros. Only two made a marked impression, Chalmers Clifton and Eugene Goossens, and they not until the last season under Verbrugghen, when comparisons were apt to favor young and more vital rivals.

These two leaders had a tonic effect on audiences long inured to Verbrugghen's procedure, Clifton impressing by a vivid account of Elgar's *Enigma Variations,* Goossens exhibiting what was termed a "transformed orchestra." The conducting of both hinted at the potentialities of an ensemble that in Verbrugghen's waning years was becoming more and more muffled.

The orchestra's economic health fluctuated during the middle twenties, but not too dangerously. Always a deficit operation, the institution was fanned to life from its triennial sinking spells when the guaranty fund agreements ran out, the losses were counted, and the behind-the-scenes money bags bled. In June 1924 the number of backers was raised from four hundred to six hundred in a whirlwind campaign by fifty businessmen, who raised a guaranty of $450,000, providing $150,000 a year for three years.

In 1926 the slowly dying "pop" concerts became an issue. The directorate, speaking through E. L. Carpenter, notified Twin Cities concertgoers, more in anger than sorrow, that the orchestra was $100,000 in the hole, and that "private generosity" was pulling it out. "The directorate refuses to continue in the position of a group of enthusiasts attempting to foist on the city an institution in which the citizens have no apparent interest sufficient to guarantee a full ticket sale," read the manifesto.

In the threatening tone of "no dessert until you finish your dinner," the board announced that no "pops" would be scheduled until six hundred Friday night seats had been sold. Whereupon campaign workers went into the field, luncheon and women's clubs rallied around tables and teacups, and even grocery stores were pressured into using space in their food ads for Symphony appeals.

Finally enough season tickets were sold to justify setting up four "test" popular concerts. But the days of twenty-four "pops" a season were over; radio, movies, and other diversions, the increasing familiarity of orchestral sound, were putting the Sunday sessions in the equivocal position of offering bargain-price music that was less and less wanted by fewer people. Popular concerts were in a sad and relentless process of becoming depopularized.

The four "test" programs expanded to twelve, just half the quota of the year before. The next season, 1927–28, the number dwindled to six, and the season after that to none at all. It was finally clear that people didn't want the "dessert." Sunday afternoons were losing their definition as a time to hear cheap but good music, and they were never to regain it to the degree that prevailed in pre-radio days. A generation was growing up for whom, alas, a visit to the Symphony "pop" was not *the* thing to do on a Sunday afternoon, as it had been in the balmy Oberhoffer days. The Sabbath, for better or worse, was growing more secular, and the concert hall suffered with the church from declining attendance. Ways of being entertained were increasing rapidly in number and variety, and music could be heard without the effort of dressing up and going out.

Radio at first was the villain in the picture, but it soon became a benefactor. Its competition had a bad effect on Sunday patronage but eventually a compensating one on expansion of the orchestra's audience and exchequer. After the Symphony's first radio sponsorship over WLAG by the Donaldson department store in 1923, the orchestra returned to its visible audience and remained with it exclusively for four years. But by the time that Sunday afternoon concert receipts had slipped from $21,000 in 1922–23 to a meager $4940 in 1927–28, radio revenue, fortunately, had begun to take up the slack.

The Dayton Company, another Minneapolis department store, played host to the Symphony in two broadcasts over WCCO in the early months of 1927, and in 1927–28 the store took on a series of six more. Noting which way the wind was blowing, the Symphony manager in 1928 broached to H. A. Bellows, former music critic now in charge at WCCO, the happy idea of presenting series of regular radio concerts, abolishing the public "pops" in favor of radio "pops" under exclusive (and paid) sponsorship.

The plan was accepted and took hold. When the regular Sunday concerts were abandoned in 1928–29, the First National Bank group sponsored twenty-two radio concerts. It did the same the following season, and the Minneapolis Honeywell Regulator Company followed in 1930–31 with thirteen broadcasts. Radio income reached a $35,000-per-annum peak in this period, showing a healthy increase over "pop" earnings in their most flush years.

Young people's concerts — that long-range investment in future symphony audiences — continued through the twenties at the rate of usually four a season, with St. Paul taking them on in mid-decade. There was a year's hiatus when Minneapolis had no children's concerts at all, but this omission was deemed so unwise from the viewpoint of the orchestra's future that they were quickly resumed, the Parent-Teachers' Association taking the initiative in drumming up audiences.

Two audience-building schemes, one of them an old and innocuous device and the other new and untried, were put into operation during the Verbrugghen regime. In 1923–24 concertgoers were asked to vote for favorite compositions to be played at the final concert of the series. From a printed ballot of "candidates" they gave a majority vote to Tschaikowsky's Fifth symphony, Grieg's *Peer Gynt* suite, Ernest Schelling's *Victory Ball* (the *What Price Glory?* of the twenties' concert hall), Liszt's *Les Préludes,* and Tschaikowsky's *1812* overture. These represented the taste and preferences of the period.

The other scheme, brain-child of Mrs. Agnes Fryberger, who served in the short-lived post of educational director, was more elaborate and ingenious. It foreshadowed today's tune-guessing radio contests, though on a considerably higher plane. It was a memory contest, promoted by the *Minneapolis Journal,* in which concertgoers competed for valuable prizes by identifying ten excerpts from musical works by title, composer, and composer's nationality. The ten were selected from a published list of forty and were performed by the orchestra March 29, 1925.

The contest generated intense public interest, without appreciably enlarging the orchestra's support fund or its regular clientele. Prizes included a grand piano, four phonographs, a reproducing piano, phonograph records, a number of musical scholarships and memberships in musical organizations, and season tickets for Symphony, Apollo Club, and Norwegian Glee Club concerts.

Complications began to develop when it was found that one hundred and twenty-one in the audience had made perfect scores.

An elimination contest set up more rigorous rules: names must be spelled correctly, and random excerpts from forty compositions were played not by the orchestra but by a cellist and a pianist. Only eleven music-wise contestants survived this ordeal, and a second elimination ranked winners on the basis not of knowledge but of neatness. Third prize winner was a boy, John Verrall, who grew up to be a composer whose works were played by the Minneapolis Symphony Orchestra.

The critical gentry showed a few shifts and changes during the decade, Davies and Nilsson becoming the Minneapolis "old guard" and Frances Boardman (spelled in 1929 by the pianist Harrison Wall Johnson) finally superseding Judd and Flandrau as the principal and trusted commentator in St. Paul. N. B. Abbott and later Lewis Miner dovetailed their music reviews into other duties on the *Daily News* in that city, while in Minneapolis a new newspaper, the *Minnesota Daily Star,* which became the *Minneapolis Star,* added two new voices to the reviewers' chorus.

The first of these — Paul Bliss, who wrote under the pseudonym of Southworth Alden — introduced a brash and breezily personal note into the music-reviewing pattern. His first reviews were written in breathless "feature" style in an evident effort to humanize a type of technical discussion having low readership, but he calmed down later, though he continued to add to the variety of viewpoints represented by the Twin Cities critics.

Bliss was capable of vivid imagery. In discussing Chaliapin (who "gave out his song numbers like a bishop") he had this to say of the Russian basso's performance in Moussorgsky's *Song of the Flea*: "How hollowly Chaliapin laughed out the bitter satire of it! It was like a carload of brass bells bumping over a railroad crossing."

Bliss's successor on the *Star* was John K. Sherman, a young newspaperman of "cub" status whose dual interest in music and writing had prompted him to enter journalism with a hopeful and greedy eye on the music-writing post. Substituting on concert dates that Bliss was willing to relinquish, he started reviewing in the fall of 1926, and when Bliss finally left for greener fields, Sherman slipped unobtrusively into the vacated post. For a time he wrote under the Southworth Alden disguise but in 1928 acquired his own signature for his reviews. Subsequently his writing spread to other cultural terrain: art, books, and the drama.

Much of the stability of the Verbrugghen chapter in Minneapolis Symphony history must be credited to the clearheaded efficiency of Arthur J. Gaines, the orchestra's first professional business manager.

Everyone knows that a good orchestra must be conducted well; it is not so clearly understood that a good orchestra must be managed well. The Symphony's affairs had never really had a strict and businesslike supervision with modern bookkeeping methods. Heighton in the previous decade had specialized largely in tour booking, being absent for long periods from home quarters; Carlo Fischer was essentially a musician and program writer and statistician who doubled as home manager and performed other necessary functions.

In 1923 the directorate decided the time had come to make the management less of a makeshift operation, and Gaines was chosen by Carpenter as the man for the job. He had managed the St. Louis Symphony for ten years and had similarly served the City Symphony of New York for a year. He came to the Twin Cities as associate manager in charge of tours for the 1923–24 season, Carlo Fischer continuing in charge of business management in Minneapolis, with Edmund A. Stein performing the same function in St. Paul. A year later Gaines assumed full management duties.

Gaines, a certified public accountant, belonged to a rare and relatively new species: the specially trained orchestra manager whose skills had been developed at first hand in orchestra offices. In him love of music was linked with business ability and a cool head for figures. He knew the delights of music but he knew also their cost, and their profit-and-loss potentials.

On his arrival Gaines found the orchestra's management operating in haphazard fashion, bills being paid by reaching into the till to see what money was there, or into Carpenter's pocket. Richard Horgan was in charge of season ticket sales at the Cable Piano Company, the Symphony office handling only single ticket sales. Money was drawn when needed from Horgan's fund of subscription receipts and from Carpenter's bank accounts.

When Gaines became full manager, he began ironing out this informality by instituting up-to-date accounting, and he soon was able not only to spell out the orchestra's financial status in plain black and white (and red) but to make his methods a basis for wiser and more profitable guidance of an institution that earned and dispersed money.

Meanwhile, in his first season, 1923–24, he discovered that as tour manager he had inherited a money-losing junket of ample dimensions, booked earlier by outside agents who had made many dates on a loose and far-flung itinerary. But worse than that, he found that Verbrugghen and his eastern manager, Daniel Mayer, had between them dreamed up a week's cycle of Beethoven programs in Carnegie Hall in New York. They had contracted for the hall for no fewer than six evenings of concerts by the Minneapolis Symphony.

Verbrugghen's motives for this ambitious project were clear and his hopes were high. In Australia he had several times taken his Sydney orchestra to Melbourne for week-long fiestas that traversed the Beethoven symphonies from One to Nine, and these had been a formidable success. New to America, Verbrugghen did not pause to reflect that whereas Melbourne was music-deficient, New York was music-wise, a cosmopolitan center that needed no concentrated applications of Beethoven.

Gaines was dismayed and shocked. After convincing Carpenter that a week's course in Beethoven by midwestern musicians in Manhattan would prove a costly fiasco and make the orchestra a target of derisive and harmful comment, he immediately set about undoing the damage before it was done. He tried unsuccessfully to substitute a single Monday night appearance for the six-night contract, but had to be content with a compromise agreement requiring payment for three nights, two of them "dark." This was a stiff price to pay for a single performance, but probably less stiff than the price of a nonattended cycle.

With his Beethoven cycle summarily canceled, Verbrugghen turned from Beethoven entirely for his New York debut as Minneapolis conductor, and chose the Brahms C minor as his major offering. There was some critical praise, but it was flecked with doubts and the usual eastern touch of revulsion. W. J. Henderson thought the delivery was "marred by force and eagerness rather than by finish," and the sharp-spoken Henry T. Finck said the first three movements were the "dryest, most literal and pedantic reading I have ever heard." Pitts Sanborn, on the other hand, found Verbrugghen "quite lily-soft in his tenderness towards Brahms . . . a thoroughly domesticated Brahms . . . that took his decorous way through the four sections of the symphony."

The custom on tours at that time was to mobilize the entire personnel for the Manhattan concert and then to shave it down for the return through the hinterland. Foreseeing certain loss in the prearranged tour in 1924, Gaines coaxed Carpenter into cutting the already reduced orchestra of sixty-five to fifty. This measure brought protest from cities where a larger complement had been expected, and some rebates were made at these disaffected points.

On this first tour under Verbrugghen, Orpheus on Wheels, as the *Minneapolis Tribune* had called the roving orchestra, ran up two memorable records. On the road seven weeks, it played to 150,000 people and returned home with a loss of nearly $20,000.

Perhaps it was a bad omen that Orpheus on Wheels had started out with a conductor on crutches. Verbrugghen never coddled himself, and after wrenching his knee at a rehearsal of *Heldenleben* in Minneapolis, he had been helped on stage by Fischer for several home concerts, conducting from a high bookkeeper's chair with his lame leg propped on a cushion. Undaunted, he began the tour while still a cripple.

Next season the tour crept out of the red, and Gaines's special knack for making barnstorming pay began to add much-needed dollars to the orchestra's coffers. Procedure was systematized and simplified, contacts were built up, service was promised, and delivered, to communities that wanted the orchestra. At the same time the conditions under which the orchestra could play were codified; printed forms sent out to local managers specified such things as "good, solid straightback or bentwood chairs, not the usual folding chairs," the amount of square-footage needed to hold the orchestra, "no carpet on stage, preferably no drapes," and other technical matters, including how to pay the fee. "Before the concert" was the rule laid down for this important technicality, and the fee was usually a straight $2000.

The management felt better when receipts exceeded outlay and traveling made money as well as friends for the orchestra and new recruits for fine music, but the profit motive was not the prime and only consideration. Years of touring, profit and nonprofit, had driven home the lesson that the orchestra was Minneapolis' most valuable piece of prestige advertising and was spreading ever farther its fair name and fame.

That name and fame hopped the Caribbean for the first time in 1929, when the orchestra gave a three-day concert series in Havana, so charming the demonstrative Cubans that an invitation was promptly extended for a return visit the following year. One of the minor but surprising discoveries made in Havana was that the orchestra, despite its multi-racial character, had not a single Spanish-speaking member to act as interpreter.

The Symphony's home quarters in the Auditorium had served the orchestra well for twenty years, but changes began to affect its desirability as early as 1924. In that year the Northwestern National Life Insurance Company moved out of the building and sold it to F. W. Clifford, who in turn leased it to a firm of motion picture operators, the Clinton-Meyers Company of Duluth. The buyers agreed to a proviso permitting the orchestra to continue its occupancy for morning rehearsals and Friday and Sunday concerts.

The Auditorium thenceforth became the Lyceum Theater, and extensive remodeling took place. A year before, a new step-up stage platform had been installed, and the old woodsy backdrop — "E. L. Carpenter's pine forest," which the lumberman was often teased about — made way for plain sidewalls. The remodeling of auditorium into theater that followed the next year was a more drastic alteration. The long-pronged horseshoe balconies were ripped out and the two upper floors, of wooden construction, were replaced by a single cement balcony. The acoustics of the old Auditorium were in great measure impaired for use as a concert hall.

At the same time — and this was the blow that nearly killed the orchestra — the yearly rental was doubled from $11,000 to more than $22,000, making the Lyceum a highly expensive practice and concert room. In the next six seasons the orchestra paid $144,000 for the space it occupied on Eleventh Street, where concerts were held usually not oftener than twice a week for a half-year's season. This charge became increasingly onerous as "pop" concert receipts fell off, subscription intake remained static (actually decreased in St. Paul), and general orchestra expenses mounted.

In the spring of 1930 the orchestra came close to the end of its trail. Carpenter called together his board of directors and talked to them with a new note of gravity in his voice. He told them he was unable to carry longer the brunt of the financial burden alone, that the Lyceum rent was ruinous, that a new blueprint for the orchestra must be formulated.

From an event of the year before came two ideas for resolving the crisis.

In October 1929 the orchestra had been a party to the dedication of the handsome new Cyrus Northrop Memorial Auditorium on the campus of the state university, playing one of three programs which formally opened the building. To add luster to the opening, the Boston Symphony under Serge Koussevitzky had been imported at a fee of $10,000 and had displayed in Ravel's *Daphnis et Chloé* suite No. 2 an orchestral virtuosity of a kind

188

rarely heard in Minneapolis and never forgotten by those who heard it. These concerts had been arranged by Mrs. Carlyle Scott, music impresario of town and campus, manager since 1919 of the University Artists Course, wife of the university's music department head, importer of the Chicago Civic Opera, and a manager-showman of pronounced and proven gifts.

In August of 1930 Mrs. Scott was called by Carpenter and soon found herself facing a sober-miened directorate that asked her bluntly to become the manager of the Minneapolis Symphony. She deliberated a few days, obtained release from a contract with the Chicago Civic Opera, and accepted the post within the week, becoming the second woman manager of a major American orchestra. (Mrs. Adele Prentiss Hughes of the Cleveland Orchestra was the first.)

Gaines, who in seven years had made a major contribution in his hardheaded financial management, his extension of tour schedules, and the profitable radio broadcasts, was asked to share managerial responsibilities with Mrs. Scott and remain in charge of touring, finances, and orchestra relations. After careful consideration of the offer he declined it. He left to become again the St. Louis Symphony manager.

Turning immediately to the question of a new home for the orchestra, Mrs. Scott and the board discussed the feasibility of moving to the huge Minneapolis Auditorium, which had opened in 1927, but it was obvious that the orchestra could secure no continuity in its rehearsal and concert schedule in a hall regularly housing conventions and mass entertainments.

Northrop Auditorium, with its campus location and 4850 seats, was unquestionably the solution, and Mrs. Scott with her university connections might be expected to find a way around the barrier to its availability: How could a state-supported institution associate itself with a subsidized performing unit that charged admission to its performances? Northrop Auditorium was university property which, according to long-standing policy, could not be rented or leased.

University officials when first approached were dubious. But the governing boards of the two institutions were partly inter-locking, and a symphony orchestra in the appropriate cultural-educational setting of a university, located moreover in "neutral" territory between the two cities where St. Paul patronage could be retained without weekly commuting to that city — this was too perfect a prospect not to inspire a legal *modus operandi* to make it come true.

The ingenious Mrs. Scott, conferring with William T. Middle-brook, university comptroller, found the *modus*. A contract was devised whereby the University of Minnesota engaged the Min-neapolis Symphony Orchestra to give concerts in Northrop Audi-torium, charging nominal fees for use of the building and office space and handling the money, but allowing the Orchestral Asso-ciation to continue its corporate existence and manage itself as it had in the past.

The contract (which is still renewed annually) was accepted and signed. Thus began the fruitful and unique partnership of university and symphony orchestra which has shed prestige on both and has made the Minnesota campus the only one in the country harboring a major professional orchestra as permanent resident. The orchestra came as house guest and is now a mem-ber of the academic family — not so closely tied as a college or department, but a valuable and respected addition to the cultural-educational facilities of the university. Along with the University Artists Course and the University Theater, the orchestra-on-campus has done much to bring town and gown together in a more cordial and understanding relationship.

The St. Paul concerts were now abandoned for the single series at Northrop Auditorium, and many St. Paulites found themselves closer to the concert hall than Minneapolitans living in the southern reaches of the city. The new auditorium had more than double the seating capacity of the Lyceum — room enough for the largest single-concert audience of any major or-chestra in America. Savings in rental allowed for a greater num-ber of cheaper seats, special ticket prices for students and staff members, and an opportunity (or so it seemed before the onset of the depression) to spend more money on an enlarged orchestra personnel and guest stars.

Opening night at Northrop Auditorium on October 17, 1930, was spectacular in a way to disrupt the cloistered campus atmosphere and shake the sedate traditions of the orchestra, at one and the same time. Mrs. Scott was never one to minimize a big event, and she gave her imagination and energetic showmanship free rein for the orchestra's campus bow. The public of both cities was apprised of the coming event in large print and small: in the newspapers and on downtown street banners announcing the "World Première of University Symphony Series."

When the big night came, concertgoers abashedly made their way up stately Northrop's steps to boom of cannon and blare of trumpet. Flags of all nations fluttered along the approaches to the auditorium, the university band under Michael Jalma played outside from the foyer's roof, and radio station WCCO broadcast a running patter of gossip as patrons trooped into the lobby. Five minutes before the concert started, artillerymen thrice loaded and fired a 75-millimeter antiaircraft gun.

Filing into the expansive interior, the audience sat facing a stage whose curtains were slowly drawn after eight soldiers, four on each side aisle, had marched down to the footlights and blown a final fanfare. For the first time the orchestra was visually dramatized by special lighting effects. As the curtains parted the eighty-seven musicians were obscurely disclosed in a bluish darkness which gradually lightened to full yellow brilliance, and Henri Verbrugghen walked to the platform.

Nearly five thousand listeners were on hand for that glittering opening, and the *Star*'s Sherman, in a glow, declared it an occasion on which the Minneapolis Symphony Orchestra met Democracy.

Other new phenomena greeted the first-nighters. There was a new author of program notes: the scholarly Donald Ferguson. There was a new and elegant podium. There was a new first cellist, Jascha Schwarzmann. Only the program was familiar and time-tested, filled with material deemed acceptable for a gala evening: Dvořák's *New World,* Ravel's *Boléro,* and Wagner's *Rienzi* overture.

That blonde goddess of song, Maria Jeritza, had been specially engaged for the first concert, and what could be more appropriate than her singing of *Dich teure Halle* (Hail, Hall of Song)? She swept from the wings in a canary yellow Grecian-style gown with belt of brilliants and necklace of pearls. Making her bow with the orchestra after her songs, she lavishly lent her picturesque charm to a ritual of curtsies, histrionic gestures, and graceful distribution of flowers from her bouquet to Verbrugghen and his men. James Gray, writing in the *St. Paul Pioneer Press,* found it all a diverting little vaudeville act.

The fates were unkind to Verbrugghen in making that first glorified season in Northrop Auditorium his eighth and last. There had been signs for some time that his grip on the orchestra had loosened, that aging and hard, unremitting work had lessened his energies. He sometimes seemed to conduct with nose in the score without much regard for what was happening in front of him in the orchestra.

His health had generally been good, and he was never a man to lay down his baton when it wasn't. A mastoid infection had once threatened his hearing, and he had undergone an ear operation. A lame leg, a severe cold, would never put him out of action unless sheer weakness or a tough doctor's orders made him desist. As time went on his health became increasingly a problem, and in 1928 he visited the Mayo Clinic in Rochester.

A bitterness seemed to have crept into his outlook in 1928 when, in several cities the orchestra played in, he declared that "our classical music is stale, worn out, and futile" — this from a man to whom the classics were the staff of life. "Not eighty per cent of the people who hear it understand it," he lamented. "I don't know why so many people attend concerts, unless perhaps it is the thing to do. If I were to wear a red vest and a yellow tie at a concert, then perhaps I could understand why people come." What music needed, he said, was a new genius, someone with a new system of music, a system which people could understand.

It was this same year that in St. Louis Verbrugghen, to quote the *Globe-Democrat* critic, "ran through the four movements of the Brahms *C minor* much as an academician of the '90s would, in those days, have expounded Browning." Of the same performance Thomas Sherman wrote that the conductor "rationalized the music to such an extent that what resulted was a display of its anatomical parts rather than as a unified, integrated whole."

Probably the severest criticism came from the late Charles Edward Russell, author of the Pulitzer Prize book *The American Orchestra and Theodore Thomas,* who in 1931 deplored the Minneapolis Symphony's fall from grace. "Today this orchestra is really beneath consideration as any factor in music," he wrote. "No persons with any ear for orchestral excellence can listen to its performances without being amazed and appalled." Russell cited raggedness of attack, harsh and ill-adjusted tone, faults in pitch, and woeful lack of unison.

But the decline of the orchestra in Verbrugghen's last years will never obscure the positive and lasting contribution he had earlier made to it. After the guidance of the poet, Oberhoffer, it was perhaps necessary to have the rule of the scholar, Verbrugghen, a musician steeped in the classics and a technician who well understood the subtle carpentry of putting a composition together when transmuting it from black notes to intangible sound.

He had shown that the classics had their base in Bach. He had introduced many modern works in a decade of musical ferment, and kept abreast of the times in intelligently planned programs which for the most part were venturesome yet solid. No one in his position has shown a kinder, a more patient and paternal interest in young musicians and their problems. This interest had its base in a personality that was impulsively generous and inherently tactful. His unaffected geniality and charm made him not only socially winning but genuinely liked by all he met.

As a chamber musician, many have said, Verbrugghen was

better than as an orchestra conductor. His string quartet concerts, including the later ones with Lemay and Roentgen filling the posts left vacant by Nichols and Messeas, gave evidence of great knowledge, experience, and skill in the chamber classics. He considered it all in the season's work, as well as a matter of duty and source of joy, to play most of the sixteen Beethoven quartets as well as numerous Haydn and Mozart works, with a sprinkling of modern quartets — all in addition to his regular labors of rehearsing and conducting symphony programs. Some may recall the characteristic and engaging gesture he always made at the conclusion of a string quartet performance. He would whip off his spectacles and turn and gaze sharply at the audience, as if to say, "There, how did you like that?"

It was an unseasonably hot autumn midday, October 26, 1931, and Verbrugghen was directing a special rehearsal of the brass section for Strauss's *Ein Heldenleben* in the basement practice room beneath Northrop's stage. The tired conductor, to whom the turbulent score of *Heldenleben* was a complex and harrowing problem requiring section rehearsals, called for a trumpet passage at one place in the score. The trumpeters shook their heads and told him they had no notes, only rests. Verbrugghen put down his stick and suddenly sat in his chair, apparently to study the score further. The men waited, their puzzlement turning to concern. For more minutes than seemed necessary he stared blankly at the score, then rose and walked uncertainly out of the room, aided by horn player Richard Lindenhahn and stage manager Sam Grodnick, to find Mrs. Scott on the stage above.

"I can't see. Everything is going black," he told her.

The fifty-eight-year-old conductor had suffered a cerebral hemorrhage, and was quickly taken to Eitel Hospital. Paul Lemay carried on acceptably in his place, finishing the rehearsals and conducting *Heldenleben* at the season's second Friday concert. By that time Mrs. Scott, working with heroic speed, had selected a rising young conductor in the East and engaged him for four guest performances, to span the gap until it could be known whether Verbrugghen would be able to resume his duties.

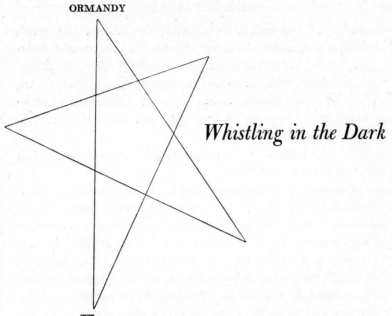

Whistling in the Dark

Eugene Ormandy's first concert in Minneapolis could be compared to an explosion, but an explosion that operated in reverse, consolidating rather than shattering, like one seen in a motion picture film run backward. The pieces not only fell in place but were pulled and magnetized into the tightest, most effective and dynamic entity the orchestra, its backers, and its hearers had so far known.

There was no mistaking what had happened that November evening in 1931, although how it happened and just who this young and blond bundle of energy was, were mysteries not to be solved till later. For a long time the orchestra had been an instrument that expounded music rather than dramatizing it, at its best a calm and thoughtful exponent, at its worst a wheezy, confused one. But its falling off had been gradual and intermittent as the vitality of its conductor declined, and the town was used to the way it sounded. The majority unconsciously accepted an occasional dullness of performance as part of the necessary pain of supporting culture and attending concerts.

Now, suddenly, the orchestra sang. It rang out with irresistible eloquence. The tone had come alive, the phrases had grown sharp and purposeful, the climaxes made the blood pound. Overnight the ensemble had acquired a youthful vigor, flexibility, and unanimity, with compelling rhythmic impulse. Many in the audience had not known, or had forgotten, that music could be so exciting and inspiring. A new spirit was there; the orchestra seemed reborn.

What had happened was plain enough, thrilling enough, but how had it come about?

The answer lay in the unique mixture of talents and ambitions possessed by the thirty-two-year-old Ormandy, linked with a fortunate combination of circumstances. Ormandy's coming to Minneapolis was a case of mutual seizure of opportunity for mutual benefit. To Ormandy was offered the gift of an orchestra to energize and shape to his will while he was acquiring invaluable conducting routine and building his repertoire. To the orchestra and its backers was granted a chance at the services of the most brilliant and promising young conductor in America.

Ormandy was the Alger hero of American music when he came to Minneapolis. He seemed absurdly, even touchingly young for a profession which had long been the province of older and seemingly wiser men, but if he was young for a conductor and virtually unknown in the Midwest, he was by no means untested or unapplauded.

Ten years before, as the story was often told, he was not known at all, having arrived in New York from Budapest with little money but carrying in his pocket what he thought was a $30,000 contract for an American tour as concert violinist. This was his first trip to America. He had grown up in Budapest as a *wunderkind,* a star pupil of violinist Jenö Hubay, having begun his musical education as a tot of five years in the Budapest Royal Academy. He made his concert debut two years later; at the age of fifteen he was awarded a state diploma for violinists by special decree of the ministry of education; and at nineteen he was appointed a flull-fledged professor. But teaching was not to his taste, nor a profession he would follow long.

Whistling in the Dark

As a child, Jenö (named by his dentist father after Jenö Hubay in hope his boy would become a concert violinist) was able to read musical notes before he could identify letters of the alphabet. There was endless practice, not much play, and he was soon thrust in front of an audience to perform on his pint-sized violin. For that formidable occasion he was dressed up in white short pants and blouse, and his blond hair was brushed up in the pompadour fashion of the period. But his teacher was a cautious man who took no chances, and he made the tactical error of placing a music stand on the stage, and putting Jenö's music on it. When the boy, making his entry, saw the stand, he was furious. This was an insult to his pride in his memorizing ability. He turned to the wings and loudly announced: "I will not play unless this stand is taken off!" It was taken off, and he played.

The boy grew up, daily running through his exercises and in time taking on exhibition pieces of the Wieniawski-Vieuxtemps stripe. He perfected his performing art and started to concertize. A few years after the war came the opportunity, or so it seemed, to make an American reputation and earn a pot of American money, and he arrived in New York with high hopes in 1921.

His rosy prospects turned to gray a few blocks from the pier. The tour vanished into thin air. The agent who had booked the tour was broke and unable to finance it.

Lacking money, friends, and a speaking knowledge of English, the lonely violinist found himself in a predicament made bleaker by the fact that it was December of the year, when all orchestra jobs were filled. By chance he met a former Budapest acquaintance who staked him to a small loan and advised him to play for Erno Rapee, a fellow Hungarian and conductor at the Capitol Theater, a large movie house (then run by a former Minneapolitan, S. L. Rothafel, "Roxy"). The audition was arranged. It resulted in a back-row post in the violin section of the Capitol's orchestra, after the conductor had voiced repugnance at assigning that lowly position to a concert violinist. The issue was an academic one to the grateful Ormandy. "I have to eat," he said.

But his talents could not long be hidden, and within a week

he found himself elevated to the concertmaster position. Thereafter Eugene Ormandy Blau (he was known then by his original
name) quickly caught the tempo of American life and, confident
of his powers, plunged into the rough-and-tumble of New York's
competitive musical world. He soon became a starring member
of Roxy's Gang, an assemblage of vocalists and Capitol Theater
musicians emceed by Rothafel and appearing regularly over the
air — one of the first radio shows to personalize, in an informal
way, the performer appearing before the microphone.

Not long after came the Alger twist, that stroke of fate which
is found in all work-and-win fiction but rarely in real life. One
of the three assistant Capitol conductors who was to lead the
orchestra a certain afternoon fell ill. What happened was related
by Ormandy ten years later to a Minneapolis magazine editor,
Virginia Safford:

"I had come to the theater with my wife [Steffy Goldner, a
harpist]. We put the car in the garage and she went around to
the front door and I went around to the back. The doorman told
me, 'You are to take the show.' I thought it was a good joke.
'What kind of a joke is this?' I asked him. 'No joke, you have
to take the show,' the doorman assured me. 'The conductor is sick.'

"It was then 1:45 and I had 15 minutes to change my suit to
a cutaway and go on stage. My wife, in the audience, had noticed
that the concertmaster's chair was removed and all the other
chairs moved up. The lights were already on and there were 80
men in the orchestra. The audience was whispering.

"She was wondering what could have happened and when she
saw me walking out on the stage, she was more surprised than
the orchestra members. We were to play the last three movements of the *Fourth* symphony of Tschaikowsky. I looked at the
score which was always opened, and then closed it. My wife by
then was ready to be carried out, but I conducted the whole
thing by heart. I knew every note."

This was the crucial episode in the Ormandy career, which
had already relegated poverty and obscurity to the status of a
brief, if painful, prelude to an American success story. His im-

pressive feat of conducting on a moment's notice a symphony score from memory won him the post of fourth assistant conductor and ever-increasing conducting duties. His march upward accelerated and he soon had the full musical direction of the Capitol orchestra. For seven years thereafter he was in charge of the orchestra, acquiring there the same kind of intensive training that an actor gains in a stock company with weekly changes of plays and roles.

The standard symphony orchestra plays a given composition one or two times and then starts practice on a new program, but the Capitol orchestra in the course of a week played the same works as many as twenty-eight times on a four-a-day basis. This repetition of performance in the big movie house, aided by the naturally retentive Ormandy mind, engraved deeply the lessons learned: the absorption of specific scores, performance techniques, keener memorization habits.

The time came for New York concertgoers to cock an ear at the sounds emanating from the stage of the Capitol, where Ormandy's vibrant baton was evoking exciting music, and they started going to his symphonic hours. Music critic W. J. Henderson gave an appreciative word to the quality concerts Ormandy was playing, and soon concert manager Arthur Judson, that collector of conductors, took notice of the strange phenomenon of good music brilliantly performed in a film emporium. Impressed with what he saw and heard, Judson gave the young musician an assignment to conduct the orchestral support for a performance by the Duncan dancers.

By 1929 Ormandy was no longer a violinist, except in private, and he cast the die which decided his future course: He resigned from the Capitol Theater and signed with Judson. Thereupon things began to happen in rapid and ascending progression. In the summer of 1929 he directed the New York Philharmonic at Lewisohn Stadium; the following summer he led the Philadelphia Orchestra at Robin Hood Dell; and he became meanwhile one of the leading maestros of the Columbia Broadcasting network.

A bigger plum fell to him in the fall of 1931 when Arturo Toscanini, delayed by illness in returning from Europe, was unable to fulfill a guest assignment with the Philadelphia Orchestra. This was a vacancy holding as much of threat as promise, for the truism was, and is, that there can be no substitute for Toscanini. But Ormandy was no weakling in the face of a large challenge, and he boldly took on the six concerts.

This was the same fall, the same week in fact, when the *Heldenleben* score blurred in front of Verbrugghen's eyes. The Minneapolis manager, Mrs. Scott, had to think and work fast when she found herself deprived of a conductor at the start of the season. Lemay jumped temporarily into the breach — and, incidentally, was chagrined that his candidacy for the vacant post was not considered. But Mrs. Scott knew that she must locate a more-than-adequate conducting talent, if to do nothing more than keep audiences satisfied until Verbrugghen returned to the podium.

She thought of Ormandy, the brilliant young man who, according to the headlines, was good enough to substitute for Toscanini. She telephoned long distance to a close friend, Willis I. Norton, long-time Minnesota legislator and political power who was in Philadelphia at the time. Informing him of Verbrugghen's collapse, she asked Norton to attend Ormandy's concert that night in the Academy of Music, and to look, listen, and report back.

Norton, admittedly a lay judge of music, returned the call late that night, his superlatives burning the wire. "You couldn't do better," he told her, and he described the rapturous reception given Ormandy by Philadelphians who rose from their seats and shouted their approval.

Next morning Arthur Judson was the recipient of a call from Mrs. Scott and he had to parry her plea for quick delivery of Ormandy with an explanation of previous commitments tying up the conductor. But he sniffed a fine opportunity for his young star, and after freeing him from his entanglements he called her back to say that Ormandy would leave Philadelphia for Minneapolis promptly after the Saturday concert.

Whistling in the Dark

And so he did. There was no time to change clothes before the train's departure that night, and Ormandy in full-dress regalia, with a suitcase hastily packed by his wife, careened via cab to the railroad station, a shrieking police guard clearing the way.

Meanwhile in Minneapolis E. L. Carpenter had called a board meeting, directors who wondered "Who the hell is Ormandy?" were briefed, and the first rehearsal under the dapper and dynamic blond, now garbed in an old blue sweater and gray slacks, started on Monday morning.

"I want to say I already know you," Ormandy told the men after Mrs. Scott introduced him. "I know of your work and I admire you very much. All I ask is your cooperation in making the concerts a success."

With that deceptively mild and modest foreword — and with the comradely suggestion that the men call him Gene because he was just a fellow fiddler — Ormandy took up the baton to begin what soon became an almost ruthless re-education of the orchestra. This turned out to be a meticulous and taxing course of study conducted by force of persuasion, exhortation, and browbeating — all adding up to the most skillful extraction of the best playing his musicians, individually and together, could produce.

The manager listened awhile to that dramatically efficient first rehearsal, then hurried out of the hall to the office phone to call Carpenter. "Come over right away if you can. We *have* a conductor." And Carpenter, always prepared to drop everything when orchestra affairs demanded his presence and personal attention, hastened to the hall for his first inspection of the man who would be his third conductor.

The nearly five thousand people who attended Ormandy's first concert were almost wholly in the dark about the young visitor from Hungary by way of New York, aside from what they may have gleaned from newspaper stories. Their anticipation mostly took the form of curiosity over an unknown who might thrill or pall. The program on paper looked fairly innocuous: the Tschaikowsky Fourth, the polka and fugue from Weinberger's

Schwanda as novelty, and for soloist, soprano Elisabeth Schumann.

So the "electrifying shock of delight" reported by one observer was stronger than if the audience had not been unprepared and largely unsuspecting. Reviewers the next day echoed the reactions of the excited and enthralled Friday-nighters. Frances Boardman in St. Paul hailed "a young genius in one of the most brilliant concerts of the orchestra's history," and extolled the "style, sweep, force, and sheer musical splendor" Ormandy evoked in his first program. Davies greeted him as a "great builder," and Sherman, quite beside himself, declared that this young maestro of a "metamorphosed orchestra" belonged up in the front row "with Toscanini, Koussevitzky, Stokowski, et al."

Ormandy's debut was a personal triumph. He had won a majority vote of confidence from that large audience as he had already received the nod from the few who had been instrumental in bringing him westward. For by this time, medical opinion on Verbrugghen's condition had advised more than a few weeks' rest for the ailing conductor and indicated that resumption of his duties would be unwise and dangerous. Between Ormandy's first and second concerts he was given a one-year contract as Minneapolis Symphony conductor at a beginning salary of $20,000. His wife Steffy soon arrived, and two weeks later his precious Balestrieri violin was brought to him from New York. The conductor then felt perfectly at home, a committed Minneapolitan.

At Ormandy's second concert, an all-Brahms program, patrons were apprised of an emergency new to the Minneapolis Symphony, that of trying to support two conductors on a budget built for one. Mrs. Scott appealed for a special contribution made necessary by the obligation of hiring a new leader while carrying the old and ill one through the season. Pledge cards netted $8000 that night; elation over the new conductor combined with sympathy for Verbrugghen to draw quick response even from depression-pinched purses.

Ormandy vitalized the musical scene and made the concerts

at Northrop Auditorium increasingly a cynosure for those to whom his interpretive methods brought rich and heady experience. One much-talked-of marvel was his memory, which enabled him to conduct virtually everything he played without benefit of score. This was not a new feat by any means (Oberhoffer had often dispensed with the score many years before), but in Ormandy's case it was a dramatic proof of his close integration with the complex tone machine under him, reacting directly to a baton unimpeded by stand or book.

But the greatest wonder to those audiences that heard him in the early thirties was the new kind of potency and persuasion of utterance he gave the orchestra, wrought by painstaking preparation and a tense, concentrated platform style not lacking in dramatic gesture. His conducting manner has become more relaxed and contained since then, but in those days it had a lashing and athletic elasticity, all compounded of youthful exuberance, intensity, and ardor.

One of the first improvements he wrought in the orchestra was a tonal one, based on an increased richness and "body" in the strings' sound, obtained by plenty of vibrato and full sweep of the bow. His most frequent conducting gesture was the crooked left arm and shaking left hand with bent fingers — a violinist's pulsating left hand, held near the heart. With larger and enriched violin tone he achieved a better string-and-wind balance in the ensemble. This helped not only the fortes and tuttis but gave an unfailing musicality to pianissimo passages.

Aside from his skills, inborn and acquired, Ormandy possessed two qualifications that carried him buoyantly from triumph to triumph in his Minneapolis appearances.

One was a sure musical instinct, a feeling for the rightness and essential meanings of the music he played, combined with the ability to achieve in living tone what his instinct told him was right. His performance seemed a case of an interpreter by-passing all the labor of working out an "interpretation" and instead merely unearthing the treasure within the score and exhibiting it in full color and potency.

Ormandy's other special attribute was also his basic source of energy: a driving ambition, a white-hot, overriding ambition that made him a tempestuous martinet, eager to build Rome in a day and make the Minneapolis Symphony play as he dreamed it ought to play — and incidentally to climb the rungs of the ladder the Minneapolis Symphony offered him. This ambition, which had landed him in Minneapolis to take charge of a symphony orchestra he could call his own, made him a madman of energy and industry and exacting discipline. His idol was Toscanini, and he had some of Toscanini's fanatic desire for perfection. He drove his musicians hard, but no harder than he drove himself, using to the hilt his ample fund of physical and nervous energy. In rehearsals he was apt to be more roughshod than suave, and it is not surprising that resentments and antipathies were built up in some of the orchestra members.

But the whip-handed disciplinarian, capable of explosion and withering rebuke, lived in the same body with an endearing, affectionate, and generous person. It was impossible not to like this blond, high-spirited boy (for so he seemed) once one came under the spell of his personality, so warm-blooded and outgiving. Tempest was quickly followed by sunshine in the weather of his temperament. The demon became the cherub, and vice versa. He was a social creature, basking with no false reluctance in admiration. To see him at recess or after the concert was to find a man all smiles, perspiration, and bubbling talk, frankly pleased at what he had done and pleased that people should tell him how well he had done it.

At intermission he would discard his damp and wilted collar and shirt and put on fresh ones. In answer to an admonition that he was working too hard he would quickly agree, and then add that he was doing so "while the iron was hot." No budding conductor ever used his opportunities more shrewdly and energetically or built them up more assiduously than Ormandy.

During his five-year regime the orchestra acquired a new and double status. It cast off the remaining vestiges of provincialism, rising from little more than an enterprising inland orchestra into what might be called the "class group" with international standing. Its recordings made under Ormandy literally carried his name and fame, and the orchestra's, around the world. (In Chungking in 1943, during World War II, George Grim, newspaperman in charge of the Chinese government's radio station, played Minneapolis Symphony recordings over the troubled air of that place and time.) In many foreign countries the name *Minneapolis*, hitherto little known (or thought to be "something to eat," Ormandy once reported), was now linked with quality symphonic music.

At the same time the orchestra became a ladder to fame and high rewards for aspiring, brilliant, but only partially tested conductors: Ormandy was to leave in 1936 to assume the baton of the Philadelphia Orchestra, Dimitri Mitropoulos would heed the call of the New York Philharmonic after his later and longer tenure in Minneapolis, and Antal Dorati doubtless was following the same upward path when he took over in 1949.

But those developments were not readily to be foreseen in the dark days of the early thirties. No one did more, or deserved more credit for the accomplishment, than did Ormandy to keep the Minneapolis Symphony a going concern during the depression, when it very nearly became a dispensable civic luxury. Years later, Oscar Kalman, long-time friend of the Symphony in St. Paul, remarked that Ormandy "would have turned handsprings on the stage if that would have helped the orchestra." As it was, the conductor put himself voluntarily on call for all the functions, social and public, boring and otherwise, that the harassed backers and campaign workers arranged in behalf of the orchestra and its hungry treasury. It was once remarked that Ormandy "kept the blood circulating in the music he played"; it can be said with equal justice that in the early thirties he kept the money circulating in an organism that needed money as badly as the body needs blood.

The affirmative and healthy tone he immediately gave a humdrum orchestra in a financially sick period was symbolized, in a way, by the warm and rowdy Weinberger *Schwanda* music, which he played at his first concert. Concertgoers have a way of associating certain conductors with certain musical pieces, trivial or otherwise, which bear the conductor's unique imprint. Verbrugghen's well-remembered souvenir when he took over the orchestra had been the Maori *Waiata Poi*. Ormandy's was this *Schwanda* polka and fugue, and later, of course, his inimitable Strauss waltzes.

On a higher level, his first season introduced Twin Citians to two modern works of satirical bent, widely different but each delightful in its way: Prokofieff's crisp and knowing paraphrase of late eighteenth-century music, the *Classical* symphony, and Kodály's humorous saga of a folk hero, *Háry János*. Among the soloists, that same year was notable for appearances of Mary Garden, Rachmaninoff, Anna Duncan the dancer (with the orchestra in the pit), pianist Eunice Norton (gifted daughter of Willis I. Norton), and Steffy Goldner Ormandy in the Mozart flute and harp concerto.

(Mary Garden had opened the season prior to Ormandy's arrival with a battery of specially installed lights illuminating a new coiffure of reddish hair laid straight and flat across the top of her head, a sylphlike figure, and a breath-taking gown. Orchestra players, facing the lights, found the diaphanous gown and the Garden silhouette distracting that night.)

The downward slope of the depression dipped to a steeper pitch in Ormandy's second season, 1932–33, when the guaranty fund took a $64,000 tumble from the previous year's figure, the midwinter tour held only twenty-one dates, and the bank holiday in March temporarily froze the flow of cash.

Mrs. Scott was equal to the emergency caused by the banks' closing. She had revived the Sunday afternoon "pop" concerts in March 1931, after a three-year lapse, and she now promptly announced a free "pop" for March 5 as the orchestra's brave answer to the scarcity of ready money. Northrop Auditorium that afternoon was jammed with happy "deadheads," most of them younger people who had very little ready money anyway, bank holiday or no. Thereafter, for a period in the thirties, Sunday concertgoing — low-priced music in the depression era — proved reasonably popular and profitable.

In Minneapolis as everywhere else, this was the time of malodorous memory when salaries submitted to surgery in payroll departments. All but the lowest paid employees of the Symphony organization, from fiddlers' ranks to manager's office, suffered a deep and heartbreaking 33⅓ per cent cut in pay. This was the time, too, when Ormandy found a way for the orchestra to whistle in the dark and get paid for the tune. He initiated the happy and avidly received idea of "Viennese afternoon" at Northrop, where the ingratiating waltzes, polkas, and marches of the Strauss family, and later the sweet melodies of Victor Herbert, took people's minds off their financial troubles.

The Strauss waltz has probably never been done better in Minneapolis, before or since, than the way Ormandy performed it. Frances Boardman, most fervent devotee of Ormandy's sorcery in this field, expatiated on the "indescribable and gorgeous sense of style" the conductor brought to Viennese fare, his faultless rhythm and fastidious respect for the composer's intentions. Sherman suggested that part of the secret was that Ormandy brought to Strauss "the full power and conviction of his musicianship," that he knew where and how to apply rubato on the one hand and strict tempo on the other.

That the *gemütlich* music of old Vienna's cafes and theaters could be converted into hard coin to help pull a midwestern orchestra through an economic bog is one of those mysterious alchemies that prove, among other things, that people will pay for what they genuinely enjoy, even if they can't afford it.

Unfortunately, many people listening to inexpensive Sunday music has never meant more than extra pennies jingling in the toe of a long, limp sock. The big money for orchestra support must be sought before tune-up time. So that 1932–33 season took an extra long head start behind scenes, buoyed by hopes that more time for the fund campaign would accumulate more contributions before opening night. As early as June the machine started rolling, and the general public, not alone the limited concertgoing public, was the object of attack. Thirty solicitors with blood in their eye took the field, and $145,000 was the goal. (This was not the first time, or the last, that the Symphony fund drive went "direct" to the general public, although each time the maneuver was regarded as positively unprecedented, and each time, too, the general public was not much touched, emotionally or monetarily, by the orchestra's plight.)

At the same time a new and grim note entered the tone of solicitation of the big donors in that dark year. Hitherto the etiquette of the request had dictated an appeal to civic pride and personal duty and responsibility; now it was a blunt, simple question cued to a hard and immediate crisis: Do you favor the continuance of the Minneapolis Symphony Orchestra? Voting for continuance, you contributed; voting for abandonment, you abstained.

The Junior Association of Commerce took up the gauntlet and with youthful resolution set out to raise $25,000 on its own initiative. "The Symphony Must Be Saved" exhorted the newspapers, and once again was voiced that incontestable statement, so often repeated it had become a bromide: "Abandonment of the orchestra would be unthinkable." Unthinkable, yes, but quite possible. The press of both cities printed subscription blanks headed "I Will Help Save Our Symphony" and footnoted with the plea, "Help 100 men keep their jobs," a refrain in tune with the times. Editorials had knell-tolling captions: "The Symphony on the Brink," "Symphony — Oblivion or Glory?"

The campaign continued with nagging persistence, reaching greedily, and by necessity, for small sums. A "dollar up" drive was instigated by the Junior Association as a "last desperate attempt" to extract from the citizenry the remaining and reluctant $12,000 needed. The schools were enrolled in an S.O.S. (Save Our Symphony) effort, the Third Minnesota Infantry Band marched weekly up Nicollet in behalf of its highbrow colleague, and finally a Symphony Tag Day was set, reducing the campaign to its lowest common denominator as an all-city project.

The wolf-crying campaigners of this 1932 drive were as near

to having a genuine, orchestra-eating wolf in the offing as any group of symphony workers ever had. Their labors were completed October 12 when, after four months of cajolery, persuasion, sales talk, and dime grabbing, the city was assured of its Symphony — for one more year anyway.

Discreetly withheld from this heartening announcement was the distasteful fact that a campaign employing every ingenuity of promotion and solicitation had netted not $145,000 but only $106,700, the smallest but one of any annual guaranty since the beginning of the Verbrugghen regime in the early twenties. Two years later, in 1934–35, the fund sank to the rock-bottom low of $100,700, demonstrating that the depression was no shorter for the orchestra than for anyone else, and that the climb out was slow and arduous. Not until well into the Mitropoulos era did the orchestra begin to show consistent surpluses at the ends of seasons.

But Ormandy's career in Minneapolis is remembered not for the hard times the orchestra went through but for the inspiration and escape from hard times that his concerts provided. As Frances Boardman put it, Ormandy seemed to be "trying to exert counter-leverage to the dark pressure of the times," reminding people that the spiritual, imaginative values in great art always transcend the rises and falls of the world's material fortunes.

These values his concerts vividly expressed. Ormandy chose his programs carefully, adjusting shrewdly what he wanted to play with what people might like to hear, striving always for balance. While his list of new and unheard works was by no means revolutionary, he achieved with good success what he once asserted were the proper proportions of symphony programming: two-fifths classical, two-fifths semimodern, and one-fifth ultramodern.

At the beginning of his second year Ormandy returned from a summer in Europe with the encouraging and patriotic statement that "our orchestra is better by far than any I heard in Europe," and the *Star*'s reviewer after the first concert notified "the future historian of the orchestra" that the thirtieth season opened with unprecedented brilliance and vitality in performance and direction. The occasion was glamorized by slim and silvery Lily Pons in her Minneapolis debut: a coloratura "without strain or torture to the audience."

Goeta Ljungberg, on the other hand, was a disappointment, the flaxen-haired soprano from Sweden forcing her tone and scooping her high notes. Other first-timers among the soloists in this low-budget season were Roland Hayes, the Negro tenor who impressed by his ethereal spirit and sensitive skill as a song craftsman, and Elsa Anneke, the gifted Duluth pianist, who played the Grieg concerto.

Despite the depression and the qualified success of the fund drive, Ormandy was signed for a three-year term. A new platform was installed on Northrop's cement-bottomed stage, raising the orchestra a few inches from the floor and giving better resonance to its tone. Ormandy retained the new orchestral pattern he had established the year before, the so-called Stokowski arrangement which put the cellos to the right of the conductor and massed the second violins with the firsts at the left front. This alignment continued, off and on, until Antal Dorati returned the second violins to the right of the stage in 1951. Ormandy also was the first to seat the orchestra flat on the platform, as a further means of giving the strings a fighting chance against the back-row brass.

Ormandy's contract allowed him frequent absences for guest assignments in the East, where he wished to retain his foothold and where audiences apparently showed no resentment at the intrusion. Four times during this season the eupeptic conductor shuttled between Minneapolis and New York and Philadelphia, each time gathering fresh encomiums. During his leaves various hands took over: Paul Lemay, Eugene Goossens, and Donald Ferguson. After an eleven-year interval, Ferguson again conducted his *Symphonic Waltz,* leading the orchestra, as he was later to lead his University Bach Society, like a scowling Svengali laying a hypnosis on his musical forces.

Whistling in the Dark

Charles Courboin, the French organist, was on hand to help dedicate the new organ in Northrop, playing Widor's Sixth symphony with the orchestra with majestic effect. One of the big premières of the season was the Rachmaninoff Third piano concerto, with Vladimir Horowitz summoning a kind of "diabolical romanticism" in his conception of the work, but using fingers and wrists which were definitely of the steel age. He was held over the weekend to play the Tschaikowsky B flat minor concerto at a Sunday "pop."

This season was also marked by one of the major and best remembered projects of the Ormandy regime: the performance, for the first time in Minneapolis, of the Verdi *Requiem*. This was prepared and performed as a tribute to Emil Oberhoffer, who died of cancer in San Diego, California, in May 1933.

Since his resignation as conductor eleven years before, Oberhoffer had led a semi-public, semi-retired life. He had filled Walter Rothwell's post as conductor of the Los Angeles Symphony for a time after Rothwell's death (this was the same Rothwell who had been Oberhoffer's rival as conductor of the St. Paul Symphony); guest-conducting appearances had frequently taken him to San Francisco, St. Louis, and Detroit; and he had been a great favorite at the Hollywood Bowl whenever he conducted there. But he had returned for long periods to his home, "The Towers," at Orchard Lake, fifteen miles south of Minneapolis in the Minnesota River valley. There he loved to put on old clothes and use his hands in cultivating his garden, laying cement walks, and even building his plumbing and electric power systems, which were his special pride. He spent much time at his piano; the writer remembers vividly the sound of a Bach *Invention* drifting through open windows as he approached the Oberhoffer door for the only conversation he ever had with that gracious and gallant music master.

A large singing aggregation was mobilized for the *Requiem* in tribute to Oberhoffer and was given the name of Twin City Symphony Chorus. It survived one more season, an extremely busy one in which it sang the *Messiah*, the Mahler *Resurrection* symphony, and the almost unsingable *Secular Mass* of Paul Nordoff.

Trained by Rupert Sircom, organist and choirmaster at Westminster Presbyterian Church, and conducted by Ormandy, who learned not only every note but every word of Verdi's semi-operatic tribute to Manzoni, the chorus sang the *Requiem* with a "proud, ringing tone that boomed like a big Bertha" when the baton flashed. The soloists were four of the ablest and best known singers of the community: Corinne Frank Bowen, soprano; Adair McRae Roberts, contralto; George Hultgren, tenor; and Berthold Busch, baritone. The performance served as a moving memorial to Oberhoffer, and as a piece of music proved such an attraction that it was repeated the following Sunday afternoon for a "pop" audience.

Less than a year later Ormandy was called upon to perform the last musical rites for the orchestra's second conductor, Henri Verbrugghen, with three of the little Belgian's favorite compositions: the prelude to *Lohengrin* and the Beethoven Seventh and Franck D minor symphonies.

Verbrugghen, like Oberhoffer, had not strayed far from the orchestra after his retirement as its conductor. Following his recovery from the cerebral hemorrhage in 1931, he had spent a spring and summer on his son's ranch in northern Minnesota and had then joined the faculty of Carleton College in Northfield, Minnesota, as head of its music department. It was in Severance Hall on the Carleton campus that he made his last concert hall appearance. He, members of his quartet, and his son, Dr. Adrian Verbrugghen, brain surgeon and cellist, were giving a chamber music program that opened with Brahms' G minor piano quartet. It was soon obvious to his colleagues that Verbrugghen's performance as first violin was erratic, with skipped passages indicating faulty vision, the telltale symptom of his earlier stroke. He could not be persuaded to leave at the pause after the first movement, so James Messeas pulled one of the strings off the bridge of his cello, then pleaded a broken string as reason for not going on. Verbrugghen was led off and

Whistling in the Dark

Jenny Cullen took over his part in the quartet. He died in North-field six months later, in November 1934.

The Symphony's memorial program in his honor followed by one week its final musical tribute to Richard Lindenhahn, veteran horn player, who had died shortly after hurrying to a rehearsal of *Ein Heldenleben*. Coincidences were noted: It had been at a rehearsal of *Heldenleben* three years before that Verbrugghen collapsed, and it had been Lindenhahn who sprang to his aid in Northrop's basement practice room.

The Ormandy years in Minneapolis are remembered more perhaps for the high and steady level of interpretive excellence extending through the whole period than for specific performances recalled as "peaks" of this or that season. But several ambitious ventures were undertaken, among them the Verdi *Requiem,* already mentioned, the Mahler Second symphony in C minor (*Resurrection*), and the Bruckner Seventh and Beethoven Ninth symphonies. These were Ormandy's heaviest productions, in point of intensive preparation and in the size of musical forces involved.

Three of these works — all but the Mahler — were presented in one season, 1933–34, which stood at about the midway point of Ormandy's Minneapolis sojourn. The Bruckner Seventh had not been exhumed for a quarter-century, and the conductor felt that its importance, and its difficulty for listeners, justified a few words on Bruckner as a preface to its performance. This, Ormandy's first talk at a symphony concert, was an engaging plea for understanding of a neglected artist and it resulted in keener attention to, if not keener enjoyment of, the maundering and disjointed symphony.

With Bruckner taken care of, the conductor turned next season to that other symphonic inflationist, Gustav Mahler, and scheduled the ninety-minute *Resurrection* symphony. This occupied a whole evening, required several tons of backstage bells, three hundred and fifty singers, and orchestras both off stage and on.

Engineering ingenuity was needed to devise a method to transmit the beat of Ormandy's baton to the smaller orchestras beyond his vision. The problem was solved by connecting wires to a push button under the foot of J. Andrew Cooper, second concertmaster, who as he played tapped his foot to Ormandy's tempos. This pedal time-beating caused nine electric lights to wink on and off in the back reaches off stage.

The search for proper equipment to make the stentorian bell tones was difficult. Varying lengths of streetcar rail were at first considered, and rejected, and finally five bells from the old St. Paul courthouse were located in a storage garage. Three of them were carted off to Northrop. They were heavy, and the heaviest of the three was swung in on cables after the backstage doors had been taken off.

Unfortunately, the net result of all this frantic search and laborious installation was an unmusical thud with no carrying power, even when the bells were struck with fifty-pound sledge hammers.

But the performance otherwise was everything that hard work, careful planning, and long drill of the choristers and orchestra could achieve in dramatic re-creation of a cumbersome and ultimately tiresome work. The *Star*'s critic, no Mahlerite, was restless and patronizing, and remarked that "we can learn more about death and resurrection in five minutes of Bach than from ten times five minutes of Mahler." A month after the Friday night performance the chorus, orchestra, and soloists (Ann O'Malley Gallogly and Corinne Frank Bowen) assembled again for a second performance for "pop" customers and also for Victor engineers, who recorded the work in its entirety at that concert.

Ormandy was the medium for introducing to the Twin Cities such central Europeans and countrymen as Zádor, Zemachson, Esterházy, Wladigeroff (the first Bulgarian in the orchestra's repertoire), and Kodály, and for first hearings of works by the more familiar Dohnányi. These represented an invasion from a new quarter. In the Verbrugghen days new compositions had stemmed largely from the French and Italian schools, represented

Henri Verbrugghen, "vigorous scholar of the podium"

Richard Lindenhahn, French horn

*Three of the mainstays
of the Verbrugghen ensemble*

Henry C. Woempner, flute

Georges Grisez, clarinet

High competence in the strings

Engelbert Roentgen, cello

Jenny Cullen, violin

Paul Lemay, viola
and assistant conductor

*A good orchestra not only must
be conducted well; it must also
be managed well*

Mrs. Carlyle Scott, a manager
of "imagination and
energetic showmanship"

Arthur Gaines, in whom "love of
music was linked with business ability and a cool head for figures"

Northrop Auditorium on the campus of the University of Minnesota,
home quarters of the Symphony since 1930

Eugene Ormandy, "a musical meteor" on the Minneapolis scene

"a great musical narrator . . . an eloquent orator with a flame-touched wand"

Sumner T. McKnight, E. L. Carpenter, and John S. Pillsbury
planning a fund-raising campaign

Emil Weflen and Sam Segal waiting with sledge hammers
to ring the bells in Mahler's *Resurrection* symphony. "The net
result . . . was an unmusical thud."

*Veteran orchestra members
whose years of service by 1952
totaled one hundred and fifty*

Henry J. Williams

Carlo Fischer, Ed Schugens, and William Faetkenheuer

Dimitri Mitropoulos, "the devout, aspiring
El Greco of the concert hall"

During the war years
a manual laborer with
the Red Cross mobile
blood donor unit

Climbing the Grand Teton — "the
high and hazardous mountain
was his symbol"

In the dual role of pianist-
conductor, a seventh wonder

"He springs down among the violins pulling out their theme . . .

. . . he points with a fierce index finger into the horns"

Mitropoulos discussing a score with Harold Ayres, concertmaster for sixteen seasons, until Louis Krasner took over in 1944

A "pop" concert in the Minneapolis Auditorium, where the lure of beer and light refreshments was added to tuneful music

Listening to the playback after recording the Tschaikowsky B flat minor piano concerto with Artur Rubinstein as soloist. Fred Lynch, left, RCA recording engineer, watches Mitropoulos' reaction

Beret and mountaineer's knapsack,
Mitropoulos' trademark on tours

The tent in Aspen,
Colorado, where Mitropoulos and
the Symphony were the main musical
inducement at the Goethe festival in the summer of 1949

Donald Ferguson, musicologist,
composer-conductor, author of the
program notes since 1930

Frances Boardman, long-time critic
for the *St. Paul Dispatch-
Pioneer Press*

Critic John Sherman listening as Benny Goodman and Dimitri
Mitropoulos form a mutual admiration society

Antal Dorati, builder for the future

by such composers as Ravel, Casella, Malipiero. That was the era when the Pro Musica organization sent into the hinterland various musical notables, including Ravel, who played an indifferent piano at the Minneapolis Institute of Arts). In a later period, after Mitropoulos arrived, the English (Walton), the Germans (Hindemith), and the Russians (Shostakovitch) were to have their innings, along with the new Americans and the exponents of atonalism.

The many Ormandy evenings remembered for their successes vie, in recollection, with the few recalled for odd and off-beat aspects, for personalities that did not fit the occasion or sometimes overwhelmed it, for those instances where for various reasons soloists and orchestra did not make close connections.

When Fritz Kreisler first shared the stage with Ormandy in Minneapolis, the difference between the impetuous introduction by the orchestra as it sailed into the Beethoven violin concerto and the violinist's almost feminine delicacy when he took up his solo was so marked as to throw the whole conception off balance, until conductor and orchestra adjusted themselves to the situation. Kreisler had arrived late that day, and there had been no time for rehearsal.

Two popular male singers were largely a disruptive influence, for different reasons. One was the Italian tenor Nino Martini, of dulcet tone and smooth delivery, who in November 1935 proved rather too saccharine for the symphonic environment. He lacked in inspiration as well as clear-cut rhythm, said Nilsson, who judged that he was indisposed because he coughed in his cuff. Sherman reported that Martini's songs were like six or seven chocolate sundaes in a row, and Davies, taking issue with the singer's encores, objected to his "telling us about some girl that he stuck in his pocket" — a reference to the song *I Carry You in a Locket in My Pocket*.

The other idol, arriving three months later, caused the largest female stampede in local musical history. He was baritone Nelson Eddy, making his bow in Minneapolis at a special Thursday afternoon concert attended by a fluttering mass of women estimated by one frightened male observer at forty thousand head, or so it seemed. An audience of housewives, schoolgirls, maiden aunts, schoolma'ams, salesgirls on furlough, comptometer operators, stenographers, dowagers, housemaids, and girl scouts made what was called "the most massive ladies matinee" in the annals of the city.

The remarkable thing about the event was that Mr. Eddy had a good voice; his only major competition was the well-worn César Franck symphony and another male blond, Eugene Ormandy, whose luster paled somewhat beside that of the glamorous Eddy. The baritone's program, far better than Martini's, included Mozart and a Mahler song cycle.

The most shocking and ludicrous evening of the Ormandy reign, and one of the most curious in the orchestra's history, was an April night in 1935 when Feodor Chaliapin, the aging Russian basso, knocked symphonic traditions galley-west and threw a dignified Friday evening program out of gear, much to the suppressed fury of Conductor Ormandy.

Chaliapin had been heard several times before in Minneapolis; on one occasion, when he was suffering from a severe cold, he had given a half-singing, half-coughing program for the Apollo Club.

This time when the actor-singer emerged on Northrop's stage, he struck a posture of amazed delight as if the concert were a surprise party arranged in his honor. This pose set the amiable and mischievous tone of the evening, and from then on Chaliapin took charge with impish irresponsibility. He served as his own announcer, apologized for his broken English (which he said was "suffering from tuberculosis"), rearranged the order of his songs and interpolated new ones, even announced the intermission, explaining with a grimace that he wanted to smoke "one cee-gar-et."

After the recess he all but reduced the concert to a shambles, singing encores wherein (1) he simulated drunkenness and (2) coyly mimicked a kiss whose explosive smack resounded to the last balcony row. "The worst of all," reported the decorous Nilsson, "was that his vitality could not be sufficiently checked to keep him from interfering with the conducting." It was this maneuver that particularly enraged Ormandy, while it kept Chaliapin in constant motion, strolling this way and that, turning his back to the audience to wave his hands at the men, and trying frantically to shush them in loud passages.

Only to those who have suffered from the oppressive gentility of conventional concert hall behavior did the eccentric basso's clowning appeal as healthily subversive. Indisputable, at any rate, was the *Star*'s comment that "such buffoonery has twice its normal effect in surroundings consecrated to the good, the true, and the beautiful."

Also to be listed among the curiosa of the Ormandy period was the first appearance of the Cecelian Singers with Minneapolis Symphony support in April 1934. These eighty lyric ladies have reformed since (and changed their name to the *Cecilian* Singers), but in those days they were angelically garbed in Grecian classic robes and swayed rhythmically in various stage patterns as they sang, meanwhile being "painted," according to Sherman, "in various soft hues applied by a very intelligent electrician." To the relief of some in the audience the Cecelians had by this time discarded one of their former memorable effects: hand-held roses each of which concealed an electric bulb that lighted up at certain passages in a song.

The chorus' appearance on stage was soothing to the eye accustomed to the severe and static uniforming of most choral groups, and the musical program it offered in 1934 was not too taxing, devoted as it was to good cheer, sentiment, vernal gaiety, religious faith, and mother love. The *Star* averred that "there was quite a bit of mother love, and we think the proportion on hand last night should not be exceeded in the future."

Another singing organization of wider fame and higher aim, the St. Olaf Lutheran Choir of Northfield, directed by F. Melius Christiansen, began its annual visits to the Minneapolis Symphony's stage after the orchestra moved from Eleventh Street to the campus in the thirties. These appearances, always well attended, regularly brought to the city the current crop of Christiansen choristers in peak vocal form, usually at or toward the end of their touring schedule, and the peremptory, unshowy directing of the stocky conductor came to be a symbol of the finest clarity, intonation, and precision in *a cappella* art.

Ormandy did not have much use for jazz; it was too closely associated with the Broadway world he had left behind. So Paul Lemay in 1934 took on the Gershwin *Rhapsody in Blue,* which returned for the first time since its dubious entry on the symphonic scene six years before. This time the piano solo benefited by the wiry and crisp style of Ramona Gerhard, but the orchestra again was too heavy and set up too large a frame for Gershwin's "blues" and his swift, whimsical figures. The *Rhapsody* marked the second appearance with the orchestra of Miss Gerhard, who was to become one of the city's prominent radio artists and a frequent pianistic aide for the Symphony. Her bow, made three months before, had been in the piano role of the Sitwell-Lambert *Rio Grande.*

The period had its landmarks also in the left-handed virtuosity of Paul Wittgenstein, who had lost an arm in the war and who played one of the compositions which had been specially written for him, the Ravel piano concerto for the left hand; in the local bow of chubby, ten-year-old Ruth Slenczynski, who played the Mendelssohn G minor concerto in a half-standing position and had to jump for her fortes and sforzandos; in the first appearance of that newest and most exciting of Brünnhildes, Kirsten Flagstad, who sang beautifully without twitching a muscle; in the debut of the latest conqueror of the cello, tall and black-browed Gregor Piatigorsky; in the visit of that amazingly coordinated union of man and violin, Nathan Milstein; in the evening dominated by the man described as the "present caretaker of the soul of Beethoven," pianist Artur Schnabel, who played the C minor concerto with granite-like rectitude and shining simplicity of purpose.

The return of Rachmaninoff to introduce his *Rhapsody on a*

Whistling in the Dark

Theme of Paganini in November 1935 was a momentous event. The "gaunt, wise ogre in evening dress" shambled to the piano to evoke from it the blazing fires of eloquence and the slow flame of poetry. And it was that somber Russian's C minor concerto which Walter Gieseking chose for his second appearance with the orchestra, playing as before with his nose nearly on the keys and summoning cascades of musical thunder and the faintest gossamers of sound. Myra Hess and Joseph Szigeti, old favorites, reaped their usual rapt tributes, and Lotte Lehmann plunged into her songs "like a diver leaping headlong into the water," although the orchestral settings of her Strauss lyrics that night seemed pretentious and heavy.

The orchestra's personnel through the Ormandy-and-depression epoch remained fairly constant; among other reasons for that situation, the employment market for orchestral musicians was anything but lively. It was a time of holding on rather than one of change and migration. The gypsy that is in most musicians hugged his hearth and job, the foot-loose became the wary and stay-at-home.

Three important shifts in principals' positions must be recorded: In 1934 Emil Opava succeeded Henry C. Woempner as first flute and became one of the most valued of the orchestra's soloists, and in 1935 Frank Miller left the Philadelphia Orchestra to succeed Jascha Schwarzmann in the first cellist's chair. Handsome and young (just twenty-five), Miller not only added markedly to the youthful good looks of the orchestra's front phalanx (for years he was a cynosure of feminine eyes) but contributed a warm tone and an athletic vigor of technique to its tonal ensemble. In the same season another veteran-to-be took up residence in the woodwind section: William Santucci, whose rich bassoon tone and faultless phrasing have been a continuing delight through the years since.

Other changes involved Jacob Heidrich, who headed the second violins in 1933; the indispensable Karl Scheurer, who became second concertmaster in 1935; and Al Rudd, returning in 1934 to the first violins after a long career as theater orchestra conductor and soloist. Rudd had been a familiar fixture for many years at the old Orpheum vaudeville house on Seventh Street.

Probably nothing that happened while Ormandy was in charge of the Minneapolis Symphony did more for its future financial health and international prestige than the recordings that RCA Victor started making in January 1934. That year marked the first real tapping of an income source which by 1951 had brought $400,000 in royalties into the Symphony's coffers (this includes receipts from Columbia records made under Mitropoulos).

The year 1934 was a low and a slack one for recording firms, as for so many other enterprises. The Radio Corporation of America had bought out the old Victor Talking Machine Company with no great enthusiasm for the profit possibilities of records, and its musical director, Charles O'Connell, was seeking some means of injecting new interest and new vitality into the company's catalogue. He felt, as he recently wrote in his book, *The Other Side of the Record,* that "new and good recordings were the only possible starting point for the rebuilding of the record business."

With that in mind, he acted on a suggestion from Arthur Judson, Ormandy's manager, that the Minneapolis Symphony would be a likely medium for these "new and good recordings." His firm was disinclined to invest much in new recordings, and to his delight O'Connell discovered that the Minneapolis orchestra could be employed for recording without extra compensation. The Orchestral Association's contract with the Symphony men specified a designated number of work hours per week in return for their salaries, and this work could be for rehearsals, concerts, broadcasts, or any other performing job. (This contract has since been changed.)

So O'Connell and his technical crew hastened to Minneapolis and spent several feverish days making a large number of recordings: a bonanza for Victor and O'Connell (who "acquired them virtually for nothing") and ultimately a rich source of revenue for the Orchestral Association — if not for Ormandy, who had relinquished his royalties and later wished he hadn't.

These first Victor recordings of the Minneapolis Symphony were skillfully made, as were those of a year later, and despite the advances in recording technique since that time, still sound brilliant and colorful today. The old acoustical Brunswick discs made in Verbrugghen's time had long since become obsolete, and they had never sold particularly well. By this time, too, Brunswick had bowed out as a recording firm, having sold this part of its business to Warner Brothers in 1930.

The sessions with O'Connell and his men were tense, concentrated, and efficient. The walls of Northrop's stage were blanketed with canvas to reduce resonance and tonal "bounce," and off stage at right the cylindrical slabs of stearin and beeswax revolved under needles that engraved the vibrations transmitted by microphones and wires from the stage. There was much rehearsal, much go-and-stop playing, many pauses for adjustments and retakes. O'Connell's buzzer frequently brought peremptory halt to the music when certain instruments or instrumental groups registered poorly, or when a distant slamming door or footsteps in the corridor intruded on the musical sound.

It was a nerve-racking ordeal, where either a sneeze or a musician's fluff could ruin six man-hours of work or four inches of grooves. Critic Frances Boardman, who attended one of the sessions, witnessed the recording in a state of virtual paralysis. Later she said she was deathly afraid that one of her stockings would run noisily during a pianissimo.

Other extracurricular activities for the orchestra during the period were mostly in front of radio microphones, and the peak in this phase of its work was reached in 1933–34 when eleven concerts were broadcast over KSTP and thirteen over WCCO.

Among the benefit concerts was one for the Wartburg Hospice which took the orchestra on a sentimental journey to the old homestead at the Lyceum Theater in November 1933. The occasion was *gemütlich* and nostalgic, the environment (not yet modernized at that time) somehow provincial after Northrop's

"Tempest . . . sunshine; demon . . . cherub"

spacious interior. Older concertgoers who were present were prompted to muse on the vast amount of great music that had been played under the old-fashioned green chandeliers on the Lyceum stage.

Touring between 1931 and 1936 encompassed much the same geography as in earlier years but the number of concerts dwindled. Some backers of the orchestra almost suffered heart failure when they saw their band take off in icicle-hung railroad cars in the dead of a depression winter, seeking to lure dollars from the pinched citizenry of cold and far-off cities. Those were the tours from which Mrs. Scott dispatched to the home office by the fastest means of postal delivery the checks she received from local managers, so as to clear them with the least possible delay. One large check from one manager was not converted into coin of the realm for a full year after issuance, but on the whole fee payments were prompt and cashable, and earned the orchestra more by traveling than if it had sat nervously at home.

The traveling orchestra then cost nearly $1000 a day, and fees ranged generally from $1500 to $2500. New Orleans paid $5000 for three concerts; Palm Beach's fee was $6000. At the other end of the scale was Wadena, Minnesota (population 2500), where the orchestra paused en route to Winnipeg to play for expenses: $1000.

The tours trod familiar itineraries through the South and Midwest, but did not chance New York. The one hundred and eighty pieces of baggage, the $100,000 worth of instruments, the eight trunks bulging with scores were trundled from city to city and town to town: Chicago, Pittsburgh, and New Orleans were the big spots (sometimes the tough ones as regards critics), while Georgia and Florida offered balmier climes for the musical troupers who for a time had left behind their bills and families and Minnesota's subzero blasts.

Pittsburgh dragged out an old and reliable metaphor: Ormandy was "Lochinvar out of the West," as Verbrugghen and Oberhoffer had been before him. The bouquets, generally, outnumbered the brickbats as the orchestra probed the southern shores of the Great Lakes and descended into the cotton and citrus belts. Chicago was on the whole receptive to the new and little-known conductor of the Minneapolis group, and at times its critics permitted themselves to be thrilled. Herman Devries of the *American* referred to the "magical baton" of Ormandy and an aggregation of players today ranking "among the 'star' orchestras." Karleton Hackett hailed the young Hungarian as "a personality" and was impressed by his sense of command, "poetic, fiery, yet self-controlled."

On the other hand, Albert Goldberg, speaking for the *Chicago Herald Examiner,* found the Brahms First essentially meaningless, lacking proportion and a sense of form, with distorted contrasts of tempos — conductorial failings one never would have suspected by reading the rapturous Twin Cities reviewers. In Pittsburgh another dissenter's voice was raised when J. Fred Lissfelt complained of monotony of conception and a hammer-and-tongs beat from a leader who was "a little obvious in his climaxes and a bit stagy altogether."

Back in Chicago Glenn Dillard Gunn of the *Herald Examiner* conceded that the orchestra had improved since Ormandy assumed control, but drawing on a long memory judged that it had not reached the artistic excellence it enjoyed under the late Emil Oberhoffer. The devotion to Oberhoffer has been tenacious and well founded, in the Twin Cities and elsewhere, and it still exists in mid-century.

Ormandy left Minneapolis almost as abruptly as he came. He was a musical meteor that flashed suddenly on the Minneapolis scene, burning there with steady brilliance for a seemingly short five years, then making swift flight back to the East whence it came. His leave-taking at the end of the 1935–36 season, to become associate conductor and later musical director of the Philadelphia Orchestra, was a stroke of the inevitable. "It was like a love affair," said one sad but resigned admirer, "that you knew couldn't last."

In the winter of 1935–36 Leopold Stokowski announced his decision to withdraw from his duties as full-time director of the

Philadelphia organization, and on January 2 Ormandy was named the new co-conductor, with a three-year contract. It was a quick coup, with Arthur Judson pulling the strings, and it happened without Mrs. Scott's foreknowledge. Relations lately between the manager and conductor ("Mother" and "Gene" to each other in the earlier years) had cooled; Ormandy's attitude oscillated between deference and rebellion. Many a stormy dialogue hinged on the issue of modern works, which Ormandy wanted to play but which Mrs. Scott deemed too costly for the budget and too advanced for a mass audience.

O'Connell is authority for the statement (in *The Other Side of the Record*) that a major motivating factor in Philadelphia's choice of Ormandy was the probability that he would carry on capably the role that Stokowski had made so lucrative to the orchestra: that of a recording conductor. Ormandy's success in this specialized function had been demonstrated in his recordings with the Minneapolis Symphony, and as it turned out he proved equally successful in keeping the Philadelphia unit one of the best and most recorded of all symphony organizations.

Ormandy's Minneapolis contract still had a year to run at the time of Philadelphia's bid. But the opportunity offered him was such a large and challenging one, and what he had done to lift the Minneapolis orchestra out of the economic mire of the early thirties had been such a unique and lasting service, that there was little quibbling about letting him go. E. L. Carpenter reported the board's unanimous decision when he announced that Ormandy would leave at the end of the 1935–36 season. "We have realized for some time," he said, "that we could not retain his services permanently."

The blow of Ormandy's precipitate departure was softened somewhat by the promise that he would return twice the following season, to open the Minneapolis series in November and to close it with a five-week visit in the spring of 1937. This promise was only half fulfilled — wisely so, since Ormandy's influence at both start and finish might have spelled domination. He did conduct four Friday concerts and one "pop" in November, but for the rest of the season his post was filled by a succession of six guest conductors — making an interregnum not unlike the transition year between Oberhoffer and Verbrugghen in 1922–23.

Ormandy's last program as regular conductor was a sold-out Strauss matinee of the kind he had made so popular in Northrop. "Ormandy gave us his prettiest baton magic, and the orchestra responded to a man, alert on every cue and ready to die for dear old Rutgers, or for Ormandy in this case," commented the *Star*. The audience was hugely pleased, one woman being so happy that she fainted from delight and had to be carried out.

The post-mortems on the Ormandy career in Minneapolis were written in contrasting moods of elation that "our" conductor had been plucked by one of the world's greatest orchestras and of rueful resignation that somebody had stolen "our" man. Davies declared that Ormandy had been a stimulant to both players and hearers, and a tower of strength to assisting soloists. And Frances Boardman in St. Paul, one of the sorriest to see Ormandy leave, noted the forlorn mien of many a concertgoer that April afternoon and quoted the sad refrain heard on all sides: "We'll never hear these things played like that again."

The *Star* summed up the music under Ormandy's baton, music which, first of all, had been dramatic. "Ormandy is a great musical narrator; he understands the 'plotting' of music so that suspense, dénouement, and climax carry the nth degree of force and conviction. He has excelled in all music in which this dramatic quality is foremost. He has been less a poet and scholar than a dramatist, an eloquent orator with a flame-touched wand."

On the Mountain Top

OBERHOFFER was the poet, Verbrugghen the scholar, Ormandy the dramatist. Dimitri Mitropoulos was the mystic and missionary. More than any other conductor before him, he regarded a concert performance as an act of faith and a spiritual necessity, a high and holy rite whereby the public was not so much to be entertained as led to the mountain top.

And while some of the public, as time went on, did not always want to climb to the peak, being of shorter wind than Mitropoulos and less eager for the heights he had charted, they were acutely aware of musical experiences the like of which they had never before undergone. There was a compulsion in this conductor's music that could be accepted or resisted, as the case might be, but never ignored.

Like Ormandy before him, Mitropoulos was a question mark when Twin Cities concertgoers first saw and heard him on the night of January 29, 1937. He was an unknown quantity to the general public and to most of the orchestra's board. And history repeated itself that night, in a heightened version, when an audience that is considered one of the calmest and coldest-handed in the country became an excited mob that staged the nearest thing to a riot ever seen in Twin Cities concert halls. Wild-eyed

227

spectators cheered and shouted bravos, clapped strangers on the back, and otherwise acted as if they were under the influence of strong stimulants.

The stimulants, as a matter of fact, were strong. The Greek on the podium seemingly had given music another dimension, a transcendence above and beyond itself, and by some spiritual fury and technical legerdemain had given a music-playing machine the tongue of angels.

To the audience that night Mitropoulos appeared to be a fanatic who had sold his soul to music and conducted the orchestra like a man possessed. Bald, lithe, and rawboned, he exploded from the wings, walked to the rostrum with the loose-limbed lope of a professional hiker, spread his long arms and tapering pianist's fingers in a mesmeric gesture.

With the first downbeat he started punching the air barehanded, unleashing a weird repertoire of frenzied gestures and scowls and grimaces that registered every emotion from terror to ecstasy. His quivering frame and flailing fists gave the picture of a man quaking with a peculiarly vital and rhythmic form of palsy. It was as if the music were an electric current that passed through his body to make it jerk and vibrate.

The impression was that of a leader pulling tone from ninety instruments by almost physical coercion, by exhortation and pleading and command, that tied him by invisible bonds to each musician before him. It was a memorable sight — especially memorable because the sound that went with it was intensely compelling, music so full of blood, muscle, and nerves as to seem alive and sentient, and bearing unmistakable overtones of great thought and aspiring spirit.

His program contained the Beethoven overture *Leonore* No. 2, the Beethoven Second symphony, his own arrangement of the Bach G minor *Fantasia and Fugue,* and — *pièce de résistance* of the evening — the Respighi *Toccata* for piano and orchestra. In this Mitropoulos performed his most spectacular sorcery, that of conducting and playing simultaneously, with what appeared to be two sets of arms and fingers.

In sum it was a virtuoso performance, and its impact on the hearers was not to be explained this time, as it had been partially when Ormandy stepped into Verbrugghen's shoes five years before, by the contrast of a brilliant ensemble with a stodgy one. This was not a case of a dull orchestra suddenly coming alive; it was a case of a skillful orchestra reaching new and higher levels of inspiration.

After his first rehearsal, Mitropoulos declared that the Minneapolis musicians had "no bad habits," that they grasped every direction given them "before I finish saying it myself" — a tribute to the Ormandyan color, plasticity, and "steam" the orchestra still possessed, and which the new leader found quickly adaptable to his purposes.

The Symphony had been in the hands of a succession of guest conductors that 1936–37 season, and it had played ably under all of them, and for some of them splendidly. Ormandy had come back to open the season and, after a first concert that was rough in performance and blatant in some swollen Bach arrangements, carried on with the special conviction and dynamism the Hungarian always brought to his concert hall tasks.

He was followed in November by square-shouldered, longlegged Artur Bodanzky, who had conducted the orchestra once before, but so long ago (in 1918–19) that most concertgoers had not heard him or had forgotten him. Bodanzky's assets of lucidity and certainty, free of temperamental distortions, were a tonic to his hearers, especially in his Wagner, and an unofficial movement was soon afoot to make Bodanzky a once-a-year guest leader.

The third guest dimmed somewhat the focus that Bodanzky had brought to such sharp definition. He was Jerzy Bojanowski from Warsaw, a man poetic in appearance and interpretation, a persuader rather than a commander. His music often lacked fiber, clarity, differentiation and contrast in mood. Bojanowski took the orchestra on a short regional tour (there were no long tours in this guest season), and after two local concerts and four on the road he turned the baton over to Leon Barzin.

Belgian-born Barzin was musical director and conductor of the National Orchestral Association, an orchestra that served, among other things, as a "feeder" and source of supply for symphony orchestras throughout the country, and he produced in Minneapolis a sound, clearheaded tonal argument. He was young, versatile, and venturesome, with a wide repertoire. Without the color of Ormandy or the authority of Bodanzky, he still seemed to personify the kind of enterprise and forward-looking ideas that Minneapolis was seeking in a conductor.

There is evidence that Barzin was considered a likely candidate for the vacant post and that he expected the appointment; he was feted at a Symphony ball, and to a students' forum at the University of Minnesota he seemed to suggest the probability of his remaining: "People ought to know their orchestras," he said. "If I ever come to Minneapolis, it will be my job to open the doors."

But when Mitropoulos arrived it became obvious that the doors were to be opened by this man from Athens, disclosing vistas of experience in which "knowing your orchestra" would be mere supplementary knowledge. He conducted five concerts — two evening and two Sunday afternoon programs, plus one concert for students — his fifth one at the finish pulling the audience to its feet in a shouting ovation.

Ten days after his departure E. L. Carpenter announced from Northrop's stage what everyone wanted to hear, that Mitropoulos had been engaged. The news brought a burst of spontaneous cheers from the house and caused one critic to so far forget himself as to shout "Yippee-ee!" at a symphony concert.

Unavoidably, the rest of the 1936–37 guest season was anticlimactic after Mitropoulos' revelations. Two conductors remained to be heard in the regular series: the young and genial Britisher, Guy Fraser Harrison (who returned later to lead the orchestra in several annual attempts to make the town relax with light music, beer, and exhibition dancing), and the Spanish pianist, José Iturbi. The latter's conducting technique was not well developed at that time, being phlegmatic in style, with a kind of loose-reined hold on the orchestral forces. Howard Hanson directed a special postseason program made up entirely of American works.

Mitropoulos had come to Minneapolis on his second visit to America, the first, in 1936, having introduced him to Boston at the invitation of Serge Koussevitzky. The enthusiasm aroused at that first American concert convinced the Boston Symphony's management that he should be imported a second time. By coincidence, just before the Boston manager dispatched a cable asking Mitropoulos to return he received a phone call from Mrs. Carlyle Scott, who also wanted the Greek as a conductor. She was searching desperately for a conductorial "star" to fill in some February dates of her incomplete guest list for the coming season, and she had heard enough about Mitropoulos to suspect that he would be big news in Minneapolis.

So the cable to Athens carried a double invitation, and within two days a reply came back accepting both bids.

Mitropoulos had appeared as a musician on a wide and shifting front before his Boston and Minneapolis adventures, but only in Europe. Born in Athens in 1896, he was strongly drawn in his early years to the far less migratory calling of priest. The attraction was powerful; both his own nature and a long family tradition impelled him toward the church. The home atmosphere was deeply religious and the family had contributed notably to the church: two of his father's brothers were Orthodox monks, his paternal grandfather was a priest, his granduncle an archbishop of the Greek church. After visits to his uncles in a monastery on Mount Athos, the boy Dimitri dreamed of the serene and consecrated life he would live on the "holy mountain" of the Greek church, and of some day serving God through his own compositions. For he had grown deeply interested in music, having started piano lessons with his mother when he was seven. His formative years in that devout household gave him what he later called his attitude of looking upon art as a religion, and the practice of it as a kind of worship.

His increasing interest in the piano finally forced the choice between two ways of life each of which had profound appeal. The Greek church did not countenance music in its instrumental forms. When Dimitri found he would not be permitted to have a little harmonium, he knew then he could not be a monk on Mount Athos.

Like most who are unusually gifted musically, he early showed an omnivorous capacity to learn, not only in his absorption of scores but in his technical mastery of his chosen instrument. Before his teens he was at home at the keyboard and had memorized many opera scores, and at the age of fourteen he entered the Athens Conservatory, where he concentrated for six years on piano and composition. An odd and irrelevant tangent in his young life was his experience as a soldier-musician in the Greek army at the time of the Greek-Bulgarian war. Because he had played percussion instruments in the conservatory orchestra, he was assigned to play the drum in an army band!

His studies in composition led to his first major musical accomplishment: his composition of an opera, *Soeur Beatrice,* based on the French text of Maeterlinck's play. This project, completed in 1919, so impressed the professors that a handsome production was decided upon. A young dramatic soprano who later became a noted stage and screen actress, Katina Paxinou, sang the title role. A happy chance found the composer Camille Saint-Saëns in the audience. The aging Frenchman was vastly impressed by what he heard, and he did not keep his enthusiasm to himself. He wrote a long and laudatory article about the work for a Paris newspaper and, more practically, offered to aid the young man in furthering his studies in France. The offer was quickly followed by the city of Athens arranging a scholarship for a native son of high and demonstrated talent. Mitropoulos left for Brussels, where he studied under Paul Gilson, and then for Berlin and the studio of the noted Ferruccio Busoni.

Mitropoulos' career from this point ascended by sure and steady steps. Completing his scholarship studies, he obtained the position of assistant conductor at the Berlin Staatsoper, where he discovered that conducting was what he liked best and could do best. In his earlier years he had never planned to be a conductor, but now he committed himself to what he believed to be his true métier. He abandoned composition and piano, the latter — fortunately for concertgoers of the future — only temporarily. He remained at the Staatsoper until 1924, when he was called back to take charge of the Athens Conservatory orchestra, the leading instrumental organization of the city. His reputation grew apace in Greece, and soon leaped national boundaries. In 1930 he was lured back to Berlin for guest appearances with the Philharmonic, and his Continental career began.

As with Ormandy, a stroke of bad luck that turned to good gave the Athenian's career a sudden lift, spreading like wildfire the reports of his virtuosity. The noted pianist Egon Petri fell ill and was unable to fulfill an assignment to play the Prokofieff Third piano concerto at a Berlin concert Mitropoulos was conducting, and in the end the young conductor had to fill the breach and take on the chore himself.

His brilliance in the double role, and in the mechanistic and capricious measures of Prokofieff, made a sensation. This was in 1934, and thereafter he found himself saddled with the concerto as his conductor-pianist's specialty. He was invited to play the work in all the major music centers, riding with it to his first high-level fame.

With all his subsequent traveling in France, England, Italy, and the Soviet Union, he continued as the director in Athens, conducting the city's symphony in annual series of winter concerts and doing much to help it financially, buying instruments and conducting without fee. Even in those early years, Mitropoulos had contracted the admirable and not-too-common habit of dispensing his own funds for philanthropic, cultural, and educational purposes. He was always to be a willing contributor to deserving causes and persons.

Eventually, in 1936, came the invitation from America, specifically from Koussevitzky. He sailed for New York, whence he made his way to Boston, to inflame the normally noninflammable patrons of the Boston Symphony. A year later he was in Minneapolis.

After his five programs as guest conductor — hailed by Davies as a series "that for sheer glory of performance has never been equaled in this city" — there was a long intermission impatiently endured by his already large band of followers. He could not return until after six of the next season's sixteen concerts had been played.

This was because his loyalty and obligation to his Athens orchestra kept him abroad until January of 1938. For the interim, to open the Minneapolis season, he had recommended Daniele Amfitheatrof, an exiled White Russian and a pupil of Respighi, scion of a cultivated family whose members had contributed significantly to history and music. Amfitheatrof was tall and serious, whole-souled but immature in his conducting style, and certainly no adequate substitute for the kinetic and inspired Mitropoulos. His concerts on the whole were not successful.

For one of his programs he unburdened a shrill work of his own titled *Panorama Americana,* composed before he came to the United States. It was a kaleidoscopic canvas that emphasized urban aspects of American life — traffic, nightclubs, jazz — but scarcely plumbed below the surface. Sherman declared it should have been called *Picture of America by One Who Has Never Been in South Dakota.* The conductor's peculiar patronymic inspired several nicknames: Dan, Amfi, Dax, and finally (for musicians who gave up trying to pronounce it) Balcony.

When Mitropoulos returned from Europe early in January, Amfitheatrof made his way to Boston for a conducting assignment, returned to Minneapolis January 30 for a "pop" program, and then left for good, becoming in time an important musical figure in Hollywood's film world.

Minneapolis welcomed its new permanent conductor with fervor. The tonal alchemist was back. And both the musical and lay public soon realized that the Symphony had snared a rare and unconventional specimen of the conductor genus. At his rehearsals, wearing a black pull-over sweater, he guided the men without aid of score or baton. ("Conducting with a stick is something like playing the piano with gloves on," he had said.) It was immediately obvious that the music he was shaping up was indelibly imprinted on his mind, note by note and bar by bar, and in such a way as to be immediately available in his mind's eye, on any page or part of the page of the score. ("Hamlet doesn't walk on the stage reading his part. Why should I?")

On the platform he stamped, he clapped, he yelled, he crouched for the pianissimos and lifted beseeching hands, palms down, for sustained passages. In the climaxes he often jumped clear off the floor, landing on beat. These leaps were not merely exercise or outbreaks of physical exuberance; they had their intended effect on interpretation. Rupert Sircom tells of the time that his symphony chorus, singing at full volume in rehearsal, simply could not achieve a sharp sforzando that would top the preceding fortissimo passage sung at full lung power. Mitropoulos jumped off the floor — and the startled choristers exploded in a reflex sforzando that was entirely satisfactory.

From Brenda Ueland, a fervent Mitropoulos devotee, comes a vivid description of one of his practice sessions: "His face is lighted with joyful excitement; he springs down among the violins, pulling out their theme, bounds to point with a fierce index finger into the horns. To whip the rhythm, he leaps high, stamps his heels in pistol shots. It makes the heart race to see the terrific and wild exaggeration of his rehearsals. . . ."

With all this gymnastic vehemence, which shot strong and exhilarating currents through his players, the conductor was anything but a despot in his working relationships with those who helped him make music. Persuasion and kindness were his tools, not ruthless commands. As an orchestra conductor he would "rather be president of a republic than a dictator." He treated his men as his colleagues, yet he was human enough, with enough of the conductor's temperament, to explode occasionally when things went wrong. The outburst was usually followed by an apology.

Mitropoulos' concerts found only slightly subdued the rehearsals' physical frenzy in transmuting dead notes on the score to the living tonal tissue. Only the platform leaps and the quick sorties into the ranks were missing. The music then became a life-giving tonic to his hearers, stepping up the levels of existence, adding new dimensions to their perceptions and consciousness.

These were the professional and public aspects of the Mitropoulos personality. It was soon evident that they issued from an unusual human being as well as an unusual musician. There was amazement when it became known that he chose to inhabit a bare cubicle at the university's Center for Continuation Study, within walking distance of his "work" at Northrop Auditorium. The crucifix he always wore at concerts beneath the white dress shirt was soon espied by reporters who sought him out in his dressing room.

He became known as the "monk in conductor's clothing," an ascetic whose monkish look was enhanced by deep-set eyes, hollow cheeks, and tonsured head. It was rumored (on the sound basis of fact) that he was a man who gave his money away and worried more about his men's income than his own. His passion for the movies, through which, as he said, he absorbed in painless form the history and mores of his adopted country, made him a familiar figure to every ticket-seller and usher in Minneapolis.

The real Mitropoulos was a far more complicated and less easily definable person than these glib and partial, popular portraits indicate. His deep spirituality was linked with a sharply objective intellectuality that ventured far beyond theological borders; his was a mind of analytical and speculative force. He was capable of ruthless and iconoclastic appraisal of himself as well as others.

He once spoke in deprecating vein of the conductor, "to whom only the spotlight is important." If you are not good enough to be a great instrumentalist, "you become a conductor," he went on. "Quickly you develop a great artistic temperament. You let your hair grow a little longer. You are a conductor!" On a later occasion he declared that the conductor was lucky in that he "could always wave his hands," while instrumentalists often found their skills leaving them as age crept up on them. "Conducting is the coward's profession," he said, "because the conductor can blame the mistakes on his players, and who knows what his are?" Such self-diminishing statements were probably only exercises in humility, for behind them were a passionate devotion to music and a deep sense of responsibility as interpreter.

Mitropoulos the would-be monk was also a sophisticate, the ascetic was a man of the world, the boy who once wished to practice humility and virtue in a mountain top retreat grew up to be an internationalist. Raised in the strict tenets of the Greek Orthodox faith, he became in Minneapolis a devoted parishioner of a Protestant, Dr. Arnold Lowe, minister of Westminster Presbyterian Church. The man who had little personal vanity once spoke of his Berlin conducting days when he strove to be a "fashion plate" — an inclination later evident in his striking and individual garb and his midnight-blue full dress. The recluse was a cosmopolite who had conducted four annual seasons at Monte Carlo, a world center of wealth and luxury. The devout, aspiring "El Greco of the concert hall" was capable also of crackling expositions of the clever and heartless examples of latter-day French music.

The man who thought much about God had also been a fervent student of Friedrich Nietzsche and in his youth had made a pilgrimage to the grave of that iconoclast philosopher to pay homage to his memory. The man who relished western movies, once chortling with naive delight at a sequence showing a cowboy leaping from a second-floor window to the saddle of his waiting cayuse, dug deep into Sören Kierkegaard and was an avid reader of Thomas Mann.

The lonely, wifeless conductor, whose apartment (in later years at 510 Groveland) was a well-appointed but functional cell where he worked in seclusion in the late night hours or early dawn ones, often used sexual analogies to express his ideas about the conductor's role. For instance, he sometimes spoke of the conductor's ministrations on his orchestra as a sublimated sex act, the two of them combining to produce the "child," that is, the performance.

Each gives to the other, he said, what each has to give; each responds to the other, and in performance the conductor must be able to draw forth the "inner genius" of the orchestra. The performance then is a creative act in itself, which can achieve in the heat of creation an aim only approached in the preliminary preparation. In brushing up a passage at rehearsal, if it was not quite right after several tries, he would say, "Never mind, we'll understand each other at the performance." And oftener than not they did.

Again he would allude to a performance, particularly a performance of a difficult score, as a purge, a cleansing rite. The sense of sin was strong in him, and expiation could be gained by self-sacrifice and struggle for perfection, which in his case meant the sternest discipline in long hours of studying and absorbing his scores. The more difficult the score the more imperative was obedience to its demands. This involved an immolation of self as a duty the gifted must assume, as payment for being gifted, and as example for the world. "A man who has something to give the world *must* do more than he is required to do," he once said. "Humanity is served by extreme examples, like that of St. Francis embracing poverty and thus dramatizing the ideals of virtue, love, and service to mankind."

He often spoke of the importance of evil, without which the good would have no dynamic role in life, no resistance, no enemy to work against. The positive pole needs the negative pole to produce a current. No one knows better than the saint the necessity of evil.

Mitropoulos' great symbol was the mountain, the high and hazardous mountain, which he climbed both in actuality when he conquered the peaks of Mounts Shasta and Whitney and the Grand Teton, and figuratively when he grappled with intricate pieces of music that were virtually unmemorizable. Both gave him a heightened sense of challenge and fulfillment. His pride in reaching the top of Wyoming's Grand Teton — "the most fierceful mountain in the U.S." as he informed his friends in the late summer of 1946 — was tinged with dark satisfaction at being near danger and death and outwitting both. The fires of his temperament sometimes turned to ice; in the depths of his nature was a death-wish, and in moods of dejection he would speak of the kind of death he preferred, that of falling into the glacial silence of a crevasse. (The writer vividly recalls the unnerving experience of interviewing Mitropoulos over the radio when the maestro, just returned from a western trip, expatiated with a kind of somber relish on this kind of death. Only with difficulty was the interview lifted to a livelier plane.)

So Minneapolis, in making Mitropoulos its first musical citizen, had captured no clever *Kapellmeister* or orchestral entertainer, but a complex and profound mind to whom the assignment of making music was no pleasant sinecure but a symbol, and a means, of struggle and suffering. He would rather lift up his hearers, lead them across the dangerous crevasses, than give them diversion and transient pleasure.

His concerts were tremendously exciting, even if at times the music in them was "Mitropoulized" — overaccented and over-guided, even jerked and flagellated when he was in a high state of tension. Occasionally his expression was so violently personal as to prevent the original intentions of the music from coming through on their own terms. He was not often the kind of conductor who "steps aside" to let the music speak for itself, and there were few compositions he played that were not refracted through his temperament.

This temperament was Mediterranean, the kind that meets all experience, music included, with ardor and a whole-souled desire to live and act fully. The tone that issued forth was animated by the warm and airier spirit of what Americans call the "Latin" personality, as opposed to the heavier accent and logic of the northern and western European. And yet the logic, the structure, of what he played was the controlling factor: logic driven toward a goal, and cued generally to urgent tempos that rarely sagged, even in andantes and adagios.

Mitropoulos often spoke of musical interpretation as largely a matter of a man's pulse rate and physiological rhythms, of how every man has his own tempo. "If I walk faster than B, or slower than C, my interpretations will naturally be different from those of B and C."

Mitropoulos' tempo on the whole was brisk, with no waste motion or lag. His quality of mind likewise was presto — eager, sharp, intense, probing. His quality of spirit was essentially philosophical-religious. He could not help regarding himself as a priest, guide, and mentor, and he looked upon his musical gift as a sacred trust he could not debase even if integrity in its service meant opposition and disaffection from his public.

With such a man at the helm of the orchestra, the concert-going public in the late thirties entered the most unorthodox period, programmatically, of Minneapolis Symphony history: twelve years of stimulating, irritating, uplifting, exhausting concerts which rose to the highest and most glorious peaks of interpretation the orchestra had attained. It was an era of greatly extended horizons in musical, emotional, and spiritual experience. It offered programs of unprecedented severity and thorny content, of music and conducting that made the city for a time both a laboratory and an international capital of contemporary, experimental, and unconventional music.

Whatever else may be said of the Mitropoulos period, it must be granted that his listeners were in the hands of a genius those twelve years. Many were putty, some were stiff and reluctant clay. It is not always comfortable to live with a genius, but to take and to understand what he gives is a lucky opportunity for those who want to grow. It was a fructifying, maturing process even for many who lagged far behind the "teacher."

Mitropoulos' program policy, in general, was not hampered by the usual precepts of balance and variety in serving an attractive tonal "menu." By the same token it was unorthodox and unpredictable, often a direct reflection of the conductor's personal tastes and interests and his desire to explore. Rarely was it audience-conscious, although there were a few occasions when he pleased his hearers so assiduously (as on one tuneful evening when he staged a miniature Puccini festival with Eleanor Steber) that some suspected he was banking good will against the day of withdrawals.

Some of his programmatic trends began to show themselves in his first season as permanent conductor. One was severity, exemplified in the three main courses of his homecoming program — the Haydn *London,* Mozart Thirty-Ninth, and Beethoven First symphonies — and again a few weeks later in a concert containing only two works, the Mahler First symphony and the Beethoven Fourth piano concerto.

Another program characteristic arose from what appeared to be a spirit of whimsical experiment in choosing, for example, seven overtures for a Sunday program; in putting two Strauss tone poems cheek by jowl, *Don Juan* and *Death and Transfiguration.* In a later season he proffered an almost indigestible mixture whose components, served in a single evening, were the austerities of Bach (two fugues from *The Art of the Fugue*), the sentiment of Dvořák (*New World* symphony), the impressionism of Debussy (*La Mer*), and a shrill example of Casella that had a battle scene climax.

Another preoccupation, manifest more in the earlier than in the later years of Mitropoulos' tenure, was chamber music swollen to the full dimensions of the string orchestra. This was exemplified in his first season by the Beethoven opus 131 quartet, in the following season by the Grieg G minor and Beethoven F minor quartets, and later, most formidable of all, by the Weingartner orchestral arrangements of Beethoven's opus 133 *Grand Fugue* and his *Hammerklavier* piano sonata.

These inflations of works in small forms were programmed as a means of bringing to the Symphony public some of the riches of chamber music literature, and of adjusting them tonally to concert halls as large as railway stations. But in the opinion of Frances Boardman (who, until John Harvey succeeded her, was almost the sole dissenter among the local critics during the Mitropoulos period) these were not entirely successful, because the "difference between chamber music and orchestral music is something more than merely a difference in volume."

The Athenian in his first year also showed a predilection for the early romantics, specifically Mendelssohn and Schumann, two composers with whom concertgoers were to become familiar through much repetition before Mitropoulos departed. The fresh and airy lyricism of romanticism's "spring" appealed greatly to a conductor whose alter ego showed a vast appetite for intellectual modern works. Schumann, who wrote awkwardly for the orchestra, always had charm and sweet suasion in Mitropoulos' treatment of him; he always "sounded."

The new man soon revealed himself also as a member of the anti-lollypop school of "pop" conductors. The Sunday programs quickly took on the character of abbreviated Friday nights and frequently offered premières that were denied to the Friday-nighters. There was no element of condescension in Mitropoulos' attitude toward his Sunday audiences. He was like a teacher who treats his pupils not as freshmen but as a postgraduate class. Duplication was abhorrent to him. When he carried over an item from a Friday to a Sunday, it was most likely to be a major offering like *La Mer,* played first in November at night and revived in January for daytime listeners. Mitropoulos considered the afternoon audience every bit as adult in their interests as the after-dark audience.

Another memorable aspect of the Mitropoulos years was his occasional resumption of the pianist-conductor role. This always provided a thrilling show that deserved its definition as "one of the seven wonders of Minneapolis." With the piano lid removed to allow visibility to and from the orchestra, his arms would wave madly in the orchestral portions but always plummet to the keyboard precisely on cue, whereupon the shiny head and darting eyes took control until the hands were again free of the keyboard. It was an amazing exhibition of quick-witted, fleet-fingered integration.

In his first four years Mitropoulos played in this fashion the Respighi *Toccata,* an Aubert *Fantaisie* for piano and orchestra,

the Prokofieff C major concerto (the work he had made his own
in his European days), a Malipiero concerto, and the Bach
Brandenburg concerto No. 5. During the early forties he took a
recess from this man-killing form of making music (he was fully
aware, too, of its grandstanding effect), but in 1945 he repeated
the Respighi *Toccata* with great success and in 1946 took on
double responsibilities in a work he had commissioned from
Ernst Křenek, a concerto for piano and orchestra.

This Křenek concerto was a première in a program made up
wholly of premières, and here again Mitropoulos achieved a record that had not been matched by any predecessor. His score
of "firsts" was so high, and he so rarely resisted the temptation
to present new works that attracted him, that the orchestra
management finally developed an acute sensitiveness to premières, local, national, and world. It started deleting from the
printed programs the stars that indicated first performances, on
the theory that the concertgoers' feelings should not be un-
necessarily ruffled before the concert started — and that what
they didn't know wouldn't hurt them.

Many of these "firsts," which still bring a retrospective thrill
or shudder to those who recall them, were the good deeds of a
self-chosen champion of difficult if not lost causes. In his zeal
to bring to light music otherwise fated to blush unseen, Mitropoulos showed his concern for the underdog quite as significantly
as in his monetary aid to struggling students, his public and outspoken grousing about musicians' low salaries, and his social-
political beliefs, which for a time made him a follower of Henry A.
Wallace, advocate of "the common man."

Young composers, notoriously the most unheeded and least
exhibited of all arts practitioners, found in Mitropoulos a friend
and promoter and a paternalistic teacher who spurred them to
hard work and ever higher aims. More to their practical ad-
vantage, they discovered that he was that *rara avis* of his kind,
the conductor who actually performed works by composers who
were not only living but, worse yet, obscure.

For some of these composers, it was a case of propinquity

leading to friendship and friendship leading to advocacy. But with his warm, impulsive sympathies toward gifted and thwarted talent, Mitropoulos was never fooled in matters of art and technical craft; his mind was a cold and sharp critical tool when he inspected a score. If the score was hopeless he would not spare the feelings of the victim, providing the victim was salvageable. If the score was good, even potentially good, the conductor was kindled, and often would come to a quick, unalterable decision to play it. Whether or not the orchestra manager's hair turned grayer as a result of these rather capricious decisions can only be conjectured.

John Verrall, who taught theory and piano at Hamline University, a thirty-one-year-old composer with a personal, dynamic idiom, was the first of the local composers to come under Mitropoulos' sheltering wing. Verrall's *Rhapsody* for orchestra was introduced in 1939, his First symphony was given the cachet of a Friday première in January 1940, and in the following season his *Portrait of Man,* revealing an advance in contrapuntal skill, was brought before the public.

In the same season another native son, Ross Lee Finney, gained a hearing of his *Slow Piece for Strings,* a song-like, communicative, and sparely built composition which bespoke the composer's integrity of purpose and skill in fulfilling it. Later a young and dark-skinned Panamanian, Roque Cordero, an exchange student at the University of Minnesota, came under the tutelage of Mitropoulos, was routed into the composition classes of Křenek, and had his *Panamanian Overture* performed by the Minneapolis orchestra.

Not since the early days of the orchestra had so much composition nurtured on home grounds been publicly exposed and subjected to the audience test. There had been a long lapse in this field of endeavor, and many years had passed since the local composers of older schools — Stanley R. Avery, Donald Ferguson, J. Victor Bergquist, and James A. Bliss — had enjoyed the honor of Minneapolis Symphony performance.

The playing of these local works had the value of proving that new music could represent not only "now" but "here" — a demonstration accepted with varying degrees of stimulation and reluctance by ticket-holders.

None of the lessons Mitropoulos offered seemed harder for his hearers to swallow, or more bitter to their taste, than the one begun soon after the arrival of Ernst Křenek at Hamline University, where the Czech-Austrian composer became dean of the arts department. Křenek's coming led Twin Cities music naturally into the realm of atonalism, although as early as 1939 Mitropoulos had given concertgoers a sample of this esoteric idiom: three excerpts from the *Lyric Suite* by Alban Berg, who has been termed the romanticist and middle-of-the-roader of the atonal school. To prepare the twelve minutes of this curious and crafty music, the orchestra's string sections had rehearsed a total of seven hours, and the performance achieved a persuasion and clarity that carried conviction even if it did not enlist complete understanding.

Three years later, not long after Křenek's arrival, the orchestra performed his symphonic movement in variations form, *I Wonder as I Wander*, based on a North Carolina folk song, and followed it the next season with the American premières of his Second symphony and his *Cantata for War Time*. In 1946–47 came the piano concerto Mitropoulos had commissioned: a more communicative article than some of Křenek's other works, epigrammatic, full of technical mischief and dissonance, a spirited and almost playful work.

Mitropoulos had a justifiably high regard for the composer of *Jonny Spielt Auf* (the successful jazz opera Křenek composed before his conversion to atonalism), and it is incontestable that Křenek, with his wide musical culture, his seriousness, and his great teaching gifts, wrote a significant chapter in Twin Cities music history before he moved on to the West Coast in 1948. His advanced idiom and his seemingly arid and cerebral musical ideas made friends among only a handful of Symphony followers, but he was a germinal force as well as an uncomfortable novelty; if most listeners abhorred his music, he nevertheless developed a small coterie of creative pupils at Hamline and furthered interest in unfamiliar new and old music.

It was, however, the engagement of Louis Krasner to succeed Harold Ayres as concertmaster in 1944 that gave Minneapolis its first sustained encounter with the keyless twelve-tone music of Arnold Schönberg. Many Symphony patrons now began to discover that there were musical languages as difficult to apprehend as French would be to an Eskimo. But intelligibility, as such, was often overridden by the eloquence, sincerity, and compelling art of great music greatly expounded. Krasner had acquired a considerable reputation as a specialist in this field, much of it based on his brilliant recording of the Berg violin concerto with the Cleveland Orchestra, and his Berg specialty was soon presented at Northrop.

The Berg concerto is really a requiem, a moving piece of music by any definition. In it the composer has used the new musical language to clothe ideas and sentiments and emotions "which the modern creators of algebraic patterns," one critic averred, "have shunned as if they were infectious diseases." The concerto's first hearing in Minneapolis was a tensely brilliant collaboration of soloist, conductor, and orchestra, in which one of the most poignant expressions in modern music was given a performance that drew deeply on the skills and insights of two rabid champions, Krasner and Mitropoulos.

But this Berg concerto was only halfway up the mountain. Soon was reached the master himself, Arnold Schönberg. First came the string orchestra arrangement of his F sharp minor quintet for strings (with difficult vocal solos taken by Nancy Ness), and then, climactically, his almost unplayable violin concerto, performed with phenomenal skill and understanding by Krasner on November 30, 1945. That date marks atonalism's high-water mark in Minneapolis, and also the most astringent evening in Minneapolis' music history.

Schönberg was doubtless the ultimate test Mitropoulos imposed on his hearers, a portion of whom by this time were alienated and in rebellious mood. But the education that took them off safe and familiar musical ground widened their experience, whether or not they appreciated the stretching process. Furthermore it gave them the distinction (which they may not have relished) of being for several years the most valiantly and progressively served concert audience in the country, not excepting those in eastern centers. While Krasner and Křenek were both in residence, with Mitropoulos an eager conspirator, the Twin Cities were one of the world's seats and citadels of atonal music.

Four other compositions — which Mitropoulos referred to as "problematical" works — must be mentioned in connection with the forced feeding of the Twin Cities public in modern music. Two of them could probably classify as pieces other conductors wouldn't touch with ten-foot poles, because of their extreme difficulty and the audience resistance they would undoubtedly arouse. But Mitropoulos all the more eagerly embraced their performance as a privilege and a duty.

One was a symphony by Artur Schnabel, the pianist and great Beethoven exponent. It was a complex, dissonant, and energetic opus of big dimensions which the orchestra, playing it in December of 1946, had slaved on since the season's opening. One commentator felt that the work had vastly more gusto and humanity than some of the bone-dry intellectual charades presented by the Schönberg school, and another critic, Norman Houk of the *Tribune,* accurately reported that "it was too strenuous an adventure on uncharted seas for some of the audience, who struck out for familiar shores. I mean they got up and walked out."

Roger Sessions' violin concerto, another "problematical" offering, came in November of the following year. With Krasner in the solo role, it revealed itself as a nonromantic, abstract, but intellectually vigorous composition from one of America's most respected and original composers, a work with lightly but tightly woven counterpoint. It proved a nondramatic but lucid argument that won a decent measure of applause and even a bravo or two for the composer, who was present for the performance.

Present, also, had been Paul Hindemith on an earlier evening for the debut of his E flat major symphony, another landmark in new music. This was a kinetic outpouring of tone and idea, with intellectual muscle and plenty of emotional ballast. The composer — bald, chubby, and beaming — took many bows in response to audience approval.

Béla Bartók, probably the greatest creative mind of all the controversial composers brought forward by Mitropoulos, was introduced by the conductor and Yehudi Menuhin in 1943 through the medium of his violin concerto. Menuhin that season was playing only this Bartók composition. Its "dark brown colors" and what was termed "the fury of the mind" at work in it made the program that carried it a historic occasion. In 1947 Mitropoulos performed the same composer's *Dance Suite*.

World War II launched still another programmatic trend in Minneapolis: the featuring of modern Russian music and specifically the music of Dimitri Shostakovitch, whose Seventh or *Leningrad* symphony was the sensation of its year locally and nationally.

Later, when the cold war succeeded the fighting war, nothing dived into desuetude and oblivion so fast as the Shostakovitch Seventh. But in 1942 the Russians were the free world's allies in the fight against fascism. Their music for several years had been on the international market and their composers were encouraged to write for export. Such younger men as Khatchaturian and Kabalevsky participated in this movement, and the older masters, Glière and particularly Prokofieff, were heard with greater frequency than before.

No symphony had ever before enjoyed the kind of promotional build-up that was given the Shostakovitch Seventh in that year. Never before had a symphony been such "hot," up-to-the-minute news. The pale, bespectacled composer was pictured in the papers in his asbestos fire warden's suit, worn during the siege of Leningrad, his native city, and it was told that he composed music between air raids on that city.

On the Mountain Top

The symphony was given its première in Kuibyshev in March and straightway was photographed on microfilm and rushed by plane to Tehran. A wide circuit around Fortress Europe then took the film by automobile to Cairo, thence by air to Lisbon, and on to America.

There had been widespread competitive bidding from American symphony orchestras for the distinction of introducing the Seventh to the Western world. Arturo Toscanini and the NBC Symphony won the honor, and on July 19 they were tuned in by the largest audience ever to hear a first performance of any symphony.

This broadcast set another precedent, making the *Leningrad* symphony the first major orchestral work to gain initial circulation and familiarity via the radio. The whole country heard the symphony that Sunday afternoon in July, many hearers taking pains to listen to it even while engaged in away-from-home diversions.

Six orchestras — in Chicago, Cleveland, Los Angeles, Washington, Boston, and Philadelphia — had played the work to local audiences and over the air waves before the Minneapolis orchestra and Mitropoulos had their turn on November 27. To understand how urgent and eloquent was the call of this symphony at that particular point of time (and perhaps appreciate why it so quickly went to limbo) one must remember the tragic and heroic events contemporaneous with it. The Russians were our comrades, standing off with great losses the Nazi onslaught.

In his column "More or Less Personal" in the *Minneapolis Tribune,* William J. McNally wrote: "Even as you listen to the symphony tonight, guns will be barking in the Surovikhino area, where a battle having an important bearing on the outcome of the war is being fought. Between the time when Mr. Mitropoulos lifts his arm to indicate the first beat, and makes his last gesture calling for the final fadeout, whole platoons of men will have been destroyed in the vicinity of the Don. What this symphony deals with is a living thing, a mighty, surging movement of which we are a part."

For that reason, listening to the work could hardly be cool or objective. Sherman commented that "if you point out that the symphony is loose, rambling, too long and too full of derivations, you're apt to be set down as a fifth columnist, or even a saboteur." (Nine years later, expressed approval of the work might have made you un-American, suspect in the eyes of an investigating committee, proving that yesterday's partisanship may be tomorrow's subversion.)

The Minneapolis Symphony played the work, with its winding and repeated themes and juggernaut climaxes, only once. The composition called "the global war theme song," the *War and Peace* of modern symphonic literature, never came back; it was discarded almost as quickly as was the newspaper bearing the date of its first performance. Its very timeliness, its intense topicality, seemingly made it a one-time visitor only, to which conductors and public bade "hail and farewell."

But Shostakovitch continued to figure prominently in symphony programs during the war and afterward, until the time when simultaneously the Soviet government changed from friend to enemy and the composer's music descended in professional and lay esteem. By the early fifties Shostakovitch, while still played now and then, seemed to have shot his bolt, and of his orchestral work only the lean and pungent First symphony of his youth weathering well the passing years' judgment and digestion.

This First symphony was introduced in Minneapolis as early as the 1929–30 season and it remained for Mitropoulos in the early and mid forties — the love-Russia period — to present the bulk of other symphonic compositions by this chained creative artist. The Fifth symphony had four performances, the Ninth one, and on a well-remembered Sunday afternoon in 1944 Ramona Gerhard was heard in the première of the concerto for piano, strings, and trumpet, playing a crisp solo in a work full of playful, insolent humor and scratchy tone colors.

One of the enjoyable by-products of a Shostakovitch performance was the dim view invariably taken by Donald Ferguson, program annotator, of bureaucratic control of musical expression. Discussing the Shostakovitch Fifth, he once wrote: "The Soviet Republics not only recognize that literature and the other arts are significant contributions to culture; they have discovered criteria by which art-works may be judged as supporting or weakening the precious consciousness of nationality. The criteria remain, apparently, a close governmental secret. Judgments are readily offered, but the basis of the judgment is not stated. It is hard for us to imagine the condition of mind in which an artist must work, in those enlightened regions."

It should not be mistakenly concluded from the foregoing that the Mitropoulos period was occupied largely with Soviet Russian heroics and Schönbergian algebra. It is a matter of record and fond memory that the concerts of Mitropoulos covered much of the standard symphonic terrain, giving his audiences many evenings of tonal splendor, of kindling and illuminating insights into the familiar masterworks.

The conductor's interpretation of Brahms was usually searching and deep-pondered, avoiding that wooliness of treatment so often heard and thus dispelling the Brahmsian murk. Occasionally, though, as in his performance of the Third symphony in 1941, the maestro's Brahms was restless and jerky, making the old man run and puff a bit, whiskers awry.

Mitropoulos' Beethoven was kinetic, light-stepping, urgent, with south-European illumination. His Mozart at its best was light as air, sweet-spirited, graceful in shape and motion, and at its less than best (as in his 1948 version of the *Jupiter* symphony) was manipulated and mannered. His Wagner, when he chose to play it (Mitropoulos found Wagner's music for the most part repugnant), had large dimensions and altitude, without drag.

His Tschaikowsky (another un-favorite composer) was apt to be, but not always, "spiked" Tschaikowsky, taken at furious tempos and given a hectic flush. What critic John Harvey once wrote about his handling of the *Hamlet* overture applied often to his Tschaikowsky: "Dry it up as much as possible, bring it into sharp focus, never let the languishing phrases languish one moment, give it everything the brass can blow into it, and get it over with quickly."

Mahler was a preoccupation of Mitropoulos during his first season, when both the First and Fourth symphonies of that prolix master were presented, the latter with Irene Opava, wife of the Symphony's first flutist, in the soprano solo role. Two Mahler symphonies in one season (plus an excerpt from his Fifth symphony) seemed to some a heavy allotment, and three seasons elapsed before the First was repeated. A year later, in April 1942, a stunning performance was given of Mahler's *Das Lied von der Erde,* with Charles Kullman and Lilian Knowles in vocal solos that sometimes were inundated by the rich floods of orchestral sound.

This performance was one of the Alps of a period that reached high altitudes with consistent and stimulating regularity. Others were an all-Ravel program and Act I of Wagner's *Die Walküre* in 1938, Hindemith's *Mathis der Mahler* in 1939, and Beethoven's Ninth symphony in 1940 with a chorus trained by Rupert Sircom and again in 1948 with the newly organized University of Minnesota Chorus trained by James Aliferis.

The harsh and noble Vaughan Williams Fourth Symphony in 1941 got a clammy response from the concertgoers but was nevertheless one of Mitropoulos' great interpretative triumphs in the early war period. This was the season, too, of a notable Brahms *Requiem* (not fully billed as *Deutsches* that year) in its first symphonic performance in Minneapolis, supported by Earle Killeen's University Chorus and Maria Montana and Herbert Gould in the solo parts. Schubert's Fifth symphony in 1943, "as light and lithe as Diana's tread through the woodland," was an unusually engaging example of the conductor's affectionate aptitude for the early romantics. The long and spacious Prokofieff Fifth symphony had a compelling première in the spring of 1947.

The 1938–49 span of the orchestra introduced many new soloists to the Twin Cities public and brought back many old friends. Among the pianists, Rudolf Serkin, Robert Casadesus, and

Claudio Arrau were the three major "discoveries" of the period. Serkin, that passionate pilgrim of the piano, made his bow with an intense and devoted account of the Beethoven *Emperor* concerto. Casadesus had a double debut in d'Indy's *Symphony on a French Mountain Air* (wherein he was submerged) and Weber's F minor *Konzertstück* (which brought him into exciting audibility). The suave Chilean, Arrau, took on the Beethoven Fourth concerto, which in the words of Grace Davies was "a spiritual conversation" between conductor and soloist.

Other first-timers among keyboard artists were Rudolf Firkusny, Edward Kilenyi, Witold Malcuzynski, Alexander Uninsky, Arturo Michelangeli, and William Kapell. Strangely enough, considering his long-standing fame, Egon Petri was among the newcomers. Cool and self-possessed, he played Mozart, looking very much "like a senior bookkeeper going over the day's accounts."

Aside from Mitropoulos' seven appearances as conductor-pianist — in a class by themselves for their almost acrobatic jugglery of orchestra and keyboard roles — the big pianistic evenings were provided mostly by the aging Sergei Rachmaninoff and the man who in 1938 suddenly became the most-in-demand symphonic pianist, Artur Rubinstein.

Rachmaninoff appeared twice during Mitropoulos' tenure, and had now become such a venerable and venerated figure that each visit was in the double role of listening composer and performing pianist. In 1939 he played two works, the Beethoven First concerto and Liszt's *Totentanz,* and heard the orchestra perform his Third symphony. Three years later, in what proved to be his farewell appearance, he took the platform for his popular Second concerto, after which his *Symphonic Dances* were played for the first time.

William McNally of the *Tribune* was present during the rehearsal of the *Dances,* and later told how the composer, standing in the wings, kept frowning and snapping his fingers as if to accelerate the tempo. Stopping the orchestra, Mitropoulos conferred with Rachmaninoff and it was quickly discovered that through some error the allegro movement had been labeled non allegro on the score. The *non* was promptly expunged, and the orchestra's leaden gait was changed to the proper quickstep.

At sixty-nine Rachmaninoff had become one of the patriarchs of the musical world, and it was a matter of wonder that a man who appeared bent, tired, and apathetic could so recently have composed the exuberant and modern *Dances* and could, unlike most pianists in their autumnal years, play with the vigor and brilliance he showed in his concerto. The audience that night was in a reverent mood, and gave him clapping, standing homage.

The following year, shortly after the Russian composer's death, Mitropoulos programmed a Rachmaninoff memorial concert and made it notable as much for his conducting as for Leonard Pennario's vibrant pianism in the Second concerto.

Artur Rubinstein had played once with the orchestra in the 1920–21 season. Then he vanished from the scene for seventeen years, not returning until 1938, when his tremendous technique and full-blooded artistry mowed down all lay and critical resistance. Thereafter he came back about as often as the Symphony management could afford him, attracting ever-larger crowds of greedy listeners at each successive appearance.

His appearance on the night of January 23, 1942, was a curious occasion. A rabid audience had been drawn to hear a serious piece of music, the Tschaikowsky B flat minor concerto, because of the popularity given it by swing bands and singers who had mauled and crooned one of its themes. The usual Symphony throng was augmented by a shiny-eyed crowd of young folk who had come to hear the original version of their beloved *Piano Concerto,* as it was known in the band treatment, and *Tonight We Love,* when sung. It may be assumed that many of them were disappointed because the theme they knew appeared only in the introduction, never returning later in the composition.

In 1945 the pyrotechnical collision of Rubinstein with two modern piano-orchestra works — the Szymanowski *Symphonie Concertante* and Rachmaninoff's *Rhapsody on a Theme of Paganini* — was compared to the Fall of Babylon at the Minnesota State Fair grandstand. It was an evening of breath-taking tonal fireworks.

No summary of piano evenings at Northrop should omit mention of Josef Hofmann's return in a neat, firm handling of the *Emperor* concerto, Vladimir Horowitz' taut and furious account of the Rachmaninoff Third concerto, and William Kapell's high-speed romp in the First concerto of Aram Khatchaturian in January of 1945. Kapell's performance, introducing both a new composition and a new pianist to the Twin Cities, was incidentally memorable for a sight rarely seen in a concert hall: a gory keyboard. Kapell split a finger tip while playing this highly percussive concerto, but carried on with savage intensity despite pain and slippery keys.

The two leading debutants among the violinists were Zino Francescatti and Isaac Stern, far different in style but both scrupulous and masterly interpreters. The Frenchman with an Italian name, a direct "descendant" in teacher-pupil relationship of Paganini (his father had studied with Paganini's star pupil), represented a break-away from older violinists like Heifetz and Milstein in his firm "dry" tone and aristocratic finesse and precision. His debut was in March 1943, and Stern's came in December of the same year in the Mendelssohn concerto, which the young violinist played "as if he had made it, owned it, and lived with it comfortably for years." The ill-starred Ginette Neveu, who was killed in a plane crash in 1949, made the Brahms violin concerto an absorbing and exciting document by her fiery musicianship.

The older names continued to exert strong appeal — Kreisler, Heifetz, Menuhin, Milstein, and Szigeti ranking in about that order in their drawing power.

Kreisler returned in November 1944 for the herculean assignment of playing two concerts and two works at each. The imperturbable Heifetz seemed somewhat tense when playing the Beethoven concerto with the scoreless conductor, but later, in the Elgar and Walton concertos, he again exhibited a skill that seemed to exist in superb self-confidence on its own lofty plane.

Szigeti returned regularly to offer his own unique gifts of intellect and fire, and the bald heads and flying hands of soloist and conductor spelled a special kind of magic the night in 1942 when Szigeti performed the seldom-heard Busoni D major concerto. The implacable poise of Milstein, that compact playing unit, was combined as usual with spotless technique and the controlled flame of his temperament. Menuhin was a biennial visitor, and the former prodigy, though sometimes listless in platform demeanor, showed increasing maturity.

Runners-up in the violin division were Tossy Spivakovsky, Carroll Glenn (a girl doing amazingly well in the utterly masculine Sibelius concerto), and Robert Virovai. The cello was ridden masterfully by Gregor Piatigorsky and Gaspar Cassado, picturesquely by Raya Garbousova.

It was not a particularly memorable decade for singers on the Symphony's platform, and this fact may be taken to illustrate the slow decline of singers' status at orchestral concerts. This trend was well advanced in eastern centers, and it seems to have crept slowly to Minneapolis. For example, to pick two Minneapolis seasons at random, the 1927–28 Friday night series contained four women singers (all sopranos, incidentally), while the 1946–47 series offered but two. The 1951–52 series under Antal Dorati had only one: Kirsten Flagstad. (These comparative statistics include only featured soloists, not those involved in choral-orchestral undertakings.)

New women singers who were more than transients were in especially short supply in 1938–49. Among those whose names and gifts survive were Blanche Thebom, Dorothy Maynor, Astrid Varnay, and Eleanor Steber. The great personalities on the distaff side were Marian Anderson, Helen Traubel, and Kirsten Flagstad.

Male vocalism at the Symphony concerts was more substantial and showed a more valiant record. Three renowned fugitives from Wagnerian opera were heard during the period: Lauritz Melchior, Emanuel List, and Alexander Kipnis (the latter singing Brahms' *Four Serious Songs*). And from the Metropolitan

Opera lists came Ezio Pinza and Salvatore Baccaloni, the roly-poly basso *buffo* injecting a droll, comic note into his first collaboration with a symphony orchestra. Paul Robeson was engaged during the height of his popularity, and a French baritone of impeccable style, Martial Singher, offered a choice menu of French song art.

In 1940 the popular Nino Martini returned, his facile but unvaried style again proving unsuited to symphonic partnership. Another instance of uncomfortable collaboration had occurred three years before when Richard Tauber, a European operetta star famous for his monocle, sang with Symphony support. Buttery tone and rubbery phrase characterized his songs. He looked "like a shadow boxer who woos his muse with clawing gestures and grimaces . . . his manner that of a man whom audiences have given too much adulation."

In 1938 Mitropoulos began going east regularly as guest conductor, taking on such assignments in and out of season. He was called upon to lead the NBC Symphony, the New York Philharmonic, and later the Robin Hood Dell Orchestra, the latter for its summer series at Philadelphia. For many years it was a regular duty of newspaper critics and reporters to track down, and of Mitropoulos to deny, the chronic and recurrent rumors that he was being snatched away by Boston, Philadelphia, and New York. From the beginning of his tenure it was persistently said that he was the heir presumptive of Koussevitzky in Boston.

As time went on, his guest-conducting bids multiplied, taking him not only to the East but to Mexico. He succeeded in conducting his concert in Mexico City only after a double effort to cross the Mexican border. On his first attempt he was turned back for lack of a special entry permit and so returned to Minneapolis. There he found apologetic telegrams explaining that the Mexican ambassador and the Department of State had now arranged for his immediate entry. So he flew back to Brownsville and this time was quickly routed through to the Mexican capital.

All these conducting chores robbed Twin Cities audiences of his continuing presence at home concerts, but they had a compensating result in the richest array of guest-conducting talent these audiences had heard.

Certainly one of the historic evenings in Symphony annals was the one in December 1940 when Igor Stravinsky conducted a program given over wholly to his own compositions. The erstwhile "wild man of modern music" turned out to be a short, prim, bespectacled gentleman with a calm, measured beat and a self-possessed, entirely unferocious manner. The most controversial figure of twentieth-century music exhibited a precise baton style and an almost pedagogical method that gave shining clarity to works which, as he remarked at the time in an interview, were too often "sensationalized" by prima donna conductors.

Only one other conductor-composer paid a call during the period: twenty-seven-year-old Leonard Bernstein, who breezed along in 1945, when he was the "boy wonder" in the conducting-composing field, not sure which role he wanted to develop. He proved to be anything but a prim batonist; he punched out the music with right hooks and left jabs and gave it kindling warmth and eloquence.

Many of the guest maestros in these years were new to the Twin Cities, and several offered major experiences. The contentious Sir Thomas Beecham led the local orchestra for the first time in 1942, thereby filling a large gap in the concert hall education of his hearers. There was some alarm on the morning of his first rehearsal when the unpredictable conductor failed to arrive at starting time, and relief mingled with concern when he limped through the stage entrance a half-hour late. He had hurt his foot and there had been a fevered search for slippers. Otherwise he was immaculately dressed in morning garb; a true Britisher, he would not think of appearing even at a practice session in American-style casuals or rolled-up sleeves.

He was in good humor, and when he sat down with the score in front of him, he ask the musicians, "What shall we play?"

"Poker!" came a quick response from the back row.

The conductor grinned, asked if there were any ladies in the orchestra, made a disparaging remark about trombone sections, and then tackled Delius' *Walk to the Paradise Garden.*

The writer, attending this first rehearsal, was amazed that the conductor after only a few minutes' playing could impart the recognizable Beecham flavor to the opening measures of the Delius, and later asked him how it was done.

"My dear fellow," Sir Thomas replied, flicking ash from his cigar, "a conductor who can't play an orchestra like a violinist plays a violin, or a pianist a piano, is no damn good. When Kreisler starts playing a violin, it sounds like Kreisler; when Rachmaninoff puts his fingers on the keyboard, it sounds like Rachmaninoff. The man in charge isn't a conductor if he doesn't know how to make an orchestra sound the way he wants it to sound."

He also went on record as approving the Minneapolis orchestra, declaring it to be plastic, experienced, and well disciplined.

Beecham's concert proved a stirring and delightful occasion, and to it he brought the gifts of one who knew that music must have both the power of logic and the power of emotion, adroitly blended and balanced in the interpretation. For the first time within memory, the audience applauded a performance of *The Star-Spangled Banner,* played by Beecham with a rousing gusto that perfectly fitted his definition of the American national anthem. It is a battle cry, he had insisted at rehearsal, and "not a widow's dirge as played by the Metropolitan Opera orchestra."

Other distinguished newcomers, famous, half-famous, and unknown, took turns in putting the Minneapolis orchestra through its paces. Erich Leinsdorf, young conductor of the Cleveland Orchestra, achieved what was called the real Wagnerian sound in an all-Wagner program, played with cool objectivity yet with a sense of drama that stayed well this side of theatricality. Wilhelm Steinberg, a Toscanini protégé, made a good impression with Mozart's *Jupiter* symphony and Strauss's *Don Quixote.* Two years after the war's end Charles Munch, the sandy-haired Alsatian who later took over the Boston Symphony, played an all-French program that contained an incandescent reading of Debussy's *La Mer*.

The guest batonists came from all points: Vladimir Golschmann from St. Louis, Arthur Fiedler from Boston, Fabien Sevitzky from Indianapolis, Alexander Hilsberg from Philadelphia, Tauno Hannikainen from Duluth. Edwin McArthur conducted while Kirsten Flagstad sang, Andre Kostelanetz conducted while Lily Pons sang, and Morton Gould and Sigmund Romberg were imported for special concerts of lighter content. (It was on one of the latter's visits to the Twin Cities that John Harvey recalled Romberg's classic bit of advice to prospective conductors: "Don't bodder de moosicians vhen dey are playing.")

The methodical but forceful Fritz Reiner paid his first call, an extended one, when he signed up for the opening weeks of Mitropoulos' last season in the fall of 1948. He played a series of staple programs with an iron authority that spelled sound yet sometimes dogmatic readings.

A great and good friend of the orchestra, the only familiar maestro from afar, returned to conduct it in three consecutive seasons between 1941 and 1943, the latter year being his fiftieth as an orchestra conductor. For twenty of those fifty years Bruno Walter had known Minneapolis and kept a soft spot in his heart for the city that had welcomed him so eagerly in 1923. When he came back for the fourth time in 1943 this humanist among conductors observed that "conducting an orchestra is more a human problem than a musical one. You are working with many men and when they are eager to give their best your task is only one of bringing out, by suggestion and persuasion, what they have to give." This philosophy of conducting was not too far from Mitropoulos' approach to the craft.

Musical Minneapolis had an opportunity to inspect its future permanent conductor, Antal Dorati, on two occasions while he was still a peripatetic maestro on the ballet circuit. The first time was in January 1943, when he was associated with the Ballet Theatre, the second in December of the following year, when he led one of the regular Friday night programs. Warmly received by critics and laity, he was appraised as being the "winning rather than the aggressive type" and made many of the friends who later urged and applauded his selection as Minneapolis' regular maestro.

By the time of Dorati's first visit in charge of the Ballet Theatre, dance madness had taken deep root in the Twin Cities region as elsewhere in the country. The year 1937 had marked the onset of this pleasant infection, with the Ballet Russe de Monte Carlo as the carrier, and thereafter hardly a Symphony season passed without the dazzling pictorial embellishment of a ballet troupe at Northrop Auditorium. It made a welcome gift to the eye inured to the visual austerities of orchestral music. The Monte Carlo organization, under S. Hurok's management, made four return appearances, and other dance companies, long- and short-lived, came and conquered.

The Littlefield Ballet made a single appearance in the Minneapolis Auditorium in 1939, and it was not long before the various split-ups and reorganizations in the chaotic ballet world gave Minneapolis a wide choice in balletic wares. Colonel W. de Basil's Original Ballet Russe came with the polished colonel in attendance, and starting with the 1942–43 season the American-complexioned and -rooted Ballet Theatre was a regular visitor.

The first intrusion of ballet into the symphonic frame happened in the last season of Mrs. Carlyle Scott's management. When Mrs. Scott resigned in the spring of 1938, comforting memories of Arthur Gaines's hardheaded and efficient handling of the orchestra's business affairs led the board to bring him back from St. Louis to resume his former position.

Gaines carried on the custom of presenting ballet with the zeal of the balletomane he had become and with the experience of a man who had been the first manager in the country to bring a major symphony orchestra and a ballet company together. This he had done in St. Louis, setting a bold precedent for what later became a common practice, that of moving a complete symphony unit to the pit so as to give big musical dimensions to the ballet's visual glory.

Music and Maestros

From the rich and varied programs the ballet troupes offered, individual ballets and personalities remain bright in recollection: Alexandra Danilova in *Swan Lake* and *Coppélia,* Tamara Toumanova as the Sugar Plum Fairy in the *Nutcracker,* Alicia Markova in *Les Sylphides* and *Giselle,* and the unforgettably piquant Tatiana Riabouchinska as the cockerel in *Coq d'Or.* Lucia Chase and Nora Kaye in *Pillar of Fire* were a dramatic triumph, and Janet Reed as the forlorn but winsome ballet duckling in *On Stage!* was a gem of characterization.

Of the male contingent, one recalls above all the electrically tense performances of Leonide Massine in *The Three-Cornered Hat* and *Beau Danube,* his maniacally dapper Peruvian in *Gaîté Parisienne,* and the pathetic puppet in *Petrouchka.* David Lichine and Frederic Franklin ranked high, and in the earlier ballet years, the Tartar warrior in *Prince Igor* and the blackamoor in *Petrouchka,* as enacted by Yurek Shabalevsky, stand out among the striking roles of the era.

The orchestra as an institution had never had dealings with staged opera, although individual musicians over the years had augmented orchestras assembled to play for local and imported opera. The Symphony retired to the pit only for ballet and, back in the Verbrugghen and early Ormandy days, for the Isadora Duncan dancers and Anna Duncan. But in 1944, three years after three-hundred-pound Salvatore Baccaloni made his solo appearance, it played the accompaniment to the basso's own opera company in performances of Rossini's *The Barber of Seville* and Donizetti's *Don Pasquale.* In this instance, as when it stepped down from the stage for the ballet, the orchestra's tone and ensemble sometimes suffered in the wide-open space of the auditorium front and its shallow pit.

In the spring of 1945 the Orchestral Association, though not the physical orchestra, became a partner in the most successful and large-scale operatic venture in Twin Cities history. At that time the Metropolitan Opera Company of New York made the first of what have become regular annual visits to Northrop Auditorium under the joint sponsorship of the Association, the

University of Minnesota, and a state-wide group of sponsors and underwriters headed by Stanley Hawks. The local management of this opera series has been under Arthur Gaines, the Symphony manager, with James S. Lombard of the university's department of concerts and lectures as associate manager.

The possible prospect of the Symphony itself participating in operatic production is a matter for hopeful conjecture. That a real hunger for more opera exists in the Twin Cities and the region is attested not only by the sellouts at the Metropolitan performances but by the continuing success of the twenty-year-old St. Paul Civic Opera and the encouraging efforts to present outdoor opera at Lake Harriet in Minneapolis. Many in the area would welcome the development of opera to the artistic level of the Symphony, with the Symphony a partner in the undertaking.

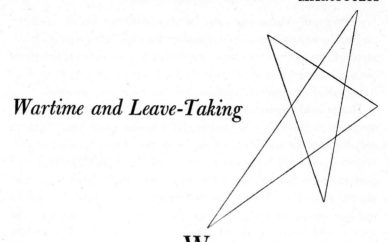

Wartime and Leave-Taking

W<small>ORLD</small> War II, with its tensions and dislocations, was the major external and overshadowing fact of Mitropoulos' mid-term in Minneapolis. In numerous ways it affected orchestral policies and arrangements, most seriously perhaps in its damage to the ensemble stability of the orchestra, whose shifting membership created new problems for the conductor and management.

The personnel of the Mitropoulos orchestra had what might be called three different phases, or complexions, each influenced in varying degree by the personalities and gifts of the men who occupied the positions of concertmaster and cello principal.

The three seasons from 1936 to 1939 constituted the "early period" or prewar orchestra, when Harold Ayres and Frank Miller were the pillars of the string sections.

The middle period from 1939 to 1944, corresponding to the war years, started with the arrival of Nikolai Graudan as first cellist, with Ayres remaining at the concertmaster's post. Graudan was a Latvian, a graduate of the St. Petersburg Imperial Conservatory, who for nine years had been cello soloist of the Berlin Philharmonic. He came to Minneapolis with his wife Joanna (Hansi Freudberg before her marriage), an accomplished pianist and pupil of Artur Schnabel, and the two of them soon made their impress on the community by superior musical gifts and considerable social charm. Mrs. Graudan's piquant clarity and delicacy of style were exhibited in delightful fashion in her performances of the Mendelssohn *Capriccio Brilliant* (which was recorded), and in Schumann and Chopin concertos.

The third or postwar period of the orchestra, 1944 to 1949, represents a more marked change, for at the outset of the 1944–45 season both Ayres and Graudan departed, and Louis Krasner and Yves Chardon and his wife arrived.

The dependable and poised Ayres, who left for California, had given twenty years of his professional life to the orchestra, had been a member for nearly half the period of its existence and its concertmaster for sixteen seasons. The man who took his place was a skillful musician and a serious if not magnetic leader. He had, as we have said, made a unique niche for himself as an exponent of *avant-garde* music, particularly in the atonal idiom.

The French Chardons, like the Graudans, were a musical couple. The wife, Henriette de Constant, was a cellist like her husband and shared the first stand with him, and Chardon had conducting aspirations and aptitudes which were soon put to work. He became the first assistant Mitropoulos had had since his arrival. (Amfitheatrof had been a temporary associate and interim conductor.)

The ambitions of these three gifted newcomers began soon to show themselves in extracurricular endeavors, not only initiating a chamber music revival in the Twin Cities (with two chamber music groups) but setting up rival if partly overlapping camps among the musicians. For a time a jostling factionalism revolved in different orbits around a common center, Mitropoulos.

A third small ensemble, having the same unofficial connections with the orchestra but destined to last longer, was the Northwest Sinfonietta, an excellent chamber orchestra. This was founded and conducted by Henry Denecke, Jr., the brilliant young tympanist who came to Minneapolis in 1941 to succeed the veteran William Faetkenheuer, who died after a stroke following a midwinter tour. Denecke and his wife Julia were the third professional couple to come to Minneapolis within a five-year span. The wife, a graduate of the National Orchestral Association and a former member of Phil Spitalny's all-girl orchestra, played frequently and ably in the orchestra's flute section, and for two of the war years was a regular member.

Many of the key men of the 1952 Minneapolis Symphony joined its ranks during the Mitropoulos regime, some of them drawn by the opportunity to play under the maestro's stimulating guidance. Rhadames Angelucci had arrived in 1936 as English horn and third oboe, and his talents soon moved him to permanent first oboe, where his tasteful phrasing and beautiful tone made him a star performer. In 1937 Walter Thalin, an exceptional clarinetist, succeeded Georges Grisez, and Waldemar Linder moved into first-horn position. John MacKay, first trombone, arrived in 1938–39, the same year that Ray Fitch, long in the bass ranks, moved to first chair and veteran Henry J. Williams retired to the relatively inactive position of second harp because of eye trouble. Thereafter the Symphony's harp was played by many fingers, male and female, the best remembered incumbent being Valerie Vitale. Carl Berglund entered the oboe section in 1939 and two years later became English horn soloist, one of the best in that role the orchestra had ever had.

The passage of time and disruptions of war particularly affected the first viola chair, occupied in turn by David Dawson, Vincent Mauricci, Peter Filerman, and again by Mauricci after his war service was over. James Greco was first trumpet beginning in 1944, and Karl Scheurer's long and skillful service was recognized when he became second violin principal in 1945.

Man shortage during the war raised the female contingent of the orchestra personnel to its highest level. Eight of the musicians wore skirts, all of them but flutist Julia Denecke playing in the string sections.

The critics' brigade too showed some new faces after the deaths of its two veterans, Victor Nilsson and James Davies, and when the entry of the Cowles organization changed the pattern of Minneapolis newspapers. Johan Egilsrud, a poet and university English instructor, shared musical commentary with the aging Nilsson and succeeded him after his death, while Grace Davies took up the pen for the *Daily Times* after her husband died.

Other short-time reviewers were Warren Wirtz, a young composer with keen discriminations; Jack Conklin, a music-wise observer; and Paul S. Ivory, cellist and music instructor at the university. Norman Houk eventually became the *Tribune* critic, and after the Minneapolis newspapers were reduced to two, he and Sherman of the *Star* carried on as Minneapolis' aisle-seaters. Houk's shrewdly perceptive observation of concerts soon made him a dependable analyst of what was heard and how it was performed.

In St. Paul Frances Boardman, after thirty years as a musical writer for St. Paul papers, relinquished her post to the young, Yale-educated, and discerning John H. Harvey.

After the rough seas and dangerous reefs of the depression, the orchestra sailed into comparatively calm waters in the Mitropoulos period. The greatest blow it suffered was less physical than psychological and emotional, when death took the man who had warded off virtually all blows except this last one to himself, which he could not control.

Elbert L. Carpenter died January 29, 1945, but for the three preceding years his tall, gallant, but now slightly stooped figure had been seen with lessening frequency in the concert hall. In 1942 he was absent for the first time in four decades from a meeting of the orchestral board. From then on he was forced to retreat more and more from active duties and concertgoing, but so persistent and insatiable was his desire to hear his cherished orchestra that arrangements were made to have him listen to it in his living room miles away. For many months a microphone could be seen at the front of the auditorium, placed there to pick up the orchestra's sound and "pipe" it to him on Friday nights and Sunday afternoons.

Among board members, backers, and management, Carpenter's death caused the same keen sense of loss that an aged father's death would produce in a son who had grown up and become self-supporting, yet felt for the first time alone in the world. The good, solid prop was gone; the orchestra and its steerers were on their own; they no longer could have recourse to the wise and material aid the father had always freely given. Whatever crises lay ahead must be solved without "the old man."

The memorial concert for the Minneapolis Symphony's great patron was a solid and noble program: Mitropoulos' arrangement of the Bach *Fantasia and Fugue*, the Beethoven First symphony, and the Brahms First symphony.

Seemingly Carpenter had chosen to go only after the orchestra's circumstances had shown enough improvement to justify his leaving. Financial emergencies had of late been only normally harrowing, never dire. In the 1941–42 season Carpenter had pointed out that the orchestra was in much better condition to face a war crisis than it had been twenty-four years before, and for several years thereafter the ready money the war put into circulation did much to keep the Symphony solvent. In April 1945 treasurer Ben Woodworth announced the good news that the orchestra was debt-free and in good financial condition.

After Carpenter's death a rotation plan went into effect for filling the office he had held since 1905. Sumner T. McKnight, long a vice-president of the Orchestral Association, became its second president in the 1945–46 season, and after three years of service was succeeded by Loring M. Staples, a Minneapolis attorney. In 1950–51 Stanley Hawks, who had been initiated into musical financing and campaigning when he was named statewide chairman of the Metropolitan Opera committee, became president.

The custom continued of making direct pleas for support to patrons at concert intermissions, usually toward the end of the season, and if the plea was cleverly scheduled for the night of a rousing program, the "take" in pledges was generally encouraging.

Various schemes were devised to develop keener and more widespread interest in the orchestra. A women's committee was active, and Mrs. John T. Baxter of Minneapolis and Mrs.

William J. Towle, Sr., of St. Paul headed the Young People's Symphony Concert Association. The matinees for youth were waxing strong. Soon after Gaines returned he put the series on a subscription basis for the first time, and they were finally oversold. In 1939–40 there were only three young people's concerts; in 1951–52 there were ten.

Other resourceful champions of the orchestra arranged for Symphony balls, parties, and appreciation dinners. One of the latter, an amusing and enjoyable affair, was sponsored by the Junior Association of Commerce, with Gilmore MacPhail handling the program. It was mainly memorable for Mitropoulos' droll and elaborate mimicry of an old-style, scowling *Kapellmeister*. The caricature was enhanced by his yard-long baton and his fussy ritual of taps and cues, by spectacles on his nose and the nose diving into the score at crucial points in the music he played. The orchestra men behaved quite in the spoofing spirit of the occasion — especially violinist Heimann Weinstine, who sawed vigorously on a four-note concerto for open strings.

Conductor and orchestra that year (1941) had another opportunity to get "out of character" when they donned velvet breeches and powdered wigs for a "period" presentation of Haydn's *Farewell* symphony. Mitropoulos keenly enjoyed these "acting" roles and entered into them with great zest and no little histrionic skill.

The war brought also the twenty per cent entertainment tax, and in 1944–45 the season ticket prices went up. Five years before, the number of Friday concerts had been increased from sixteen to eighteen, and there had been a three-year experiment, finally abandoned, of shifting the "pop" concerts to the loop.

These downtown "pops," held in the municipal auditorium, strove to lure the musically unlettered by "easy" music and eventually by the supplementary temptations of beer, light refreshments, and exhibition ballroom dancing. Mitropoulos conducted three straight concerts in the loop in the spring of 1938, and the following season a more ambitious plan was hazarded: twelve concerts in winter and early spring, six for each city, followed by "Ten Nights in Old Vienna" in June at the Minneapolis Auditorium under Guy Fraser Harrison.

The inducements to relax and have a good time were varied and original. They ranged all the way from the Arthur Murray dancers and open nights for candid camera fans to bridge games played right under the footlights. To all these ideas the complaisant Harrison lent himself with right good will. On one occasion Cedric Adams, columnist and radio personality, appeared in the narrator's role of *Peter and the Wolf*. A non-music-lover who found himself in the fairly baffling position of Minneapolis Symphony soloist, Adams dispatched his duties in the Prokofieff fairy tale with fine address and good timing. (He had once been a trap drummer but he watched for Harrison's cues with an eagle eye.) His diction, resonance, and variations in pitch, his geniality and stage poise, all contributed to an ingratiating performance.

But the downtown venture finally faltered to a stop. Out-of-season "pops" away from home base had never proved irresistible fare to the Minneapolis citizenry, and unlike the summertime combination concerts and skating shows so popular in St. Paul, they provided little to look at and no refreshing view of ice and ice frolics on warm nights. The orchestra reached rather low to win new friends and draw in the nonmusical: it made itself an accompanist for strutting baton twirlers; it beguiled university youth with the Big Ten college songs; it played the *Beer Barrel Polka* to audiences that broke out in cheers and clapping in the second measure. Being pals with its hearers could go no farther than that.

Meanwhile there had been considerable complaint, and rebuttal, on the subject of customers' "guzzling beer in presumably Viennese style" at concerts played by a respectable orchestra of high standards. But this issue had less effect than declining attendance on the fate of the "pops." In May 1940 they suddenly stopped, two weeks short of their scheduled close. This was the time of the Nazis' blitz invasion of the Low Countries and France, and the disastrous war news made relaxing at the auditorium temporarily unpopular — permanently so far as the orchestra was concerned.

Thus ended the out-of-season popular series, but the following year a new and successful approach to the in-season "pops" was devised by manager Gaines. The "twilight concerts" were born November 24, 1940. These were a series of six late Sunday afternoon concerts lasting hardly more than an hour without intermission. (The intermission, a desirable "breather" and social period for concertgoers, was introduced in 1951.) The four thirty starting time was chosen as a convenience for those who wanted to hear the New York Philharmonic's weekly broadcast before the concert, and to make ticket buying more convenient, "twilight" tickets for two years were placed on sale in business firms, industrial plants, and social centers.

The opening "twilight" had a near-capacity audience. Over the years since that time there has been fluctuating but fairly substantial attendance on the whole, reaching its peak each season at the joint concert by the orchestra and the St. Olaf Lutheran Choir.

In the 1940–41 season another annual institution was founded, the pension fund concert, whose proceeds go into a fund for disbursement to aging musicians retired from the orchestra. Orchestral players, employed by a nonprofit association, did not then come under the provisions of government social security, as they do now, and thus were denied the assurance of old age security available to workers in industry. The pension concert, a program of light content featuring a popular artist like Alec Templeton or Oscar Levant, was the beginning of an answer to this retirement problem.

In the earlier years of Mitropoulos' regime several series of radio programs kept the Symphony before the living-room public. Outstanding among these were the so-called March of Minnesota broadcasts over WCCO, saluting twenty-one towns and cities of the state and linked with the Sunday "pops" so that concertgoers could hear the live broadcasts. Another ambitious series was fifteen Sunday morning programs rebroadcast over

271

regional radio stations in Minnesota and Wisconsin in 1939–40. In more recent years both the radio industry and radio advertisers have grown increasingly cool to "classical music" as a selling medium with mass appeal, so that the orchestra's radio income has declined.

After the last Ormandy recordings for RCA Victor, there was a five-year holiday in the Symphony's record-making, terminated when a Columbia crew headed by Moses Smith, a former Boston music critic then in charge of Columbia's Masterworks, arrived at Northrop with $20,000 worth of equipment in the last week of 1939. Thenceforth until Victor took over again eight years later, new Minneapolis Symphony recordings carried Columbia's blue labels instead of Victor's red seals. By the fall of 1941 the orchestra's recording activities had accumulated seventeen titles in the Columbia catalogue, and thirty-six remained in the Victor lists.

One of the best, and most difficult, of all the Symphony's disc performances was the Mahler First symphony, waxed in the fall of 1940. The first two hours of playing into the microphones found a tense and edgy orchestra still bogged down in the opening movement, fluffs and inaccurate estimates of playing periods having ruined many grooves in the revolving acetate that received the sound.

In the main the Mitropoulos-Columbia product did not measure up to the earlier Ormandy-Victor recordings. It was wartime, methods of recording were not always painstaking, and a shortage of shellac resulted in poorer quality discs. Also, at that time Mitropoulos was less aware than Ormandy of the technical procedures of putting a symphony into the rotating grooves and less tractable to the demands of the process. Using no stopwatch and no score, he often ran over the prescribed four minutes and twenty seconds in making a "side," which meant scrapping what had been played and starting over again.

There was one especially nerve-racking afternoon on Northrop's stage in November 1946, when Artur Rubinstein and the Symphony played the Tschaikowsky B flat minor concerto into recording microphones. The session was set for a Saturday — unfortunately the noisy and traffic-jammed Saturday on which Minnesota played Iowa in a football game at the university stadium. Rubinstein arrived late at the hall after a series of misadventures which had so dampened his normal good nature and high spirits that for a while he was unable to perform.

He had been unable to get lunch at his Minneapolis loop hotel because it was overrun by out-of-town football fans. The hotel's management for some reason had declined to cash a personal check tendered in payment of his room bill, and this failure of courtesy had irritated Rubinstein no end. Worse yet, he had found it all but impossible to hail a taxicab to take him to Northrop, and he was finally forced to share one with several noisy inebriates who were stadium-bound. So he reached the auditorium at last in an advanced stage of jangled nerves and hungry exhaustion — certainly in no condition to play the piano.

A twenty-minute breathing spell and a round of sandwiches and coffee restored the pianist's spirits and he finally felt ready to proceed. But as the recording got under way it was discovered that the roar of airplanes over the football field was intruding into the concerto and spoiling side after side. Anguished pleas were relayed by telephone to Wold-Chamberlain Airport, base of the planes, and at length the pilots were called home. Then the recording went on and was completed in the late afternoon.

An interruption in all recording began January 1, 1948, as the result of an order issued by James C. Petrillo, president of the American Federation of Musicians. This order, banning "forever" the making of records and radio transcriptions by union musicians, was Petrillo's answer to provisions of the Taft-Hartley Act, passed six months before, which put a stop to direct payments of royalties to unions by recording companies. The ban was lifted eleven months later after an agreement had been worked out whereby royalties were paid into a "music performance trust fund," administered by a trustee named by the recording industry, and passed on from there to union members. The fund was later to provide free concerts, and extra employment to musicians, in the Twin Cities and elsewhere. In 1952 Minneapolis musicians' extra income from this source amounted to between $17,000 and $18,000.

The most marked physical and acoustical change involving the orchestra and its home on Northrop's stage was initiated singlehandedly by Mitropoulos himself. This was the new shell installed at the start of the 1941–42 season. It was built of seasoned wood on scientific principles developed by Leopold Stokowski, with ceiling and sidewalls set at angles and with a floor of terraced platforms.

Mitropoulos was so eager for this improvement that he impulsively broke all the rules that would call for committee hemming and hawing, public campaigning, and benefit teas and performances and launched the project by a large money contribution from his own pocket. Then he formed a solicitation committee of one, himself, and started a fund drive which in a few weeks of the summer of 1941 netted the $5000 needed to build the shell. This good work accomplished, Mitropoulos went out west in a jubilant frame of mind and climbed two mountains in a row: Mount Shasta and Mount Whitney.

Now the orchestra, for the first time, had wood instead of canvas backing. The shell, hung on steel cables with which to hoist it out of the way when not in use, improved vastly the orchestra's tone, mixing and blending it to better effect. The sound was more alive, and there was heightened individuality of solo instruments and their timbres. The first fall concert gave vivid demonstration of these qualities; it was as if "a veil had been lifted from in front of the orchestra."

Two years after the Mitropoulos shell was set up, the stage that at every rehearsal and concert held 14,000 pounds of musicians, 10,000 pounds of shell, and a ton of instruments underwent needed repairs and strengthening. Another three years later, in August 1946, the rather crass "institutional yellow" of the shell's walls was replaced with what Johns Hopkins, the university's colorist and interior decorator, termed "eggplant purple," a dark grayed blue. This soothing tint, which did much to soften yet dramatize the visual severities of an orchestra on stage, harmonized with the new color treatment of Northrop's interior. An added grace was the streamlining and de-tasseling of the thirteen hundred yards of maroon velvet hanging from the proscenium arch.

Touring had fallen into the doldrums in the three-year transition between the Ormandy and Mitropoulos commands and the Scott and Gaines managements. But Gaines, a resourceful and experienced symphonic trouper, soon had the out-of-town schedules patched up and in 1940 started a profitable if rugged period of far-flung travel for the orchestra.

Government restrictions and wartime priorities, coupled with difficulties in obtaining transportation equipment, added new and painful handicaps to the normal exigencies of touring. Discomforts and makeshifts were common, and it was soon borne in on the roving orchestra that GI's were more important than musicians and ordnance more important than musical instruments. One morning at a station in the South the Symphony's baggage car was requisitioned by the army and the orchestra's instruments were summarily removed. There was nothing to do but transfer the fragile and expensive musical equipment to a freight car.

Never before had touring been such a scramble to meet the next engagement by any means of locomotion. Day coaches and even buses took the place of the former comfortable Pullmans. Mitropoulos, inured to travel and instinctively democratic, rode with the men, catching cat naps on the dusty mohair seats as did his flutists and fiddlers. And he met the problem of personal luggage by stuffing all his effects into a mountaineer's knapsack which he strapped on his back. For two or three years an odd but familiar sight in hotel lobbies and railroad stations on the orchestra's itinerary was the conductor of the Minneapolis Symphony loping to his destination with a beret on his bald skull and a heavy pack on his back. (His disguise gave him somewhat the look of a hitchhiking vagrant, and once caused a brief

On tour, backstage at the Chicago Opera
House (sketch by Oz Black)

crisis at a railroad station. The train conductor stopped him: "Here you, you can't get on that train! That's taken by the Minneapolis Symphony Orchestra.") Virtually the only luxury the maestro allowed himself was a jug of Minnesota spring water, which was under the stage manager's supervision, and which the conductor habitually quaffed from when he came off stage on concert nights.

Response to Mitropoulos in the orchestra's "trade territory," where his intensity and unorthodox platform style spelled a new and spectacular kind of conductor, was almost unanimously and fervently favorable. On his first visit in 1939 to Chicago, a city whose adoration was not always assured, observers detected a note of frenzy in his playing. But in succeeding years a more mellow and relaxed style was perceived, and praised. The outspoken Claudia Cassidy, then critic of the Chicago *Journal of Commerce,* was pleased with a concert "more spontaneous and infinitely more brilliant than its predecessor," while Eugene Stinson of the *Daily News* found the conductor had "drastically curbed the style of conducting" he displayed in 1939.

Five thousand concertgoers in New Orleans, the orchestra's "second home," stood and cheered at the conclusion of a concert there. The Symphony, incidentally, had many "second homes," first rank in the second-home honors probably belonging to Winnipeg.

Visiting Chattanooga for the first time, Mitropoulos was bothered by a chattering, restless audience that refused to quiet down when he walked on stage for the second half of the program. Waiting patiently and vainly for a few minutes, he walked off stage, then walked on again for a second try. The chattering turned into an abashed ovation and finally a silence that allowed the downbeat. In Elmira, New York, the maestro turned about and gave an unruly juvenile audience a firm but tactful talk on decorum which magically changed his hearers into three thousand Little Lord Fauntleroys.

These were comparatively minor unpleasantnesses on the historic seven-thousand-mile trek in the winter of 1943, an odyssey which for dire and exhausting vicissitudes surpassed any other tour in Symphony annals. All other American orchestras timorously stayed home or close to home that year, but the travel-happy Minneapolis band had never been cowed by the hardships and miseries of trouping. At midday most of the orchestra members would be in a state of coma from lost sleep and general fatigue, but in the evening the stimulus of performance would pull them out of their torpor and gear them up to their best efforts.

In Indiana there was a stretch of eighteen hours without food or sleep, when the men stood in a travel-weary daze in aisles and vestibules. A lap between Birmingham and Tuscaloosa was ridden in a grimy prison car with bars on its windows. Two incipient cases of pneumonia were nipped en route. In a New York town cellist Graudan was hit in the eye with a chocolate lollypop flung by a juvenile music lover. And there was one good fist fight, caused largely by frayed nerves, that resulted in a dismissal.

Mitropoulos' toe was an episode in itself. He stubbed and broke it one dark night on the train and was limping painfully for most of the trip. Despite the pain he walked briskly to the concert platform at every public appearance. And more than once he conducted a concert while in fever. He was a seasoned traveler, and a touch of hardship and pain harmonized with his ideas of suffering and self-sacrifice. His soldiering in the Greek army as a youth had taught him to "rough it" with not only good grace but good technique, which quickly adapted itself to the situation at hand. In eating he could be either an epicure who relished fine viands, or a man-in-a-hurry who bolted a hamburger and a cup of coffee in the White Castle nearest the concert hall.

He reserved his right, however, to be occasionally the problem conductor who almost wasn't there. In Savannah, Georgia, he bought himself an alarm clock which made it unnecessary, so he said, to be called at 6 A.M. for an early getaway to make a Sunday matinee date in Augusta. The alarm never went off and the train left without him. But a half-hour after the Symphony musicians assembled in the Augusta hotel lobby, he showed up beaming; he had hired a taxicab for the hundred-and-twenty-mile trip.

There were compensations for all the difficulties, of course. The slow train in Florida allowed the men to hop off at every station to savor the oranges and grapefruit of the region, and the oyster crop in New Orleans was the best in years. Audience appreciation helped too. Mitropoulos' experience with the noisy children of Elmira encouraged him to speak informally to his youthful audiences along the way, calling on leaders in the various orchestra sections to play their instruments to illustrate themes and instrumental color. He interpolated jocular remarks that won over the youngsters, and one moppet in Atlanta was heard to say, "Gee, this is fun!"

Tours continued after the war, but traveling expenses that zoomed up twenty to thirty per cent in 1948 put to stringent test manager Gaines's ingenuity in the art of coming home with a profit. This was the year the orchestra returned to Boston's Symphony Hall after an absence of thirty-two years and there heard the proper Bostonians shout and stamp their feet after Mitropoulos conducted the Mozart *Jupiter* and cellist Chardon, a former resident, played Bloch's *Schelomo Rhapsody*. It was "an ovation of extraordinary intensity for this city," reported Cyrus Durgin of the *Globe,* "and every decibel of it was deserved by orchestra and conductor."

Experience on this tour pointed up the truism that no symphony orchestra and no conductor can please all audiences all the time. Bloch's *Schelomo* aroused considerable audience resistance in Toledo, where it was classed with Morton Gould's *Concerto for Orchestra* as noisy and uncomfortable. But a few days later a Boston observer found the *Schelomo* "a bit old-fashioned," a piece that "showed the ravages of time."

New York was the next stop, the tough and critical town that had not been on the Symphony's calling list since 1927. Here the chief praise went to the orchestra's executive skill and Mitropoulos' conducting mastery ("altogether big league," said the

Post), and most of the heckling was directed at the program and at some of the conductor's interpretive ideas. Virgil Thomson declared the Rachmaninoff Second a poor choice of a symphony, calling it a work "long since discarded from the winter programs of metropolitan orchestras," but Olin Downes hailed it rapturously as an inspired score superbly played. The Mozart *Jupiter* was generally criticized for distortions of phrase and tempo.

Mitropoulos hated to skimp in the number of compositions he took on tour, and librarian Herman Boessenroth with his many trunks of scores (all of them so packed as to make distribution of parts a quick and efficient job) was a harried man, mentally and physically juggling a thousand details. Eleven symphonies were taken on the 1944 tour. Three years later the orchestra management offered no fewer than thirty-five different programs — a far cry from the three or four taken on tour in the orchestra's early days. These programs comprised a dozen symphonies and thirty-eight other works arranged in numerous combinations. The Rachmaninoff Second was the most played symphony on that tour — it was presented seven times — while Ibert's *Escales* held the record of fourteen performances.

The orchestra that year, 1947, found itself in an environment not often associated with musical art, paying its first call on the United States Military Academy at West Point. This was the first concert of its kind in the post's history arranged entirely by the cadets, who not only sponsored the event but hustled all the baggage, instruments, and scores from the station to the war department theater.

The 1947 tour came in a hard winter, and is remembered chiefly for the bus trip from Pittsburgh eastward over the Alleghenies through a blinding snowstorm and the late arrival at Johnstown — so late that the musicians made straight for the concert hall without dinner to start a program long overdue. Hearing of their guests' plight, the Johnstownites made a quick raid on restaurants and rounded up two hundred sandwiches and a five-gallon pot of coffee, which were ravenously consumed at intermission.

Wartime and Leave-Taking

Undoubtedly the Symphony's most extraordinary out-of-town pilgrimage was made in July 1949, when Mitropoulos and the orchestra functioned as the main musical inducement at the Goethe bicentennial convocation and music festival in the picturesque mountain town of Aspen, Colorado. This cultural rodeo in a former mining town, surrounded on all sides by the lofty peaks of the Rockies, drew noted scholars, educators, and writers from all over the world: men like José Ortega y Gasset from Spain, Robert M. Hutchins from Chicago, Thornton Wilder from New England, and, as the featured personality, Dr. Albert Schweitzer, the musician-philosopher-missionary from Lamba-réné, French Equatorial Africa, who spoke on Goethe in two languages, French and German.

In prestige and in the extension of its reputation, the orchestra probably gained more by its part in this Goethe festival than by two or three tours of the kind it customarily took every winter. For the world went to Aspen that summer in the person of some of its best and most noted brains. Mitropoulos and the Symphony shared the platform in the amphitheater tent on the meadow near Roaring Fork River with the cream of scholarship from many lands. Their concerts there helped to make the city's name more than ever an international symbol of cultural enterprise and excellence.

The engagement reassembled the Minneapolis Symphony at a time when normally it did not exist physically, and the trip to scenic Aspen, west of Denver, was seized upon by many of the orchestra members as an opportunity for a combined family vacation and working assignment. Housing was difficult in the overcrowded community, which not many years before had been a ghost town, and the musicians were lodged all over the town and the surrounding mountainsides, some in cabins near trout streams, some in motor courts, some in a former bordello converted into a hotel.

The altitude of this hinterland Salzburg, nearly eight thousand feet, affected the breath of the wind players at first, and the mountain climate offered considerable meteorological interference in the tent where the Aspen pilgrims daily congregated. One Sunday afternoon a sudden cloudburst literally washed out a concert, interrupting Schumann's *Rhenish* symphony (whose pronunciation, "rainish," seemed appropriate to the emergency). Hail pelted through the pole holes and peppered the Steinway. Henry Denecke's kettledrum heads went soggy, and Mitropoulos finally waved Schumann to a stop when the beat of rain and the boom of thunder drowned him out. An hour-and-a-half intermission ensued, during which the tentmaster clambered up the canvas to bail out the heavily sagging big top.

Almost daily mountain showers did not dampen the enthusiasm of the Aspen culture seekers, who came in spite of them to hear the orchestra and the many big-name soloists and to give ear also to the theories and discussions of the imported scholars. The festival's conjunction of great ideas and great music, the hovering shade of Goethe, plus the incongruity of noted intellectuals mingling with leather-faced cowhands in hotel lobbies and restaurants, made the Aspen adventure one of the truly extraordinary experiences of the orchestra.

This session of music in the mountains marked the end of Mitropoulos' association with the Minneapolis Symphony. In blue jeans, white tee shirt, and gum-soled shoes he daily rehearsed the group he had headed for twelve years, and in more formal garb he leaped gazelle-like down the stairways that led from backstage to platform to conduct with his usual fury and devotion. On a July day he made his farewell appearance, with Nathan Milstein playing the Beethoven violin concerto. There were standing ovations for the soloist and the departing orchestra, and at the end of the program the audience remained long and noisily in the amphitheater, calling the conductor back again and again. Backstage there were some tears: Mitropoulos was leaving, as were Louis Krasner, Yves Chardon, Jenny Cullen, and some others.

The recurrent rumor that the conductor was being snatched away by the possessive and prosperous East had finally proved true. Seven months before, in the last week of December 1948, had come the unexpected announcement that Mitropoulos had been engaged to share the conductorship of the New York Philharmonic-Symphony with Leopold Stokowski and would leave Minneapolis at the end of the season. The conductor at first wished to continue in Minneapolis, splitting his time between the two cities, since the New York assignment was for a short term that might allow him considerable time at his old post.

But after some discussion the orchestra board decided that a full-time conductor would be best for the city and the orchestra, and Mitropoulos readily perceived the wisdom of its decision. Antal Dorati, conductor of the Dallas Symphony Orchestra, headed a long list of candidates for the Minneapolis post, and within a week's time arrangements had been concluded to engage him.

Some objection was made to the speed with which Mitropoulos' offer to conduct part time was declined and the new man selected. In an editorial in the *Minneapolis Star,* editor Gideon Seymour, a member of the Symphony's board, outlined the problem that faced the orchestra and explained the need for the quick and forthright solution that was reached:

"The orchestra board put just one thing ahead of its desire to keep Mitropoulos for at least part of another season. That is the permanence of the orchestra as a civic institution. It engaged Antal Dorati of the Dallas Symphony because it concluded, after the most conscientious study, that a permanent, full-time conductor is the best guarantee that the orchestra can ride safely through the financial rapids."

Seymour pointed out that keeping Mitropoulos part time would not solve the problem of who would conduct the annual tour, which even in a period of high traveling cost produced a financial return sufficient to pay salaries for eight of the twenty-six weeks prescribed in the orchestra members' contracts. "And there was some fear," he went on, "that a season of guest conductors, in quest of a Mitropoulos successor, might create factions in behalf of this candidate or that, among the orchestra and in the community, which would weaken the orchestra in a time of financial tension."

These were the sound reasons in favor of acquiring a good conductor immediately and against a "transition" season in which two or more conductors, none in full charge, would preside on Northrop's podium.

But the wrench was a hard one: for Mitropoulos, who had made a second home and many friends in Minneapolis, and for his many stanch advocates, who did not soon recover from the blow of his going. He had become musical Minneapolis' possession and pride, and had grown to be a part, an unconventional and picturesque part, of the community's life. He had never been the usual civic or social display piece his position and gifts would have made him had he been less wary. He had avoided all but hand-picked members of the Minnetonka society set. An able dowager-dodger who abhorred small talk over cocktails or tea, he had rarely intruded in the social activity of the town; his depression when caught in a chattering, lionizing circle was fathoms deep, his expression registering a profound and despairing ennui.

He was not often trapped in such gatherings. The agreement made at the time of his arrival had held pretty firm. He had asked whether the city wanted a musician devoted to his task or an agreeable conductor and society man. Minneapolis chose good music and a non-"party" man.

But Mitropoulos was far from being antisocial. With friends of his own choosing whom he liked, where the conversation took quick flight in speculation on the state of music and the world, he was happy and talkative, his darting mind and deep sympathies, his keen logic and bold deductions, all making a breathtaking experience for those who talked with him — and tried to keep up with him. Against those who voiced fallacies and prejudices, he could quietly marshal an adroit and demolishing argument that outpointed his adversary every step of the way.

He was eager always for new experience. The speed with which he had taken root in his American home revealed his capacity for absorbing the new and strange. His quick orientation to a northern, Nordic locale, so distant geographically and ethnically from the land of his fathers, reflected the eagerness and whole-souled manner of his plunge into American life, his acceptance of the New World. In the summers of 1938 and 1939 he returned to Greece to conduct open-air concerts in the ancient amphitheaters, but on the day the Nazis invaded Poland he embarked for America on an overcrowded boat, sleeping in the lounge, and returned to a country he would fully adopt as his own. Soon thereafter he took the first steps toward acquiring his citizenship papers.

If the calls of duty and curiosity were both involved in the prospect of a new experience, Mitropoulos would gladly plunge into it. His interest was piqued by jazz — he called it "the apotheosis of the syncope" — and he had a high respect for skillful practitioners of the craft. He once had a long backstage talk with Benny Goodman after hearing his concert at the Hennepin Orpheum Theater, the two of them that night forming a mutual admiration society. The writer recalls hauling him off one night to hear "Fats" Waller play at an upper Nicollet Avenue nightclub. Waller later visited the conductor's apartment and, exclaiming enviously at the sight of the big grand piano there, sat down immediately to play it.

Another time Mitropoulos was snared by some eager boogie-woogie fans at the University of Minnesota, where a new song, *Beat Me, Dimitri,* was unveiled in his special honor. After listening to the piece, he graciously but firmly told the young people that it was not good enough, making the point that funny music must be approached seriously to realize its purpose.

He once conducted the North High School band, making him probably the only conductor of his stature ever to concern himself with a secondary school's musical curriculum. This assignment followed by only a week or two his guest conductorship of the New York Philharmonic on tour!

He was ever on call for chamber music concerts, either conducting or playing the piano, and these performances were for him both recreation and duty: doing a bit more, as musical leader of the community, than was expected of him. ("One must be more than an opportunist," he once said, "who makes all the correct moves and no more.") One of the greatest performances in Twin Cities history was his conducting of Stravinsky's *L'Histoire du Soldat* at Hamline University in April 1944. The Twin Cities chapter of the Society for Contemporary Music, based at that school, found him a hard-working and eager accomplice in many of its musical evenings.

Besides this ceaseless activity on the musical fringes, he was seen and heard with increasing frequency at public meetings, where he spoke out bluntly what was on his mind, often to the point of indiscretion, particularly when he was aroused by the war or orchestra deficits or low salaries for musicians.

The war was not something Mitropoulos merely deplored, and the fate of his family in far-off Greece had been a deep and constant worry. At the close of the 1942–43 season he volunteered to work for the Red Cross mobile blood donor unit and for five months became a skilled manual laborer in blue denim trousers. He worked as a blood custodian, spending four or five days a week and often as long as twelve hours a day on a truck that visited dozens of small towns and war plants within a sixty-mile radius of Minneapolis. On days when he was not on the road he was busy at the Minneapolis blood donor center. He performed with high seriousness and diligence his duties of collecting bottles of blood in cloth bags, storing them in refrigerated containers, and sterilizing the blood-collecting tubes.

If Mitropoulos had an Achilles' heel, it was his programming, which more than once became a bone of public contention. A feverish debate of the pros and cons developed as early as 1942, when the Sunday *Tribune* opened up several columns to the controversy. His programs were variously criticized for being too severe, too odd a mixture of old and new, too monopolized by noisy modernism, too "educational" for a public that yearned for more of the entertaining and the familiar. The argument waxed hot between traditionalists who asked, "Is familiarity a sin?" or pleaded piteously for three old standbys rarely heard any more (the Brahms First, the Tschaikowsky Fifth, and the Beethoven Fifth), and the progressive-minded who stoutly defended their right as symphony-goers to continue hearing the "relatively small amount" of modern music that Mitropoulos played.

At a Friday night concert three years later Mitropoulos gave such a persuasive and disarming answer to the antimodernists that many of them were won over in spite of themselves, at least temporarily. He had been asked to make a brief appeal for the Red Cross at intermission, which he did in an earnest and graceful talk. Then, having just conducted the "harrowing" Tansman Fifth symphony, he proceeded to make a comparison between the universal use of modern invention and the contrasting and illogical rejection of modern music. For example, travel today, he said, moves at dizzying speed over routes formerly traced by slower means of locomotion, which allowed for a more leisured and pleasant view of the scenery. New music is analogous to the new means of travel. Then he made his principal point: a plea to his hearers to adopt a "sporting interest" in modern music, to accept the challenge of giving it a receptive ear and only then choosing to like it or dislike it. The experiment of listening to a new work can be its own reward, he said, and concluded: "We don't have to ask that all modern works we hear should be supremely great works of art. Most of them aren't, and we'd be naive to expect them to be, but we are more naive to close our ears to them."

When Mitropoulos spoke for the last time to his long-suffering, long-adoring audience, all was forgiven. His closing words, at his final Minneapolis concert on March 18, 1949, were as memorable and moving, if not so mournful, as Oberhoffer's "farewell address" in 1922. Forty-seven hundred listeners were there to hear Mitropoulos' valedictory to the city where he had spent "the best years of his life." He had just conducted the Mahler First symphony and had returned several times to bow and kiss his hand to the crowd roaring its affection and respect. Finally he paused at the stage-side microphone and spoke in low and husky tones: "You have helped me to grow, and you have grown with me. . . . The inexorable laws of destiny tell me that I must follow my duty and not my heart's desire, that I must climb the mountain. . . . All these years my colleagues have been like my kids and I their father. If I have been harsh at times, please forgive me, and if you, the audience, have been hurt by my playing modern compositions [laughter] don't keep it in mind. . . . And so I say to you, so long, and may God be always with you."

The Minneapolis experience had given Mitropoulos "mastery and relaxation," he told a friend the next day. "When I came here, I was very tense. But the conditions here, and the way I have been able to work with the orchestra, have helped me immeasurably in all the things that help a conductor and a man."

So Minneapolis again relinquished a symphony conductor to the East that wanted him and had offered the steeper, higher pinnacle and the greater world. The inland orchestra had again proved to be a conductor-maker. But it, too, had been made and re-made by the conductor, in a reciprocal process of growth.

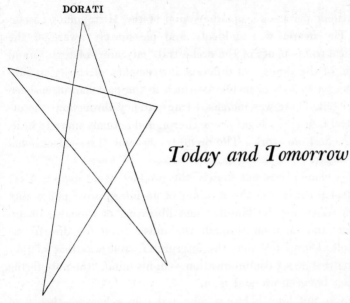

Today and Tomorrow

W_{HEN} he arrived in the fall of 1949, Antal Dorati brought down the high blood pressure of the Minneapolis Symphony's interpretations, which became temperate, with normal urgency of feeling and less strain. What was lost in throbbing tension and excitement was gained in a compelling but orderly unfolding of the music's thought and emotion.

The contrast with the style of his predecessor seemed that of reason, of ardent but clearheaded persuasion, as against an over-riding eloquence, ecstasy, and occasional frenzy. In a curious way, the interest shifted from the interpretation of the music to the music itself, which seemed more palatable if occasionally less rousing.

It was evident after two or three of his concerts that the man who occupied the large and rather menacing vacancy left by Dimitri Mitropoulos had brought things of substantial value to the orchestra, had restored several desirable features which had been underemphasized and even lacking at times during the exciting Mitropoulos regime.

Immediately apparent was an "open" tone as compared to the

sometimes percussive, opaque sound of the Mitropoulos ensemble. The hearer was suddenly and pleasurably aware of the physical components of the orchestral "mixture," of texture and depth, of the timbres of different instruments, of clarity in subsidiary passages and incidents which in the past had often been blanketed. There was increased transparency throughout the orchestral fabric which gave new charm, and actually more to hear, in new and old works. The orchestra became three-dimensional to the ear.

This change was not merely the product of an expert in orchestral tone; it was the medium of an interpretive philosophy which called for the kindling and liberating of thought, imagination, and emotion through the music itself, as directly as possible. Dorati felt that the interpreter's role was that of producing this direct communication — in his mind, "the only fertile contact between art and man."

It was not long before a new and comprehensive theory of programming also revealed itself, awakening interest and anticipation about the compositions played and the way they were selected and arranged. There was enticement here, an eye for variety, a shrewdness in pairing the difficult with the familiar. Mitropoulos had given scant attention to the art of programming; his interest and stimulus arose more from the individual composition than from the program composite. As a result, he sometimes put together almost indigestible programs.

Dorati came to Minneapolis with deep convictions and a definite policy on program-making, and a great zeal for it; he restored what could be called the Oberhoffer formula of balancing the established old with the provocative new in a long-range scheme embracing the entire orchestral literature. He gave long and painstaking study to the past programs of the orchestra before drafting his own schedule for the 1949–50 season. Indeed, it was his practice to ponder his program strategy as carefully as a general mapping out an invincible offensive. "New" music — which could mean anything that audiences had not heard, from seventeenth-century Monteverdi to twentieth-century Villa-

Lobos — was gently but insistently tucked into almost every program.

These two features, open tone and inviting programs, were the most noticeable changes brought about by the Symphony's new master, along with an artistry that seemed at once both relaxed and disciplined. The orchestra was less driven, less forced. While this calming down struck some hearers at first as prosy after the power and intensity of Mitropoulos, others were glad to be more "on their own" as listeners, making their own meanings out of explicit, undistorted music that laid no hypnosis on them. Dorati's concert hall was less the mountain top of the days gone by but also less the exhorter's platform.

The orchestra's fifth conductor was its second to come from Hungary — the first, of course, having been Eugene Ormandy. Born of musical parents in Budapest in 1906, Antal made the brilliant scholastic records all future conductors seem to make in their early years, studying composition, conducting, and piano at the city's Academy of Music and being graduated as one of the youngest to receive a degree there. It was in these years that he studied under Hungary's outstanding composers, Zoltán Kodály and Béla Bartók.

Dorati was only eighteen when he won an appointment in 1924 as conductor of the Budapest Royal Opera House, and four years later he became Fritz Busch's assistant at the Dresden Opera. His next assignment was that of musical director and chief conductor of the Municipal Opera at Münster, in West-phalia. There he remained three seasons, through 1932, making frequent trips to conduct at opera houses in Frankfurt, Düsseldorf, Dessau, and other German cities, and in Brünn, Czechoslovakia.

Meanwhile, in 1930, he took on his first symphony perform-ance, making his debut with the Budapest Philharmonic, and for seven years thereafter he served from time to time as guest con-ductor of that noted organization. This marked his entry into the profession he wished most to follow, and did follow on a freelance basis for fifteen years. But in 1933 came a call which steered the Dorati career into an entirely new direction and ultimately brought him to the notice of an international audience.

This was an invitation to the post of conductor for the Ballet Russe de Monte Carlo, which had just been organized by René Blum and Colonel Wassili de Basil. The chief lure in that invitation was that the company was about to start its first American tour, and Dorati could not resist the temptation to join it, though it meant leaving a remunerative position with the French government radio in Paris. He conducted this brilliant and roving company of dancers through the middle thirties, transferring to the Original Ballet Russe in 1938 and to the American-based Ballet Theatre in 1941. It was during these years that he composed most of his colorful ballet arrangements, including the well-known *Bluebeard* and *Helen of Troy*, with Offenbach's music, and *Graduation Ball*, to music of Johann Strauss.

Although ballet held him off and on for twelve years, Dorati continued to build his symphonic repertoire and to develop his skill in this field. He conducted in Paris, London, Florence, and Barcelona and made his American bow as guest maestro of the National Symphony Orchestra in Washington in 1937 in a Beethoven program. From then on he extended his guest-conducting circuit to four continents, adding cities in South America and Australia to his conductor's logbook. For two seasons, returning to an old love, he took charge of the New Opera Company in New York in 1941 and 1942, and while there arranged and directed Offenbach's *La Vie Parisienne*.

The second major turning point in a career now in danger of being swallowed up by ballet (Dorati was identified primarily as a ballet maestro by most American concertgoers) came in 1945, and was brought about by two decisions, one made by Dorati and one by the city of Dallas, Texas. The conductor decided to quit the Ballet Theatre in order to accept the increasing number of bids for his services as a symphonic leader. That summer he conducted in Montreal, Toronto, Lima, Peru, and Havana, Cuba, and took charge for his eighth consecutive season at the Hollywood Bowl. And that fall Dallas was shopping for a first-rate man to take charge of its reorganized orchestra, dormant during the war.

As early as 1937, Arthur Gaines had recommended Dorati for the Dallas post, and now Dallas had grown up to the point where it was ready to want and need him.

John Rosenfield, music editor of the *Dallas Morning News*, has recounted the events that led to a four-year musical boom the like of which the city had never before experienced. Reorganization of the orchestra on thrice the scale of the season before had been undertaken by an executive committee, whose hardheaded chairman asked the candidate point-blank: "How do we know you can give us a good orchestra, Mr. Dorati?"

"If I can't I cut my throat," Dorati replied.

This startling threat of success-or-suicide impressed the Texans, who like hyperbole, and he was signed up.

From then on, according to Rosenfield, the town was treated to high musical adventure: "world premières, daring excerpts from operas, the commissioning of new works." Only two months after Dorati took up the Dallas baton, the orchestra he conducted was making the first of numerous recordings for RCA Victor.

"Dallas and Dorati were names indivisible, each giving the other a glory that detonated through four continents," wrote the admiring Rosenfield. "It was a love affair for four breathless seasons."

(This fond attachment, incidentally, continued long after the engagement was broken off. Seven years later when Dorati returned to Dallas as guest conductor, William P. Steven of the *Minneapolis Star* and *Tribune* heard his concert while on a trip to the South. "I came to protect our property," Steven was quoted as saying, "but now I feel like an interloper. This love affair of Dallas and Dorati rather shames outsiders.")

What Dorati was later to do in Minneapolis he started to do in Dallas, his first "home town" in America. "I have to push programs both ways," he said, meaning that he had to provide a classic background and a modern one at the same time in his concerts. It was in Dallas that this long-time musical vagabond, now at last settled down, first had an opportunity to put into practice his programming philosophy: that of (1) making of each program a well-rounded unit, (2) presenting each season a balanced ration from all schools and periods of music, and (3) planning a series of seasons which, without repeating individual works, gave the symphony subscriber a comprehensive background in what the world of music offers.

Dorati's four years in Dallas were memorable both for the community, which enjoyed a forced growth in musical understanding and enjoyment, and for the conductor, who for the first time found himself cast in the double role of civic and musical hero in an American city. He proved himself a builder, a promoter and campaigner American style, as well as a musician who carefully studied his notes and thrillingly played them. Dallas was won over by the man and relinquished him with regret.

In luring Dorati from Texas the Minneapolis Symphony board did something it had not hitherto done: it "raided" another American orchestra in its search for a conductor. The fact that it could do so was a significant commentary on the increased stature, richness, and distribution of civic symphonic music in America of the late forties as compared with the situation of two or three decades before, and it indicated the generally higher caliber of the musicians in charge. It also dramatized the Minneapolis Symphony's status as an orchestra to step up to, as well as one to step up from.

So it happened that a world-noted, world-traveled musician was found in that outsize corner of the United States which had supplied many things, but never conductors. And Minneapolis soon found its new maestro to be a progressive-minded leader and a fine orchestral craftsman.

Dorati brought with him his wife (Klara Korody) and small daughter Antonia, and Minneapolis again had a "family man" to lead its Symphony. Tall, boyishly handsome, well built, with black wavy hair that became tousled in *furioso* passages, the forty-three-year-old maestro made a quick and creative adjustment to the new environment and its demands and potentialities. And Dorati soon grew deeply attached to Minneapolis, finding it more of a personal home than Dallas was. He had ideas and energy to apply to the orchestra and its program, and enough left over of both to "stump" for the orchestra whenever called upon, becoming in his spare time the orchestra's best friend and advocate in its own town.

Dorati's basic impulse was to build strongly and surely for the future. As the fiftieth Symphony anniversary approached he made it plain that he hoped to be known not as the last conductor of the orchestra's first half-century but as the first conductor of its second half-century. He looked ahead, and his strategy involved not only carefully constructed programs but the improvement and strengthening of his instrument — what he called the "re-tooling" of the orchestral machine. This was a gradual process calling for no drastic personnel changes at the start. The first move in this direction was his choice of concertmaster, Rafael Druian, who came with him from Dallas.

Druian at twenty-seven was as gifted a concertmaster as the orchestra has ever had. Born in Russia and reared in Cuba, he had enrolled at Philadelphia's Curtis Institute and studied under Efrem Zimbalist, and was hardly more than a boy when he made his American concert debut in 1938, playing with the Philadelphia Orchestra under Eugene Ormandy.

Druian brought the air, and fact, of command back to the Minneapolis concertmaster's position, his skill and mere presence at the post doing much to solidify the strings, which soon acquired new morale, luster, and authority. He was a virtuoso violinist with fire in his bow, precision technique in his fingers, and infallible taste and musicianship in his head, and he was also a dependable orchestra captain and ensemble man.

Henry Kramer, a conscientious and artful violinist, had worked his way up the ranks to the position of assistant concertmaster under Dorati. Veteran Karl Scheurer continued as second violin principal, and in Dorati's second season, 1950–51, Rolf

Persinger was engaged as viola principal and Lorne Munroe as cello leader. These newcomers, along with Bernard Adelstein as new first trumpet, seemed amazingly young, considering the experience and craftsmanship apparent in their work. Young too was the new assistant conductor, Gerard Samuel, a violinist who showed authority and style on the few occasions when he took the orchestra's reins. The Symphony had begun to assume a younger look; youth had seized some of the key posts, although others remained in able older hands.

Two developments gave character, renewed interest, and a real sense of progress to the orchestra's programs under the Dorati dispensation. One was an extended exploration into the creative mind of Béla Bartók, whose enthusiastic partisan the conductor had been since his student days and to whose works he brought a special gift of perceptive exposition. Dorati's first Minneapolis season offered no fewer than three Bartók works: the concerto for orchestra, the concerto for viola and orchestra (with William Primrose), and the *Divertimento*; the second season brought the *Music for Strings, Percussion, and Celesta*.

The other development was the increased use of the three-hundred-voiced University of Minnesota Chorus, which had been brought to a high degree of interpretive and vocal power by James Aliferis, the brilliant choral director who had joined the University of Minnesota faculty in 1946. Aliferis' first appearance on the Symphony platform was in the fall of that year, during the Mitropoulos regime, when he directed his student singers in Brahms' *Song of Destiny* and the choral finale of Wagner's *Die Meistersinger* at a twilight concert.

Aliferis prepared four other works, including the Beethoven Ninth finale, which Mitropoulos took over in the last stages and conducted, and after Dorati arrived his projects became even more venturesome and large scale: the coronation scene from Moussorgsky's *Boris Godounov*, Vaughan Williams' *Dona Nobis Pacem*, the Verdi Requiem, Honegger's *King David*, Bach's Magnificat in D, the Beethoven Ninth again, Haydn's *Creation*, and the Beethoven *Missa Solemnis* in a belated Twin Cities première.

Today and Tomorrow

These performances by the University Chorus did much to draw closer together the Symphony, the university, and the community, and invariably attracted large audiences.

Minneapolis' choral renascence had the result of bringing the all-female Cecilian Singers into the symphonic fold in Mahler's Third symphony and the third Debussy orchestral nocturne, *Sirènes*. It also found the all-male Apollo Club (that ancient rival of the Philharmonic Club) returning to the Symphony stage after a quarter-century's absence to sing in Verretti's *Sinfonia Sacra*. And it mobilized a miniature army of high school pupils for a vivid performance of Handel's *Messiah*.

Besides the Bartók and choral performances, Dorati's big achievements in his three seasons with the orchestra have included Stravinsky's *Sacre du Printemps* and *Song of the Nightingale*, Hindemith's *Symphonic Metamorphosis on Themes of Carl von Weber* and *Symphonia Serena*, the Barber violin concerto, Messiaen's *The Ascension*, Piston's Fourth symphony (commissioned for the University of Minnesota centennial concert), an all-Wagner program with Kirsten Flagstad, and Strauss's *Salome* in semidramatic concert form.

Guest conductors during these three years have been Aliferis, Tauno Hannikainen, Fritz Busch, Vladimir Golschmann, Leopold Stokowski, and Bruno Walter.

Another renascence has taken place during this recent period: a zealous and well-organized renewal of women's interest in the orchestra. The Women's Association of the Minneapolis Symphony Orchestra, vigorous successor to many past women's committees, was headed by Mrs. Leo Pflaum and set about telling "the orchestra story" to women throughout the state who had never heard it before. While devoting itself more to public relations than fund-raising, the group collected sums running into five figures by its ingenious idea of "chain luncheons," and it also revived the old idea of getting public and orchestra together for social fun.

A newly organized group, Junior Symphony Associates, with Louis N. Zelle as president, has done a similar good work among younger adults, unmarried or recently married, who like music but need help on ticket-budget and baby-sitting problems. And the Young People's organization has continued to "pack the hall" regularly with eager youngsters. It has lately picked up an idea of Dorati's — original paintings by children inspired by hearing musical compositions — and developed it into annual exhibitions hung in Northrop's halls.

Telecasts over WTCN-TV, one each in 1949–50 and 1950–51 and a series of five in 1951–52, have proved vastly interesting and informative to a large lay and musical public, with a "rating" that came close to that of the televised football games in estimated number of viewers.

Touring has continued during Dorati's first three seasons, and while mounting transportation costs have prohibited the long itineraries of yore, one hundred and ten cities have been visited in an area extending as far east as New York State, south to Missouri, and north into Canada. Dorati, a foot-loose maestro most of his life, has been entirely in character as a traveling conductor, and the reception of him and his orchestra in the region has been consistently favorable.

In the early months of 1952 the orchestra transferred its recording allegiance to a comparatively new firm, the Mercury Record Corporation, which staged two recording sessions at Northrop and subsequently issued long-play discs of unusual realism and spaciousness of sound.

Reaching its fiftieth season, the Minneapolis Symphony has achieved the unique record of being an "older" orchestra, in relation to the age of its sponsoring city, than any other of its rank in America. Minneapolis' corporate existence dates from 1867, so that in 1952 the city had harbored an orchestra playing consecutive seasons for nearly sixty per cent of its life as a city and for almost exactly half of its life as a population center.

Such statistics are bound to please chauvinistic Minneapolitans, but their real significance lies in the fact that the orchestra was a natural and relatively early consequence of the urgency of the city's musical aspirations and activities. Far from being imposed on the city, the new orchestra in 1903 had long, tenacious roots in the community's cultural soil. It was sustained by a tradition that extended backward to Frank Danz in the nineties and eighties, to the timorous Minneapolis Musical Society in 1872, even unto the earnest Mr. Messer's production of *Flora's Festival* in 1854. Luck and favorable circumstance, zealous civic leaders and devoted musicians, these certainly were needed to bring the Symphony into being, but they could hardly have created an orchestra had not the civic impulse been there in the first place.

Theories about the "personality" of that many-faced, chameleon creature, the symphony orchestra, should not be pushed too far, but they can be plausible and at least partially true. Interesting is the appraisal of the Minneapolis organization by David Hall, well-known record critic and recording executive and author of several editions of *The Record Book,* who recently wrote:

"Among the major orchestras of America, the Minneapolis Symphony has had a particularly distinctive 'personality' — in the sense that its style of performance and texture and sonority can be mistaken for no other. It is the zest of its rhythmic drive and the vital warmth of its lyrical playing which constitute the major factors in the collective personality of the Minneapolis ensemble. . . . This 'personality' has been maturing, deepening and gaining added refinement and subtlety, the latter qualities having been the special contributions of Antal Dorati. . . ."

The distinctive personal character of the Minneapolis orchestra may well have some underlying relationship with geography and rugged climate, for the organization through all its changes of conductor and personnel has been a lively, quick-learning, adaptable unit, expressing in the spirit of its work a certain "midwestern" forwardness, candor, and impetuosity.

That forwardness in its nature has reflected, from its earliest days, a dogged will to survive and improve, a conviction of perfectability. The problems facing the orchestra grow no easier, but the challenges, the need, are greater. The present need must be served; the potential need, among those who can be nourished and inspired by great music but have not yet discovered the diet, must be anticipated and met. Meanwhile, nothing has taught Minneapolis more convincingly the old biblical lesson that "man doth not live by bread only" than its own orchestra, which has given to a business city a spiritual elevation, an overtone and extra dimension that have contributed to making the town worth living in. The next fifty years may be as difficult as the first fifty, but if difficulty had ever meant anything more to its supporters than obstacles to overcome, the orchestra would have died in infancy. The hard road has proved the high road to a high goal, and the best hope for the future is that the journey ahead, whatever its difficulties, will be as exciting, as rewarding individually and communally, as the trip so far has been.

The history of the Minneapolis Symphony Orchestra is not only a midwestern story. In a real sense it is an American story, the oft-repeated one that tells of free citizens in a free land who, wanting to do more than thrive and be comfortable, have willingly assumed the obligation to build for themselves, their neighbors, and their children, the good life.

Listings for Reference

Personnel

OF THE MINNEAPOLIS SYMPHONY ORCHESTRA
FIRST THROUGH FORTY-NINTH SEASON, 1903–1952

Conductors

Emil Oberhoffer, 1–19; Henri Verbrugghen, 21–28*; Eugene Ormandy, 29–33; Dimitri Mitropoulos, 35–46; Antal Dorati, 47–49.

Associate and Assistant Conductors

Engelbert Roentgen, 19–27; Paul Lemay, 28–33; Daniele Amfitheatrof, 35; Yves Chardon, 42–46; Gerard Samuel, 48–49.

Guest Conductors

James Aliferis, 44P, 45P, 46P, 47P, 48P; Leon Barzin, 33P, 34&P; Sir Thomas Beecham, 40; Leonard Bernstein, 43, 45; Artur Bodanzky, 16&P, 34&P; Jerzy Bojanowski, 34&P; Felix Borowski, 18; Carl Busch, 7P; Fritz Busch, 48; Alfredo Casella, 19; George W. Chadwick, 13; F. Melius Christiansen, 34P; Chalmers Clifton, 28; Albert Coates, 20; Walter Damrosch, 20; Antal Dorati, 42; Arthur Fiedler, 42; Ossip Gabrilówitsch, 20, 31P, 32&P; Vladimir Golschmann, 39, 48; Eugene Goossens, 28, 30&P; Morton Gould, 42; Glenn Dillard Gunn, 20P; Tauno Hannikainen, 43P, 47; Howard Hanson, 34, 39P; Guy Fraser Harrison, 34&P, 36P, 37P; Alfred Hill, 23P; Alexander Hilsberg, 46&P; José Iturbi, 34&P; Andre Kostelanetz, 37P; Erich Leinsdorf, 43; Edwin McArthur, 38; Dimitri Mitropoulos, 34&P; Charles Munch, 45; Eugene Ormandy, 34&P, 45; Erno Rapee, 34†; Fritz Reiner, 46&P; Sigmund Romberg, 43; Hugh C. M. Ross, 20P; Louis Victor Saar, 17P; George Schick (Baccaloni Opera Co.), 41; Fabien Sevitzky, 45; Wilhelm Steinberg, 40; Leopold Stokowski, 49; Igor Stravinsky, 38; Henri Verbrugghen, 20&P; Bruno Walter, 20&P, 38, 39, 40, 49; Adolf Weidig, 16&P.

Concertmasters

Frank Danz, 1–5; Fram Anton Korb, 6; Richard Czerwonky, 7–15; Guy H. Woodard, 16–18; Vladimir Graffman, 19; Alfred Megerlin, 20; Elias Breeskin, 21; Gustave Tinlot, 22; Pierre Henrotte, 23; E. Joseph Shadwick, 24–25; Harold Ayres, 26–41; Louis Krasner, 42–46; Rafael Druian, 47–49.

Orchestra Members ‡

ADAM, Claus (Cello), 38–40
ADAMS, Merle (Violin), 27–48
ADELSTEIN, Bernard (Trumpet), 48–49

ALBRECHT, Fred (Violin), 1–9
ALEXANDER, Joseph P. (Violin), 6–7
ALLEN, Blain (Violin), 3–5
ALPERT, Dorothy (Violin), 43–45

* Conducted first concert in twenty-ninth season. Illness prevented further activity.
† General Motors Radio Broadcast.
‡ Each season the orchestra member appeared with the Symphony is included in this list, although he may have played for only part of the season.

Music and Maestros

Orchestra Personnel

CONSTANT, Henriette de (Cello), 42–47

COOKE, Glenn R. (Tuba, Percussion, Personnel Manager), 21–49

COOPER, J. Andrew (Violin), 24, 26–32

COSTA, Benedetto (Violin), 18

COTE, E. E. (Violin), 3

CRASSAS, Stelly (Violin), 14–15

CULLEN, Jenny (Violin), 21–29, 42–46

CUNNINGTON, Henry (Bassoon), 1, 14–31

CUNNINGTON, Syd (Bassoon, Contra-Bassoon, Bass), 16–21, 23–49

CURRIER, Frank S. (Violin, Viola), 11–12

CZERWONKY, Richard (Violin), 7–15

DAHL, Anton (Viola), 1–3

DAHLGREN, Marvin (Percussion), 49

DALMAN, Conrad (Cello), 7–8

DAMM, Alfred, Sr. (Violin, Percussion), 12–24

DAMM, Alfred, Jr. (Clarinet, Bass Clarinet), 18

DANZ, Frank, Jr. (Violin), 1–5

DAVENPORT, Kenneth (Bass), 37–40, 43–49

DAVIS, Lester (Bassoon, Contra-Bassoon), 48–49

DAWSON, David P. (Viola), 35–38

DELLONE, Loretta (Harp), 1–4

De LORENZO, Leonardo (Flute), 12–16

DEMKIER, Albert (Violin), 2, 6

DENECKE, Henry, Jr. (Tympani), 38–49

DENECKE, Julia (Flute), 42–43

DePALMA, Emilio (Bass), 41–42

D'ESTE, Charles (Oboe), 22

DICKS, Franz (Violin), 5–17

DIRCKS, William E. (Violin), 6–7

D'ISERE, Guy (Clarinet), 18

DORAN, R. (Trumpet), 28

DOSCH, William M. (Violin), 10–16

DOST, Oscar (Clarinet), 11

DOTZEL, John (Flute, Piccolo), 12–16

DOUCET, Alfred (Oboe), 11

DOUCET, Louis L. (Oboe), English Horn), 18–22

DOUGLAS, Meyer (Violin, Viola), 23–24, 30–34

DRUIAN, Rafael (Violin), 47–49

DUBOIS, Gaston (Cello), 20

DUMONT, Adolphe (Violin), 12–13

DUPUIS, Andre (Oboe), 18

DUVOIR, Alexandre (Oboe), 18–35

EDDY, Cynthia (Cello), 43–49

EDMUNDS, F. T. (Bass), 9

ELEFTHERAKIS, Eleftherios (Viola), 45

ELSON, Joseph (Viola), 26

ELST, Richard O. (Trombone), 19–35

ERCK, Christian (Cello), 3–7, 9–37

ERCK, Edward J. "Bill" (Violin, Horn), 1–26

ESSER, Walter (Cello), 44–48

EURIST, Harry (Viola), 21–24

EVENSON, P. E. (Trumpet), 27–31

EVENSON, S. (Clarinet), 10

EVERS, Hermann (Viola), 4–5

EWART, Hugh (Violin), 43

FAETKENHEUER, William (Tympani), 1–38

FALLICK, Louis (Violin), 41–49

FANTOZZI, William (Violin), 17

FARMER, Virginia (Violin), 43–44

FEILER, Maurice (Cello), 17

FIELDS, Dall (Bassoon), 17–18

FILERMAN, H. (Viola, Horn), 11

FILERMAN, Peter (Viola), 23–41

FINNEY, Theodore M. (Viola), 21–22

FISCH, Burton (Viola), 39

FISCHER, Carlo (Cello, Assistant Manager, Manager, Program Editor), 1, 4–49

FISHMAN, Bernard (Oboe), 44–49

FITCH, Ray W. (Bass), 23–49

FITZGERALD, James (Violin), 20, 25–49

FLOR, Samuel (Violin), 45–49

FOX, Fred (Horn), 32–34

FRANK, Joseph (Viola), 1–4

FRANKSON, Roy E. (Violin), 21–23

FREEMAN, Charles (Flute), 4–6

FREIWALD, Arthur (Viola), 47–49

FRENGUT, Leon (Viola), 34

FROHN, Otto (Violin), 35–41

FROMMELT, Alfred (Cello), 12–15

FUNNEKOTTER, Adrian (Violin), 13–15

FUST, Carl J. (Violin), 7–9, 14

GALLICCHIO, Joseph (Violin), 16–17

GANGELHOFF, John (Viola), 1–8

GARFINKLE, Paul (Violin), 25–39

GATSCHA, John (Violin), 10–31

GAUTHIER, Roger (Oboe, English Horn), 24–31

305

Orchestra Personnel

KNUTSEN, Christian (Cello), 16–31, 33–37
KNUTSON, Erling (Violin), 17
KOCH, Jean (Viola), 6–15, 18–20
KOCH, Oscar (Cello, Trombone), 9–10 15, 18, 28–49
KOEHLER, Albert (Trumpet), 7–18, 20–22
KOEHLER, George (Clarinet, Violin), 1–12
KOEHLER, Lawrence (Violin), 6
KOERNER, Carl (Violin), 19
KOLTUN, Alexander (Violin), 36–42
KOMAROVSKY, Constantin (Cello), 18–19
KONRAD, Robert (Violin), 39–42
KOPP, Edouard C. (Violin), 11–15
KORB, Fram Anton (Violin), 6
KOSTELECKY, Gustave (Violin), 16
KOVARICK, Frank J. (Viola), 5–18
KOVARIK, John P. (Viola), 2–4
KRAMER, Henry (Violin), 39, 43–49
KRASNER, Louis (Violin), 42–46
KRAUSSE, Otto H. (Bass), 10–12
KRUCZEK, Leo (Violin), 22
KRUSE, Paul (Cello), 43–47
KUCHYNKA, Frank (Bass), 11–35
KUEHLE, Alfred (Cello), 27–28, 33–42
KUEHNE, Carl (Clarinet), 12–16
KURTZ, Arthur (Bassoon, Contra-Bassoon), 46–47
KURZ, George A. (Viola), 35–49
KUYPERS, John (Viola), 24–29
LABATE, Bruno (Oboe), 12–17
LAH, Radivoj (Bass), 41–46
LAMBERT, John C. (Violin), 23–35
LAMPING, Willy (Cello), 9
LANGSTADT, Moritz (Violin), 2
LANTZ, William H. (Horn), 1–10
LARSEN, T. Nils (Cello), 17
LARUSSON, Harry (Trumpet, Cornet), 2–8, 19
LATISCH, Emil (Bass), 5
LATISCH, Isa (Harp), 5
LAU, Paul (Viola, Trumpet, Violin), 12–14, 30–49
LAWRENCE, P. J. (Flute), 1
LeBARBIER, Henri (Trumpet), 18, 21–23
LEMAY, Paul (Viola), 19–33
LETVAK, Phillip (Violin), 18, 21–22
LEVAKOFF, Lawrence (Violin), 25–31

LEVINE, Harold (Violin), 47–48
LEVY, Harry (Violin), 8
LHOEST, Fernand (Cello), 12–16
LIEBERMAN, Harold (Violin), 25
LIEGL, Ernest (Flute), 17–25
LIEGL, Leopold (Clarinet), 26–31
LIND, Carl M. (Violin), 10–14, 17
LINDAMAN, John R. (Violin), 40–49
LINDEN, Anthony (Flute), 17
LINDENHAHN, Richard (Horn), 11–32
LINDER, Waldemar C. (Horn), 35–49
LINDHOLM, Fridolph (Viola), 5–6
LINKE, Charles (Violin), 8–9
LISOWSKY, Peter (Violin), 17, 19, 24–35
LLEWELLYN, E. B. (Trumpet), 9
LOESERMAN, Arthur (Violin, Viola), 24–32
LOMBARDI, Astorre (Oboe, English Horn), 4
LONG, Richard A. (Violin), 9
LUBOVISKY, Calmon (Violin), 7–9
MACCIOCCHI, Rudolph (Horn), 48
McIVER, Felix (Trombone), 1–11
MacKAY, James S. (Trumpet), 41–47
MacKAY, John G. (Trombone), 36–49
MacPHAIL, William S. (Violin), 1, 5–6
McREYNOLDS, George W. (Flute, Piccolo), 5–6, 23–25
MADDEN, Claude (Violin), 1–3
MADDY, Harry D. (Violin), 7–20, 30–49
MADDY, Joseph E. (Viola, Clarinet), 8–11
MADSON, Lawrence M. (Violin), 19–20
MALA, Stephen (Bass), 14–17
MANZELLA, Onofrio (Violin), 32
MARLOWE, W. C. (Trumpet, Cornet), 2–7
MARSHALL, W. S. (Organ), 3
MARTIN, Theodore (Violin), 7
MARTINEZ, Genario (Viola), 43
MATHIEU, Harvey F. (Horn), 18, 21–35
MATHIEU, Max (Horn), 1–10
MATTOX, Gurney (Violin), 16
MAURER, C. C. (Bass), 4
MAURICCI, Vincent (Viola), 36–39, 42–47
MAY, Louis L. J. (Violin), 7–11
MAYR, Edward (Flute, Piccolo), 7–8
MEGERLIN, Alfred (Violin), 20
MELBY, Chester D. (Bass), 22, 35–37

Orchestra Personnel

TETZLAFF, Jane (Cello), 48–49
TETZNER, Henry (Violin, Trumpet), 8–10
THALIN, Walter R. (Clarinet), 20, 35–49
THIECK, William A. (Trumpet), 10–17
THIES, Fred (Violin, Clarinet), 11–37
THOMAS, Paul (Cello), 48
THORDARSON, Lorado (Cello), 45–47
TINLOT, Gustave (Violin), 22
TONKIN, Milton (Bass), 43–45
TOWER, W. L. (Percussion), 1
TREBACZ, Leon (Violin), 19
TRIEBEL, August (Viola, Bass Clarinet), 1–22
TRNKA, Alois (Cello), 25–26
TROBAUGH, Joan (Harp), 49
TSAGGARIS, Thomas (Violin), 43–44
TSUJI, Tom (Percussion), 47
TUCKER, Irwin (Cello), 17
TWEEDY, Robert (Cello), 49
UTERHART, Carl (Violin), 10–11, 17–18
VAN BUSKIRK, John (Bass), 38
VAN VLIET, Cornelius (Cello), 10–15
VAN ZANTEN, Peter (Flute), 41
VITALE, Valerie (Harp), 44–46
VIVIER, Felix (Clarinet), 19
VOIGT, A. (Violin), 1
VOLLMER, Harry (Violin), 23
VOLONINIS, Frederick (Violin), 44–46
WAGNER, Frank (Trombone), 12–28
WAGNER, Harold (Trumpet), 26–28
WAGNER, Richard (Cello), 11
WAHLIN, Eric (Cello), 48–49
WALKER, Ernest (Violin), 42
WALSTON, Cragg (Violin), 1
WALTER, Otto (Cello), 1
WALTON, Paul (Tuba), 49
WANKA, Carl (Violin), 19–25
WARDLE, George P. (Horn), 40–43
WARMELIN, C. (Clarinet), 2
WATERHOUSE, John (Violin), 10–11

WAXMAN, Henri (Violin), 27–28
WECKL, Christian (Bassoon), 21–22
WEFLEN, Emil (Percussion), 23–24
WEIDENHAMMER, Charles (Flute), 4
WEINSTINE, Heimann (Violin), 25–40
WEISEL, Clay (Viola), 15–17, 29
WELCOME, Harry (Viola), 46
WEST, Walter W. (Viola, Clarinet), 13 16–18, 20–49
WIDOFF, Gerald (Violin), 49
WIEDRICH, Fernand (Violin), 10–13
WIEGAND, F. G. (Violin), 9–10
WIGLER, Jerome (Violin), 40, 43
WILBER, Weldon G. (Horn, Violin), 29–35
WILL, Fred (Violin), 1–2
WILLIAMS, Henry J. (Harp), 6–40
WILLOUGHBY, Clarence (Cello), 2–3, 5–8
WINKLER, Anton (Flute), 44–49
WINSLOW, Irving L. (Violin), 34–40, 43–49
WINSOR, Frank (Horn), 49
WISTRUM, Emanuel (Violin), 5
WITTMAR, Friederich von (Bass), 1–17
WITZ, Victor (Viola), 34
WOEMPNER, Carl, Sr. (Flute), 7–11
WOEMPNER, Carl, Jr. (Flute), 27–41
WOEMPNER, Henry C. (Flute, Violin), 7–31
WOHL, Harry (Violin), 25–26
WOLFE, Joseph (Oboe, English Horn), 36–38
WOLFF, Louis (Violin), 18–22
WOLTER, Matt A. (Trombone), 41
WOODARD, Guy H. (Violin), 16–18
WRIGLEY, A. (Violin), 1–2
WUERZ, Herman (Oboe, Viola), 1–11
ZAWISZA, Leon (Violin), 34
ZEDELER, Franz (Violin), 2–17
ZIEBEL, Sigmund (Violin), 18–20
ZWOLANEK, Joseph (Percussion), 2–3, 7
ZINN, William (Violin), 48

Out-of-Town Engagements

FIRST THROUGH FORTY-NINTH SEASON, 1903–1952

Figures in Parentheses Indicate Additional Visits during the Same Year.

ALABAMA. Auburn, 1924. Birmingham, 1912, 1916, 1921, 1925, 1926, 1928, 1930, 1932, 1933, 1934, 1935, 1941, 1943, 1944, 1945. Florence, 1912. Huntsville, 1912. Mobile, 1929, 1930, 1942, 1945. Montevallo, 1941. Montgomery, 1925, 1926, 1928, 1931, 1932, 1941, 1945, 1946. Selma, 1931, 1932. Tuscaloosa, 1929, 1943, 1946. Tuskegee, 1931, 1932.

ARIZONA. Phoenix, 1917, 1918, 1920. Tucson, 1917, 1918, 1920.

ARKANSAS. Eldorado, 1928, 1929. Fort Smith, 1916, 1918. Little Rock, 1916, 1918, 1928, 1929.

CALIFORNIA. Berkeley, 1918. Fresno, 1917, 1920. Long Beach, 1918, 1920. Los Angeles, 1917, 1918, 1920. Oakland, 1917, 1918, 1920. Pasadena, 1918. Redlands, 1917, 1920. Sacramento, 1920. San Francisco, 1917, 1918, 1920. Santa Barbara, 1918. Venice, 1920.

COLORADO. Aspen, 1949. Boulder, 1923, 1928, 1946, 1947, 1949. Colorado Springs, 1918, 1923, 1928, 1930, 1946. Denver, 1910, 1917, 1918, 1920, 1923, 1928, 1930, 1946, 1947, 1949. Fitzsimmons (U.S. General Hospital), 1923. Fort Collins, 1928. Grand Junction, 1918, 1923, 1947. Greeley, 1928, 1949. Pueblo, 1920, 1928, 1946.

CONNECTICUT. New London, 1948. Norwalk, 1948. Stamford, 1948.

DISTRICT OF COLUMBIA. Washington, 1912, 1913, 1927, 1930, 1931.

FLORIDA. Daytona Beach, 1929, 1930, 1931, 1932, 1935, 1936. Gainesville, 1929, 1930, 1933, 1934, 1936. Jacksonville, 1924, 1929, 1930, 1931, 1932, 1933, 1934, 1935, 1936, 1943, 1944. Miami, 1929, 1930, 1931. Miami Beach, 1931. Orlando, 1943, 1944. Palm Beach, 1929, 1930, 1931, 1932. Pensacola, 1929, 1930. St. Petersburg, 1931. Tallahassee, 1929, 1930, 1936. Tampa, 1932.

GEORGIA. Athens, 1943. Atlanta, 1926, 1927, 1931, 1932, 1933, 1934, 1935, 1943, 1944, 1945. Augusta, 1944. Columbus, 1948. Macon, 1924. Savannah, 1930, 1943, 1944. Valdosta, 1924.

IDAHO. Boise, 1947, 1949. Lewiston, 1920, 1947. Moscow, 1920.

ILLINOIS. Alton, 1917, 1920. Aurora, 1914, 1931, 1932. Beverly Hills, 1951. Bloomington, 1913, 1918, 1919, 1920, 1942, 1947. Bloomington Normal, 1942. Cairo, 1912. Carbondale, 1926. Centralia, 1911, 1912, 1914, 1915, 1916. Charleston, 1913, 1915, 1916, 1925, 1928. Chicago, 1911, 1912(2), 1913, 1914, 1915, 1916, 1917, 1918, 1921, 1924, 1928(2), 1929(2), 1930, 1931, 1932, 1934, 1936, 1939, 1940, 1941, 1942, 1943, 1944, 1945, 1946, 1947, 1948, 1949, 1950. Cicero, 1949. Danville, 1910, 1911, 1920, 1928, 1932. Decatur, 1911, 1912, 1913, 1914, 1915, 1916, 1917, 1918, 1919, 1920, 1924. Elgin, 1917, 1918, 1919, 1920. Elmhurst, 1951. Evanston, 1911, 1914, 1917, 1918, 1919, 1952. Freeport, 1929, 1951. Galesburg, 1909, 1910, 1911, 1912, 1913, 1914, 1918, 1919, 1920, 1931, 1952. Highland Park, 1948. Jacksonville, 1915, 1916, 1917, 1918. Kewanee, 1920. La Salle, 1917. Mattoon, 1916. Moline, 1910, 1911, 1912, 1913, 1914. Monmouth, 1909, 1911, 1913, 1914, 1920. Ottawa, 1931. Peoria, 1910, 1911, 1912, 1913(2), 1914, 1915, 1917, 1918, 1945, 1946, 1952. Quincy, 1911, 1929, 1947. Ravinia Park, 1912. Rockford, 1917, 1918, 1920, 1934, 1935, 1936. Rock Island, 1915. Springfield,

Music and Maestros

1911, 1913, 1919, 1920, 1941. Streator, 1911, 1912, 1914, 1918, 1919. Urbana, 1910, 1911, 1914, 1915, 1916, 1917, 1918, 1920, 1921, 1924, 1925, 1926, 1927, 1928, 1931, 1940, 1941, 1945, 1949, 1951.

INDIANA. Anderson, 1912, 1915. Bloomington, 1912, 1913, 1925, 1927, 1929, 1931, 1932, 1943, 1945, 1946. Crawfordsville, 1911. Elkhart, 1948. Evansville, 1913(2), 1914, 1915, 1920, 1927, 1930, 1931. Fort Wayne, 1912, 1915, 1918, 1919, 1930, 1932, 1942, 1944, 1946, 1950. Gary, 1931. Greencastle, 1911, 1912, 1913. Indianapolis, 1913, 1914, 1919, 1920, 1925, 1926, 1929, 1931, 1933, 1934, 1936, 1947. Kokomo, 1910. Lafayette, 1913, 1915, 1916, 1920, 1926, 1931, 1932, 1935, 1946, 1948. La Porte, 1915, 1916, 1927, 1949. Logansport, 1911, 1912. Michigan City, 1928. Muncie, 1946. Richmond, 1913. South Bend, 1910, 1911, 1912, 1913, 1914, 1916, 1919, 1920, 1935, 1943. Terre Haute, 1915, 1916, 1925, 1947, 1949. Valparaiso, 1913, 1914, 1919.

IOWA. Algona, 1912. Ames, 1914, 1919, 1920, 1924, 1935, 1936, 1940, 1941, 1942, 1943, 1944, 1945, 1946, 1947, 1949, 1950, 1951, 1952. Boone, 1911, 1912. Burlington, 1913, 1914, 1918, 1919, 1926, 1928, 1940, 1951. Cedar Falls, 1915, 1917, 1919, 1920, 1923, 1924, 1925, 1926, 1928, 1946. Cedar Rapids, 1913(2), 1914, 1915, 1916, 1917, 1918, 1919, 1920, 1924, 1925, 1926, 1940, 1941, 1942, 1945, 1946, 1947, 1949, 1951, 1952. Centerville, 1910, 1917. Charles City, 1917. Clarinda, 1919, 1920. Clinton, 1909, 1910, 1915, 1919, 1920. Davenport, 1916, 1941. Decorah, 1940. Des Moines, 1909, 1910, 1911, 1912, 1913, 1914, 1915, 1917, 1925(2), 1927, 1928, 1929, 1940, 1941, 1942, 1943, 1944, 1945, 1946, 1947, 1949, 1950. Dubuque, 1915, 1917, 1943. Emmetsburg, 1915. Fort Dodge, 1910, 1911, 1912(2), 1915, 1923, 1925, 1926, 1949. Grinnell, 1910, 1911, 1912, 1917, 1920, 1924, 1927, 1928. Iowa City, 1909, 1910, 1911, 1912, 1916, 1917, 1918, 1919, 1920, 1924, 1925(2), 1927, 1928, 1929, 1931, 1946, 1947, 1948, 1949, 1950, 1951, 1952. Iowa Falls, 1916. Keokuk, 1913, 1919. Marshalltown, 1923, 1924. Mason City, 1911, 1912(2), 1915, 1919, 1920. Oskaloosa, 1913, 1914, 1917, 1919, 1924. Ottumwa, 1930, 1940, 1946. Sioux City, 1909, 1910, 1911, 1912, 1913, 1914, 1915, 1916, 1918, 1919, 1923, 1924, 1927, 1928. Waterloo, 1912, 1916. Waukon, 1920. Waverly, 1951. Webster City, 1915, 1916, 1924.

KANSAS. Abilene, 1920. Atchison, 1913, 1914. Baldwin, 1909, 1910. Chanute, 1915, 1916, 1928. Concordia, 1924. Emporia, 1914, 1915, 1916, 1918, 1919, 1925, 1926, 1929, 1930. Fort Scott, 1915, 1917, 1927. Hays, 1923. Hutchinson, 1912, 1913, 1914, 1915, 1917(2), 1918, 1924. Independence, 1911. Lawrence, 1909, 1910, 1911, 1912, 1913, 1915, 1916, 1917, 1918, 1920, 1923, 1925, 1926, 1927, 1928, 1929. Leavenworth, 1913, 1923. McPherson, 1928. Manhattan, 1911, 1912, 1923, 1924, 1925. Newton, 1915, 1916. Pittsburg, 1911, 1912, 1916, 1917, 1918, 1926. Pratt, 1920. Salina, 1910, 1911, 1917, 1920, 1924. Sterling, 1924. Topeka, 1909, 1910, 1911, 1915, 1916, 1924, 1929. Wichita, 1909, 1910, 1911, 1913, 1920, 1927, 1942, 1945. Winfield, 1916, 1928, 1929, 1942.

KENTUCKY. Bowling Green, 1929. Lexington, 1916, 1927, 1929. Louisville, 1912(2), 1913, 1915, 1916, 1919, 1920, 1921, 1928, 1929, 1942, 1945.

LOUISIANA. Alexandria, 1929. Baton Rouge, 1942, 1946. New Orleans, 1916, 1917, 1918, 1920, 1924, 1925, 1926, 1927, 1928, 1929, 1930, 1931, 1932, 1933, 1934, 1935, 1936, 1941, 1942, 1943, 1944, 1945, 1946.

MAINE. Portland, 1948.

MARYLAND. Cumberland, 1924.

MASSACHUSETTS. Boston, 1916, 1948. New Bedford, 1948. Pittsfield, 1948. Springfield, 1916, 1948. Worcester, 1948.

MICHIGAN. Adrian, 1916. Ann Arbor, 1941, 1942, 1948. Battle Creek, 1912, 1916,

Out-of-Town Engagements

1945, 1952. Bay City, 1941, 1948, 1951. Benton Harbor, 1910, 1911, 1912, 1913, 1915, 1917, 1918, 1919, 1944. Dearborn, 1949. Detroit, 1913, 1914, 1947, 1949, 1951. East Lansing, 1945, 1949, 1951. Escanaba, 1916. Flint, 1916, 1917, 1930, 1948. Grand Rapids, 1910, 1911, 1912, 1915, 1924, 1936, 1943, 1947. Houghton, 1916. Ironwood, 1928. Ishpeming, 1951. Jackson, 1918, 1947, 1951. Kalamazoo, 1910, 1911, 1912, 1913, 1914, 1915, 1917, 1918, 1943, 1947. Lansing, 1916, 1917, 1918, 1930, 1943, 1947. Marquette, 1916. Midland, 1948, 1951. Mount Pleasant, 1915, 1916, 1917. St. Joseph, 1914. Saginaw, 1912, 1943, 1947, 1949, 1951. Ypsilanti, 1914.

MINNESOTA. Albert Lea, 1909, 1910(2), 1912, 1923, 1940. Austin, 1911, 1912, 1947, 1949. Bemidji, 1924, 1939. Brainerd, 1908, 1910. Crookston, 1911, 1919, 1951. Duluth, 1907, 1908, 1909, 1910, 1911(2), 1912, 1913, 1915, 1916, 1922, 1925, 1927. Faribault, 1910, 1912(2), 1915. Fergus Falls, 1912, 1913, 1915. Fort Snelling, 1942(2). Glen Lake, 1933, 1934, 1935. Hibbing, 1911, 1924, 1947. International Falls, 1951. Litchfield, 1913, 1914. Little Falls, 1913. Mankato, 1908, 1909, 1911, 1912(2), 1914, 1918, 1923(2), 1950. Moorhead, 1907, 1929, 1930, 1936, 1937, 1940, 1942, 1943, 1944, 1946, 1947, 1950, 1951, 1952. New Ulm, 1911, 1912. Northfield, 1913, 1914, 1915, 1920, 1925, 1926(2), 1927, 1932, 1933, 1934, 1935, 1936(2), 1938(2), 1939, 1940, 1941, 1942, 1943, 1944, 1945, 1946, 1947, 1948, 1949, 1950, 1951. Owatonna, 1910, 1912, 1915. Red Wing, 1912, 1914. Rochester, 1909, 1910, 1911, 1912, 1915, 1920, 1923, 1940, 1941, 1946(2), 1948, 1949, 1950, 1952. St. Cloud, 1909, 1910(2), 1911, 1913, 1918, 1919, 1920, 1925, 1933, 1934, 1941, 1947, 1948. St. Peter, 1949, 1950. Stillwater, 1910, 1911. Thief River Falls, 1911, 1913. Virginia, 1921. Wadena, 1935, 1936. Willmar, 1939. Winona, 1915, 1924, 1925, 1936, 1951.

MISSISSIPPI. A. and M. College, 1927, 1928. Columbus, 1929, 1941, 1942. Jackson, 1918, 1925, 1936. Laurel, 1927.

MISSOURI. Brookfield, 1915. Cape Girardeau, 1918. Carthage, 1910, 1912. Columbia, 1912, 1913, 1914, 1917, 1919, 1920, 1925, 1926, 1927, 1928, 1940, 1947, 1951, 1952. Hannibal, 1920. Jefferson City, 1920. Joplin, 1909, 1911, 1914, 1917, 1918, 1919, 1920, 1928, 1929. Kansas City, 1909, 1910, 1911, 1915, 1916, 1917, 1919, 1920, 1923(2), 1924, 1925(2), 1928, 1929. Kirksville, 1909, 1910, 1911, 1912, 1913, 1914, 1915, 1916, 1920, 1927. Lexington, 1909. Maryville, 1916, 1917, 1925. St. Joseph, 1909, 1911, 1913, 1915, 1916, 1917, 1918, 1919, 1920, 1923, 1925, 1926, 1927, 1928, 1929, 1930, 1945. St. Louis, 1913, 1926, 1927, 1928, 1940, 1944, 1945, 1949, 1951. Sedalia, 1915, 1916, 1917, 1926. Springfield, 1912, 1913, 1914, 1917, 1927. Tarkio, 1910, 1911. Warrensburg, 1912, 1915, 1916, 1917.

MONTANA. Billings, 1920, 1923, 1947, 1949. Bozeman, 1920, 1923. Butte, 1920, 1923, 1947, 1949. Deer Lodge, 1920. Great Falls, 1920, 1923, 1947, 1949. Helena, 1920, 1947, 1949. Miles City, 1920. Missoula, 1920, 1923, 1947, 1949.

NEBRASKA. Beatrice, 1949. Falls City, 1915, 1918. Fremont, 1949. Grand Island, 1913, 1914, 1920. Hastings, 1925, 1926, 1946, 1947. Kearney, 1928. Lincoln, 1909, 1910, 1913, 1914, 1918, 1920, 1924, 1925, 1946. Omaha, 1908, 1909, 1910, 1913, 1914, 1915, 1916, 1917, 1919, 1920(2), 1923, 1924, 1941, 1943, 1945, 1946, 1947.

NEVADA. Reno, 1917, 1918, 1920.

NEW JERSEY. New Brunswick, 1948.

NEW YORK. Albany, 1947. Aurora, 1913, 1914. Brooklyn, 1914. Buffalo, 1912, 1913, 1914, 1942, 1943, 1945, 1946, 1947, 1948, 1949, 1950. Corning, 1943. Elmira, 1943. Ithaca, 1913, 1914, 1946, 1947, 1949, 1951. Jamestown, 1949. New York City, 1912, 1913, 1914, 1916, 1924, 1927, 1948. Niagara Falls, 1932. Oswego,

313

1916. Rochester, 1914. Rome, 1914, 1916. Syracuse, 1916, 1946, 1951. Utica, 1946. West Point, 1947.

NORTH CAROLINA. Asheville, 1933, 1934. Chapel Hill, 1936. Charlotte, 1930. Durham, 1932, 1935. Greensboro, 1924, 1931, 1932, 1933, 1934, 1935, 1936. Raleigh, 1948. Winston-Salem, 1933, 1935, 1936.

NORTH DAKOTA. Bismarck, 1914, 1915, 1920, 1947, 1952. Devils Lake, 1913, 1914. Fargo, 1908, 1909, 1910, 1912, 1914, 1915, 1918, 1919, 1920, 1922, 1935. Grand Forks, 1907, 1908, 1909, 1910, 1912, 1913(2), 1914, 1915, 1918, 1919, 1920, 1922, 1929, 1949, 1950, 1951, 1952. Jamestown, 1911. Minot, 1919, 1920, 1930, 1950, 1951. Valley City, 1909, 1910, 1911, 1912, 1913, 1914, 1920, 1925. Wahpeton, 1914.

OHIO. Akron, 1913, 1914, 1919, 1932. Athens, 1926. Bluffton, 1918. Bowling Green, 1918, 1919, 1947. Cincinnati, 1912, 1929. Cleveland, 1912, 1913, 1914, 1916, 1942, 1947. Columbus, 1912, 1913, 1914, 1915, 1916, 1924, 1928, 1930, 1931, 1932, 1933, 1934, 1935, 1936, 1940, 1941, 1942, 1943, 1944, 1945, 1946, 1947. Dayton, 1914, 1915, 1916, 1919, 1927, 1928, 1931, 1932, 1943, 1944. Delaware, 1946. Findlay, 1918, 1942, 1944. Lima, 1918, 1944. Mansfield, 1920, 1945. Newark, 1946. Oberlin, 1914, 1916, 1946. Oxford, 1925. Piqua, 1920. Springfield, 1915, 1919, 1924, 1926, 1949. Toledo, 1913, 1920, 1924, 1929, 1934, 1935, 1936, 1940, 1941, 1942, 1943, 1944, 1945, 1946, 1947, 1948, 1949, 1950, 1951. Youngstown, 1916, 1928, 1932, 1933. Zanesville, 1924, 1947.

OKLAHOMA. Bartlesville, 1917. Durant, 1929. Edmond, 1915, 1916. Guthrie, 1929. Muskogee, 1915, 1916, 1918. Norman, 1924. Oklahoma City, 1916, 1924, 1945. Tulsa, 1913, 1916, 1928, 1929, 1945.

OREGON. Eugene, 1923, 1947, 1949. Medford, 1923. Monmouth, 1920. Pendleton, 1947, 1949. Portland, 1920, 1923, 1947, 1949. Salem, 1947.

PENNSYLVANIA. Altoona, 1926. Beaver Falls, 1947. Carlisle, 1926. Erie, 1932, 1942, 1944. Harrisburg, 1948. Johnstown, 1947. Lancaster, 1927. New Castle, 1927, 1949. Oil City, 1916. Philadelphia, 1913. Pittsburgh, 1912, 1913, 1914, 1924, 1925, 1926, 1927, 1928, 1929, 1930, 1931, 1932, 1933, 1934, 1935, 1936, 1942, 1948. Wilkes-Barre, 1948. York, 1926, 1948.

SOUTH CAROLINA. Charleston, 1924. Clemson, 1948. Columbia, 1924. Rock Hill, 1924, 1930. Spartanburg, 1948.

SOUTH DAKOTA. Aberdeen, 1909, 1910, 1911, 1912, 1913, 1914, 1915, 1916, 1917, 1918, 1919, 1925, 1926, 1927, 1947, 1949, 1952. Brookings, 1908, 1909, 1910, 1911, 1926, 1927. Deadwood, 1910. Huron, 1908, 1909, 1911, 1914, 1925, 1927. Madison, 1917. Mitchell, 1908, 1909, 1910, 1911, 1912, 1913, 1916, 1924, 1925, 1926. Pierre, 1910, 1911, 1926. Rapid City, 1911. Sioux Falls, 1911, 1912, 1913, 1914, 1918, 1923, 1924, 1926, 1947, 1952. Vermillion, 1910, 1911, 1912, 1917, 1924, 1949. Watertown, 1911, 1912. Yankton, 1908, 1910, 1912, 1914, 1917, 1927.

TENNESSEE. Chattanooga, 1943, 1944, 1945, 1946. Knoxville, 1943, 1944. Memphis, 1916, 1917, 1918, 1920, 1925, 1928, 1931, 1932, 1934, 1935, 1944, 1945. Nashville, 1916, 1921, 1925, 1926, 1929, 1930, 1940, 1941, 1942, 1945.

TEXAS. Austin, 1920, 1924, 1945. Corsicana, 1924. Dallas, 1929, 1941, 1945. Denton, 1929, 1941, 1942. El Paso, 1917, 1918, 1920. Fort Worth, 1924, 1929, 1945. Galveston, 1941, 1942. Houston, 1917, 1918, 1920, 1924, 1929, 1941, 1942, 1945. San Antonio, 1917, 1918, 1920, 1929. Waco, 1929. Wichita Falls, 1945.

UTAH. Logan, 1918, 1923. Ogden, 1917, 1920, 1923, 1947. Provo, 1918, 1923, 1947, 1949. Salt Lake City, 1917, 1918, 1920, 1923, 1947.

VIRGINIA. Charlottesville, 1924. Danville, 1924. Lynchburg, 1932, 1934.

Out-of-Town Engagements

WASHINGTON. Aberdeen, 1923. Bellingham, 1920, 1949. Centralia, 1920. Everett, 1947, 1949. Grandview, 1920. Pullman, 1920, 1947, 1949. Seattle, 1920, 1923, 1947, 1949. Spokane, 1920, 1923, 1947, 1949. Tacoma, 1920, 1923. Walla Walla, 1920. Yakima, 1920, 1947, 1949.

WEST VIRGINIA. Charleston, 1928, 1949. Huntington, 1928, 1949. Wheeling, 1914, 1934, 1935.

WISCONSIN. Appleton, 1912, 1913, 1916, 1917, 1921, 1923, 1925, 1926, 1927, 1928, 1950. Ashland, 1916. Beloit, 1913, 1919, 1932. Eau Claire, 1911, 1919, 1921, 1923, 1925, 1926, 1940. Fond du Lac, 1925. Green Bay, 1912, 1921, 1929, 1947. Janesville, 1912, 1915. Kenosha, 1911. La Crosse, 1910, 1911, 1912, 1914, 1915, 1920, 1923, 1925, 1940, 1941, 1943, 1944, 1945, 1946, 1947, 1949, 1950, 1951(2). Lancaster, 1924. Madison, 1912, 1913, 1914, 1915, 1918, 1920, 1921, 1923(2), 1924(2), 1925(2), 1926, 1940, 1941, 1942, 1943, 1944, 1945, 1946, 1947, 1948, 1950, 1951. Manitowoc, 1942. Menomonie, 1911. Milwaukee, 1912, 1914, 1917, 1920, 1921, 1923, 1925, 1927, 1930, 1936, 1942, 1943, 1944, 1945, 1946, 1947, 1949, 1950, 1951, 1952. Neenah, 1912(2). Oshkosh, 1912, 1913, 1920, 1929. Racine, 1912, 1919, 1929. Ripon, 1920, 1923, 1925. Sheboygan, 1912, 1943. Stevens Point, 1925, 1926. Superior, 1911, 1921. Watertown, 1925. Wausau, 1926, 1947, 1949, 1950. Waukesha, 1925.

WYOMING. Cheyenne, 1928, 1947, 1949. Laramie, 1917, 1928, 1946.

CANADA. Brandon, Man., 1912, 1913. Calgary, Alta., 1920, 1950, 1952. Edmonton, Alta., 1920, 1950, 1952. Hamilton, Ont., 1942, 1943, 1944, 1949, 1951. Kingston, Ont., 1945, 1946. Lethbridge, Alta., 1952. Montreal, Que., 1944, 1945, 1946. Moose Jaw, Sask., 1950. Ottawa, Ont., 1943, 1944, 1945, 1946. Quebec, Que., 1944, 1945. Regina, Sask., 1920, 1925, 1930, 1950, 1952. Saskatoon, Sask., 1920, 1950, 1952. Toronto, Ont., 1942, 1943, 1944, 1946. Vancouver, B.C., 1920, 1923, 1947. Victoria, B.C., 1920. Winnipeg, Man., 1908, 1909, 1910, 1911, 1912, 1913, 1914, 1918, 1919, 1920(2), 1922, 1924, 1925, 1929, 1930, 1935, 1936, 1937, 1939, 1940, 1941, 1942, 1943, 1944, 1945, 1946, 1947, 1948, 1949, 1950, 1951, 1952.

CUBA. Havana, 1929, 1930.

Summary

UNITED STATES	No. of Cities	No. of Concerts
Alabama	10	58
Arizona	2	9
Arkansas	3	18
California	11	36
Colorado	9	54
Connecticut	3	3
District of Columbia	1	5
Florida	11	47
Georgia	7	32
Idaho	3	8
Illinois	34	299
Indiana	19	129
Iowa	29	372
Kansas	22	185
Kentucky	3	25
Louisiana	3	58
Maine	1	1

Music and Maestros

UNITED STATES continued	No. of Cities	No. of Concerts
Maryland	1	1
Massachusetts	5	7
Michigan	23	124
Minnesota	29	233
Mississippi	4	13
Missouri	17	179
Montana	8	32
Nebraska	8	71
Nevada	1	3
New Jersey	1	1
New York	16	43
North Carolina	7	31
North Dakota	8	104
Ohio	20	137
Oklahoma	8	27
Oregon	6	14
Pennsylvania	13	54
South Carolina	5	7
South Dakota	12	155
Tennessee	4	40
Texas	11	54
Utah	4	26
Virginia	3	4
Washington	11	28
West Virginia	3	9
Wisconsin	24	189
Wyoming	2	6
Total	425	2931
CANADA		
Alberta	3	5
British Columbia	2	5
Manitoba	2	181
Ontario	4	20
Quebec	2	7
Saskatchewan	3	13
Total	16	231
CUBA		
Havana	1	6
Grand total	442	3168

Repertoire (abridged)

FIRST THROUGH FORTY-NINTH SEASON, 1903–1952

COMPILED BY CARLO FISCHER

The seasons during which a work was performed are indicated by the numbers following the title. A number standing alone indicates the regular evening symphony series; P following the number indicates the work was played at a popular, twilight, pension fund, or extra concert; a double dagger (‡) preceding the number indicates a joint concert of the Philharmonic Club and the orchestra (during the first six seasons). If a work was repeated during the season, (2) follows the number. To ascertain the years in which listed works were played, add 2 to the season number: thus, season 1 was the season of 1903–4, season 10 the season of 1912–13, and so on.

To keep this list of performed works within reasonable bounds, it has been necessary to delete songs (except a few important song cycles), arias, instrumental solos, numerous inconsequential works of slight musical quality or outmoded idiom, some display pieces for solo instruments with orchestral support, arrangements of vocal and instrumental solos, a cappella numbers, musical comedy and operetta potpourris, and many scenes from Wagner operas and music dramas. Omitted also, in most cases, are excerpts from works if the complete works were played.

ADAM, Adolphe. Overture to *Si J'Etais Roi*, 15P, 22P, 24P.

ALBENIZ, Isaac. *Iberia:* Suite, 49; *Triana*, 34, 35, 41; *Holiday in Seville*, 34. *Navarra*, 32, 36, 41. *Catalonia*, 41.

ALBERT, Eugène d'. Overture to *Der Improvisator*, 2, 3, 4P, 5P, 6P, 7P, 9P, 11P, 15P, 17P, 19P. Overture to *Die Abreise*, 8P. Concerto for Violoncello in C major, 10, 13.

ALFVEN, Hugo. Symphony No. 3, in E major, 12, 13, 17. *Midsommarvaka*, Swedish Rhapsody, 8P, 10P, 11, 14P, 15P, 16P, 17P, 19P, 22P, 27, 29P, 30P. *Drapa*, Symphonic Poem, 12P. *Festspel*, Polonaise, 12P.

ALIFERIS, James. Symphony No. 1, 45. *Minnesota 1849*, A Fantasy for Orchestra, 47.

AMBROSIO, Alfredo d'. Concerto for Violin, in B minor, 7P, 15P.

AMFITHEATROF, Daniele. *Panorama Americana*, 35.

ANROOY, Peter van. *Piet Hein*, Dutch Rhapsody, 22&P, 25P, 27.

ARENSKY, Anton. Ballet Suite, *A Night in Egypt*, 17P. Concerto for Piano, in F minor, 8P.

ATTERBERG, Kurt. Symphony No. 2, in F major, 18. Symphony No. 3 (*West Coast Pictures*), 19, 24. Symphony No. 6, in C major, 26. Rhapsody, *The Foolish Virgins*, 21P.

AUBER, Daniel. Overture to *Masaniello*, 5P, 11P, 13P, 18P, 22P, 24P. Overture to *Fra Diavolo*, 16P, 23P. Overture to *The Bronze Horse*, 16P, 22P, 35P.

AUBERT, Louis. Fantaisie for Piano and Orchestra, 35.

AULIN, Tor. Swedish Dances, Nos. 1, 2, and 4, 11P. Concerto for Violin, No. 3, in C major, 7P.

Music and Maestros

AVERY, Stanley R. *A Joyous Prelude*, 12P.

BACH, Christopher. *Wedding March*, 7P.

BACH, Johann Sebastian. *Brandenburg* Concerto No. 1, in F major, 42, 45. *Brandenburg* Concerto No. 2, in F major, 26. *Brandenburg* Concerto No. 3, in G major, 5, 22&P, 26, 29, 31, 41. *Brandenburg* Concerto No. 4, in G major, 22. *Brandenburg* Concerto No. 5, in D major, 22, 37, 42. Suite No. 1, in C major, 21P, 28. Suite No. 2, in B minor, 22, 33. Suite No. 3, in D major, 24, 41, 48. (Arr. Mahler) Suite, 8, 11. (Arr. Goossens) Suite in G (transcriptions from the French suites), 30. (Arr. Abert) Prelude, Chorale, and Fugue, 4, 19. (Arr. Verbrugghen) Prelude and Fugue in E flat major (*St. Ann's*), 25, 27. (Arr. Schönberg) Prelude and Fugue in E flat major (*St. Ann's*), 31. (Arr. Cailliet) Prelude and Fugue in F minor, 34. (Arr. Respighi) Prelude and Fugue in D major, 34, 36, 45. (Arr. Mitropoulos) Prelude and Fugue in B minor, 35, 40. (Arr. D'Antalffy) Prelude and Fugue No. 18, in E minor, 30. (Arr. Ormandy) Toccata and Fugue in D minor, 31(2), 32. (Arr. Weiner) Toccata No. 1, in C major, 38&P, 41, 44, 47. (Arr. Mitropoulos) Fantasia and Fugue in G minor, 34, 36&P, 37P, 39, 42. (Arr. Boessenroth) Passacaglia and Fugue in C minor, 32, 33, 34P, 36, 44, 47. (Arr. Ormandy) Passacaglia and Fugue in C minor, 45. (Arr. Stokowski) Passacaglia and Fugue in C minor, 49. (Arr. Kes) Three Preludes, Nos. 8, 22, and 3, from *The Well-Tempered Clavier*, 25. (Arr. Guerrini) Adagio and Fugue (arranged for strings), 45. (Arr. Verbrugghen) Prelude and Fugue in C sharp minor, from *The Well-Tempered Clavier*, 26, 28. (Arr. Darmstadt) Two Fugues from *The Art of the Fugue*, 38. (Arr. Nabokoff) *Goldberg Variations*, 36. Choral Fantasy, from Cantata No. 41, 47. (Arr. Schönberg) Two Choral Preludes: *Schmücke Dich, O Liebe Seele,* and *Komm Gott, Schöpfer, Heiliger Geist,* 30. (Arr. Cailliet) Organ Choral Prelude, *Herzlich Thut Mich Verlangen,* 32, 33. (Arr. Boessenroth) Choral-Prelude, *Wir Glauben All' an Einen Gott,* 33, 36, 38, 40. (Arr. Reger) Choral-Prelude, *O Man, Thy Grievous Sin Bemoan,* 37, 42. (Arr. Cailliet) Choral, *Jesu, Joy of Man's Desiring,* 34. (Arr. Boessenroth) Prelude in E major, from Sonata No. 6 for Solo Violin, 33. (Arr. Hubay) *Chaconne,* 30(2), 32. Concerto for Piano in F minor, 24, 44. Concerto for Two Harpsichords in C major, 25. Concerto for Three Pianos in C major, 21. Concerto for Violin in G minor, No. 2, 20, 49. Concerto for Two Violins in D minor, 20P, 32P, 34P, 35. *Magnificat,* for Chorus, Soloists, and Orchestra, 48.

BACH, Karl Philipp Emanuel. (Arr. Steinberg) Concerto in D major, 42&P.

BALAKIREFF. Symphonic Poem, *Russia,* 32.

BANTOCK, Granville. Prelude to *Sappho,* 18&P. Comedy Overture to *The Pierrot of the Minute,* 25.

BARBER, Samuel. Overture to the *School for Scandal,* 39&P. Second *Essay* for Orchestra, 44. Adagio for Strings, 38&P, 42. Concerto for Cello, 45. Concerto for Violin, 47. *Knoxville: Summer of 1915,* for Soprano and Orchestra, 46.

BARRATT, Edgar. (Arr. Verbrugghen) *Coronach,* Scottish Highland Lament, 23P, 24P.

BARTOK, Béla. Concerto for Violin and Orchestra, 41. Dance Suite for Orchestra, 45. Concerto for Orchestra, 47, 48. Concerto for Viola, 47. Music for Strings, Percussion, and Celesta, 48. Divertimento for Strings, 47.

BAX, Arnold. Fantasy for Viola and Orchestra, 22P.

BEACH, Mrs. H. H. A. Symphony in E minor (*Gaelic*), 15. Concerto for Piano in C sharp minor, 15.

BEACH, John Parsons. *The Asolani,* Three Pieces for Strings, Woodwinds, and Harp, 24.

BEETHOVEN, Ludwig van. Symphony No. 1, in C major, 2, 6P, 12, 13P, 15, 18P,

Repertoire

19P, 21&P, 28, 29P, 35, 36P, 38, 41&P, 42, 44P, 49P. Symphony No. 2, in D major, 1, 10, 12, 21, 22, 27, 33, 34, 36, 38P, 39, 44, 49. Symphony No. 3, in E flat major (*Eroica*), 5, 7, 9, 12, 13, 16, 18, 19, 20, 21, 23, 26, 29, 31, 35, 38, 40, 42, 46, 48. Symphony No. 4, in B flat major, 7, 12, 18, 21, 32, 36, 38, 42, 45, 48. Symphony No. 5, in C minor, 3, 4, 6, 7P, 9, 11&P, 12, 14, 15, 16, 18P, 19&P, 20P, 21, 24, 26, 29&P, 30P(2), 31P, 32, 33, 34P, 35, 36P, 38, 40, 43&P(2), 47, 48, 49P. Symphony No. 6, in F major (*Pastoral*), 1, 8, 10, 12, 14, 17, 19, 21, 22, 33, 36, 37, 41, 44, 47. Symphony No. 7, in A major, 3, 6, 8, 10, 12, 13, 16, 18, 19, 21&P, 25, 28, 29, 30P, 32, 34P, 35, 36, 39(2), 43&P, 47. Symphony No. 8, in F major, 9, 12, 15, 17, 20, 21, 25, 31, 34P, 37, 40, 42, 45, 49. Symphony No. 9, in D minor (*Choral*), 5, 12, 21&P, 22&P, 24, 31&P, 37&P, 45, 48. *Jena* Symphony, 9P. Overture, *Coriolanus*, 12, 13, 15, 20, 22, 27, 37, 41&P, 45. *Leonore* Overture No. 1, 12, 21, 39, 43. *Leonore* Overture No. 2, 34, 36, 41&P. *Leonore* Overture No. 3, 6, 8, 9, 12, 13, 14P, 15, 16, 17P, 18, 19, 20&P, 21&P, 23&P, 25&P, 27, 29&P, 30, 31P, 32, 34P, 42, 43, 45, 46, 48. Overture to *Fidelio*, 12&P, 14P, 17, 18P, 21&P, 24, 33, 37, 43. Overture to *Egmont*, 5, 7, 10&P, 12, 13, 14, 18, 20&P, 21&P, 22P, 25, 28, 29, 30P, 31, 32, 33, 34(2)&P, 35P, 36P, 38, 41, 44&P, 46, 48, 49. Overture, *Namensfeier*, 49. Overture, *King Stephan*, 24. Overture, *Weihe des Hauses*, 37P. Suite from the ballet *Prometheus*, 5, 35P. Overture to *Prometheus*, 23, 38&P, 43&P, 45, 48. Concerto for Piano, No. 1, in C major, 15, 22P, 37, 43. Concerto for Piano, No. 3, in C minor, 16, 17, 21, 22P, 24P, 31, 33, 34P, 40P, 48. Concerto for Piano, No. 4, in G major, 12, 21, 24, 27, 35, 40, 42, 44, 47. Concerto for Piano, No. 5, in E flat major, 4P, 5, 7, 10, 12, 13, 20, 21, 25, 30, 35, 38, 41, 45, 46, 47, 49. Concerto for Violin in D major, 3, 8, 11, 12, 14, 17, 18P, 19, 21, 23, 29, 30, 31, 34, 35, 38, 43, 44, 45, 46, 47, 49. Concerto for Piano, Violin, and Violoncello in C major, 14P. Romance for Violin in G major, 12. Romance for Violin in F major, 12. Turkish March from *The Ruins of Athens*, 5P, 7P, 11P, 14P, 22P, 24P. Rondino for Wind Instruments in E flat major, 5, 19, 21&P. Trio for Two Oboes and English Horn, 24. Three Equales for Four Trombones, 24. Theme and Variations from Quartet No. 5, in A major, 5P, 8P, 9P, 10P, 11P, 17P, 18P, 19P, 22P. Quartet No. 11, in F minor, 36. Quartet in C sharp minor, 35. (Arr. Weingartner) Grand Fugue in B flat, 36. (Arr. W. Damrosch) Polonaise from Serenade for String Trio, 20. (Arr. Weingartner) Sonata in B flat major, 36. *Missa Solemnis*, 49. Terzet, *Tremate, Empi, Tremate*, 5. Elegiac Song for Vocal Quartet, 24.

BEREZOWSKY, Nicholai. Symphony No. 1 (in one movement), 34.

BERG, Alban. Three Extracts from *Lyric* Suite (for strings), 37. Fragments from *Wozzeck*, 45. Concerto for Violin and Orchestra, 42.

BERGQUIST, J. Victor. Oratorio, *Golgata*, 3P.

BERLIOZ, Louis Hector. *Symphonie Fantastique*, 9, 20, 30, 38, 44, 48. Symphony No. 3 (*Harold in Italy*), 12, 23, 36, 39, 42, 49. Symphony, *Romeo and Juliet*: Scherzo, *Queen Mab*, 13, 22&P, 32, 33, 41: Love Scene, 14P, 35P, 41. Overture to *King Lear*, 40, 43. Overture to *Roman Carnival*, 6&P, 7&P, 8&P, 9P, 10, 11&P, 12, 13, 14, 16, 18P, 20&P, 22P, 25, 27, 29, 30P, 31&P, 32P, 33, 35P, 39&P, 42&P(2), 44, 46, 48, 49. Overture to *Benvenuto Cellini*, 13, 22P, 30, 34, 37, 43, 47. Overture to *The Corsair*, 36. Overture, *Rob Roy*, 45. Overture to *Beatrice and Benedict*, 46. March, *Marocaine*, 10P. *The Damnation of Faust*: Dramatic Legend, ‡5; Minuet of the Will-o'-the Wisps, Dance of the Sylphs, Rakóczy March, 1, 6P, 7P, 8P, 9P, 12P, 15P, 16P, 17, 19P, 20P, 23P, 24P, 29, 30P, 32&P, 34P, 36P, 41, 45. Trio for Two Flutes and Harp from *The Infancy of Christ*, 16P. Overture to *The Flight into Egypt*, 41.

319

Music and Maestros

BIZET, Georges. Symphony in C major, 40. Dramatic Overture, *Patrie*, 20P. *L'Arlésienne*, Suite No. 1, 5P, 8P, 9P, 11P, 12P, 20P, 23P, 34P, 35P. *L'Arlésienne*, Suite No. 2, 23P, 29P, 33P. Suite, *Children's Games*, 9P, 45. Suite, *Roma*, 11P, 13P, 24P. Selections from *Carmen*, Suites Nos. 1 and 2, 4P(2), 5P, 7P, 10P, 14P, 22P, 23P, 25P, 35P. Egyptian Dance from *Djamileh*, 12P.

BLEYLE, Karl. Tone Poem, *Flagellantenzug*, 9.

BLISS, James A. (Arr. Verbrugghen) Two Sketches from Sonata for Piano, 22P.

BLOCH, Ernest. *America*, An Epic Rhapsody, 26, 27, 43. Two Poems, *Hiver, Printemps*, 16. Three Jewish Poems, 16. *Schelomo*, Hebrew Rhapsody for Cello, 22P, 38, 45, 48.

BOCCHERINI, Luigi. Symphony in A major, 38. Overture in D major, 41P. Suite in C major for Strings (string quintet), 35.

BOELLMANN, Léon. *Variations Symphonique*, for Cello, 5&P, 10P, 12P. *Fantasy Dialogue*, for Organ and Orchestra, 6P, 12P.

BOIELDIEU, François. Overture to *La Dame Blanche*, 21&P, 27. Overture to *The Calif of Bagdad*, 15P.

BONVIN, Ludwig. Festival Procession, 13P.

BORODIN, Alexander. Symphony No. 2, in B minor, 13, 19, 20P, 34, 35P, 39&P, 41&P, 46, 49. *A Sketch of the Steppes of Central Asia*, 3, 9P, 17P, 23, 34, 35P, 38. *Prince Igor*: Overture, 41P; Polovetzian Dances, 13P, 16P, 28&P, 29&P, 30P, 31P, 33P, 34, 35P, 38P, 43P(2).

BOROWSKI, Felix. *Trois Peintures*, 15&P, 17. *Elégie Symphonique*, 15&P. *Marche Triomphale*, 15P, 16P. Suite from the ballet-pantomime *Boudour*, 18. Fantasie-Overture, *Youth*, 27.

BORTKIEWICZ, Sergei. Concerto for Piano in B flat minor, 12P, 19P.

BOSSI, Marco Enrico. *Intermezzi Goldoniani*, for Strings, 8.

BOTTESINI, Giovanni. Grand Duo for Violin and Contra-Bass, 30P.

BOURGUIGNON, Francis de. *Jazz Triumphant*, Symphonic Poem, 28.

BRAHMS, Johannes. Symphony No. 1, in C minor, 6, 7, 9, 10, 12, 13, 14, 15, 16, 17, 18, 19, 20&P, 21, 23, 25, 27, 29&P, 30, 31, 32, 33P, 34, 36, 38, 40&P, 42, 43, 45, 46, 47, 49. Symphony No. 2, in D major, 7, 9, 11, 13, 15, 16, 18, 19, 20, 21P, 23(2), 26, 28, 30, 32, 33, 34, 35, 37, 41(2)&P, 43, 45, 46, 48, 49. Symphony No. 3, in F major, 10, 11, 14, 17, 19, 24, 31, 33, 35, 38, 41&P, 44&P, 47. Symphony No. 4, in E minor, 8, 12, 17, 18, 19, 22, 25, 26, 28, 29, 30, 32, 33P, 34, 36, 39, 42, 45, 46. *Academic Festival* Overture, 4, 8, 12P, 21&P, 22P, 24P, 27, 29, 30P, 31, 32P, 33P, 34, 35, 39, 41, 46. *Tragic* Overture, 21, 36. Variations on a Theme by Haydn, 11, 18, 19, 23, 26, 31, 32P, 39&P, 42&P, 47. Hungarian Dances (first set), 4P, 5P, 6P, 7P, 8P, 9P, 10P, 11P, 12P, 15P, 16P, 17P, 19P, 20P, 22P, 24P, 28P, 29P, 30P, 33P. (Arr. Dvořák) Hungarian Dances (Nos. 19, 20, 21), 32. Concerto for Piano, No. 1, in D minor, 11, 18, 27, 36, 40, 41, 43, 48. Concerto for Piano, No. 2, in B flat major, 23, 29, 31, 38, 39, 43, 47, 49. Concerto for Violin in D major, 10, 11, 12, 19, 22, 24, 26, 29, 32, 33, 36, 38, 41, 43, 45, 46, 48. Concerto for Violin and Cello in A minor, 15, 35, 39, 46P, 48. *Requiem*, for Soprano, Baritone, Chorus, and Orchestra, 38. Rhapsody for Contralto, Male Chorus, and Orchestra, 21. *Schicksalslied* ("Song of Destiny"), for Chorus and Orchestra, 44P. *Nänie*, for Vocal Quartet and Orchestra, 23P. *Vier Ernste Gesänge* ("Four Serious Songs"), 38, 43.

BRAUNFELS, Walter. Fantastic Variations on a Theme of Berlioz, 24. *Taubenhochzeit*, from *Die Vögel*, 22.

BRITTEN, Benjamin. *Sinfonia da Requiem*, 43. Three Sea Interludes from *Peter Grimes*, 47. *The Young Person's Guide to the Orchestra*, Variations and Fugue

Repertoire

on a Theme of Purcell, 46, 48. Scottish Ballad for Two Pianos and Orchestra, 45.

BRUCH, Max. Introduction to *Die Loreley*, 21&P. Concerto for Violin, No. 1, in G minor, 5, 6P, 11&P, 13&P, 14P, 17P, 18P, 20, 21P, 25, 36, 48. Concerto for Violin, No. 2, in D minor, 12&P, 19P, 23. Scotch Fantasie, for Violin, 9, 20P, 22P. *Kol Nidrei*, for Violoncello, 4P, 6P, 8P, 12P, 13P, 14, 18P. *Ave Maria*, for Violoncello, 21P.

BRUCKNER, Anton. Symphony No. 4, in E flat major (*Romantic*), 27, 34, 40. Symphony No. 7, in E major, 7, 31, 33.

BRUNEAU, Alfred. Symphonic Poem, *La Belle au Bois Dormant*, 8P, 10P, 12P, 16P.

BRUNSWICK, Mark. Symphony in B flat, 44.

BRUSSELMANS, Michel. Suite after the Caprices by Paganini, 39.

BURGMEIN. Suite, *The Romance of Pierrot and Pierrette*, 5P.

BURLEIGH, Cecil. Suite, *Mountain Pictures*, 21P. Concerto for Violin, No. 1, in C minor, 16P. Concerto for Violin, No. 3, in C minor, 23P.

BUSCH, Carl. Indian Suite, *Sequentahre* ("Memories"), 7P. *Indian Rhapsody*, 22P. Symphonic Poem, *Minnehaha's Vision*, 13P, 21P. Symphonic Poem, *The Song of Chibiabos*, 16P. *A Chippewa Vision* (for strings), 9P. Prologue to *The Passing of King Arthur*, 7P. Rhapsody, *Negerleben*, 7P. (Arr. Foster) Variations on an American Folk Song, 8P. Concerto for Violoncello in C minor, 17P.

BUSONI, Ferruccio. Concerto for Violin in D major, 19P, 39.

BUTTERWORTH, George, Rhapsody, *A Shropshire Lad*, 20P.

CADMAN, Charles Wakefield. Suite, *The Thunderbird*, 19P.

CALOMIRIS, Manolis. Two Movements from *Hellenic* Suite, 36.

CAPLET, André. *Epiphanie*, Fresco for Cello and Orchestra, 43.

CARPENTER, John Alden. Suite, *Adventures in a Perambulator*, 14, 20P, 22&P. Concertino for Piano and Orchestra, 18P.

CARRILLO, Julian. *Horizontes*, 49.

CASADESUS, Robert. Suite No. 3, 42. Concerto for Piano in E major, 44. Concerto for Cello in C minor, 46.

CASELLA, Alfredo. Rhapsody, *Italia*, 19, 23&P. Suite from *The Convent by the Water*, 19&P. Second Suite from *La Donna Serpente*, 38. *Paganiniana*, 49.

CASTAGNONE, Ricardo. *Prelude Giocoso*, 37.

CASTELNUOVO-TEDESCO, Mario. *Italiano*, Concerto for Violin in G major, 26.

CATALANI, Alfredo. Prelude to Act IV of *La Wally*, 35P.

CECE, Antonio. Passacaglia, 37.

CHABRIER, Emmanuel. Rhapsody for Orchestra, *España*, 3, 6P, 7P, 8, 9P, 11P, 14P, 15P, 16P, 17P, 18P, 19P, 20P, 22P, 27, 29P, 30P, 31P, 32P, 33P. *Marche Joyeuse*, 5P, 7P, 8P, 9P, 11P, 12P, 14P, 16P, 18P, 19P, 23&P, 35P. (Arr. Mottl) *Bourée Fantasque*, 45.

CHADWICK, George. *Suite Symphonique*, in E flat major, 9. Suite, *Symphonic Sketches*, 5. Dramatic Overture, *Melpomene*, 15. Symphonic Ballad, *Tam O' Shanter*, 13, 15. Ballad for Baritone and Orchestra, *Lochinvar*, 5P.

CHAMINADE, Cécile. Concertino in D major, for Flute, 17P, 43.

CHARPENTIER, Gustave. Suite, *Impressions of Italy*, 12P, 24, 37, 46.

CHASINS, Abram. Period Suite, 48.

CHAUSSON, Ernest. Symphony in B flat major, 13, 18, 33, 37, 43, 45. Symphonic Poem, *Viviane*, 12. *Poème*, for Violin and Orchestra, 14, 27, 31, 37, 49. *Poème de l'Amour et de la Mer*, for Contralto and Orchestra, 17.

CHERUBINI, Maria Luigi. Overture to *Ali Baba*, 49. Overture to *Anacréon*, 5, 21P, 33P, 35P, 44. Overture to *The Water Carrier*, 25. Overture to *Les Abencérages*, 40.

Music and Maestros

CHOPIN, Frédéric. Piano Concerto No. 1, in E minor, 10P, 13, 19, 26, 28, 39, 46. Piano Concerto No. 2, in F minor, 2, 10P, 17P, 22, 25, 34, 38, 42, 44P. Andante Spianato and Polonaise, for Piano and Orchestra, 19P, 20.

CHRISTIANSEN, Paul. Symphonic Movement, *The Vials of Wrath*, 39P.

CIMAROSA, Domenico. Overture to *The Secret Marriage*, 47.

CLAPP, Philip Greeley. *Norge,* Tone Poem for Orchestra and Piano, 22P. Prelude, *Summer,* 23P. Overture to a Comedy, 46.

COLE, Rossetter G. Symphonic Prelude, 14P. Ballad for Violoncello and Orchestra, 6P.

COLERIDGE-TAYLOR, Samuel. *The Bamboula,* A Rhapsodic Dance, 11P, 12P.

COLLINS, Edward. *1914,* A Tragic Overture, 26.

CONUS, George. Suite, *Scenes from Child Life,* 7P.

CONUS, Jules. Concerto for Violin in E minor, 16.

CONVERSE, Frederick. Romance for Orchestra, *Endymion's Narrative,* 7.

COPLAND, Aaron. *A Dance Symphony,* 36. Suite from the ballet *Appalachian Spring,* 44. *El Salón Mexico,* 37, 43. *A Lincoln Portrait,* 41. *An Outdoor Overture,* 39.

CORDERO, Roque. *Panamanian* Overture No. 2, 43.

CORELLI, Arcangelo. (Arr. Pinelli) Suite for Strings, 35. (Arr. Dorati) Concerto Grosso No. 1, in D major, 48. *La Folia,* Variations for Violin, 30, 39.

CORNELIUS, Peter. Overture to *The Barber of Bagdad,* 27, 40.

COUPERIN, François. (Arr. Milhaud) Overture and Allegro, 39, 42, 45.

COWEN, Sir Frederic Hymen. *The Fjords* (Andante), from Symphony No. 3 *(Scandinavian),* 23P. Overture, *The Butterfly's Ball,* 14P. Four English Dances in the Olden Style, 18P.

CRESTON, Paul. Choric Dance No. 2, 49.

CZERWONKY, Richard. *Questions,* Two Modern Sketches, 17P, 22P. *A Carnival of Life,* 22P. Serenade, 14P.

DAMROSCH, Walter. Prelude to Act II of *Cyrano de Bergerac,* 11P.

DARGOMIJSKY, Alexander. *Cosatchoque,* Russian Dance, 9P, 14P, 16P.

DEBUSSY, Claude. Prelude to *The Afternoon of a Faun,* 11(2), 14, 16, 17, 19, 20P, 24&P, 27, 28, 29, 30&P, 32, 35P, 37P, 40, 43, 45, 47, 48P. *La Mer,* Three Orchestral Sketches, 19, 26, 30, 33, 34, 36, 38&P, 45, 47, 48. Three Nocturnes: *Clouds, Festivals, Sirens,* 41, 49. *Clouds, Festivals,* 13, 16, 28, 29, 31, 32, 33, 34&P, 35, 37, 45P. *Gigues (Images,* No. 1), 48. *Ibéria (Images,* No. 2), 31, 39, 43, 45, 48. *Rondes de Printemps (Images,* No. 3), 17, 48. Symphonic excerpts from *The Martyrdom of Saint Sebastian,* 47. *Marche Ecossaise,* 8&P(2), 11P, 12P, 15. (Arr. Molinari) *L'Isle Joyeuse,* 31, 38. (Arr. Ravel) *Danse,* 42P. (Arr. Büsser) Petite Suite, 7P, 11P. (Arr. Caplet) Suite, *Children's Corner,* 35P. *Jeux,* 49. (Arr. Chardon) *La Cathedrale Engloutie,* 45. *Danse Sacrée et Profane,* for Harp and Strings, 47. First Rhapsody, for Clarinet and Orchestra, 24P, 37P.

DeLAMARTER, Eric. Symphony No. 2, in G minor, after Walt Whitman, 24, 25P. *For the Children,* suite after the story of *Alice in Wonderland,* 17P. Suite from the ballet *The Betrothal*: Overture, 20P; Dance of the Sweethearts, 20P.

DELIBES, Léo. Overture to *Le Roi l'a Dit,* 17P. Ballet Suite, *Coppélia,* 5P. Ballet Suite, *Sylvia,* 23P.

DELIUS, Frederick. *A Dance Rhapsody,* 13(2)&P. English Rhapsody, *Brigg Fair,* 24, 31. *Summer Night on the River,* 27, 35. *On Hearing the First Cuckoo in Spring,* 27. *A Song of Summer,* 42. *The Walk to the Paradise Garden,* from *A Village Romeo and Juliet,* 40.

DeSWERT, Jules. Concerto for Violoncello in D minor, 8P.

Repertoire

DETT, Robert Nathaniel. (Arr. Verbrugghen) *Juba* Dance, 23P.

DIAMOND, David. Rounds for Strings, 42.

DICKS, Franz. A Concert Overture, 8P.

DOHNANYI, Ernest von. Suite in F sharp minor, 12, 15, 23&P, 28&P. *Ruralia Hungarica,* 31, 46. Adagio, from Concertpiece for Cello, 8P.

DUBENSKY, Arcady. Fugue for Eighteen Violins in Nine Groups, 31.

DUKAS, Paul. Symphony in C major, 40. Scherzo, *The Sorcerer's Apprentice,* 6, 7, 9, 12&P, 15, 16, 18, 20P, 25&P, 27, 29&P, 30P, 31, 32P, 33P, 34P, 35P, 36P, 37P, 44, 48P. *La Péri,* A Dance Poem, 37, 46.

DUNN, James P. Fantasy Overture, *We,* 28.

DVORAK, Antonin. Symphony No. 4, in G major, 39, 49. Symphony No. 5 (*From the New World*), in E minor, 1, 2, 3, 6, 7P, 9, 12, 13P, 17, 18, 19P, 20&P, 22&P, 25&P, 28, 29P(2), 30P, 31P, 32P, 33P, 34P, 35P, 38&P, 46. Dramatic Overture, *Husitzka,* 26. Overture, *Nature,* 20P. Overture, *Carneval,* 8, 9P, 10P (2), 11, 12P, 13P, 14P, 15P, 16&P, 17P, 18, 19P, 20P, 22, 25P, 29P, 31P, 32P, 37, 42, 46, 48. *Scherzo Capriccioso,* 4, 5, 7P, 10P, 14, 29, 30P, 31P, 33P, 40(2), 44. Symphonic Variations, 22. Slavonic Rhapsody, in A flat major, No. 3, 49. Slavonic Dances Nos. 1, 2, 3, 11P, 12P, 14P, 15P, 23P, 30P, 38P. Slavonic Dance No. 3, 29, 38P. Slavonic Dance No. 1, 11P. Concerto for Piano in G minor, 41P. Concerto for Violin in A minor, 37, 39, 45, 48. Concerto for Violoncello in B minor, 16P, 20P, 23, 28, 33, 36, 39, 46. (Arr. Zimmer) *In den Spinnstuben,* No. 1, 10P(2), 13P. *Stabat Mater,* for Chorus, Soloist, and Orchestra, 46P.

EICHHEIM, Henry. *Oriental Impressions,* 22. *A Chinese Legend* (about 600 A.D.), 23&P.

ELGAR, Edward. Suite, *The Wand of Youth,* No. 1, 6&P, 8P. *Enigma* Variations, 20, 28, 30. Concert Overture, *Cockaigne,* 25, 41&P. Introduction and Allegro for Strings and Solo String Quartet, 31. Three Bavarian Dances, from the choral suite *Scenes from the Bavarian Highlands,* 19P, 27. March, *Pomp and Circumstance,* No. 1, 1, 2, 3, 4P, 5P, 7P, 8P, 10P, 15P, 16P, 17P, 20P, 24P(2), 29P, 30P, 34P, 35P, 40. March, *Pomp and Circumstance,* No. 2, 3. March, *Pomp and Circumstance,* No. 4, 7P. Concerto for Violin in B minor, 40. Two Recitations with Orchestra: *Carillon, The Belgian Flag,* 16.

ENESCO, Georges. Roumanian Rhapsody, No. 1, in A major, 13&P, 18P, 30, 31&P, 32, 33&P, 42. Roumanian Rhapsody, No. 2, in D major, 10&P, 11P, 12P, 14, 17P, 20P, 23P.

ERICKSON, Robert. Introduction and Allegro, 46.

ERNST, Heinrich. Concerto for Violin in F sharp minor, 33P.

ESTERHAZY, Franz von. Capriccio for Orchestra, 30.

FALLA, Manuel de. Three Dances from *The Three-Cornered Hat,* 22, 26, 30, 32, 33, 34P, 37, 39, 42P, 46, 48. Suite from *El Amor Brujo,* 48. Interlude and Dance from *La Vida Breve,* 47P. *Nights in the Gardens of Spain,* for Piano and Orchestra, 27, 48.

FARWELL, Arthur. Suite, *The Gods of the Mountain,* 27.

FAURE, Gabriel. Suite from *Pelléas et Mélisande,* 40, 45.

FERGUSON, Donald. Symphonic Waltz, 19P, 30P. Symphonic Poem, *America — A Dream,* 25P.

FETLER, Paul. A Comedy Overture, 49P.

FINNEY, Ross Lee. Slow Piece for Strings, 38.

FLOTOW, Friedrich von. Overture to *Stradella,* 5P(2), 10P, 13P, 16P, 18P. Overture to *Martha,* 4P, 5P, 13P, 15P, 18P, 19P, 23P.

Music and Maestros

FOOTE, Arthur. Four Character Pieces after the *Rubáiyát* of Omar Khayyám, 11P, 15P. Suite for String Orchestra in E major, 8P.

FRANCK, César. Symphony in D minor, 3, 4, 6, 7, 9, 11, 12P, 13P, 15, 16, 18, 19P(2), 20&P, 22, 23, 24, 28, 29P, 30, 31&P, 32&P, 33, 34, 35P, 37, 40, 42&P, 44, 47, 48P. Symphonic Poem No. 1, *Les Eolides*, 16, 42. Symphonic Poem No. 2, *Le Chasseur Maudit*, 9&P, 27, 44. Symphonic Variations for Piano and Orchestra, 9P, 16, 18, 20P, 22, 28, 41P, 44, 46. (Arr. Gui) Prelude, Air, and Finale, 37. Quartet for Strings in D major, 36. Prelude to Part II of *The Redemption*, 30, 38, 44.

FRANCKENSTEIN, Clemens von. Variations on a Theme of Meyerbeer, 26.

FRID, Géza. *Paradou*, A Symphonic Fantasy, 49.

FULEIHAN, Anis. Pastorale (second movement), from Symphony, 39.

GARDINER, H. Balfour. *Shepherd Fennel's Dance*, 20P, 30P.

GEORGE, Earl. Introduction and Allegro, 48.

GERMAN, Edward. Welsh Rhapsody, 7P. Three Dances from *Henry VIII*, 2, 4P, 8P, 9P, 16P. Three Dances from *Nell Gwyn*, 18P.

GERSHWIN, George. *An American in Paris*, 27, 39P, 47. Excerpts from *Porgy and Bess*, 35P, 39P. (Arr. Bennett) A Symphonic Picture, *Porgy and Bess*, 41&P, 44P, 47. *Rhapsody in Blue*, 25P, 31P, 32P, 35P, 39P, 42P, 47. Concerto for Piano in F, 38P, 47, 49P.

GILLIS, Don. Short Overture to an Unfinished Opera, 43P.

GLAZOUNOFF, Alexander. Symphony No. 6, in C minor, 14. Overture on Three Greek Themes, 35P(2). Overture, *Carneval*, 15P. Suite, *Scènes de Ballet*, 7P, 8P, 9P, 10P, 11P, 15P, 16P, 18P. Suite from the ballet *Ruses d'Amour*, 10P. *Cortège Solennelle*, 11P. *Valse de Concert*, No. 1, 8P, 9P, 10P, 12P, 14P, 15P, 16P, 18P, 31P, 47P. Variations on a Russian Theme, Var. 6, 4, 5, 8P, 14P. Concerto for Violin in A minor, 10, 21P, 23, 31, 46.

GLIERE, Reinhold. Symphonic Poem, *The Sirens*, 17, 19&P, 25. Russian Sailors' Dance from *The Red Poppy*, 31, 32P.

GLINKA, Michael. Overture to *Russlan and Ludmilla*, 29, 32P, 33P, 34, 35P, 36P, 41&P, 45P. *Caprice Brilliant*, on Theme of the *Jota Aragonese*, 40P. Fantasia, *Kamarinskaya*, 7P, 8P, 16P, 23P.

GLUCK, Christoph von. Dance of the Happy Spirits, from *Orpheus and Eurydice*, 10, 20P, 22P, 36P, 43. *Iphigenia in Aulis*: Overture, 7, 20P, 24&P, 27, 39, 44, 47; Dance of the Slaves, 9P. Overture to *Alceste*, 38, 40. (Arr. Mottl) Ballet Suite, 21P, 30P.

GODARD, Benjamin. Suite from *Jocelyn*, 17P. *Kermesse*, 17P. Suite for Flute and Orchestra, 24P.

GOLDMARK, Karl. Symphony No. 1, *Rustic Wedding*, 1, 2, 7P, 10P, 12P, 13P, 14P, 15&P, 18P, 19P, 23P. Overture, *Sakuntala*, 1, 3, 7&P, 9P, 10, 11P, 13P, 16P, 18P, 19P, 25P. Overture, *In Springtime*, 12, 13P, 14, 16P, 17P, 18P, 19P, 23P, 25P, 28, 29P, 30P, 32P, 37. Overture, *Sappho*, 20, 23P. Scherzo, 8&P, 9P, 10&P, 11P, 12P, 13P, 15P, 23P. Prelude to Act III of *Cricket on the Hearth*, 27. Ballet Music from *The Queen of Sheba*, 5P, 10P, 23P. Concerto for Violin in A minor, 8, 17, 19, 40.

GOLDMARK, Rubin. *The Call of the Plains*, 25P.

GOLTERMANN, Georg. Concerto for Violoncello, No. 1, in A minor, 9P, 12P, 19P.

GOOSSENS, Eugene. Suite from *Kaleidoscope*, 30. Scherzo, *Tam O'Shanter*, 22.

GOULD, Morton. Symphony (No. 2) on Marching Tunes, 42P. Rhumba, from *Latin-American Symphonette*, 42P. Concerto for Orchestra, 43, 45. Cowboy

Repertoire

Rhapsody, 42P. *Minstrel Show*, 44&P. Spirituals, for String Choir and Orchestra, 41&P. *American Salute (When Johnny Comes Marching Home)*, 41&P. *Philharmonic Waltz*, 46.

GOUNOD, Charles. *Petite Symphonie*, for Woodwinds, 15P. Funeral March of a Marionette, 5P, 23P, 24P. March, *Religious Festival*, 8P, 10P(2), 11P, 14P, 18P. Meditation, *Hymn to Ste. Cecile*, 7P, 21P. *Faust*: Introduction, 7P; Ballet Music, 4P, 5P, 14P, 16P, 20P, 23P, 28P, 29P, 33P, 34P. *The Queen of Sheba*, March (Cortege), 24P. Overture to *Mireille*, 23P.

GRAINGER, Percy. *The Warriors*, for Orchestra and Three Pianos, 24. *In a Nutshell*, Suite for Orchestra, Piano, and Percussion Instruments, 14. English Dance, for Orchestra and Organ, 27. March, *Over the Hills and Far Away*, for Piano, Wind and Percussion Instruments, and Basses, 17&P. *Colonial Song*, 16P, 17. *To a Nordic Princess*, 33P. *Spoon River*, American Folk Dance, for Orchestra and Piano, 33P. *Handel in the Strand*, Clog Dance for Piano and String Orchestra, 33P. *Shepherd's Hey*, A Morris Dance, 13P(3), 14P, 15P, 16P, 19P, 20P, 22P, 29P, 30P, 31P, 33P, 45. *Country Gardens*, An English Dance, 29P, 30P, 31P, 32P, 33P(2), 45. *Molly on the Shore*, Irish Reel, 18P, 30P, 31P, 33P(2), 45. *Irish Tunes from County Derry*, for Strings, 11P, 13P, 15P, 19P, 30P, 31P, 33P, 45. *Mock Morris*, for Strings, 11P, 12P, 13P, 15P.

GRANADOS Y CAMPINA, Enrique. Intermezzo, from *Goyescas*, 15P, 16P, 34, 46. (Arr. De Grignon) *Rondallo Aragonesa*, 28.

GREEF, Arthur de. Four Old Flemish Songs, for Orchestra, 16, 20P.

GRETRY, André. (Arr. Mottl) Ballet Suite from *Céphale et Procris*, 31P, 36, 48.

GRIEG, Edvard. Suite, *Aus Holbergs Zeit*, 21P. *Peer Gynt*, Suite No. 1, 1, 2, 4P(2), 5P(2), 6P, 7P, 8P, 9P, 10P, 11P, 12P, 13P, 14P, 15P, 16P(2), 17P, 18P, 19P, 20P, 21&P, 23P, 28P, 29P, 30P(2), 34P, 49P. *Peer Gynt*, Suite No. 2, 22P. *Lyric Suite*, 5&P, 6P, 7P, 8P, 9P, 10P, 11P, 12P, 14P, 15P, 16P. Overture, *In Autumn*, 14P, 41. Two Elegiac Melodies, for Strings, 5P, 6P, 7P, 9P, 10P, 12P, 13P, 16P, 19P, 22P, 33P, 35P(2). (Arr. Halvorsen) Norwegian Bridal Procession, 4P, 5P, 12P, 15P, 16P, 18P. Concerto for Piano in A minor, 3, 5P, 7P, 8, 10P, 11P, 14, 18P, 19P, 22, 30P, 33P, 41, 45. String Quartet in G minor, 36.

GRIFFES, Charles Tomlinson. *The Pleasure Dome of Kubla Khan*, 18, 22, 41.

GUILMANT, Félix. Symphony for Organ and Orchestra, No. 1, in D minor, 4, 5P, 25.

GUIRAUD, Ernest. Scene and Waltz from *Gretna Green*, 11P(2), 12P, 13P, 17P. Melodrama from *Piccolino*, 20P, 22P. Air de Ballet, *Danse Persane*, 17P.

GUSIKOFF, Michael Joseph. *American* Concerto for Violin, 32P.

HADLEY, Henry Kimball. Symphony No. 3, in B minor, 7. Symphony No. 4, in D minor, 11. *The Culprit Fay*, Rhapsody for Orchestra, 8&P, 9. Overture, *In Bohemia*, 10P, 11P. Tone Poem, *The Ocean*, 19. *Silhouettes*, A Little Suite, 16. *Scherzo Diabolique*, 32P.

HAHN, Reynaldo. *Le Bal de Béatrice d'Este*, Suite for Wind Instruments, Harp, and Piano, 13P.

HALVORSEN, Johan. Suite, *Vasantasena*, 11P. March, *Entrance of the Boyards*, 8P(2), 9P, 11P, 12P, 13P, 14P, 15P, 16P, 18P, 22P, 23P, 30P.

HANDEL, George Frederick. Concerto Grosso in B flat major, 47. Concerto Grosso in C minor, 49. Concerto Grosso in D minor, 36, 41. Concerto for Organ in D minor, No. 10, 24. (Arr. Harty) Suite from *Water Music*, 25, 27, 32, 33, 37, 39, 43, 48. (Arr. Harty) Suite from *Music for the Royal Fireworks*, 34. (Arr. Beecham) Suite, *The Faithful Shepherd*, 40. (Arr. Beecham) Suite, *Origin of Design*, 40. (Arr. Elgar) Overture in D minor, 30. (Arr. Henri Casadesus) Concerto for Viola in D minor, 43. Oratorio, *The Messiah*, ‡1, ‡2, ‡3, ‡4, ‡5, ‡6, 7, 9, 10, 11, 12, 13, 14, 15, 22, 23, 32, 47, 49.

HANSON, Howard. Symphony No. 1, in E minor (*Nordic*), 23. Symphony No. 3, 39P. Symphonic Poem, *Pan and the Priest*, 25. Suite from the opera *Merry Mount*, 34.

HARRIS, Roy. Folk Rhythms of Today, 40.

HAYDN, Franz Joseph. Symphony No. 31, in D major (with horn call), 48. Symphony No. 39, in G minor, 33P. Symphony No. 45, in F sharp minor (*Farewell*), 5P, 6P, 22P, 35P, 38P. Symphony No. 48, in C major (*Maria Theresa*), 49. Symphony No. 73, in D major (*La Chasse*), 40. Symphony No. 80, in D minor (*1784*), 38&P. Symphony No. 82, in C major (*L'Ours*), 23. Symphony No. 83, in G minor (*La Poule*), 22. Symphony No. 85, in B flat major (*The Queen of France*), 18. Symphony No. 86, in D major, 40. Symphony No. 88, in G major, 21&P, 42. Symphony No. 92, in G major (*Oxford*), 38. Symphony No. 93, in D major, 29. Symphony No. 94, in G major (*Surprise*), 7P, 8P, 15, 20P, 31. Symphony No. 95, in C minor, 20P, 28. Symphony No. 96, in D major (*The Miracle*), 47. Symphony No. 97, in C major, 32. Symphony No. 100, in G major (*Military*), 12P, 24, 40. Symphony No. 101, in D major (*The Clock*), 25, 29, 33, 37. Symphony No. 102, in B flat major, 20. Symphony No. 103, in E flat major (with tympani roll), 42. Symphony No. 104, in D major (*London No. 7*), 35, 44. *Symphonie Concertante*, for Solo Violin, Cello, Oboe, and Bassoon, and Orchestra, 28, 35. Concerto for Clavecin in D major, 21P. Concerto for Violoncello in D major, 9P, 11, 18, 24, 34P, 38. *The Creation*, 2, 49P.

HERBERT, Victor. Suite, *Romantique*, 16. *Serenade*, Suite for Strings, 17P. American Fantasy, 10P, 16P, 17P, 21P. Irish Rhapsody, 8P, 10P, 11P, 13P, 14P, 15P, 30P(2), 31P, 32P. *Pan-Americana*, 16P, 30P(2), 31P, 32P, 33P.

HEROLD, Louis. Overture to *Zampa*, 5P(2), 9P, 10P, 12P, 13P, 16P, 19P, 22P.

HILL, Alfred. *Tangi* (Maori Funeral Lament), 20P, 23P. *Waiata Maori*, 23P(2). (Arr. Verbrugghen) *Waiata Poi*, 20P(3), 22P, 26.

HINDEMITH, Paul. Symphony, *Matthias the Painter*, 36, 39. Symphonic Metamorphosis on Themes of Carl von Weber, 47. Symphony in E flat, 39. *Symphonia Serena*, 48. Concert Music for Strings and Brass Instruments, 43. Overture to *Neues vom Tage* ("News of the Day"), 41. Ballet Overture, *Cupid and Psyche*, 42. *Der Schwanendreher*, Concerto for Viola and Small Orchestra, 38. Concerto for Violin, 49.

HINTON, Arthur. Symphony No. 2, in C minor, 11. Three Orchestral Scenes from *Endymion*, 8P, 14P. Concerto for Piano in D minor, 6.

HOLBROOKE, Joseph. Symphonic Variations on *Three Blind Mice*, 23P.

HOLST, Gustav. *The Planets*, 25. *St. Paul's Suite*, for String Orchestra, 22, 25, 43.

HONEGGER, Arthur. Symphonic Poem, *Pastorale d'Eté*, 27, 34. *Pacific 231*, A Symphonic Movement, 22, 48. *Rugby*, A Symphonic Movement, 30. *King David*, A Symphonic Psalm for Chorus, Soloists, and Orchestra, 48P.

HUMPERDINCK, Engelbert. *Hänsel and Gretel*: Prelude, 2, 6P, 8P, 9P, 11P, 18P, 19P, 20P, 27, 29P, 33P; Dream Pantomime, 9P, 14P, 30P.

HUTCHESON, Ernest. Fantasie (Concerto) for Two Pianos and Orchestra, 24.

IBERT, Jacques. *Escales* ("Ports of Call"), 24&P, 33, 44. Divertissement, for Small Orchestra, 42.

INDY, Vincent d'. Symphony for Orchestra and Piano on a French Mountain Air, 19, 22, 37. Symphonic Variations, *Istar*, 19, 23, 33. *A Summer Day on the Mountain*, 45. Trilogy, *Wallenstein*, 15. Introduction to Act I of *Fervaal*, 27.

INGHELBRECHT, Desiré Emile. Symphonic Poem, *La Valse Retrouvée*, 34.

Repertoire

IPPOLITOV-IVANOV, Mikhail. Suite, *Caucasian Sketches*, 22P, 23P, 40P.

JACOBI, Frederick. *A California Suite*, 16P.

JAMES, Philip. Suite, *Station WGZBX*, 33.

JAQUES-DALCROZE, Emile. Concerto for Violin in C minor, 18P.

JOACHIM, Joseph. Concerto in Hungarian Style for Violin, 7, 24.

JONCIERES, Victorin de. Hungarian Serenade, 23P.

JONGEN, Joseph. Fantasy on Two Walloon Carols, 22. *Ronde Wallonne* (Ms.), 23.

JUST, Robert. Two Symphonic Poems, for Two Pianos, 25.

KABALEVSKY, Dmitri. Overture to *Colas Breugnon*, 42, 45.

KALAFATI, Vassili. Polonaise, 11P.

KALINNIKOFF, Vassili. Symphony No. 1, in G minor, 14(2), 15P, 17P, 18P, 19P, 26, 31P, 34P. Symphony No. 2, in A major, 16.

KAUN, Hugo. Festival March and Hymn to Liberty, 8&P, 9P, 12, 14P, 19P.

KELLEY, Edgar Stillman. Symphony No. 2 (*New England*), in B flat minor, 12. Tone Poem, *The Defeat of Macbeth*, 8P. *Aladdin*, A Chinese Suite, 13P.

KERN, Jerome. Scenario for Orchestra on Themes from *Show Boat*, 41P.

KHATCHATURIAN, Aram. Concerto for Piano, No. 1, 42. Three Dances from the ballet *Gayne*, 43(2).

KISTLER, Cyrill. Prelude to Act III of *Kunihild*, 9P, 10P, 12P, 14P, 15P.

KLENGEL, Julius. Concerto for Violoncello, No. 2, in D minor, 18P. Gavotte, for Four Violoncellos, 9P.

KODALY, Zoltán. Suite from *Háry János*, 29, 31, 32P, 47, 48P. Dances from *Galánta*, 34. *Peacock* Variations, 48.

KOLAR, Victor. *Americana*, Symphonic Suite, 13P(2), 16P.

KREISLER, Fritz. (Arr. Sevitzky) Praeludium and Allegro, in E minor, 45. Concerto in C minor for Violin, in Style of Antonio Vivaldi, 42P.

KRENEK, Ernst. Symphony No. 2, 41. Symphonic Movement in Form of Variations on a South Carolina Folk Tune, *I Wonder as I Wander*, 40. Concerto for Piano, No. 3, 44. *Cantata for War Time* (for orchestra and women's chorus), 41.

KROEGER, E. R. Suite, *Lalla Rookh*, 5&P. Symphonic Poem, *Mississippi, Father of Waters*, 23P.

KUBELIK, Jan. Concerto for Violin, No. 1, in C major, 18.

KURTHY, Zoltan. Overture, 38.

LACOME, Paul. Spanish Suite, *La Verbena*, 18P.

LALANDE, Michel Richard de. *Musique pour les Soupers du Roi*, 49.

LALO, Edouard. Norwegian Rhapsody, 18&P. Overture to *Le Roi d'Ys*, 9P, 10&P, 11P, 12P, 13P, 14P, 15P(2), 18P, 19P, 20, 23P, 26, 32P, 36, 37, 40, 42P. Suite No. 1, from the ballet *Namoune*, 13P. Two Aubades for Small Orchestra, 24P. Concerto for Violin, No. 1, in F minor, 15, 26. *Symphonie Espagnole*, for Violin, 7, 9, 11, 13P, 15, 16, 17, 18P, 20&P, 28, 30, 34, 36, 41P, 42, 45. Concerto Russe for Violin in G minor, 22P. Concerto for Violoncello in D minor, 5, 12, 14, 25.

LAMBERT, Constant. *The Rio Grande*, for Chorus, Orchestra, and Piano, 31P.

LASSEN, Eduard. *Festival* Overture, 2.

La VIOLETTE, Wesley. *Penetrella*, for Strings, 26.

LEE, Dai Keong. *Hawaiian Festival* Overture, 40.

LEKEU, Guillaume. Adagio, for String Orchestra, 20, 28, 35.

LEVANT, Oscar. Overture *1912*, 38P. Caprice for Orchestra, 38P. Concerto for Piano and Orchestra, 39P.

LIADOFF, Anatole. Tableau Musical, *Baba Yaga*, 7, 26. Two Legends for Orchestra: *The Enchanted Lake*, 9P, 10P, 14P, 16P, 18P; *Kikimora*, 9&P, 17P, 18P.

Music and Maestros

Eight Russian Folk Songs, 31, 32P, 33, 40(2). Intermezzo, 18P. Variations on a Russian Theme, Var. 3, 4, 5, 8P, 14P.

LIAPOUNOFF, Sergei. Concerto for Piano, No. 2, in E minor, 17, 35P. Ukrainian Rhapsody, for Piano and Orchestra, 19P, 29P.

LISZT, Franz. *A Faust Symphony,* 9, 16, 34. A Symphony after Dante's *Divine Comedy,* 10, 25. Symphonic Poem No. 2, *Tasso, Lamento e Trionfo,* 1, 10, 13. Symphonic Poem No. 3, *Les Préludes,* 1, 2, 4&P, 5P(2), 6P, 7P, 8&P, 9, 10&P, 11P, 12P, 13P, 14P, 16P, 17P(2), 18, 19P, 20P, 21&P, 23&P, 25&P, 28, 29P, 30P, 31P, 32&P, 33, 34P, 36P. Symphonic Poem No. 6, *Mazeppa,* 8, 12P, 38. Symphonic Poem No. 11, *Battle of the Huns,* 6. *Mephisto* Waltz, 10&P, 22, 30P, 35P. Hungarian Rhapsody No. 1, 5&P, 11, 23P, 29P. Hungarian Rhapsody No. 2, 2(2), 4P, 5P, 6P, 7P, 8P, 9P, 10P, 11P, 12P, 13P, 14P, 15P, 16P(2), 17P, 18P, 19P, 21P, 24P, 29P, 30P, 31P, 32P. Hungarian Rhapsody No. 3, 3, 4P, 5P, 7P. March of the Magi, from the Oratorio *Christus,* 9P, 14P. (Arr. Mottl) *St. Francis of Assisi's Sermon to the Birds,* 16P. (Arr. Weiner) *Feux Follets,* 33. Concerto for Piano, No. 1, in E flat major, 1, 5P, 8P, 9P, 11P, 12P, 13P, 14P, 17P, 20&P, 23P, 24P, 25, 32P, 36, 38P, 46. Concerto for Piano, No. 2, in A major, 3, 8P, 9, 15, 20, 21P, 22P, 41P, 43, 47. Hungarian Fantasy, for Piano and Orchestra, 12P, 15, 17P, 18P, 25, 32P, 43P(2), 46. (Arr. Busoni) Spanish Rhapsody, for Piano and Orchestra, 10P, 37. (Arr. Siloti) *Totentanz,* for Piano and Orchestra, 37.

LITOLFF, Henry. Overture, *Robespierre,* 9P, 25P. Scherzo from *Concerto Symphonique,* for Piano, 4, 7.

LOEFFLER, Charles. *A Pagan Poem* (after Virgil), 26.

LUIGINI, Alexandre. Egyptian Ballet Suite, 10P, 14P, 22P.

LULLY, Jean-Baptiste. (Arr. Mottl) Ballet Suite, 38. (Arr. Weingartner) Concerto (Suite) for Strings, 34P.

McCOY, William J. *Naiad's Idyl,* from *The Hamadryade,* 17P. Prelude to Act III of *Egypt,* 22P.

MacCUNN, Hamish. Overture, *Land of the Mountain and the Flood,* 7P(2), 8P(2), 9P, 10P, 12P, 14P, 16P, 17P, 24P.

McDONALD, Harl. Procession of the Workers, from the suite *Festival of the Workers,* 32P.

MacDOWELL, Edward. *Lancelot and Elaine,* Symphonic Poem No. 2, 5, 8P(2), 12P, 14P. Suite in A minor, 9&P, 10P, 11P, 12P, 13P, 15P, 16P, 17P, 18P, 34P. Suite, *Indian,* 10P, 15, 22P. (Arr. Oberhoffer) Suite, *Woodland Sketches,* 12P(2), 15P. Concerto for Piano, No. 1, in A minor, 7P, 12P. Concerto for Piano, No. 2, in D minor, 7, 10P, 16P, 18P, 20P, 22P.

MAHLER, Gustav. Symphony No. 1, in D major, 35, 38, 46. Symphony No. 2, in C minor, 32&P. Symphony No. 3, in D minor, 47. Symphony No. 4, in G major, 19, 35, 49. Adagietto, for Strings and Harp, from Symphony No. 5, 35P, 42&P. *Das Lied von der Erde,* Symphony for Tenor, Contralto, and Orchestra, 39. *Kindertotenlieder,* 47. *Lieder Eines Fahrenden Gesellen,* 33, 38, 48.

MALIPIERO, Francesco. *Impressions from Nature,* Suite No. 1, 24. Concerto for Piano and Orchestra, 36. Concerto for Violin and Orchestra, 32P.

MANCINELLI, Luigi. Overture to the drama *Cleopatra,* 35P.

MANFREDINI, Francesco. *A Christmas Pastoral,* for Strings, 30.

MARSICK, Armand. Prelude to Act II of *Lara,* 35P.

MARTIN, Frank. Concerto for Seven Wind Instruments, Tympani, Percussion, and Strings, 49.

Repertoire

MARTINU, Bohuslav. Symphony No. 2, 41. Concerto for Piano, No. 3, 49. Concerto for Two Pianos, 48.

MARTUCCI, Giuseppe. Nocturne, 35P.

MASON, Daniel Gregory. Symphony No. 1, in C minor, 21. Overture, *Chanticleer*, 28.

MASSE, Victor. Overture to *The Marriage of Jeannette*, 11P, 23P.

MASSENET, Jules. Overture, *Phèdre*, 6P, 10P, 12P, 14P, 15P, 16P, 22P, 23P, 42&P. Suite, *Les Erinnyes*, 3, 4, 9P, 10P, 14P, 19P. Suite, *Scènes Pittoresques*, 1, 4P, 5P, 13P, 18P, 20P, 22P, 23P, 25P, 30P. Suite, *Scènes Napolitaines*, 29P. Suite, *Scènes Alsaciennes*, 7P, 8P, 16P, 17P, 43. Prelude, *The Last Dream of the Virgin*, from the cantata *The Virgin*, 10P, 11P, 14P, 21P. *Le Cid*, Ballet Music, 8P(2), 11P, 15P. *Thaïs*, Meditation, 3, 7P(2), 8P, 9P, 10P, 12P, 14P, 16P, 19P, 29P, 30P.

MAYSEDER, Joseph. (Arr. Hellmesberger) *Ball Scene*, after Etudes, 5P, 14P, 16P, 33P.

MENDELSSOHN-BARTHOLDY, Felix. Symphony No. 3, in A minor (*Scotch*), 5, 21P, 27, 29P, 30, 34, 35P, 41&P, 44, 46, 48, 49. Symphony No. 4, in A major (*Italian*), 6, 19P, 21P, 28, 31, 34P, 35P, 40&P, 46. Symphony No. 5 (*Reformation*), 42&P. Symphony-Cantata, *The Hymn of Praise*, for Orchestra and Chorus, 20. *A Midsummer Night's Dream*: Complete, with Chorus and Reader, 4; Overture, 3, 4P, 6, 9P, 12, 13P, 14P, 16P, 17&P, 18P, 19, 20&P, 21P, 23P, 29, 30P, 32P, 35P, 40, 44P, 49P; Nocturne, 2, 11P, 12P, 13P, 14P(2), 16P, 17P, 19, 21P, 23P, 24P, 29&P, 30P, 31P, 32P, 33P, 36P; Scherzo, 11P, 12P, 13P, 14P(2), 16P, 17P, 19, 21P, 24P, 29&P(2), 30P, 31P, 32P, 33P, 36P; Wedding March, 2, 4P, 5P(2), 6P, 11P, 12P, 13P, 14P, 17P, 18P, 19, 21P. Overture, *Fingal's Cave*, 7P, 8, 13, 18, 20P, 23P, 27, 34P, 36P, 38, 43, 46, 48. Overture, *Calm Sea and Prosperous Voyage*, 23P. Overture, *The Lovely Melusine*, 15P. Overture, *Ruy Blas*, 5, 6P, 7P, 10P, 13P, 14, 16P, 17P, 18P, 23P, 35P, 39P, 42, 45. Overture to Oratorio, *Paulus*, 44. Scherzo from Octet, 36. Concerto for Piano, No. 1, in G minor, 32. *Capriccio Brilliant*, for Piano, 12P, 38P. Concerto for Violin in E minor, 3, 6P, 9, 10P, 12P, 17, 18P, 20P, 22P, 25, 28(2), 33P, 34P, 36P, 40P, 41, 43P, 44&P, 46P, 49P. Oratorio, *Elijah*, 1, 4, 13, 22, 46.

MENOTTI, Gian-Carlo. Overture to *Amelia Goes to the Ball*, 48. Suite from the ballet *Sebastian*, 44.

MESSIAEN, Olivier. *The Ascension*, Four Symphonic Meditations, 47.

MEYERBEER, Giacomo. Overture to Drama, *Struensee*, 18P.

MIASKOWSKY, Nicolas. Symphony No. 6, 24.

MILHAUD, Darius. *Suite Provençale*, 39(2), 41. *Suite Française*, 43. *Le Boeuf sur le Toit*, Rhapsody on South American Tunes, 42&P. *Le Bal Martiniquais*, 44. Two Marches: *In Memoriam, Gloria Victoribus*, 45. Concerto for Cello, No. 1, 48. Concerto for Piano and Orchestra, 36.

MILLER, Charles. *Appalachian Mountains*, An American Folk Rhapsody, 42.

MLYNARSKI, Emil. Symphony in F major, 26.

MOOR, Emanuel. Concerto for String Quartet and Orchestra in E major, 22.

MOSZKOWSKI, Moritz. Ballet Music from *Boabdil*, 6P, 12P. Concerto for Piano in E major, 4.

MOUSSORGSKY, Modest. Fantasie, *A Night on Bald Mountain*, 26, 32, 35P, 40. Turkish March, 9P, 13P. (Arr. Ravel) *Pictures at an Exhibition*, 28, 30, 33, 37, 40, 42, 47, 48P, 49. *Khovantchina*: Prelude, 23(2)&P(2), 25P, 32P, 34(2), 36P, 39, 42, 45; Entr'acte, 33. Persian Dances, 17P.

MOZART, Wolfgang Amadeus. Symphony No. 25, in G minor, 42P. Symphony No. 31, in D major (*Parisian*), 47. Symphony No. 34, in C major, 47. Symphony No. 35, in D major (*Haffner*), 20P, 26, 38, 40, 43, 45, 49. Symphony No. 36, in C major (*Linz*), 48. Symphony No. 38, in D major, 18. Symphony No. 39, in E flat major, 2, 3, 12P, 18P, 22, 35, 39, 46, 49. Symphony No. 40, in G minor, 5, 10, 16, 21, 23, 28, 29, 30P, 31, 32P, 33P, 39, 41&P, 44, 46P, 49. Symphony No. 41, in C major (*Jupiter*), 2, 13, 19&P, 20&P, 27, 34, 37, 40, 42, 45. Symphonie Concertante for Violin and Viola, in E flat major, 15, 25P, 34P, 48P. Serenade No. 7, in D major (*Haffner*), 22. Serenade No. 12, in C minor, for Winds, 20P. Serenade, *Eine Kleine Nachtmusik*, 7, 8P, 9, 16P, 19&P, 21, 29P, 30P, 31P, 32P, 33P, 35, 43&P, 47P. Adagio, from Divertimento No. 15, in B flat major, 24&P(2). Divertimento No. 17, in D major, 33, 34P. Minuet from Divertimento No. 17, 7P, 8P, 23P. Six German Dances, 48. (Arr. Steinbach) Eight German Dances, 31P. Suite from the ballet *Les Petits Riens,* 7&P, 20, 26. Two Entr'actes from *Thamos, King of Egypt*, 38P. (Arr. Busoni) Suite from *Idomeneo*, 40. Overture to *Idomeneo*, 48. Overture to *Der Schauspieldirektor*, 8&P, 30P. Overture to *Die Entführung aus dem Serail*, 24&P, 38&P. Overture to *Così Fan Tutte*, 26, 46P. Overture to *The Magic Flute*, 1, 5&P, 6P, 7&P, 8&P, 9, 11, 12P, 14P, 15, 16, 18P, 19P, 20, 21&P, 23&P, 28, 29, 34, 35P, 36, 39&P, 41, 43, 45, 47. Overture to *The Marriage of Figaro*, 14, 20, 21P, 22P(2), 23, 25, 26, 27, 29, 30, 31P, 33P, 34P, 35, 37, 39&P, 41P, 44&P, 46, 47. Overture to *Don Giovanni* (ending by Busoni), 14, 38, 41P, 44. Music to a Masonic Ritual, 47. Concerto for Piano, No. 7, in G major, 47. Concerto for Piano, No. 19, in F major, 37. Concerto for Piano, No. 20, in D minor, 19, 23P, 25, 28, 31P. Concerto for Piano, No. 21, in C major, 29, 44P. Concerto for Piano, No. 23, in A major, 19. Concerto for Piano, No. 26 (*Coronation*), 24P, 42. Concerto for Two Pianos, in E flat major, 15, 18P, 23P, 24, 32, 45, 48. Concerto for Violin, No. 4, in D major, 30, 42, 44. Concerto for Violin, No. 5, in A major, 34P, 40. Concerto for Violin, No. 6, in E flat major, 18, 21P, 23P, 27. Concerto for Violin, No. 7, in D major, 49. Concerto for Flute and Harp in C major, 15P, 21P, 29, 30P, 34P. Concerto for Clarinet in A major, 22P. Concerto for Bassoon in B flat (first movement), 36. Concertante Quartet for Oboe, Clarinet, Bassoon, and Horn, 13P, 47. *Romanza*, from Concerto for Horn, 12P. Andante in C major, for Flute, 36. Larghetto, from Clarinet Quintet, 10P, 11P. (Arr. Labate) Concerto for Oboe in F major (arranged from quartet for oboe and strings), 15P. *Ave Verum*, Motet for Chorus and Strings, 47.

NABOKOFF, Nikolai. Symphonic Suite, *The Life of Polichinelle*, 35.

NICOLAI, Otto. Overture to *The Merry Wives of Windsor*, ‡2, 4P, 5P, 6P, 8P, 9P, 10P, 11P, 12P, 13P, 14P, 15P, 16P, 17P, 18P, 21P, 23P, 24P, 29P, 30P, 32P, 33P, 40P.

NOGUES, Jean. *Le Baiser d'Eunice,* from *Quo Vadis?* 15P.

NORDOFF, Paul. Secular Mass (Orchestra, Chorus, and Soloists), 32.

NOSKOWSKI, Sigismunt. Symphonic Poem, *The Steppe*, 34P.

OBERHOFFER, Emil. Overture Romantique, 15&P. *Americana*, Festival March of Homage, 13&P.

OFFENBACH, Jacques. Overture to *Orpheus in Hades*, 4P, 30P. (Arr. Dorati) Suite from the ballet *Helen of Troy*, 47P, 48P.

OLDBERG, Arne. Overture, *Paolo and Francesca*, 12. *June*, Rhapsody for Orchestra, 15.

O'NEILL, Norman. Prelude and Call, from the Incidental Music to Barrie's *Mary Rose*, 23P.

PADEREWSKI, Ignace Jan. Symphony in B minor, 28. Concerto for Piano in A minor, 11, 28. Polish Fantasy, for Piano and Orchestra, 19.

Repertoire

PAGANINI, Niccolò. Concerto for Violin, No. 1, in D major, 6P, 19P, 23P, 24P, 40. (Arr. Kreisler) Concertpiece for Violin in D major, 42.

PALMGREN, Selim. Finnish Lullaby, for Strings, 22P. Concerto for Piano, No. 2, *The River*, 18, 26. Concerto for Piano, No. 3, *Metamorphoses*, 19P.

PATTON, Willard. Andante, from the suite *The Spirit of '61*, 22P.

PAULY, Francis. Concerto for Piano in E flat, 13P. *Rosalind and Celie*, Pastoral for Harp and Orchestra, 16P.

PERSICHETTI, Vincent. Dance Overture, 47.

PIATIGORSKY, Gregor. (Arr. Cohn) Variations on a Theme of Paganini for Cello and Orchestra, 44.

PICK-MANGIAGALLI, Riccardo. Nocturne and Rondo Fantastique, 43.

PIERNE, Gabriel. Entrance of the Little Fauns from *Cydalise and the Satyr*, 24, 25P, 30P. Serenade (arranged for strings), 10P, 14P. *Concertstück*, for Harp and Orchestra, 11P, 18P. Musical Legend, *The Children's Crusade*, ‡6, ‡16.

PIKET, Frederick. *Curtain Raiser to an American Play*, 46.

PILATI, Mario. Preludio, Aria, e Tarantella, 35P.

PISTON, Walter. Concerto for Orchestra, 44. Symphony No. 4, 48, 49.

POGOJEFF, Nicolai. Small Suite, *Morceaux de Ballet*, 10P.

PONCHIELLI, Amilcare. Ballet Music, Dance of the Hours, from *La Gioconda*, 10P(2), 12P, 14P, 16P, 30P.

POOT, Marcel. Overture, *Joyeuse*, 34.

POULENC, Francis. *Sinfonietta*, 47.

PROKOFIEFF, Sergei. Classical Symphony in D major, 29, 32, 37, 39, 41&P, 44&P, 47. Symphony No. 5, in B flat major, 44, 45, 49. Suite from *Love for Three Oranges*, 28, 31, 41&P. *Scythian* Suite, 48. Suite, *Lieutenant Kije*, 39, 45. Russian Overture, 40(2). *Peter and the Wolf*, An Orchestral Fairy Tale, 37&P. Concerto for Piano, No. 1, in D flat major, 44. Concerto for Piano, No. 3, in C major, 35, 49. Concerto for Violin, No. 2, in G minor, 46, 48.

PUCCINI, Giacomo. Intermezzo from Act III of *Manon Lescaut*, 44.

PURCELL, Henry. (Arr. Wood) Suite for Orchestra, 20P. *Dido and Aeneas*: (Arr. Mitropoulos) Prelude and Final Air (arranged for string orchestra), 34P, 35P, 39, 44P. (Arr. Wood) Trumpet Voluntary, 47, 48. (Arr. Barbirolli) Suite for Strings, Four Horns, Two Flutes, and English Horn, 49.

QUILTER, Roger. *A Children's Overture*, 26.

RABAUD, Henri. Symphony No. 2, in E minor, 15. Symphonic Poem, *La Procession Nocturne*, 17, 46.

RACHMANINOFF, Sergei. Symphony No. 2, in E minor, 11, 12, 13, 16, 17, 19, 24, 29, 30, 31P, 33, 40P, 41&P, 44, 45. Symphony No. 3, in A minor, 37. Symphonic Poem, *Die Toteninsel* ("The Island of the Dead"), 14, 15, 42. Symphonic Dances, 40, 46. Concerto for Piano, No. 1, in F sharp minor, 36, 48. Concerto for Piano, No. 2, in C minor, 11P, 17, 19P, 20, 21P, 22P, 23&P, 29, 31, 34, 40&P(2), 47. Concerto for Piano, No. 3, in D minor, 30, 32, 41, 42P, 45. Rhapsody on a Theme of Paganini, for Piano and Orchestra, 33, 41P, 42, 47, 48.

RAFF, Joseph. Symphony No. 3, *Im Walde*, 3. Symphony No. 5, *Lenore*, 22.

RAMEAU, Jean Philippe. (Arr. d'Indy) Suite from *Dardanus*, 48.

RAVEL, Maurice. Symphonic Fragments from *Daphnis et Chloé*, First and Second Series, 22, 35. Second Series, 28, 29, 30, 32, 33, 39, 42, 45, 46, 48, 49P. *Rapsodie Espagnole*, 17(2), 23, 33, 34, 38, 47. *La Valse*, A Choreographic Poem, 24, 29, 31, 32, 35, 49. *Valses Nobles et Sentimentales*, 40. *Alborada del Gracioso*, 31, 41(2), 49. *Pavane pour une Infante Défunte*, 20&P, 35, 41, 49. *Boléro*, 27, 28, 29&P, 30, 31P, 33&P, 34P, 36P, 43P, 47P. Suite, *Le Tombeau de Couperin*,

331

31, 35, 39. Suite, *Ma Mère l'Oye* ("Mother Goose"), 14P, 19P, 25, 33P, 35, 39P. Concerto for Piano in G major, 35, 48P. Concerto for Piano (for the left hand), 32P, 42. Introduction and Allegro, for Harp, Strings, Flute, and Clarinet, 36. *Shéhérazade*, Three Songs with Orchestra, 38P. Song Cycle, *Don Quichotte à Dulcinée*, 44.

REBIKOFF, Vladimir. *Suite Miniature*, 18P.

REGER, Max. Four Tone Poems after Pictures by Böcklin, 37. A Ballet Suite, 11. Variations and Fugue on a Theme of Beethoven, 41. Variations on a Theme by Mozart, 28(2), 34, 37. (Arr. Fritz Busch) Fantasie on a Chorale, 48. Concerto for Piano in F minor, 43.

REINECKE, Karl. Prelude to Act V of *King Manfred*, 9P.

RESPIGHI, Ottorino. Symphonic Poem, *The Fountains of Rome*, 19, 26, 30, 33, 35P, 37. Symphonic Poem, *The Pines of Rome*, 24&P, 25, 27, 29, 30P, 31, 32P, 35, 45, 48. Symphonic Poem, *Roman Festivals*, 28. Suite, *Gli Uccelli* ("The Birds"), 49. Old Airs and Dances for the Lute, 18. Toccata for Piano and Orchestra, 34&P, 42. Concerto, *Gregoriano*, for Violin, 22, 43.

REZNICEK, Emil. Overture to *Donna Diana*, 9&P, 14P, 34P.

RHEINBERGER, Josef von. Concerto for Organ, No. 1, in F major, 8P.

RIMSKY-KORSAKOFF, Nicholas. Symphonic Suite, *Schéhérazade*, 10&P, 18&P, 20, 24, 29P, 30, 35P, 38P, 41, 43P, 49. Overture, *The Russian Easter*, 26, 28, 29P, 30P, 33P, 36, 40P, 44, 47. Overture to *A Night in May*, 5, 12. *Sadko, A Musical Picture*, 18. *Capriccio Espagnol*, 6&P, 7&P, 9P, 10P, 11P, 13P, 14, 15P, 16P, 17P, 18P, 19P, 21P, 24P, 29P, 30&P, 31, 32, 33P, 34&P, 35P, 36P, 42P, 45P. Concerto for Piano in C sharp minor, 19P, 23P. *The Fairy Tale of Tsar Saltan*: Tsar Saltan Goes to War, 24; Introduction to Act II, Lament of the Tsaritsa, 24; Scherzo, *Flight of the Bumble-Bee*, 23P(2), 24, 29P, 30P. *Le Coq d'Or*: Suite, 42; Introduction and Wedding March, 33P, 48; King Dodon and Queen Shemhka, 35P. *Christmas Eve*, Polonaise, 30.

RODGERS, Richard. *Carousel* Waltz, 46.

ROENTGEN, Engelbert. Concerto for Violoncello in C minor, 23P.

ROENTGEN, Julius. Suite, *Old Holland*, 24P. Concerto for Violoncello in G minor, 20P.

ROGERS, Bernard. *The Dance of Salome*, 43.

ROPARTZ, Joseph Guy. Symphony No. 4, in C major, 12. Symphonic Sketch, *A Marie Endormie*, 17P.

ROSSINI, Gioacchino. Overture to *Le Scala di Seta*, 45. Overture to *Il Signor Bruschino*, 48. Overture to *L'Italiana in Algeri*, 49. Overture to *La Gazza Ladra*, 10P(2), 13P, 14P, 16P, 18P, 26, 33, 44&P, 49P. Overture to *Semiramide*, 2, 4P, 5P, 6P, 7P, 10P, 14P, 18P, 22P, 30P, 33P, 34, 35P, 43. Overture to *La Cenerentola* ("Cinderella"), 47. *William Tell* Overture, 1, 2, 3, 4P(2), 5P(2), 7P, 8P, 9P, 10P, 11P, 12P, 13P, 14P, 15P, 16P, 17P, 18P, 19P, 20P, 21P, 24&P, 25, 28&P, 29P, 30P, 32P, 33P, 35P, 36P. Overture to *The Barber of Seville*, 22P, 24&P, 30, 34P, 39, 42P. *Stabat Mater*, ‡2.

ROUSSEL, Albert. Symphony No. 3, in G minor, 45. Symphonic Fragment from the ballet *Le Festin de l'Araignée* ("Spider's Banquet"), 21&P, 41. Suite in F major, 46.

ROZYCKI, Ludomir. Symphonic Scherzo, *Stanczyk the Jester*, 34P.

RUBINSTEIN, Anton. Ballet Music from *Feramors*, 22P. Concerto for Piano, No. 4, in D minor, 8, 9P, 12, 14, 15P, 18, 26. Concerto for Piano, No. 5, in E flat major, 6.

SAAR, Louis Victor. Suite, *Rococo*, 17P.

Repertoire

SABATA, Victor de. Symphonic Poem, *Juventus*, 18.

SAINT-SAENS, Camille. Symphony No. 2, in A minor, 17. Symphony No. 3, in C minor, 10, 11, 25, 43&P. Symphonic Poem No. 1, *Le Rouet d'Omphale*, 2(2), 4P, 5P, 7P, 9P, 10P, 14P, 15P, 16P, 19P, 20P, 28P, 30P, 46. Symphonic Poem No. 2, *Phaëton*, 2, 5P, 6P, 8P, 9P, 11P, 12P, 19P, 20P, 24P, 27. Symphonic Poem No. 3, *Danse Macabre*, 4P(2), 5P, 7P, 8P(2), 9&P, 11P, 14P, 16P, 19P(2), 20P, 22P, 23P, 24P, 29P, 30P, 35P. Suite, *Algérienne*, 15P, 21P. Suite, *Carnival of Animals*, 20P. Ballet Suite from *Ascanio*, 26. Ballet Divertissement from *Henry VIII*, 9P(2), 10P, 19P, 20P, 22P, 23P. March, *Orient and Occident*, 9P. March, *Héroïque*, 15P, 17P. Prelude to *The Deluge*, 7P, 9P, 14P, 15P, 17P, 19P(2), 20P, 21P, 31P, 44P. Barcarolle, *A Night in Lisbon*, 5P, 16P. *La Jota Aragonaise*, 10P, 12P, 14P, 16P. Serenade for Small Orchestra, 5P. Concerto for Piano, No. 2, in G minor, 1, 7P, 9P, 10, 13P, 15P, 16, 18&P, 24, 33P, 36P, 44, 46, 48P. Concerto for Piano, No. 4, in C minor, 6, 18, 21P, 23&P, 39P. Concerto for Piano, No. 5, in F major, 19P, 25. Variations for Two Pianos on a Theme by Beethoven, 15. Concerto for Violin, No. 1, in A major, 19P. Concerto for Violin, No. 3, in B minor, 1, 6P, 8P, 11&P, 12, 14&P, 18, 21, 24P, 29P. Introduction and Rondo Capriccioso, for Violin, 2, 3, 9P, 12, 15P, 18, 19P, 24P, 49P. Concerto for Violoncello, No. 1, in A minor, 7P, 11P, 14P(2), 17P, 22P, 29P, 33P, 41P, 44. Allegro Appassionato, for Violoncello, 19P, 21P. Tarantella for Flute and Clarinet, 3.

SANDERS, Robert L. Little Symphony in G, 37.

SATIE, Erik. (Arr. Debussy) Two Gymnopédies, Nos. 1 and 3, 40&P.

SAUER, Emil von. Concerto for Piano, No. 1, in E minor, 19P.

SCALCOTAS, Nicos. Three Greek Dances, 36.

SCHARWENKA, Xaver. Concerto for Piano, No. 1, in B flat minor, 10.

SCHEINPFLUG, Paul. Overture to a Comedy of Shakespeare, 7&P, 8, 9P, 12&P, 13, 14P, 19, 25, 27, 37.

SCHELLING, Ernest. *A Victory Ball*, Fantasy for Orchestra, 21(2)&P, 22&P(2), 23, 25, 30. Fantastic Suite for Piano and Orchestra, 19. *Impressions from an Artist's Life*, for Piano and Orchestra, 23.

SCHENCK, Elliot. Four Pastels for Orchestra, 21P.

SCHIASSI, Gaetano Maria. *Christmas* Symphony, 42.

SCHILLINGS, Max von. Prelude to Act II of *Ingwelde*, 13P. *Das Hexenlied*, Recitation with Orchestra, 5.

SCHMITT, Florent. *The Tragedy of Salome*, 38. Suite, *Feuillets de Voyage*, 17P. Suite, *Pupazzi*, 17P. *Rapsodie Viennoise*, No. 3, 11&P.

SCHNABEL, Artur. Symphony No. 1, 44.

SCHOENBERG, Arnold. *Verklärte Nacht*, for Strings, 23(2), 25, 32, 39. Concerto for Violin and Orchestra, 43. String Quartet No. 2, in F sharp minor, with Soprano (arranged for string orchestra), 42.

SCHOENFELD, Hermann. Characteristic Suite for Strings, 17P.

SCHUBERT, Franz. Symphony No. 2, in B flat major, 40. Symphony No. 5, in B flat major, 33, 41, 48. Symphony No. 6, in C major, 43. Symphony No. 7, in C major, 8, 13, 18, 20, 26, 29, 30, 33, 36, 39, 42, 47, 49. Symphony No. 8, in B minor (*Unfinished*), 1, 2, 4, 6P, 7P, 8P, 9P, 10P, 11, 12P, 13P, 14P, 15P, 16P(2), 17P, 18P(2), 19P(2), 20P, 23, 25, 28P, 29P, 30P(2) 31P, 32&P, 33P, 34P, 41P, 46P, 49P. Overture to *Des Teufels Lustschloss*, 26. *Rosamunde*: Overture, 12&P, 13P, 14P, 17P, 19P, 22P, 26, 29P, 32P, 33P, 34P, 35P, 44&P; Ballet Music No. 1, in G major, 7P, 8P, 9P, 11P, 12P, 15P, 16P, 20P(2), 23P, 30P; Entr'acte, in B flat major, 10P, 15P, 16P, 17P, 20P, 23P, 26, 29P, 30P,

31P, 36P. Theme and Variations from D minor Quartet, 23P(2), 29P. (Arr. Herbeck) German Dances (first set), 34P. (Arr. Liszt) *Wanderer* Fantasy (transcribed for piano and orchestra), 44. (Arr. Cassado) Concerto for Cello in A minor (transcribed from the Arpeggione Sonata), 36, 44P.

SCHUETT, Eduard. Concerto for Piano in G minor, 14P.

SCHUMAN, William. *American Festival* Overture, 40. *A Circus Overture*, 46. Symphony No. 3, 47. *A Free Song*, Secular Cantata, No. 2, for Chorus and Orchestra, 45P.

SCHUMANN, Georg. Overture, *Liebesfrühling*, 6, 7, 9, 11, 14, 19. Dance of Nymphs and Satyrs, from *Amor et Psyche*, 9P(2), 10&P, 11P, 12P, 13P, 14P, 18P(2), 24P, 25P, 28P, 30, 31P, 32P, 33P.

SCHUMANN, Robert. Symphony No. 1, in B flat major, 4, 5, 11, 12P, 14P, 17P, 18P, 19P, 20, 30, 40&P, 43. Symphony No. 2, in C major, 8, 34, 35, 38, 45, 48. Symphony No. 3 (*Rhenish*), in E flat major, 33, 35, 39&P, 42, 44&P, 46. Symphony No. 4, in D minor, 10, 14, 19P, 25, 31, 34, 37, 41, 44P, 48. Overture, Scherzo, and Finale, 37. Overture, *The Bride of Messina*, 8, 35. Concerto for Piano in A minor, 9, 12, 16P, 18, 20&P, 22, 26, 28, 29, 32P, 37, 40, 43P, 45. Concerto for Violin in D minor, 37. Concerto for Violoncello in A minor, 14, 35, 44.

SCHYTTE, Ludwig. Concerto for Piano in C sharp minor, 8P.

SCLAVOS, G. *The Eagle*, Fantasy on a Greek Theme, 36.

SCRIABIN, Alexander. Symphony No. 2, in C minor, 17. Symphony No. 3, *The Divine Poem*, 32. *The Poem of Ecstasy*, 26, 27, 34, 47. *Reverie*, in E minor, 17P.

SEAY, Virginia. Theme, Variations, and Fugue, 43.

SESSIONS, Roger. Concerto for Violin in B minor, 45.

SEVERN, Edmund. Concerto for Violin in D minor, 16P.

SHEPHERD, Arthur. Fantasy on Down East Spirituals, 46.

SHOSTAKOVITCH, Dimitri. Symphony No. 1, 27, 41&P. Symphony No. 5, 38, 39, 42, 45, 48. Symphony No. 7, 40. Symphony No. 9, 44. Suite from the opera *The Nose*, 34. Suite from *The Bolt*, An Industrial Ballet, 33P. Concerto for Piano, Strings, and Trumpet, 42P.

SHULMAN, Alan. *A Laurentian Overture*, 49.

SIBELIUS, Jan. Symphony No. 1, in E minor, 8, 10, 13, 15, 17, 19P(2), 26, 29, 32, 34, 38&P, 43, 47. Symphony No. 2, in D major, 10, 30, 33, 34, 36, 39, 43P, 44, 48. Symphony No. 4, in A minor, 36. Symphony No. 5, in E flat major, 32, 37. Symphony No. 6, 39. Symphony No. 7 (in one movement), 38, 41. Symphonic Poem, *En Saga*, 38P. Legend, *The Swan of Tuonela*, 11P, 17P, 26, 33P, 43. Tone Poem, *Finlandia*, No. 7, 10P(2), 11, 12&P, 13, 14, 15P, 16P, 17&P, 18P, 19P, 20P, 25P, 29P, 30P, 32P, 33P, 43P. *Valse Triste*, from *Kuolema*, 7P(2), 8P(2), 9P, 10P, 11P, 12P, 13P, 16P, 17&P, 18P, 19P, 20P, 22P, 24P, 29P, 32P, 33P(2). Concerto for Violin in D minor, 39P, 44, 47, 48P.

SIEGMEISTER, Elie. *Ozark Set*, 42P. *Wilderness Road*, 43.

SINIGAGLIA, Leone. Overture, *Le Baruffe Chiozzotte*, 16, 22&P, 40&P, 44. Two Piedmontese Dances, Nos. 1, 2, 7P.

SKILTON, Charles Sanford. Symphonic Legend, 24P. Suite, *Primeval*, on Tribal Indian Songs, 19P. Two Indian Dances (Deer Dance, War Dance), 14P(2), 22P.

SMETANA, Bedřich. Symphonic Poem, *The Moldau*, 7&P, 8P(2), 9P, 10, 11P, 12P, 13P, 15P(2), 16P, 17P, 18P, 19P, 26, 29, 31, 32P, 33P, 38P, 47. Symphonic Poem, *Sárka*, 27. *The Bartered Bride*: Overture, 5, 6&P, 7, 8P, 9P, 11P, 14, 17P, 18P, 20P, 24, 29P, 30P, 31P, 32P, 33P, 35, 37P, 45; March of the Comedians, 9P, 14P, 18P; Three Dances, 23P, 29P, 30P, 33P. (Arr. Szell) *From My Life*, String Quartet No. 1, in E minor (transcribed for orchestra), 44.

Repertoire

SMITH, David Stanley. Overture, *Prince Hal*, 13. *Impressions*, Four Pieces for Orchestra, 16P. Cathedral Prelude for Organ and Orchestra, 23P.

SOKOLOFF, Nikolai. Variations on a Russian Theme, Var. 5, 4, 5, 8P, 14P.

SONZOGNO, Giulio. Tango for Orchestra, 33.

SOUSA, John Philip. March, *Stars and Stripes Forever*, 15P, 22P. March, *Washington Post*, 43P. Wedding March, 16P.

SOWERBY, Leo. Suite, *From the Northland*, 23. Overture, *Comes Autumn Time*, 18&P, 19P, 22. Symphonic Poem, *Prairie*, 30. *The Irish Washerwoman*, 20P, 22P, 30P, 33P. Concerto for Piano in F major, 18P. Ballad for Two Pianos and Orchestra, 21, 32.

SPOHR, Ludwig Louis. Overture to *Jessonda*, 11&P, 23P. Concerto for Violin, No. 8, *Gesangscene*, in A minor, 10P, 22, 26. Concerto for Violin, No. 9, in D minor, 20.

STANFORD, Charles. *Irish* Symphony, in F minor, 8. Irish Rhapsody No. 1, 6P, 7P, 8P, 9P, 14P.

STENHAMMAR, Wilhelm. Tone Poem, *Midvinter*, 11.

STOCK, Frederick. Symphonic Waltz, 8P, 9P, 12.

STOESSEL, Albert. Suite, *Hispania*, 30P. Concerto Grosso for String Orchestra and Piano, 36.

STRAUSS, Johann, Sr. March, *Egyptian*, 30P(2), 31P(2). March, *Radetzky*, 30P(2), 31P(2), 33P.

STRAUSS, Johann, Jr. Overture to *Die Fledermaus*, 8P, 14P, 23P, 24P, 29P, 30&P, 31P(2), 32P, 33P(2), 34P, 35P, 43P. Overture to *The Gypsy Baron*, 31P, 32P(2), 33P(2). Overture to *Waldmeister*, 32P, 33P. Overture to *The Queen's Lace Handkerchief*, 34P, 48. Waltz, *The Beautiful Blue Danube*, 2, 5P, 6P, 8P, 10P, 11P, 12P, 13P, 16P, 17P, 18P, 19P, 20P, 23P, 28P, 29P, 30P(2), 31P(2), 33P(2), 34P. Waltz, *Tales from the Vienna Woods*, 7P(2), 8P, 9P, 10P, 11P, 12P, 14P, 17P, 18P, 19P, 20P, 30P(2), 31P(2), 32P(2), 34P, 35P, 39, 43P, 45. Waltz, *Roses from the South*, 13P, 14P, 15P, 17P, 20P, 23P, 29P, 30P, 33P. Waltz, *Emperor*, 12P(2), 14P, 30P(3), 31P(2), 32P, 33P, 42P. Waltz, *Artist's Life*, 22P, 29P, 30P, 31P(2), 33P. Waltz, *Frühlingsstimmen*, 17P, 30P, 33P. Waltz, *Wine, Women, and Song*, 30P, 33P, 48. Waltz, *Acceleration*, 31P, 33P. Waltz, *Wiener Blut*, 30P. Waltz, *Liebeslieder*, 34P. Waltz, *Wo die Citronen Blühen*, 42. Polka, *Hail the Magyar*, 30P(2), 31P(2). Polka, *Annen*, 31P, 33P, 48. Polka Française, *Feuerfest*, 34P. Fast Polka, *Leichtes Blut*, 31P. Fast Polka, *Tritsch-Tratsch*, 32P, 33P(2). Fast Polka, *Bahn Frei*, 34P. New Pizzicato Polka, 31P, 32P, 33P. *Perpetuum Mobile*, 30P(2), 31P(2), 32P, 33P(2).

STRAUSS, Johann, Jr., and Josef. Pizzicato Polka, 30P(2), 31P(2), 32P, 33P(2).

STRAUSS, Josef. Waltz, *Dorfschwalben*, 15P, 31P. Waltz, *Aquarellen*, 32P(2). Waltz, *Sphärenklänge*, 33P. Polka-Mazurka, *Frauenherz*, 30P(2), 31P(2), 32P, 33P.

STRAUSS, Richard. Symphonic Fantasia, *Aus Italien*, 8. Sinfonia Domestica, 38. An Alpine Symphony, 14. Tone Poem, *Don Juan*, 7, 10, 12, 13, 15, 17, 19, 20, 25, 27, 29&P(2), 30, 32, 34, 35P, 39&P, 43&P, 46, 47, 49P. Tone Poem, *Death and Transfiguration*, 5, 6, 9, 13, 18, 19, 20, 24, 28, 30, 31, 33P, 34, 35P, 37, 38, 39, 41, 44, 47. Rondo, *Till Eulenspiegel's Merry Pranks*, 11(2), 13, 20&P, 24&P, 26, 29, 31, 32, 33, 34P, 35P, 36&P, 38, 40, 42, 45, 47, 49. Tone Poem, *Thus Spake Zarathustra*, 27, 33, 37, 45, 48. Fantastic Variations, *Don Quixote*, 22, 25, 33, 40, 47. Tone Poem, *Ein Heldenleben*, 21&P, 29, 32, 34, 46. Festival Prelude for Organ and Orchestra, 11(2)&P, 12. Imperial Military March, No. 1, 7P, 8P. Serenade for Wind Instruments, 5, 19, 42P. (Arr. Dorati) Suite from

Der Rosenkavalier, 42, 48. Suite from *Der Rosenkavalier* (Boosey and Hawkes edition), 44&P, 46P. Waltzes from *Der Rosenkavalier,* 9P, 11P, 19P, 29&P, 30P, 32, 33P, 35P, 40. Burleska, in D minor, for Piano and Orchestra, 24, 29. Concerto for Horn and Orchestra, 22P, 35. *Salome:* Opera (in concert form), 49; Dance of the Seven Veils, 29, 47; Final Scene (Vocal), 14.

STRAVINSKY, Igor. Suite from the ballet *The Fire Bird,* 19&P, 25, 29, 31, 33, 34, 37, 38, 43, 45P, 46P, 49. Suite from the ballet *Petrouchka,* 22, 30, 34, 38, 48. *Le Sacre du Printemps,* 47. *Apollon Musagètes* ("Apollo, Leader of the Muses"), 46. Suite from *Jeu de Cartes,* 38. Divertimento from *Le Baiser de la Fée,* 38. Symphonic Poem, *Song of the Nightingale,* 48. *Fireworks,* Fantasy for Orchestra, 14, 32. Four Norwegian Moods, 41P. Circus Polka, 41&P. Ragtime, for Small Orchestra, 22P.

STRINGHAM, Edwin. Symphony No. 1, in B flat minor, 27. Symphonic Poem, *Visions,* 25P. Symphonic Poem, *The Ancient Mariner,* 26.

STRUBE, Gustav. Comedy Overture, *Puck,* 8P, 12P.

SUK, Josef. *Scherzo Fantastique,* 13P. Fantasie for Violin and Orchestra in G minor, 44.

SUPPE, Franz von. Overture to *The Beautiful Galatea,* 13P, 33P. Overture to *Poet and Peasant,* 5P, 13P, 16P, 17P, 19P, 30P, 34P. Overture to *Morning, Noon, and Night,* 5P.

SVENDSEN, Johan. Episode, *Carneval in Paris,* 18&P, 19P, 20P, 33P. Legende, *Zorahayda,* 9P, 15P, 37P. Norwegian Rhapsody No. 3, 7P, 8P, 9P, 11P, 35P. Festival Polonaise, 17P. Coronation March, 9P, 10P, 11P, 12P, 13P, 14P, 16P. Norwegian Folk Song, *I fjol Gjette Gjettene,* for String Orchestra, 4P, 5P, 7P.

SZYMANOWSKI, Karol. Symphonie Concertante, for Piano and Orchestra, 42. Concerto for Violin (in one movement), 28.

TANEIEV, Alexander S. Festival March, 13P, 14P.

TANSMAN, Alexander. Symphony No. 5, in D minor, 42. Polish Rhapsody, 40. *Triptych,* for String Orchestra, 29. Variations on a Theme of Frescobaldi, 47.

TAYLOR, Deems. Suite, *Through the Looking Glass,* 21, 22P, 27. Fantasy, *Circus Day,* 32P.

TCHEREPNIN, Alexandre. *Rapsodie Géorgienne,* for Cello and Orchestra, 42P.

THOMAS, Ambroise. Overture to *Raymond,* 23P, 43P. *Mignon:* Overture, 2, 4P, 5P, 7P, 9P, 10P, 11P, 12P, 13P, 14P, 15P(2), 16, 18P, 20P, 21P, 22P, 29P, 30P; Polonaise, 6P, 8P; Entr'acte, Gavotte, 7P, 11P.

THOMSON, Virgil. *The Plow That Broke the Plains,* 45.

TINEL, Edgar. *Danse Sacre* and *Danse Profane* from the dramatic legend *Katharina,* 11P.

TIRINDELLI, Pietro. *Interludio,* 15P.

TOCH, Ernst. *Pinocchio,* A Merry Overture, 40&P.

TSCHAIKOWSKY, Peter Ilich. Symphony No. 1, in G minor, 18&P. Symphony No. 2, in C minor, 27, 43&P. Symphony No. 4, in F minor, 5, 8, 12, 13, 14P, 16P, 17, 18P, 19P(2), 20&P, 21, 24, 27, 29&P(2), 32P, 33P, 35, 37, 43, 46, 49. Symphony No. 5, in E minor, 4, 7, 9, 11, 14, 15P, 16, 18, 19, 21(2)&P, 23&P, 25, 28&P, 30, 31P, 32&P, 33P, 34P, 36&P, 39&P, 42P, 44P, 46, 47, 48, 49. Symphony No. 6, in B minor (*Pathétique*), 5, 6, 7, 8, 9, 10, 11P, 12P, 13P, 15P, 16, 17P, 18, 19&P, 20&P, 22&P, 24&P, 26, 28, 29&P, 30P, 31, 33P, 34&P, 37, 40P, 45, 46. Symphony after Byron's *Manfred,* 12, 14, 15, 23. Fantasia, *Francesca da Rimini,* 13, 19, 31, 40, 46. Overture-Fantasia, *Romeo and Juliet,* 10&P, 12P, 19P, 20, 21&P, 25, 29, 30P, 33, 34P, 36, 37P(2), 41, 44, 47, 48P, 49. Overture-Fantasia, *Hamlet,* 23&P, 43. Overture, *1812,* 1, 4&P, 5P(2), 6P, 7P, 8P, 9, 10P,

Repertoire

11P, 15P, 16P, 17P, 19P, 20&P(2), 21P(2), 22P, 23P, 24P, 27, 29P, 30P, 31P, 33P, 34P, 40&P, 47P. Overture to *Opritchnik* ("The Body Guard"), 49. *Marche Slave*, 8P(2), 9P, 10&P, 11P, 12P, 13P, 15P, 16P, 17P, 18P, 19P, 22P, 23P, 29P, 30P(2), 35P. *Capriccio Italien*, 3, 7, 14P, 18P, 20P, 22P, 23P, 29P(2), 30P, 32P, 33P. Introduction and Fugue from Suite No. 1, in D minor, 23, 27. Theme and Variations from Suite No. 3, in D minor, 16, 17, 18&P, 20P, 21P, 26, 28P. Suite No. 4, *Mozartiana*, 43&P. Suite from the ballet *Swan Lake*, 41P. Suite from the ballet *La Belle au Bois Dormant* ("The Sleeping Beauty"), 10P, 11P, 30P. Suite from the ballet *Casse-Noisette* ("Nutcracker"), 4, 5P, 6P, 7P, 8P, 9P, 10P, 12P, 13P, 14P, 15P, 16P, 18P, 19P, 20P, 21&P(2), 24P, 29P, 30P(2), 31P, 33P, 34P, 41. Serenade for Strings in C major, 33P, 42. Elegy in G major, for String Orchestra, 23&P, 24P. Concerto for Piano, No. 1, in B flat minor, 5, 6P, 9&P, 10, 11P, 12, 13, 15P, 17, 18P, 19, 20P, 21P, 22P, 23, 25P, 27, 30P, 31P, 32P, 39&P, 43, 44, 45P, 47P, 48, 49. Concerto for Piano, No. 2, in G major, 11. Concerto for Violin in D major, 4, 6, 10, 13, 14&P, 15P, 16, 18, 19, 21, 24, 27, 32, 34P, 35, 41, 43, 47, 48. *Sérénade Mélancholique*, for Violin, 7, 24P. *Rococo* Variations, for Violoncello, 9P, 13P, 19P, 37. *Eugen Onegin*: Waltz, 13P, 30P; Polonaise, 7P, 13P, 18P.

VAN DER STUCKEN, Frank. Festival March, *Louisiana*, 16P.

VARDELL, Charles. *Joe Clark Steps Out*, American Folk Dance Setting, 34P.

VAUGHAN WILLIAMS, Ralph. *A London Symphony*, 20, 21, 25, 42. *Pastoral Symphony*, 27. Symphony No. 4, in F minor, 38. Norfolk Rhapsody, No. 1, in E minor, 28. Fantasia on a Theme by Thomas Tallis, for Double String Orchestra, 27, 40(2), 42P, 47. *Dona Nobis Pacem* for Chorus, Soloists, and Orchestra, 47P.

VERBRUGGHEN, Henri. Fantasia on British Sea Songs, 20P.

VERDI, Giuseppe. Overture to *Nabucco*, 45. Introduction to Act III of *La Traviata*, 38. Overture to *I Vespri Siciliani* ("Sicilian Vespers"), 12P, 31P, 35P, 45. Overture to *La Forza del Destino*, 8P. *Manzoni Requiem*, 31&P, 47.

VERETTI, Antonio. *Sinfonia Sacra*, for Orchestra and Male Chorus, 48.

VERRALL, John. Symphony No. 1, in E, 37. Symphonic Suite, *Portrait of Man*, 38. Rhapsody for Orchestra, 36P.

VIEUXTEMPS, Henri. Concerto for Violin, No. 1, in E major, 19. Concerto for Violin, No. 4, in D minor, 2, 6P, 8P, 11P, 15P, 18P, 25P, 37, 41P. Concerto for Violin, No. 5, in A minor, 5P, 20P.

VILLA-LOBOS, Heitor. *Bachianas Brasileiras*, No. 2, 47P.

VIOTTI, Giovanni. Concerto for Violin, No. 22, in A minor, 15, 42.

VIVALDI, Antonio. Sinfonia No. 3, in G major, 47. Concerto for Violin in A minor, 28. Concerto for Four Violins and Strings in B minor, No. 10, 27, 47P. Concerto for Flute in G major, No. 4, 36. Concerto for Flute in F major, No. 5, 36.

WAGENAAR, Bernard. Divertimento, 34.

WAGNER, Richard. Overture to *Die Feen*, 30, 44. *Rienzi*: Overture, 3, 4, 5P, 7P, 9P, 10&P, 11P, 12, 13P, 14P, 15P, 18P, 19, 20&P, 21P(2), 23P, 24, 26, 28, 29P, 31P(2), 33P, 34P, 39; Peace March, 9P, 10P. Overture to *The Flying Dutchman*, 6, 8P, 9, 11P, 14, 18, 19P, 20P, 21, 22P, 23, 26, 29P, 30&P, 31, 33P, 34P, 36, 38, 41. *Tannhäuser*: Overture, 1, 3, 4&P(2), 5P(2), 6P, 7&P, 8&P, 9&P, 10P, 11P(2), 12&P, 13P, 14P, 16P, 17P, 18P(2), 19P, 20&P, 21P, 22P(2), 24&P, 28P, 29, 30, 32P, 34P(2), 36P, 37P, 38P, 39, 45, 47; Bacchanale (Parisian version), 5, 6&P, 7, 9&P, 14, 17P, 18&P, 19, 20, 39; (Boessenroth) Overture and Bacchanale, 21&P, 23, 26, 28, 30P, 34P, 36, 41, 48; Introduction to Act II, 25; Introduction to Act III, 21P, 25, 35P, 36, 46. *Lohengrin*: Acts I and III, complete, 23; Prelude, 3, 4&P, 5P, 6, 7P, 8&P, 10, 11P, 12&P, 13P, 14, 15P, 16P,

18P, 19P, 20P, 21P(2), 25, 27, 32, 34P(2), 35, 36(2), 41, 45, 48; Introduction to Act III, 4P(2), 6, 7P, 20&P, 21P(2), 24P, 25, 27, 28&P, 29P, 30P(3), 31P; Act III, Scene I, Elsa and Lohengrin, 6. *Tristan und Isolde*: Prelude (with concert ending), 49; Prelude and *Liebestod*, 1, 3, 5, 7P, 9, 10, 11, 12, 13, 14P, 15, 16, 17, 18P, 19P, 20(2), 21, 23&P(2), 24P, 25&P, 26, 27, 29&P, 30&P, 31P, 32P, 33P, 34&P, 35P, 36, 38, 39, 41, 44, 46, 47; Introduction to Act III, 8P, 20P, 21, 24, 49; Concert version, 47. *Die Meistersinger von Nürnberg*: Prelude, 1, 2, 4, 5, 6, 7, 8, 9, 10, 11&P, 12, 13, 14, 15P, 16P, 17, 18, 19, 20&P, 21, 23&P, 25, 28, 29&P(2), 30P, 31P(2), 32, 33P(2), 34&P(3), 35P, 36, 38&P(2), 40P, 44&P, 46, 48; Introduction to Act III, 26; Introduction to Act III, Dance of Apprentices, and Entrance of Mastersingers, 7&P, 11P, 12P, 22P, 29, 31, 37, 43, 45, 47. *Das Rheingold*: Finale, Entrance of the Gods into Valhalla, 8(2), 9, 10, 12, 13P, 14, 15P, 17, 18, 19P, 20&P, 22, 25, 26, 29&P, 37, 44, 49. *Die Walküre*: Act I (complete), 22, 35&P; Ride of the Valkyries, 4&P, 5P, 7P(2), 8P, 9, 10, 11P, 12, 13P, 14, 15, 17P, 18P, 19P, 20&P, 22&P, 24, 29P(2), 30P(2), 31P, 32P, 33P, 34&P, 36, 46; Wotan's Farewell and Magic-Fire Scene, 5, 8, 11P, 13P, 18P, 21, 27, 29, 31, 33P, 34, 35, 43. *Siegfried*: *Waldweben* ("Forest Murmurs"), 5, 6, 7P(2), 9, 12, 13&P, 14, 22, 27, 29&P, 30, 31P, 33P, 37P, 43, 47P. *Götterdämmerung*: Siegfried's Rhine-Journey, 5, 11, 20, 22&P, 23P, 26, 29&P, 32P, 34&P, 35P, 36, 38&P, 41, 46, 47, 48, 49; Siegfried's Funeral March, 5, 13, 14, 20, 22, 23P, 26, 32, 33, 34P, 35P, 36, 38, 41, 46, 47, 49; Finale, Brünnhilde's Immolation, 13, 22, 24, 25, 36, 38, 41, 43, 46, 49. *Parsifal*: Prelude, 21, 23, 25, 33, 34P, 41, 45; Prelude and Glorification, 1, 5, 10P, 15P, 18P; Good Friday Spell, 4, 20, 23, 25, 29, 33, 34P, 37, 38, 41, 45; March of the Knights of the Holy Grail, 5P, 41; Klingsor's Magic Garden and Flower Girl Scene, 23, 44. *A Faust Overture*, 4, 20&P, 23, 25, 32P, 33P, 43, 45. Overture, *Rule Britannia*, 5. *Siegfried Idyl*, 4, 8, 10, 14, 20&P, 24, 25, 32P, 33P, 34&P, 35P, 40, 45P. *Kaisermarsch*, 5, 8. *Huldigungsmarsch*, 21P, 23P.

WALDTEUFEL, Emile. Waltz, *Les Patineurs* ("The Skaters"), 9P.

WALTON, William Turner. Overture, *Portsmouth Point*, 43. Concerto for Violin and Orchestra, 42. Concerto for Viola and Orchestra, 36, 49.

WEAVER, Powell. Symphonic Poem, *The Vagabond*, 28.

WEBER, Carl Maria von. Overture to *Der Freischütz*, 2, 3, 4P, 6P, 8P, 9P, 10P, 11P, 12P, 13, 16P, 17P, 18P, 19P, 20&P, 21P, 22, 23P, 25P, 26, 27P, 30, 33, 34P, 37P, 39&P, 44, 46. Overture to *Euryanthe*, 4, 7, 9P, 10, 11, 12&P, 16P, 18, 20, 21P, 23&P, 27, 29, 30, 32P, 33P, 34, 37&P, 41&P, 44P, 46, 48P, 49. Overture to *Oberon*, 1, 2, 4P, 5P, 6P, 7P, 8P, 9P, 10P, 11P(2), 12P, 13P, 14, 15P, 16P, 17P, 18P, 19P, 20&P, 21P, 23, 24&P, 26, 28&P, 29, 30P, 32P, 34&P, 35P, 36P, 38P, 43, 47P. Overture to *Preciosa*, 10P. Overture, *Jubilee*, 4, 12P, 26, 43&P(2). Overture, *Beherrscher der Geister* ("Ruler of the Spirits"), 35, 45. (Arr. Berlioz) *Invitation to the Dance*, 5P, 34P. (Arr. Weingartner) *Invitation to the Dance*, 4, 8P, 9&P, 10P, 11P, 12P, 13P, 14P, 15&P, 19P, 20P, 22P, 29P, 30P, 32P, 33P, 37P. (Arr. Bodanzky) *Momento Capriccioso*, 17P. (Arr. Zell) *Perpetuum Mobile*, 41. *Konzertstück* for Piano in F minor, 2, 7, 27, 37.

WEBERN, Anton von. Passacaglia for Orchestra, No. 1, 46.

WEIDIG, Adolf. *Capriccio*, 11P. Symphonic Fantasy, *Semiramis*, 16. Three Episodes, 10&P. Symphonic Suite, 13. Concert Overture in F major, 16P, 19.

WEINBERGER, Jaromir. Polka and Fugue from *Schwanda*, 29&P(2), 30, 31P, 32P, 36P, 37, 44&P(2). *Under the Spreading Chestnut Tree*, Variations and Fugue on an Old English Tune, 37.

WEINER, Leo. Serenade for Small Orchestra in F minor, 6&P, 7.

Repertoire

WEINGARTNER, Felix. *Merry Overture,* 13.

WHITE, Paul. Five Miniatures, 34P.

WHITHORNE, Emerson. Two Nature Sketches (*Night, Rain*), 18P.

WIDOR, Charles Marie. Symphony No. 6, for Orchestra and Organ, 23, 30. Suite from the ballet *La Korrigane,* 13P. Serenade, in B flat major, 15P, 18P, 23P.

WIENIAWSKI, Henri. Concerto for Violin, No. 2, in D minor, 9P, 13P, 15&P, 16P, 19P, 20P, 39, 47P.

WIHTOL, Joseph. Variations on a Russian Theme, Var. 3, 4, 5, 8P, 14P.

WILSON, Mortimer. Overture, *New Orleans,* 22P.

WINDERSTEIN, Hans. *Valse Caprice,* 15P.

WLADIGEROFF, Pantscho. Bulgarian Suite, 30.

WOLF, Hugo. Italian Serenade, for Small Orchestra, 13P.

WOLF-FERRARI, Ermanno. Overture to *The Secret of Susanna,* 8, 14P, 26, 28&P, 29, 35P, 36P, 40P, 43P, 48P. Two Intermezzi from *The Jewels of the Madonna,* 9P, 10P, 14P, 19P, 24P, 29P, 32P, 33P, 44. Dance of the Angels, from *The New Life,* 10P.

WOLTMANN, Frederick. Symphonic Poem, *The Coliseum at Night,* 37. Rhapsody for Horn and Orchestra, 36.

YSAYE, Théophile. Fantasy, *Wallonne,* 8&P, 14, 21&P.

ZABEL, Albert. Concerto for Harp in C minor, 6P, 19.

ZADOR, Eugene. Variations on a Hungarian Folk Tune, 30. Hungarian Caprice for Orchestra and Tarógáto, 32&P. Suite from the ballet *Der Maschinenmensch,* 33.

ZANDONAI, Riccardo. Medieval Serenade for Solo Cello, Horns, Harp, and Strings, 19P.

ZEMACHSON, Arnold. Choral and Fugue in D minor, 32&P.

Recordings

Mercury Records, Olympian Series, Conducted by Antal Dorati
Berlioz, *Roman Carnival* Overture. Borodin, Symphony No. 2, in B minor. Debussy, Three Nocturnes: *Nuages, Fêtes, Sirènes.* Ravel, *Alborada del Gracioso.* Ravel, *Pavane pour une Infante Défunte.* Stravinsky, *The Fire Bird.* Rimsky-Korsakoff, *Schéhérazade.* Tschaikowsky, Symphony No. 5, in E minor. Mendelssohn, Symphony No. 4, in A major (*Italian*). Mozart, Symphony No. 40, in G minor.

RCA-Victor Red Seal Records, Conducted by Antal Dorati
Offenbach-Dorati, Suite from the ballet *Helen of Troy.* Bartók, Divertimento for Strings. Dvořák, Violin Concerto in A minor, with Nathan Milstein. Kodály, Suite from *Háry János.* Mozart, Symphony No. 31, in D major (*Parisian*).

RCA-Victor Red Seal Records, Conducted by Dimitri Mitropoulos
Rachmaninoff, Symphony No. 2, in E minor. Schumann, Symphony No. 3, in E flat major (*Rhenish*). Tschaikowsky, Piano Concerto No. 1, in B flat minor, with Artur Rubinstein. Weinberger, Polka and Fugue from *Schwanda.*

RCA-Victor Red Seal Records, Conducted by Eugene Ormandy
Grainger, *Country Gardens, Londonderry Air, Molly on the Shore, Irish Reel, Shepherd's Hey.* Smetana-Riesenfeld, Comedian's Dance, Furiant, and Polka from *Bartered Bride.* Johann and Josef Strauss, Waltzes *Blue Danube, Fledermaus, Vienna Woods, Acceleration, Gypsy Baron, Aquarellen, Pizzicato Polka.* Richard Strauss, Waltzes from *Der Rosenkavalier.* Tschaikowsky, *Andante Cantabile* (String Quartet No. 1).

Columbia Masterworks Records, Conducted by Dimitri Mitropoulos
Bach-Mitropoulos, Fantasia and Fugue in G minor. Bach-Weiner, Toccata No. 1, in C major. Beethoven, Symphony No. 6, in F major (*Pastoral*). Beethoven, *Leonore* Overture No. 3. Borodin, Symphony No. 2, in B minor. Brahms, Variations on a Theme by Haydn. Chausson, Symphony in B flat major. Chopin, Piano Concerto No. 1, with Edward Kilenyi. Dukas, *The Sorcerer's Apprentice.* Franck, Symphony in D minor. Glazounoff, Overture on Three Greek Themes. Liszt-Busoni, Spanish Rhapsody, with Egon Petri. Mahler, Symphony No. 1, in D major. Massenet, *Scènes Alsaciennes.* Mendelssohn, Symphony No. 3, in A minor (*Scotch*). Mendelssohn, *Capriccio Brilliant,* with Joanna Graudan. Milhaud, *Le Boeuf sur le Toit.* Prokofieff, *Symphonie Classique,* in D major. Rachmaninoff, *The Island of the Dead.* Ravel, *Le Tombeau de Couperin.* Rimsky-Korsakoff, Suite from *Le Coq d'Or.* Schumann, Symphony No. 2, in C major. Siegmeister, Ozark Set. Tschaikowsky, Symphony No. 2, in C minor (*Little Russian*). Tschaikowsky, Symphony No. 4, in F minor. Vaughan Williams, Fantasia on a Theme by Thomas Tallis.

Index

Index

ment, 79–82; incorporation of Orchestral Association, 88–89; of tours, 90–91, 115–16; dispute with American Federation of Musicians, 142–44

Under Verbrugghen, 180–83: Arthur Gaines as manager, 184–87; and change of home quarters, 188–91; Mrs. Scott becomes manager, 189

Under Ormandy, 206–9, 222

Under Mitropoulos, 267–74: sensitivity to premières, 243; and opera, 262–63; of tours, 279

Busoni, Ferruccio, 137, 145, 146, 232, 256

Cable Piano Company, 185
Calgary, Alta., 114
Calvé, Emma, 32, 84
Campanari, Giuseppe, 88
Campanini, Italo, 32, 141
Canada, 90, 97, 114, 131
Cantata for War Time, 245
Capitol Theater, Ormandy at, 197–99
Carleton College, 212
Carmen, 23, 29, 64, 84
Carnegie Hall, 113, 185
Carpenter, Elbert L., 108, 137, 187: appointed to Philharmonic's board of directors, 50; early years, 76–78; on Symphony's board of directors, 78, 79; and Oberhoffer, 78–79, 147; as chairman of committee of management, 79–82; and "pop" concerts, 85, 180; becomes president of Orchestral Association, 89; and St. Paul performances, 132–33; and AFM dispute, 143–44; and Verbrugghen, 156, 157; and Brunswick recordings, 167–68; and programming, 172–73; and Gaines, 184; "pine forest" of, 188; and financial crisis in *1930,* 188–89; and Ormandy, 201, 225; and Mitropoulos, 230; death of, 267–68
Carpenter, Mrs. Elbert L. (Florence Welles), 78, 79
Carpenter, John Alden, 136
Carpenter, Judson E., 76, 77
Carpenter, Lawrence, 137
Carpenter, Vincent Welles, 137
Carreño, Teresa, 19, 32, 117
Caruso, Enrico, 55, 92
Casadesus, Robert, 252–53

Casella, Alfredo, 137, 146, 215, 241
Cassado, Gaspar, 256
Casse-Noisette (Nutcracker), 120, 262
Cassidy, Claudia, quoted, 277
Cavalleria Rusticana, 29
Cecelian Singers (*later* Cecilian), 217, 297
Cedar Falls, Iowa, 77
Cedar Rapids, Iowa, 108
Chadbourn, Charles N., 52, 80
Chaliapin, Feodor, 183, 216–17
Chamber music, 175: Verbrugghen and, 151, 155, 162, 193–94; Mitropoulos and, 241–42, 265, 285–86
Chamberlain, Arthur M., 68
Chardon, Mrs. Yves, 265
Chardon, Yves, 265, 279, 282
Chase, Lucia, 262
Chattanooga, Tenn., 277
Chausson, Ernest, 136
Chicago, Ill., 35, 36, 45, 51, 77, 92, 98, 108, 109, 116, 141, 142, 168, 171, 222, 224, 249, 277, 281
Chicago American, quoted, 224
Chicago Civic Opera, 189
Chicago Daily News, quoted, 277
Chicago Herald Examiner, 224
Chicago Opera House, 276
Chicago Symphony Orchestra, 92, 110
Children's concerts, 92, 118–19, 182, 269, 277, 279, 298
Chimes of Normandy, The, 40
Chopin, Frédéric, 26, 34, 178, 265
Choral music

Pre-Symphony, 9: Harmonia Society, 17, 32; Philharmonic Chorus, 19, 32; Apollo Club, 32, 36, 38, 40; Mendelssohn Club, 34, 36; Filharmonix (Philharmonic Club), 36, 37, 38, 44–45, 46, 49; Ladies' Thursday Musicale, 36, 40; University Choral Union, 41

Under Oberhoffer: Philharmonic Club appearances with Symphony, 67–68, 69, 70, 82, 84, 86, 87, 118, 136; with Apollo Club, 89; on tour, 92, 114–15

Under Verbrugghen, 169–70: Minneapolis Choral Society, 162

Under Ormandy: Twin City Symphony Chorus, 211–12; *Resurrection* performance, 213–14; Cecelian Sing-

343

Index

Index

Index

Music and Maestros

Index

Index

Index

355

Music and Maestros

Index

357